TRADOC Historical Monograph Series

A HISTORY OF ARMY AVIATION – 1950-1962

by
Richard P. Weinert, Jr.

edited by
Susan Canedy

Office of the Command Historian
United States Army Training and Doctrine Command
Fort Monroe, Virginia
1991

TRADOC HISTORICAL MONOGRAPH SERIES
Henry O. Malone and John L. Romjue, General Editors

TRADOC Historical Monographs are published by the Office of the Command Historian, U.S. Army Training and Doctrine Command. These studies of training and leader development, and doctrinal and combat developments subjects provide historical perspective to support the Command's mission of preparing the Army for war and charting its future.

Library of Congress Cataloging-in-Publication Data

Weinert, Richard P.
    A history of army aviation, 1950 – 1962 / by Richard P. Weinert, Jr.
  ; edited by Susan Canedy.
ISBN:978-1-78039-131-1
       p.   cm. — (TRADOC historical monograph series)
    Includes bibliographical references and index.
    1. United States.   Army—Aviation—History.   I. Canedy, Susan.
  II. Title. III. Series.
UG633.W36   1991
358.4—dc20   91-8199
                                                                       CIP

U.S. ARMY TRAINING AND DOCTRINE COMMAND

General John W. Foss	Commander
Major General James W. van Loben Sels	Chief of Staff
Dr. Henry O. Malone, Jr.	Chief Historian
Mr. John L. Romjue	Chief, Historical Studies and Publication

Table Of Contents

Foreword xi
Preface xiii

Chapter I - Early History of Army Aviation 1
    Balloons and Dirigibles 1
    Development of Military Aviation 2
    Establishment of Organic Army Aviation 3
    World War II Training 6
    The Separation of the Army and the Air Force 10
    Joint Regulations 10
    Training Agreements 11
    Flight Training 11
    Endnotes 14

Chapter II - The Evolution of Army Aviation 15
    Planning for Organic Air Transport 16
    Department of the Army Proposals 16
    Army Field Forces Board No.1 Projects 18
    The Memorandum of Understanding of 1951 19
    Development of a Long Range Program 21
    Chief of Transportation Study 22
    Endnotes 25

Chapter III - The Formative Years 27
    Helicopter Units 27
        Unit Activations 27
        Field Training 29
    Materiel Requirements Review Panel 33
    Memorandum of Understanding of 1952 38
    OCAFF Review of the Army Aviation Program 39
    Army Aviation Plan 41
    Endnotes 45

Chapter IV - Research, Development, and Procurement 47
    Early Procurement Activities 47
    Army Observation Aircraft 48
    Fixed Wing Utility Aircraft 49
    Rotary Wing Aircraft 51
        H-13 Sioux 51
        H-23 Raven 51

      H-19 Chickasaw 52
    Development of the Cargo Helicopter 53
    Procurement Planning 56
    Endnotes 58

Chapter V - The Organization of Army Aviation 59
    Army Field Forces 59
    Army Field Forces Board No. 1 61
    Staff Organization 63
        Organization in the Field Army 64
        Corps Aviation Organization 65
        Army Aviation within the Division 65
    Tactical Aviation Units 66
        Medical Service Helicopter Ambulance Detachments 66
        Light Cargo Fixed Wing Aircraft Company 67
        Division Combat Aviation Company 67
    Cargo Helicopter Units 69
    Supply Support 72
        Division of Responsibility 72
        Expansion of Responsibility 72
        Shortage of Parts 72
        Incompatibility of Army and Air Force Supply Structures 73
        Depot Transfer 73
    Endnotes 75

Chapter VI - Early Aviation Training 77
    The Impact of the Korean Conflict 77
    Helicopter Pilot Training 79
    Expansion of Courses 80
    Liaison Pilot Training 81
    Fixed Wing and Helicopter Mechanic Training 82
    Development of Instrument Training 84
    Endnotes 87

Chapter VII - The Foundation of the Army Aviation School 89
    Planning for Expansion 89
    Establishment of the Army Aviation School 93
    Organization of the School 94
    The First Year of Operation 95
        Class Schedules 95
        Estimated Training Requirements 96
        Suspension of Transfer of Air Forces Training 97

    Duplication of Training Activities 98
    Shortage of Fixed Wing Pilots 98
    Training of Mechanics 99
Movement of the Army Aviation School 99
Endnotes 102

Chapter VIII - Plans and Programs 103
Army Aviation Plan 104
Department of Defense Policies 109
Personnel Policies 112
    Review of Officer Grades for Army Aviators 112
    Recommendations for Warrant Officer Aviators 114
    Aviator Requirements 114
Planning for Future Development 115
    Army Aircraft Requirements Review Board 115
    Rogers Committee on Army Aviation 119
The Berlin Crisis 121
    Aviator Shortages 122
    Mobilization of Reserve Aviation Units 122
    Deployments to Europe 123
Southeast Asia Deployments 124
Accomplishments of the Period 124
Endnotes 126

Chapter IX - Organizational Development 129
Organization Changes in the Department of the Army 130
Organization Changes in the Transportation Corps 130
Organization Changes in CONARC 133
    Establishment of Army Aviation Section 133
    1962 Reorganization 137
    Establishment of the Army Aviation Center 137
Aircraft Systems Management 138
Doctrine on Employment of Army Transport Aviation 139
Army Aviation in the New Division Organizations 140
AFTA and PENTANA 140
    Aviation in the Pentomic Divisions 141
    Fixed Wing Light Transport Companies 144
    Medium Helicopter Aviation Company 144
Army Aviation in the ROAD Organization 145
    Development of the ROAD Concept 145
    Basic Concept for Assignment of Aircraft 147
    The Army Aviation Battalion 147
    Aviation in Separate Brigades 148

      Army Organization for the Period 1965-1970 148
      Composite Aviation Battalion 149
      Special Warfare Aviation Detachment 149
  Army Aviation Air Traffic Operations 150
      Army Aviation Operating Detachments 150
      Use of Restricted Airspace 152
      U.S. Army Tactical Air Navigation and Landing Aids 153
      Common TA for Army Airfields 154
  Organizational Progress 155
  Endnotes 156

Chapter X - Development of Aircraft Armament 159
  Weapons System Development 159
      Project ABLE BUSTER 159
      Army Aviation School Experiments 160
      Aerial Combat Reconnaissance Company 163
      Formal Armament Program 164
      Airborne Troop Test of the SS-10 Missile System 167
  Adoption of the Armed Helicopter 168
  CDEC Experiments 169
  Army Aircraft Armament Ad Hoc Committee 174
  Armament and Airmobility 177
  Endnotes 179

Chapter XI - The Beginning of Airmobility 181
  Development of the Air Cavalry Concept 181
      Sky Cavalry 182
      Exercise SAGE BRUSH 183
      Exercise SLEDGE HAMMER 187
  The Armair Brigade Study 190
  Helicopter Carrier Tests 193
  Organizational Developments 195
  Endnotes 197

Chapter XII - Materiel Development 199
  U.S. Army Aviation Board 199
  The Development and Procurement Cycle 200
  Developmental Objectives for Army Aviation 202
  Helicopter Development 203
      HU-1 Iroquois 203
      Light Observation Helicopter 205
      Cargo Helicopters 207

      Flying Crane 209
   Development of Fixed Wing Aircraft 209
      T-37 Troop Test 210
      AO-1 Mohawk 214
      AC-1 Caribou 216
   Convertiplanes and Vertical Lift Research Vehicles 219
      Convertiplanes 219
      Flying Saucer 220
   The Status of Aircraft Development 221
   Endnotes 222

Chapter XIII - Development of Aviation Training 225
   Transfer of Training from the Air Force 225
      Early Interest in Training Consolidation 225
      Army Assumption of Training Responsibility 226
   Army Aviation Unit Tactical Training 231
   Revision in Helicopter Company Activation Schedule 232
   Growth of the Army Aviation School 235
      Organization 235
      Operations 236
   Training Developments 239
      Courses for Senior Officers 239
      Mountain Flight Training for Army Helicopter Pilots 240
      Instrument Training 240
   Army ROTC Flight Training Program 242
   Endnotes 244

Chapter XIV - Supply and Maintenance 247
   Transfer of Depot Responsibility 248
   Army Aviation Depot Plan 249
      Provisions of the Plan 249
      Implementation of the Plan 250
   Army Procurement of Aircraft 252
   Maintenance Personnel Problems 252
   Depot Maintenance Support 254
      Fifth Echelon Maintenance 254
      Fourth Echelon Maintenance 256
   Maintenance Training 257
      Army Aviation School 257
      Transportation School 261
   Endnotes 264

Chapter XV - Summary 267
List of Abbreviations 275
Appendix 277
    Fixed Wing Aircraft 1942-1962 278
    Rotary Wing Aircraft 1942-1962 279
    Convertiplanes and Vertical Lift Vehicles 1953-1962 .. 280
    Army Aviation School Courses 281
    Army Aviation School Maintenance Courses 282
    Transportation School Maintenance Courses 283
    Headquarters, CONARC 1 Feb 1955 284
    Headquarters, CONARC 10 Oct 1957 285
    Headquarters, CONARC 1 Jan 1959 286
    Aviation in the ROAD Division 287
    United States Army Aviation School 288
    Army Aviation Organization 289
    Directors of Army Aviation .... 290 - 293
    Pictorial Display of Army Aircraft .... 294 - 313
Index 315

List Of Illustrations

Piper Cubs used during 1941 maneuvers 5
L-4 Grasshopper during Carolina Maneuvers in 1942 6
L-20 and two L-19 aircraft in flight near Ft Monmouth 7
Wounded trooper evacuated during Exercise Southern Pine 30
Division Support helicopter & tanks on Exercise Longhorn ... 31
509th Transportation Company airlifting troops during
    Exercise Flashburn 34
First attempt to fire rockets from H-13 helicopter 162
H-25 Army Mule firing 1.5 inch rocket 164
Armed H-34 166
UH-1 helicopter armed w/ SS-11 antitank rockets 170
Friendly infantry troops boarding an H-34 for Exercise Sage Brush 184
Headquarters, USA primary helicopter school and Camp Wolters 227
Ozark Army Airfield, Ft Rucker, 1955 238

Foreword

Since their publication in the 1970s, the two separate works, *The History of Army Aviation, Phase I: 1950-1954*, and *The History of Army Aviation, Phase II, 1955-1962*, have been in steady demand by U.S. Army and other military researchers in the Army aviation field. Appearing in June 1971 and September 1976, respectively, those volumes were written by Mr. Richard P. Weinert, Jr., a staff historian in the Historical Office of the U.S. Continental Army Command until 1973, then Deputy Chief Historian in the Historical Office of the Army Training and Doctrine Command. The two volumes detail the early, formative years of Army aviation following the separation of the ground and air forces of the United States Army and the establishment of the United States Air Force as an independent service by the National Security Act of 1947. The call for this documented study has repeatedly exhausted printings of the two works. Prior to his retirement from federal service in 1988, Mr. Weinert took initial steps to organize his earlier work into a single publication. Since then, Dr. Susan Canedy, Research Historian and Archivist in the Office of the Command Historian, edited the combined manuscripts and completed the many other tasks necessary to bring the work to publication. The resulting volume is a reorganization of the two volumes, in which only redundancies of introduction and conclusion have been deleted. This single volume provides a useful record of the earliest stages of the battlefield function that would come into its own so dramatically in Vietnam and that would eventually be designated an Army branch in 1983.

HENRY O. MALONE, JR.

Author's Preface

Army aviation has grown dramatically in both size and breadth of activities since its inception in 1942. No comprehensive history of this growth has appeared. This monograph attempts to delineate the activities of Army Ground Forces (AGF), the Office of the Chief of Army Field Forces (OCAFF), and the United States Continental Army Command (CONARC) in the development of the aviation program from 1950 to 1962.

The period from 1950 to 1954 witnessed a critical phase in the growth of Army aviation. During this period the helicopter first began to perform a major tactical role, combat experience in Korea pointed the way to future developments, and the formation of the Army Aviation School provided a firm training base for expansion. Following 1954, Army aviation not only introduced new aircraft which significantly improved its capability, but also began development of new doctrinal concepts. The work on helicopter armament and airmobile concepts provided the ground work for the large scale airmobile combat operations which the Army would conduct during the following decade.

Because of the complexity of the subject, it has been necessary to organize this monograph topically rather than chronologically. Cross references are inserted where it is considered necessary to provide clarity.

Most of the primary documentary sources cited in the footnotes are located in the Civil Branch of the National Archives in Suitland, Maryland. Copies of many of these documents have been retained in the files of the United States Army Center of Military History and the TRADOC Command Historian. The published reports and secondary sources dealing with the Transportation Corps may be found in the library of the United States Army Transportation School at Fort Eustis, Virginia. The semiannual historical reports of AGF, OCAFF, and CONARC are in the files of the TRADOC Command Historian and the Center of Military History. The annual historical summaries of the Department of the Army staff elements are also located in the files of the Center of Military History.

The preparation of this monograph would not have been possible without the cooperation and assistance of the staffs of the Transportation Museum and library of the United States Army Transportation School, the United States Army Aviation Museum, *United States Army Aviation Digest*, the library of the United States Army Aviation School at Fort Rucker, Alabama, the National Archives, the United States Army Center of Military History, and the Historical Office, United States Army Materiel and Readiness Command.

The cooperation and assistance of many individuals contributed significantly to the research on this project: Mr. William D. Shaver, Jr., formerly of the CONARC Historical Office; LTC Donald F. Harrison, formerly with the Office of the Chief of Military History; Mr. Thomas E. Hohmann and Mrs. Ruth Nester of the Modern Military Records Division, National Archives; Mr. James Craig of the Army Aviation Museum; and COL W. R. Mathews, Aviation Division, Office of the Deputy Chief of Staff of Operations and Reserve Forces, Headquarters, CONARC.

RICHARD P. WEINERT, JR.

Chapter I

EARLY HISTORY OF ARMY AVIATION

Army organic aviation augments the capability of the Army to conduct effective combat operations. It is under the full and immediate control of, and subject to the direct orders of, the commander responsible for ground operations. Army aviation as it is known today dates from 1942, although aviation in various forms has been used by the Army for reconnaissance and observation since the Civil War. The capabilities of observation aircraft were developed during World War II and following that war, the helicopter began to play an increasingly important role. It was not until the Korean conflict, however, that Army aviation began to assume its present form. The period from 1950 to 1954 saw the emergence of Army aviation as a separate entity. During this period, the foundation was laid upon which the vast aviation structure of the Vietnam War period was built.

Balloons and Dirigibles

Aerial observation had its beginning in the United States Army on 6 June 1861 when Thaddeus S. C. Lowe brought his balloon to Washington to demonstrate its military potential. On 18 June, Lowe successfully sent a telegraph message from his balloon which in the presence of President Abraham Lincoln and War Department officials, he had maneuvered to an altitude of 500 feet. The War Department then asked Professor Lowe to ascend his balloon near Falls Church, Virginia, to determine the location of Confederate troops menacing the Capital. He began making ascensions on 22 June and eased the tense situation in Washington by reporting no offensive movement following the Confederate victory at Bull Run. He later used the balloon for artillery spotting with some success. The Balloon Corps was added to the Army of the Potomac on 25 September 1861. The corps expanded from four to seven balloons by early 1862 as operations spread out from Old Point Comfort, Virginia, west to the Mississippi River, and south to Mobile. Despite the initial success of the Balloon Corps, it was disbanded in June 1863, following a disagreement over placing it under the jurisdiction of the Signal Corps.[1]

Balloons were not again used by the Army until 1892 at which time the Signal Corps had only one balloon and no trained personnel. A balloon was in Cuba during the Spanish-American War. Its observers provided the Army with valuable information concerning the roads to the front lines and the location of the Spanish fleet, but the presence of the balloon bobbing above the advancing troops provided an ideal target for the Spanish artillery. The balloon was finally destroyed by enemy fire, much to the relief of the infantry. By 1907, the Signal Corps had increased its number of balloons to ten, but by the beginning of World War I only five free balloons were serviceable.[2]

At the outset of World War I, the training program for the Balloon Corps was stepped up with balloon companies organized and sent to the field artillery centers and schools in Texas, Oklahoma, California, and Virginia. As of 15 April 1918, the Army had only 2 balloon companies in operation, but by the armistice 33 companies and 117 officers had been sent overseas. Of the 265 balloons sent to France, 77 participated in combat, 48 of which were lost in action. During actual fighting, observation balloonists, who ascended as high as 4,500 feet and were able to see about eight miles in all directions, reported locations of enemy batteries, hostile aircraft, demolition behind enemy lines, and movement of enemy supplies and troops.

After the armistice, the Army canceled a number of lighter than air projects, and by the summer of 1920, the authorized balloon strength was cut to twenty-nine companies. The introduction of the fighter plane in World War I made the balloon exceedingly vulnerable, eliminating it as an effective means of aerial observation.[3]

The War Department also had been interested in dirigibles, providing $25,000 in November 1907 to procure an experimental model for the Signal Corps. A contract for $6,750 was awarded to Thomas Scott Baldwin, who after successfully completing a series of performance trials, taught three officers to fly the airship, which was designated U.S. Army Dirigible No.1. Although the airship made several demonstration flights around the country, it was not used after 1909 and was condemned and sold in 1912. The Army waited until 1919 to purchase its next airship, and by 1920 it had seven dirigibles. But like the balloon, the airship was supplanted by the airplane.

Development of Military Aviation

The United States became the first country in the world to contract for military aircraft when in December 1907 it called for bids on a military airplane. Of the three bids accepted by the Army, only the Wright brothers delivered. The Army accepted the aircraft on 2 August 1908, after its successful test in July by Orville Wright. By the summer of 1911, the Army had five airplanes. Another milestone was reached in November 1912 when the Army used airplanes for observation and adjustment of field artillery fire. An act of Congress of 18 July 1914 created the Aviation Section within the Signal Corps, thus increasing the strength and scope of Army aviation and giving it definite status.

The First Aero Squadron, the first tactical United States aviation unit, was organized on 5 March 1913. It began practical operations in 1916 in conjunction with the Mexican Punitive Expedition against Pancho Villa. Its achievements were not impressive, as most of the obsolescent aircraft broke down during preliminary reconnaissance missions.

American aerial reconnaissance experience in World War I centered around the First Aero Squadron, which arrived in France in September 1917. After training under French direction, the squadron went into action in the Toul Sector in April 1918 as the first American air unit to fly reconnaissance and observation missions in France. Brig. Gen. William Mitchell, commander of all air units of the American Expeditionary Force, added two other squadrons to the First, thus forming the 1st Corps Observation Group which reconnoitered for the artillery with distinction. By the end of the war, there were fifteen observation squadrons in Europe.[4]

With legislative authority granted by the Overman Act of 20 May 1918, President Woodrow Wilson by executive order removed Army aviation from the jurisdiction of the Signal Corps. Responsibilities for training and operations were vested in a Director of Military Aeronautics and the new organization was soon officially recognized as the Air Service. This designation was changed on 2 July 1926 to the Army Air Corps, but there were no fundamental changes in mission or organization. The tables of organization as of April 1926 called for a squadron of thirteen observation aircraft per division, while each corps headquarters was to have an observation group of two observation squadrons, a service squadron, and a photo squadron. Each Army and the General Headquarters of the Army was to have an observation group.

By 1930, emphasis began to shift to corps and division observation in coordination with ground units along the front lines. During this prewar decade, observation aircraft progressed from a series of small biplanes to the O-47, an all metal, 3-seat monoplane with retractable landing gear, and a 550 horsepower engine.

The Army Air Corps also considered a multi-engined, amphibious aircraft which would be used to observe and adjust coast artillery fire, but the Navy objected to Army encroachment on its mission of protecting the nation's shores. Subsequently, an agreement was reached which set the Army's sphere of operation and observation at 100 miles, thus forcing it out of the long range reconnaissance role.

Because of a change in organization, corps observation groups had doubled in number of aircraft by 1936, with four observation squadrons and a service squadron; however, at division level an officer and a small enlisted staff remained to assist the division commander on air matters. Under a further reorganization at a later date, the division air officers' function became centralized at corps headquarters.

Observation training in the thirties was neglected as pilots avoided this program because they felt that a successful and rewarding career in observation aviation was doubtful. As a result, the program faltered, morale sagged, and many officers transferred to bomber and fighter duty. The lack of funds during the thirties, along with a misunderstanding of the urgency of the requirements, served to delay the development of observation aviation.[5]

Establishment of Organic Army Aviation

After purchasing a Kellett K-2 autogiro for testing in 1930, the Army waited until 1936 to obtain the Kellett YC-1 and Pitcarn YU-2 and start combat tests at Langley Field, Virginia, and Fort Bragg, North Carolina. The Army was particularly interested in the potential use of the autogiro in tactical observation and command and liaison flights because of its ability to get in and out of small areas. Several serious accidents, weight limitations, failure to install additional observer type equipment, and failure in flight tests caused the cancellation of the autogiro program of development.

The answer to the problem of rotary powered flight seemed to be the helicopter. Encouraged by German success in this field in 1937, Congress appropriated $2,000,000 for the Army Air Corps to procure a helicopter. The XR-1, developed by Platt La Page Company, emerged in 1941, followed closely by the XR-1A later in the year. The advent of the war delayed any significant developments in rotary aircraft.[6]

After 1939, certain field artillery officers made a concerted effort to obtain efficient aircraft for their branch to be used for artillery observation. Proposals to include light observation planes organically in field artillery units were first advanced as a consequence of experience in the Louisiana Maneuvers of September 1941. In these maneuvers, the observation aircraft provided by the newly created air support commands proved to be inadequate. During the 1941 maneuvers, conducted in Tennessee, Kansas, Louisiana, Texas, and the Carolinas from April through October, 8 Piper Cubs, 4 Aeroncas, and 4 Taylorcraft were tested. The aircraft, their pilots, and mechanics were supplied by the aircraft manufacturers at no cost to the government, except that in the final stages of the Louisiana Maneuvers the Army contracted for the use of the so-called "Grasshopper Squadron" to assure their availability for a period after the date which the manufacturers had decided to withdraw them. According to Maj. Gen. Robert M. Danford, Chief of Field Artillery, the only uniformly satisfactory report of air observation during those Louisiana Maneuvers came from those artillery units which used light commercial planes (Piper Cubs) operated by civilian pilots. General Danford renewed a previous recommendation to the War Department to make light liaison planes, operated by field artillery officer-pilots, organic in the artillery component of each division and in each corps artillery brigade. Division and corps commanders who had participated in the Louisiana Maneuvers were unanimously in favor of this change.

Lt. Gen. Lesley J. McNair, Chief of Staff, General Headquarters, was well aware of the value of tactical air support for the ground forces and the importance of good aerial adjustment of artillery fire, but until the 1941 maneuvers he believed this was a responsibility of the Air Corps. After the maneuvers, General McNair recommended to General George C. Marshall, the Chief of Staff of the Army, that commercial planes be purchased to relieve the shortage of liaison aircraft.

In November 1941, General Marshall agreed that the commercial aircraft were of merit in regard to cost and availability and would relieve the current pressure on the production program of heavier tactical aircraft. As a result of this decision, the Materiel Division, General Headquarters, began negotiating for the purchase of 617 light aircraft. This initial procurement was increased more than tenfold in the next year.[7]

On 10 December 1941, General Marshall directed General Danford to test out his theory of organic aircraft. Two units—the 13th Field Artillery Brigade of the First Army and the 2d

Piper Cubs used during 1941 maneuvers.

Division Artillery of the Third Army—received twelve TO-59 Piper Cubs with each aircraft assigned a pilot and a specially trained mechanic. During the tests, which lasted all winter, the artillerymen trained enthusiastically under their civilian instructors. On 1 May 1942, Maj. Gen. Mark W. Clark, General McNair's Chief of Staff, received a favorable test report and promptly added his recommendation for approval.

The Secretary of War approved organic aviation for the field artillery on 6 June 1942. This action authorized 2 aircraft per light and medium artillery battalion, 2 per heavy artillery battalion normally assigned to brigade, 2 per field artillery group, and 2 for the headquarters and headquarters battery of each field artillery brigade and division artillery. Thus, Army aviation became a reality in the early days of World War II.[8]

Light aircraft were utilized for almost every conceivable mission during World War II. Every major command unit, except the Antiaircraft Command, established a requirement for organic assignment of aircraft. The period, 1942-1947, was characterized by the absence of any clear-cut basic understanding among the agencies concerned regarding the organic assignment of aircraft outside of the Army Air Force. Continuous difficulties over organization and control of these

An L-4 Grasshopper Observation plane of the 11th Observation Squadron taxis on a road during the Carolina Maneuvers in August 1942.

aircraft, referred to as liaison aircraft during this period, were further complicated by the questions of what type aircraft were to be used for the observation mission.

The nearest approach to any degree of accord on the light aviation issue during the war was contained in a set of principles recommended by the Army Air Force, generally accepted by Army Ground Forces, and given due consideration by the War Department in handling decisions on Army aviation. The salient features of these principles were: maximum sustained utilization of aircraft assigned organically to the Army Ground Forces; minimum detachment of individual aircraft from the main body; minimum duplication of Army Air Force units and equipment with a compensating increase in the ability to wage war; and, last, it was generally agreed that separate airdromes, depot maintenance facilities, and training facilities would not be required.

World War II Training

Early in World War II, responsibilities for the equipment, maintenance, and training associated with organic aviation were divided between the Army Ground Forces, which supervised tactical training of pilots and mechanics, and the Army Air Forces, which handled basic flight training of student pilots and their rating.

An L-20 (foreground) and two L-19 aircraft (background) in flight near Fort Monmouth, New Jersey.

On 14 January 1942, fourteen officers and twenty enlisted men of the Field Artillery, who were holders of civilian pilot licenses, reported to the Field Artillery School, Fort Sill, and were organized as the Air Training Detachment under the command of Lt. Col. W. W. Ford. Between 14 January and 28 February, these individuals received basic instruction in short field flying techniques and maintenance of liaison airplanes from seven civilian flying instructors and three civilian maintenance instructors. Thirteen officers and eight enlisted men successfully completed the course. When the War Department approved the adoption of organic air observation for the field artillery, it directed that the Field Artillery School conduct training of pilots and mechanics to be procured from the Ground Forces. Trainees had to have prior flight and mechanical experience. In the organization of the Department of Air Training, highly skilled flight instructors and maintenance instructors were hired from civilian life to give pilots intensive training.

Courses necessary for tactical training were organized in the Department of Air Training, set up in the Field Artillery School at Fort Sill, Oklahoma. The first eighteen pilots graduated on 18 September 1942. Controversy developed between the Ground Forces and the Air Forces over the recruiting of pilots and their qualification. The original plan provided that field artillery pilots might be noncommissioned officers with the rating of staff sergeants, as were all Army Air Force liaison pilots, but the majority of those recruited from the Army Ground Forces were commissioned officers. Beginning in September 1942, the Army Air Forces was to send 100 qualified liaison pilots a month to Fort Sill. This plan failed because the Army Ground Forces had difficulty finding qualified volunteers, while the Army Air Forces challenged the qualification of those admitted to the courses at the Field Artillery School. Those student pilots supplied by the Army Air Forces often failed to measure up to flying requirements of the Field Artillery School. There was constant disagreement whether or not the pilots should be observers trained to adjust artillery fire. The Air Forces contended that adjustment of artillery fire from a multi-seated aircraft could best be performed by an observer rather than by the pilot.

In September 1942, the commandant of the Field Artillery School made a concerted effort to assign responsibility for the procurement and rating of field artillery pilots to the Army Ground Forces. By November 1942, it was agreed that the Army Ground Forces should begin sending twenty-five ground officers per week to the Army Air Forces for training. These officers eventually would be included in the quota of forty which the Air Forces would send to Fort Sill every week.[9]

The first class under the Department of Air Training began on 3 August 1942 and was composed of officers up to captain, and enlisted volunteers who held or recently held Civil Aeronautics Agency private pilot licenses, had logged sixty hours pilot time, and weighed 170 pounds or less. The first basically trained pilots arrived at the Field Artillery School on 19 September. Twenty-five field artillery officers began Primary Flight Instruction at Denton, Texas, on 3 December, with the same number reporting each week thereafter for seven weeks of training as liaison pilots before reporting to Fort Sill for the 5-week advanced course. The duration of the primary flight course was changed to five weeks in February 1943.

Early in 1943, the War Department began to straighten out the difficulties over personnel and training that had arisen between the Army Ground Forces and the Army Air Forces and approved certain changes in the organic aviation program as requested by the Army Ground Forces. The most important change was that pilots were to be officers, trained to adjust fire. The pilot would be accompanied by a radioman-mechanic who was to watch for hostile planes and transmit fire directions to the ground. The new system assured Army Ground Forces control of and responsibility for the supply of pilots. Under the new arrangement, the Army Air Forces trained AGF volunteers as liaison pilots at the Army Air Forces flying schools at Denton and Pittsburg, Kansas, in a manner acknowledged by Army Ground Forces to be very satisfactory. The Field Artillery School no longer had to prolong its courses by giving its student pilots basic military training.

Late in February 1943, Army Ground Forces expressed its desire to include organic liaison aviation in tank destroyer units and mechanized cavalry units. It also wanted to provide divisions with airplanes, in addition to those with the artillery, for the use of the division commander and his staff and for work with division reconnaissance elements. About half of the planes and men requested were to be assigned organically to divisions and the remainder to tank destroyer and mechanized cavalry forces. The War Department estimated in March, that in order to implement the proposed extension of organic aviation in ground force units, approximately 1,500 liaison planes would be required in addition to the 2,500 necessary for the existing field artillery program. The War Department turned down the AGF proposal on 28 June, thereby stabilizing the organic ground force aviation program until almost the end of World War II.

During the period, 16 March - 19 April 1943, the Army Air Forces supplied the Artillery School with forty liaison pilots weekly. First priority on the weekly input of trainees went to all Field Artillery officers supplied by Army Ground Forces who had successfully completed the flight training course and had been rated liaison pilots. Second priority was given to enlisted graduates of the civilian pilot training-liaison pilot training course. These men were to have completed basic military training and were to be rated liaison pilots prior to their transfer to Fort Sill. Third priority was reserved for well qualified enlisted volunteers who had completed basic military training and who were rated liaison pilots.

On 20 April 1943, the War Department decided it would be better for enlisted men to attend officer candidate school before going to flight school. This decision was made because the enlisted men who were capable of doing an acceptable job as liaison aviators usually were officer candidate school material and left troop units for OCS shortly after reporting for duty.

The duration of the course at the Field Artillery School increased from seven weeks in February 1943 to fourteen in June 1945. Stress was placed on cross country flying and the lessons learned in the combat zones. Training was suspended from the fall of 1944 to January 1945 because a sufficient number of pilots had been trained to meet Army requirements. Contracts with civilian flying schools were cancelled and Army Air Force primary flight training at Pittsburg was discontinued.

Seaplane training for pilots and mechanics was begun in April 1944. Training in the use of the Brodie device was ordered by Army Ground Forces in October 1944. The Brodie device was a cable launching and landing apparatus which enabled aircraft to get in and out of confined or unimproved areas and to operate from Naval landing craft.

Following the resumption of training in January 1945, pilot losses in combat necessitated an increased input of from thirty to forty students every two weeks and a reduction of basic training to eleven or twelve weeks. Tactical instruction was cut to five weeks, and liaison pilots were rushed overseas until the situation eased. Beginning with Class Number 101, enrolled on 18 June 1945, the department reduced the student input from forty to thirty per class.[10]

By the end of World War II, 2,630 pilots and 2,252 mechanics had been trained. The cessation of hostilities interrupted the procurement and training programs and subsequently reduced the aircraft inventory from 1,600 to approximately 200 aircraft by late 1945.

The Separation of the Army and the Air Force

The National Security Act of 1947 established the United States Air Force as an independent service. Army Regulation 95-5 set forth the missions of Army aviation under the new arrangement in the following terms: expediting and facilitating the conduct of operations on land; improving mobility, command, control, and logistic support of Army forces; and facilitating greater battlefield dispersion and maneuverability under conditions of atomic warfare. At the same time, the provisions prevented infringement upon those areas of responsibility delegated to the Air Force by the Key West Agreement of 21 April 1948.

Joint Regulations

The Army and the Air Force, acting jointly, issued a number of so-called adjustment regulations, one of which amounted to a basic agreement on the question of Army organic aviation. On 29 May 1949, Joint Army and Air Force Adjustment Regulation 5-10-1, Combat Joint Operations, Etc.: Employment of Aircraft for Performance of Certain Missions, was issued. This regulation provided for two types of Army aircraft—fixed wing, not exceeding 2,500 pounds in weight; and rotary wing, weighing no more than 3,500 to 4,000 pounds. Organic aircraft could be utilized by the Army for the purpose of expediting and improving ground combat procedures in forward areas of the battlefield. Specific functions were very similar to those of light Army liaison airplanes during World War II. They included: (1) maintenance of aerial surveillance of enemy forward areas in order to locate targets, adjust fire, and obtain information on hostile defense forces; (2) aerial route reconnaissance; (3) control of march columns; (4) camouflage inspections of ground forces areas and installations; (5) local courier and messenger service; (6) emergency aerial evacuation; (7) emergency aerial wire laying; (8) limited aerial resupply; and (9) limited front line aerial photography. The agreement specified that the Air Force would provide liaison aircraft units to perform for the Army courier service, messenger service, aerial evacuation, aerial photography, aerial supply, and aerial wire laying.

Soon after publication of JAAFAR 5-10-1, the Ordnance Corps was assigned the major responsibilities for the logistical support of Army aircraft. The Army actively entered the aircraft supply field the following March when, in conjunction with the Air Force, it prescribed certain policies and procedures to be followed in "matters related to the development, procurement, supply, and maintenance of Army aircraft and allied aircraft equipment." On 23 March 1950, these took the form of identical documents, Army Regulation 700-50 and Air Force Regulation 65-7, Supplies and Equipment: Army Aircraft and Allied Equipment.[11]

Training Agreements

In late February 1947, General Jacob L. Devers, the Commanding General, Army Ground Forces, and Lt. Gen. J. K. Cannon, the Commanding General, Air Training Command, reached an agreement on the training of Army Ground Forces pilots. The Army Air Forces would conduct technical flight training to produce liaison pilots capable of operating AGF aircraft during daylight, darkness, and under marginal weather conditions from landing strips and roads normally used by AGF units. Also, the Air Forces would rate Army Ground Forces student pilots as liaison pilots upon successful completion of the Army Air Forces Liaison Pilot Course.

The Army Ground Forces agreed to conduct operational and tactical flight training; conduct instruction in the performance of first and second echelon maintenance of its aircraft; and conduct instruction in adjustment of fire, aerial reconnaissance, aerial photography, amphibious, airborne, and mountain operations, and any additional areas which might be required for Army Ground Forces pilots to accomplish their missions. All training was to be conducted at Fort Sill. Also, the AGF would evaluate the products of the Army Air Forces Liaison Pilot School through certain operational and tactical flight evaluation tests conducted by the Artillery School. The results of those tests, along with comments and constructive recommendations, were to be sent to the Army Ground Forces for transmittal to Air Training Command headquarters.

Flight Training

While the Army and the Air Force attempted to work out a division of their responsibilities, important changes had been taking place in Army organic aviation. On 7 December 1945, the Department of Air Training at the Field Artillery School had been redesignated the Army Ground Forces Air Training School, a change which resulted from an agreement to extend organic aviation to cavalry, infantry, engineer, armor, and tank destroyer units. An agreement between General Devers and General Ira C. Eaker, the Commanding General, Army Air Forces, also called for additional light aircraft for the AGF.

Training provided for the Army by the Air Force was conducted at several installations during the post-war period. Primary fixed wing training, which had been conducted at Sheppard Air Force Base, was transferred to Gary Air Force Base at San Marcos, Texas, in May 1946. Gary Air Force Base was closed in 1949 and all Army training was transferred to Connally Air Force Base, Waco, Texas. With the expansion of Army aviation after the outbreak of war in Korea, Gary Air Force Base was reopened and all primary flight training was transferred there, as was the training of mechanics which had been conducted at Sheppard Air Force Base.

The Air Training School at Fort Sill began operation early in 1946, but by June the demobilization of the Armed Forces brought about a severe shortage of personnel. As a result, the Air Training School had to eliminate seaplane training and had to reduce sharply the time devoted to the Brodie device. In November, the Department of Air Training again was established, and the Army Ground Forces Air Training School was discontinued. The department offered training support for all of the ground arms, rather than just for artillery as it had prior to 7 December 1945. During the period from 1946 to 1949, 486 officers graduated from the Army Ground Forces Pilot Course, while 461 enlisted men graduated from the Air Mechanic Course.

As a result of the February 1947 agreements, the program of instruction of the Army Air Forces Liaison Pilot Course was lengthened from four to five and one-half months. The maximum capacity of the Artillery School under the new program of instruction would be sixty students per class. The Army Ground Forces, anticipating a 40 percent attrition rate during the Army Air Forces Liaison Pilot Course, recommended that the maximum capacity of each class be established initially at 100 for reporting and 60 for graduation. Based upon pilot replacement requirements and experience gained in conducting the revised pilot courses, AGF also recommended changes in class capacities one month prior to the starting date of each class. It anticipated that classes would not be filled to maximum capacity because of shortages of company grade officers in the ground arms.

The Army Ground Forces Pilot Course conducted by the Artillery School was to be reduced from four to three months in order to maintain a continuous student load at the Artillery School of four 3-month classes per year. The Army Ground Forces proposed that the Artillery School attach an AGF combat-experienced pilot of field grade to the Army Air Forces Liaison Pilot School to serve as the AGF liaison officer to provide timely assistance and advice for the instructors.[12]

By far the most significant development of this period was the introduction of the helicopter into Army aviation. Early in 1945, the Army began investigating the feasibility of adapting rotary wing aircraft to the Army aviation mission. In 1946, the Army obtained its first helicopters—thirteen Bell YR-13s. In February 1947, the Bell Helicopter Corporation began the first formal Army helicopter pilot training course under contract at its factory facilities. Primary rotary wing training began at San Marcos on 1 September 1947 under Air Force direction.[13]

Army personnel qualified as helicopter pilots after twenty-five hours of flight instruction. Feeling that twenty-five hours were inadequate and that its pilots needed training in advanced techniques in helicopter flight, the Army established an advanced tactical training course at Fort Sill on 1 November 1948. Men who had taken their helicopter flight training from either the Air Force or Bell were the first instructors for the tactical helicopter training course.

During 1949 and early 1950, the training of helicopter pilots by both the Army and the Air Force had low quotas, none of which exceeded ten students per class. In August 1949, the Air Force Helicopter School program for Army Field Forces officers was extended from four to five weeks in duration, with a class capacity of six. Flight training increased from 25 to 30 hours and academic training increased from 40 to 51 hours. Officers selected to attend the course were Regular Army or selected reservists rated as liaison pilots, currently on flight status. Beginning in January 1950, all students, upon successful completion of the Air Force Pilot Helicopter Course, were required to enter the Army Field Forces Helicopter Pilot Course at the Artillery School. In December 1949, the Commanding General of the Artillery Center had recommended that the Army Field Forces Helicopter Course be extended from four to five weeks in order to provide increased instruction in maintenance, technical inspections, and practical field exercises. The Office of the Chief of Army Field Forces[14] approved this plan in late December and received Department of the Army approval in January 1950. Army Field Forces also authorized attendance at the Army Field Forces Helicopter Pilot Course for those officers who were trained as field artillery pilots during World War II in order to familiarize them with new tactical doctrine applicable to combat arms other than field artillery, new types of liaison airplanes, helicopters, communications equipment, and new conduct of fire procedures.

In view of the possible consolidation of helicopter training, the Artillery School in March 1950 pointed out that the existing facilities at Connally Air Force Base, where the first phase of training was then being conducted, were inadequate because of air congestion. If the course were to be consolidated at Fort Sill, eight weeks would be required to train a helicopter pilot, as duplication of time in performing basic maneuvers and allowing instructor pilots to become familiar with the students would be eliminated. Also, a considerable savings in funds and a subsequent increase in output would result from consolidation. Any real progress in consolidation was nevertheless stymied by the impact of the Korean conflict.[15]

Endnotes
Chapter I

1. (1) Alfred Goldberg, ed., *A History of the United States Air Force* (Princeton: D. Nostrand Inc., 1957), pp. 1-4. (2) Richard Tierney and Fred Montgomery, *The Army Aviation Story* (Northport, Ala.: Colonial Press, 1963), pp. 12-20. (3) For a detailed study of balloon operations in the Civil War, see F. Stansbury Haydon, *Aeronautics in the Union and Confederate Armies* (Baltimore: The Johns Hopkins Press, 1941), Vol. I.

2. Tierney and Montgomery, *The Army Aviation Story*, pp. 20-23.

3. Ibid., pp. 24-25.

4. (1) Ibid., pp. 26-29. (2) Goldberg, *A History of the U.S. Air Force*, p. 23. (3) Capt. Irving B. Holley, Jr., *Evolution of the Liaison Type Airplane, 1917-1944* (Maxwell AFB: Army Air Force Historical Office, 1946), pp. 1-2. (4) Irving B. Holley, Jr., *Ideas and Weapons* (New Haven: Yale University Press, 1953), pp. 49, 172.

5. (1) Goldberg, *The History of the U.S. Air Force*, pp. 29-38, 43. (2) Holley, *Evolution of the Liaison Type Airplane, 1917-1944*, pp. 7, 11, 26-27. (3) Tierney and Montgomery, *The Army Aviation Story*, pp. 39-43. (4) Robert F. Futrell, "Command of Observation," *U.S. Air Force Historical Study No. 24* (Maxwell AFB: Air University, 1952), pp. 6, 8. (5) James C. Fahey, ed., *U.S. Army Aircraft 1908-1946* (New York: Ships and Aircraft, 1946), p. 31. (6) Air Corps Advanced Flying School, *Observation Aviation*, p. 13.

6. (1) Col. H. Frank Gregory, *Anything a Horse Can Do, The Story of the Helicopter* (New York: Reynal and Hitchcock, 1941), pp. 7-89. (2) Holley, *Liaison Type Airplanes*, p. 47. (3) Futrell, *Command of Observation Aviation*, p. 16. (4) Army Air Forces, Vol. I, *The AAF Helicopter Program* (Wright Field: October 1946), pp. 11-22.

7. (1) Kent Roberts Greenfield, *Army Ground Forces and the Air-Ground Battle Team Including Organic Light Aviation*, AGF Study No. 35, 1948, p. 23. (2) Harrison, *History of Army Aviation* (Draft), pp. 40-43.

8. (1) Harrison, *History of Army Aviation* (Draft), pp. 44-45. (2) AGF Study No. 35, pp. 23-24. (3) Memo for CG AGF, WDGCT 320.2 (2-5-42), 6 Jun 42, subj: Organic Air Observation for Field Artillery.

9. AGF Study No. 35, pp. 24-28.

10. (1) History of the U.S. Army Artillery and Missile School, Vol. II, pp. 169-176. (2) Tierney and Montgomery, *The Army Aviation Story*, pp. 65-76.

11. R. Earl McClendon, *Army Aviation, 1947-1953*, Documentary Research Division, Research Studies Institute, Air University, Maxwell AFB, pp. 6-7.

12. Memo, CG AGF to CG Air Training Command, Barksdale Field, LA, 9 Apr 47, subj: Training and Rating of Army Ground Forces Pilots.

13. (1) Tierney and Montgomery, *The Army Aviation Story*, pp. 29-80, 93-96. (2) History of the U.S. Army Artillery and Missile School, Vol. III, pp. 10-18, 223-227, 349.

14. Headquarters, Army Ground Forces, was reorganized and redesignated as the Office of the Chief of Army Field Forces on 10 March 1948.

15. (1) Tierney and Montgomery, *The Army Aviation Story*, pp. 94-96. (2) History of the U.S. Army Artillery and Missile School, Vol. III, pp. 235-239. (3) Ltr ATTNG-12 360/83 (31 Aug 49), OCAFF to distr, 31 Aug 49, subj: H-13 Helicopter Pilots Course. (4) Ltr ARPSIAT 352.11, CG Artillery Center to OCAFF, 6 Dec 49, subj: Army Field Forces Helicopter Pilot Course, with 1st Ind CGSOT 352 (6 Dec 49), O&T Div to OCAFF, 10 Jan 50. (5) Ltr AKPSIAT 452.1, Comdt Artillery School to OCAFF, 14 Mar 50, subj: Army Helicopter Pilot Training.

Chapter II

THE EVOLUTION OF ARMY AVIATION

Organic Army aviation had emerged from World War II with a vast amount of both training and tactical experience. During the following five years the drastic reduction in the size of the Army had caused a major curtailment in aviation activities. It was during this period, however, that the Army began to give serious consideration to the use of the helicopter. Partially shackled by agreements with the Air Force, the Army in 1949 began to take the first tentative steps in expanding its aviation program. The outbreak of war in Korea gave an impetus to this expansion which resulted in a rapid growth of Army aviation in both size and importance.

Late in 1949, the Office of the Chief of Army Field Forces (OCAFF) conducted studies which indicated the need for various types of helicopters to provide short-haul air transport to corps, division, and smaller tactical units of the ground forces. This proposal received strong support in a Department of the Army G-3 study prepared in May 1950. It was therefore recommended that the Army provide funds in the fiscal year 1952 budget for the organization and equipping of five transport helicopter companies which would be placed with divisions in the United States for the purpose of developing doctrine for their employment.

The Transportation Corps' role in organic Army aviation stemmed from the development of this experimental program in the summer of 1950. Transportation Corps functions, largely of a staff nature, involved planning and coordination with the Army Field Forces and the Army General Staff regarding the activation, equipping, and formulation of doctrine for the employment of cargo helicopter units.[1]

The outbreak of the Korean conflict resulted in quick action in the development of the helicopter program. Provision was made for five Army helicopter transport companies in the Emergency Supplemental Budget for fiscal year 1951. In order to organize such units as soon as practicable and to gain combat experience in Korea, OCAFF was instructed on 9 August 1950 to undertake the early activation and training of four of the five units. These four companies were to be equipped with the H-19 CHICKASAW helicopter. The fifth company was planned to be organized in the latter part of fiscal year 1951 and would be equipped with H-21 WORKHORSE helicopters which were expected to become available in the fall of 1951.

Cross-servicing orders for the procurement of these helicopters were placed with the Air Force in late August and September.[2]

Planning for Organic Air Transport

On 8 September 1950, General J. Lawton Collins, the Chief of Staff of the Army, requested the Air Force to lift the weight restrictions imposed by JAAFAR 5-10-1. General Collins emphasized that there was no intention on the part of the Army to infringe on the agreed roles and missions of the Air Force. But he believed that it was essential for the Army to have organic helicopters to be used for short haul transport in corps, divisions, and smaller tactical units. And the H-21, which was a basic component of the expansion plan, exceeded the weight allowed the Army. Unless the Army obtained permission from the Air Force to lift the weight restriction, the aviation expansion program would not be possible.[3]

Department of the Army Proposals

In October 1950, the Assistant Chief of Staff, G-3, Department of the Army, prepared a study to determine the desirability of forming experimental units to be equipped with helicopters instead of ground transport. The study also explored the development procedures and doctrine for the use of organic air transport in Army units and the feasibility of converting a portion or all of the ground transportation of certain special Army units to helicopter air transport.

The Department of the Army study group concluded that it was feasible to provide certain Army units with helicopters, which would not require prepared landing fields. With the aircraft currently being procured, the Army would have sufficient helicopters, pilots, and maintenance personnel by 1 January 1952, exclusive of the five authorized helicopter transport companies, to be in a position to experiment with the use of short haul organic air transport in Army units. Helicopter transport companies then being organized would perform as units for transport purposes in divisions or corps and not be broken up or utilized to provide organic unit transport on a permanent basis to company or battalion-size units.

The G-3 study group recommended that as helicopters became available for operation above the requirements of the five helicopter transport companies, an experimental infantry battalion be equipped with helicopter transport in lieu of ground vehicles. The Army Airborne Center would use this battalion to test the feasibility of providing organic short haul transport. An experimental field artillery battery equipped with helicopters in lieu of vehicles would be placed under the control of the Artillery School for the same purpose.

The group further recommended that an experimental infantry battalion equipped with helicopters be formed at the Infantry School which would be used to test the feasibility of providing organic air transportation to infantry units for special purposes such as mountain, arctic, and jungle operations. The group recommended the Army Field Forces explore uses for Army organic air transport which could operate without prepared landing fields. Whenever practicable, the Army Field Forces should include the use of this special air transport in training exercises and maneuvers. All reports of tests and special training exercises utilizing helicopters would be submitted to the Department of the Army.[4]

The Chief of Staff of the Army approved these recommendations in January 1951, directing that the experimental units at Forts Bragg, Benning, and Sill be placed in operation as rapidly as possible. As helicopters became available over and above those needed for the original five units, they would be used instead of ground vehicles in the experimental infantry and artillery battalions and in training exercises and maneuvers. Preliminary training and tests were to be conducted as soon as small helicopters were available, pending the receipt of cargo-type helicopters. The implementation of the project was to proceed on a high priority since the results might form the basis of important changes in Army transport.[5]

In the weeks that followed, plans for the employment of the five helicopter companies were developed. To facilitate rapid development of techniques and doctrine, one company each was to be assigned to the Far East Command and the Transportation School and to an airborne division, an armored division, and an infantry division in the United States. Five additional companies were included in the fiscal year 1952 troop basis. On the basis of planned augmentation of the Army in fiscal year 1951, anticipated future requirements totaled four helicopter transport battalions and fourteen helicopter transport companies.[6]

The experimental program, and also the original five helicopter transport companies, were held up because of the continuing disagreement with the Air Force regarding the size of Army aircraft. General Collins in November requested that the Air Force expedite procurement of H-19s and H-21s for the Army. On 13 December 1950, General Hoyt S. Vandenberg, the Chief of Staff of the Air Force, replied that he would not agree to the elimination of weight limitations on Army aircraft. He believed that the necessary air transport support of ground forces could be furnished by placing helicopters and other required equipment in Air Force assault squadrons. Following this nonconcurrence, the Air Force halted procurement of the helicopters ordered by the Army. At about the same time, the 1st Helicopter Company (later redesignated the 6th) was activated without equipment at the Artillery School.[7]

General Mark W. Clark, the Chief of Army Field Forces, urged that the weight restrictions for Army aircraft be removed and that helicopters be obtained as soon as possible. General Clark recommended that the four remaining helicopter companies be activated so that they could be field tested. These field tests would provide the basis for further consideration of the most profitable employment of helicopters.[8]

Since the Chiefs of Staff of the Army and the Air Force had reached an impasse in regard to the weight restriction, the matter was referred to the service secretaries for decision. On 24 January 1951, Frank M. Pace, the Secretary of the Army, and Thomas K. Finletter, the Secretary of the Air Force, met to discuss the proposed revision of JAAFAR 5-10-1. They failed to reach an agreement either in the form of a new joint regulation or a special memorandum of agreement between themselves on the general subject of Army aircraft. Secretary Finletter felt that the position of the Army represented an encroachment into the area of responsibility assigned to the Air Force which would have a far-reaching effect on the field of air transport.

Besides its interest in cargo helicopters, the Army in the following months requested the procurement of 284 L-20 fixed-wing airplanes weighing around 3,000 pounds each, or approximately 500 pounds over the limit previously set. The Air Force continued to insist that in the field of air transport it alone had broad encompassing responsibilities. In the view of the Air Force, the Army functions were restricted to primary or local responsibilities, including courier and messenger services; limited responsibilities, principally aerial supply and aerial photography; and emergency responsibilities, mainly aerial evacuation and aerial wire laying. Secretary Finletter contended that although it might perform the operations indicated in the latter two categories with aircraft on hand, the Army could justify its organic aircraft program only upon the basis of local or primary responsibilities. On 1 August 1951, however, he agreed to waive the weight restriction in order to procure the L-20s, which was done with the understanding that "the Air Force does not abrogate any of its functions," and upon the assurance by the Secretary of the Army that the "Army does not intend to build an organic Army Air Force to perform functions of the USAF."[9]

Army Field Forces Board No. 1 Projects

In mid-November 1950, Army Field Forces, realizing the increasing need for aircraft in Korea, directed Army Field Forces Board No. 1, which was a part of the Research and Development Section, G-3, to reevaluate the needs for Army aircraft in the various types of units. The board prepared and circulated a questionnaire to interested agencies for comment. The entire scope of the project, which was broken down into three related studies, was discussed at an Army aviation conference held at Fort Bragg, North Carolina, between 8 and 10 January 1951. Representatives from the Department of the Army, Army Field Forces, the CONUS armies, and the principal service schools and boards attended. Two major proposals were presented. One of these recommended that Army aviation in infantry, airborne, and armored divisions be centralized in divisional aviation companies which would serve all division needs for organic aircraft. The second proposal was the creation of an Army Aviation Corps which would embrace all elements currently present in Army aviation, including field maintenance functions then performed by the Ordnance Corps and aerial transport functions contemplated for the Transportation Corps. Because neither of the proposals carried, they were not at that time made a part of the Army Field Forces Board report.

The report made by the board in March 1951 represented the consensus of both the questionnaires and the January conference. Study Number 1, which was to determine the need for additional types of aircraft in Army Field Forces units and the extent to which these aircraft should supplement or replace present types, concluded that 2- and 4-place utility helicopters should be in the TOE of units, but that light cargo helicopters should, for the present, be limited to experimental organizations such as transportation helicopter companies. The board recommended that research on medium helicopters be promoted. The study indicated that a requirement existed for a light, multi-passenger, fixed wing, multi-engine aircraft for use at corps, army, and comparable headquarters, but that no requirement existed for a special aircraft for the adjustment of long range artillery fires.

Study Number 2 had as its purpose the determination of the aircraft requirements of Army Field Forces units assuming a decentralized organization and proven types of aircraft. No organization which answered the questionnaire reported the number of aircraft presently assigned to be excessive; in fact, many agencies desired additional aircraft. The conferees recommended twenty-six aircraft for the infantry division. The representatives of the Artillery School disagreed, contending that 2 helicopters were required in the division artillery headquarters and 1 additional 2-place, fixed wing aircraft was needed in each artillery battalion, thereby bringing the aircraft in the division to 32.

Although the majority of agencies which answered questionnaires reported in favor of the organic assignment of aircraft to regiments and battalions, neither the conference nor Army Field Forces Board No. 1 concurred with this principle, which they considered an uneconomical method of aircraft distribution.

In order to determine which type of Army aviation organization would produce the greatest efficiency in its assigned role, Army Field Forces Board No. 1 undertook Study Number 3. The board recommended that under battle conditions at least 50 percent of the aircraft assigned to a division (13 of 26) should be operational. The proposal for this number of aircraft obviously originated from the feeling by each commander that he must have his own organic aircraft; he could not rely upon someone else, such as the artillery or the division headquarters, to furnish aircraft when it would be needed. The commander also had a feeling that if he needed one aircraft he had to have two to protect against periods when some would be nonoperational. In the opinion of Army Field Forces Board No. 1, this reasoning was unsound. Additional items of equipment should not be provided by the table of organization to guard against their misuse.

Army Field Forces Board No. 1 in its Study Number 3 concluded that decentralized organization of Army aviation was uneconomical as it required more aircraft, more associated equipment, and more personnel than a central organization would require for the same job. The board also concluded that decentralized organization was inefficient because it would not provide adequate technical command supervision over training, maintenance, or operations; it could not afford to provide all the technical skills needed; it made it hard to to take up the slack in maintenance when mechanics were in short supply; and it did not conform to common use of basic field equipment.

Following up on the recommendations of the Army Field Forces Board No. 1 regarding the needs for Army aircraft in the various types of units, Army Field Forces on 19 June 1951 forwarded its revision of proposed aircraft requirements to the Department of the Army. The latter approved these requirements on 26 June and included them in its current procurement planning.[10]

The Memorandum of Understanding of 1951

The negotiations with the Air Force finally resulted in Secretaries Pace and Finletter signing a Memorandum of Understanding on 2 October 1951. The most significant aspect of this memorandum was the elimination of the maximum weight restrictions on Army organic aircraft in favor of a definition solely in terms of the functions to be performed. Army organic aircraft were to be used "as an integral part of its components for the purpose of expediting and improving ground combat and logistical procedures within the combat zone." The combat zone could vary in depth according to conditions, but it was understood that it would normally not exceed fifty to seventy-five miles.

Army organic aircraft were to perform the following functions: (1) aerial observation for the purpose of locating, verifying, and evaluating targets, adjusting fire, studying terrain, and obtaining information on enemy forces not otherwise obtained by air reconnaissance agencies of the other services; (2) control of Army forces; (3) accomplishment of command, liaison, and courier missions; (4) performance of aerial wire laying; and (5) transportation of supplies, equipment, and small units within the combat zone. The Air Force was still assigned the primary function of supplying the necessary airlift to the Army. Army aircraft were not to duplicate the functions of the Air Force in providing close combat support, assault transport and other troop carrier airlift, aerial photography, tactical reconnaissance, and interdiction of enemy land power and communications.[11]

The friction between the two services was somewhat eased later in the month when the Army decided to seek the procurement of cargo helicopters for only five, rather than ten, companies. The establishment of firmer requirements and the need for any expansion of production would be contingent on the evaluation of tests with the five companies and on the progress of aircraft development.

Only limited progress was made in implementing the five company program. The 6th Helicopter Company had been assigned veteran officer pilots. Training classes for warrant officer pilots and enlisted mechanics were initiated at Fort Sill in June 1951, and in August a second unit, the 13th Transportation Helicopter Company, was activated. Neither unit had cargo helicopters, and it was necessary to provide small utility-reconnaissance types for use in training and in maneuvers held in the late summer and winter. The lack of suitable equipment adversely affected the operational readiness of the units and delayed the activation of the other companies.[12]

Although the Memorandum of Understanding had marked a milestone in the development of Army aviation, it did not settle the basic dispute with the Air Force. Renewed discussions began on 10 November 1951 when the Army approved an urgent Far East Command request for 122 additional helicopters in Korea. Far East Command proposed that the Air Force receive fifty of the cargo helicopters and that the Army receive seventy-two. The Air Force objected that the requirements in Korea were identified largely with its own functions. Secretary Pace replied that the Air Force had not made appropriate allocation of helicopters between the two services. In order to carry out the function of transporting its "supplies, equipment, and small units within the combat zone" the Army had decided that it was necessary to organize an adequate number of transportation helicopter companies and air evacuation units. The Secretary of the Air Force maintained that the role of the Army was still limited and secondary.

According to its interpretation of the Memorandum of Understanding, the Department of the Army programed transportation helicopter companies for several types of missions. The Army envisioned that a primary mission of the helicopter companies would be the transportation of high priority Class I, II, and V supplies from Army depots located in the rear of the army area to supply points located immediately in the rear of the divisions. The emergency issue of all classes of supply from depots or supply points to divisions by attaching helicopters to divisions to replace conventional transportation would also be of vital importance. Another crucial mission would be the emergency lateral shifting of supplies and troops to meet unforeseen situations. Helicopters also were to be used to transport troops and critical Class IV supplies in support of such operations as river crossings, where speed and deception were vital. The transportation of supplies, equipment, and small units anywhere within the combat zone where terrain conditions or other obstructions made ground means of transportation inadequate also would be the job of the helicopter.

In order to properly employ needed helicopters, the Army maintained that commanders required command and control of transportation units. Only then could they analyze their available resources and requirements and assign premium transportation to the area of maximum benefit. Because helicopter support would have to be made readily available to the unit which required assistance, helicopter units were to be assigned to the field army and temporarily attached by that headquarters to support whatever subordinate unit had the requirement, just as additional motor vehicles and tactical resources were available at the field army level to meet peak demands of subordinate echelons.

The use of helicopters was expected to reduce the requirements for other transportation equipment and units. The facility with which helicopters were able to overcome obstacles such as streams, snow, and poor roads would reduce the requirement for special equipment such as amphibious trucks, assault boats, and Weasels. The helicopter, in assuming the missions of ground transport, would be under the direct operational control of the tactical unit commander.[13]

Development of a Long Range Program

The continuing dispute with the Air Force had not only delayed completion of the original five transportation helicopter company program, but it had also slowed the development of a long range program for Army aviation.

In February 1951, the Air Force agreed to procure a limited number of cargo helicopters sufficient for the original five companies in the program. The delays in completing the equipping of the authorized companies were mainly the result of the limited production capacity of the helicopter industry. The helicopters being produced at that time were for the most part already committed to various Air Force and Navy programs. The Transportation Corps believed that it was necessary to order a substantial number of helicopters in line with the Army's ultimate expectation of its use, rather than to await complete development of doctrine, employment, and aircraft. In June, the Chief of Transportation proposed the adoption of a 3-year program for 3,000 helicopters to meet the Army's current needs and provide a base for mobilization requirements.

For various reasons, there was an unwillingness at the Department of the Army level to undertake an expanded cargo helicopter program. Aside from the Air Force's reluctance to procure larger transport helicopters, there appeared to be opposition within the Army to the large outlay of money required. And in some quarters there was still some doubt that the helicopter was a practical vehicle for the transportation mission.

In November, the Department of the Army G-3 recommended the reinstitution of a 10-company program, and money was provided to support the expanded program. To facilitate planning, the recommendations of Far East Command were requested regarding its needs for current operations and the requirements for a type field army. Far East Command set its requirements for current operations at 4 battalions of 3 companies each, and recommended 10 battalions for the type field army.

To support the 10-company program, G-3 included 97 H-19s and 85 H-21s in the fiscal year 1951 and 1952 budgets, and 80 H-19s were added to the fiscal year 1953 budget. No further expansion was recommended by G-3, Department of the Army, until field experience with Army transportation helicopters proved that the advantages of additional helicopter companies justified the necessary expense in funds and manpower. In addition, G-3 urged that caution would have to be taken to assure that each expansion in number or size of aircraft by the Army was preceded by an increase in the ability of the Army to operate and maintain the aircraft. Experience with four utility helicopters sent to Korea in the fall of 1950 had shown that there would be a continuous requirement in combat for Army air evacuation units operating small helicopters.[14]

Chief of Transportation Study

The Department of the Army requested Maj. Gen. Frank A. Heileman, Chief of Transportation, to submit his comments on the recommendations of the Far East Command. The comments were to include the basis of assignment of transportation helicopter companies or battalions to divisions, corps, and armies and the possible reduction in the number of other units, such as truck companies, to provide the necessary personnel spaces needed to implement an expanded helicopter program. General Heileman concurred with the requirements for transportation helicopter battalions recommended by the Commander in Chief, Far East Command (CINCFE), and supported the contention that procurement should be instituted immediately on such a scale so as to increase the production rate of the helicopter industry.

The Chief of Transportation believed that the request of CINCFE was tempered by a knowledge of the present availability of helicopters, but concurred in the requirement of ten transportation helicopter battalions. He also agreed that the helicopters of a type field army should be capable of producing a total lift which would be equivalent to ten battalions of H-21s, or other medium cargo helicopters, with approximately 14,000 pounds payload. In order to allow greater versatility and to achieve a proper balance of equipment, the Chief of Transportation recommended that the ultimate assignment to field armies consist of 3 light cargo helicopter battalions (3,000 pounds payload per helicopter), 6 medium cargo battalions (4,000 - 6,000 pounds), and 1 heavy cargo battalion (8,000 - 20,000 pounds). The Chief of Transportation mentioned in passing that the CINCFE apparently overlooked the requirement for administrative helicopters in battalion headquarters. Proposed tables of organization and equipment allowed two cargo models and two utility helicopters per battalion headquarters. Each operating company had twenty-one cargo models for task use and one utility type, in line with the CINCFE proposal.

Regarding tactical deployment of troops, General Heileman surmised that the Army might use its helicopters as did the Marines in Korea. The lack of roads, railways, and prepared airfields in Korea, as well as the adverse battle conditions facing surface transportation, might necessitate the replacement of a certain number of trucks and relieve the necessity for costly road construction and maintenance. In addition, any tactical needs such as movement of reserves, redeployment of front line units, and the extraction of troops in tactical difficulties could be satisfied by the use of helicopters. Helicopters also could be relied upon to carry emergency and high priority cargoes amounting to an average of 10 percent of the total supply movement, thus allowing an adequate reserve for troop movement, tactical movements, and evacuation tasks.

The Chief of Transportation further recommended that ten helicopter battalions be assigned to each field army with control exercised by the G-4 through his Transportation Movement Section. Control at the field army level was ruled essential in order to permit concentration of the entire fleet upon a single project and to allow shifting within the army area as required. The introduction of ten helicopter battalions into the transportation system of a field army would reduce to some extent the number of truck units required in the organization. Availability of helicopters would also completely eliminate the necessity for such expedients as human bearers and pack animals.

The Chief of Transportation recommended an immediate program of production and the organization to fulfill the Army mobilization requirement for 2,500 helicopters. In order to protect foreseeable mobilization requirements, a minimum of 1,000 helicopters of the largest available type would have to be included in the 1953 budget with a similar quantity to be included in the budget for the following year. He also suggested that thirty to fifty million dollars should be made available to the three primary helicopter manufacturers for the expansion of production facilities and for expediting their production engineering program. In conclusion, General Heileman recommended that a Department of the Army panel be formed and charged with the development of a transportation helicopter program for the Chief of Staff.

While concurring in the basic concepts set forth by the Chief of Transportation, the Army Field Forces commented that transportation helicopter units would be used primarily in a tactical role to provide logistical support within the forward combat areas by providing troop and supply movement. OCAFF agreed with the Chief of Transportation that helicopters of a type field army should be capable of producing a total lift equivalent of ten battalions of H-21 or other medium cargo helicopters, each with approximately 4,000 pounds payload. However, in the face of the current helicopter supply situation, a more realistic breakdown for the next several years would be 6 light helicopter battalions, 3 medium helicopter battalions, and 1 heavy helicopter battalion. OCAFF was of the opinion that for the next several years industry would be able to support 2,000-pound class helicopters (H-13s and H-23s) in greater quantities than 4,000- to

6,000-pound machines (H-19s and H-21s). To prevent delay in organizing and equipping battalions, consideration should be given to the use of the preponderance of helicopters which would be more readily available. The use of a more readily available helicopter would cut down the ton-mile capability, which could remain equivalent only by increasing the number of light helicopters which in turn would require additional pilots and mechanics.

The Army Field Forces did not agree with the proposal for having two cargo helicopters per battalion headquarters. Each operating company already was authorized two utility helicopters in order to ensure one operational utility helicopter at all times. OCAFF also stated that because of limitation of helicopters operating at high altitudes and under certain extremely bad weather conditions, alternate forms of transportation such as human bearers and pack animals could not be completely eliminated from use at that time. According to OCAFF, consideration should be given to the availability of any operational aircraft when determining their equivalent to truck companies. The large amount of maintenance required on cargo helicopters would materially affect such comparisons. Regarding limitations of large helicopters, OCAFF agreed with the Chief of Transportation, but recommended that a proportionate ratio of various sizes be considered. While agreeing with the recommendation to establish a Department of the Army panel to develop the doctrine and quantitative and qualitative standards for a helicopter program, OCAFF felt that such a panel should cover not only transportation helicopter problems but also consider the entire Army aviation structure and concept.[15]

Endnotes
Chapter II

1. Joseph Bykofsky, *The Support of Army Aviation, 1950-1954*, Office of the Chief of Transportation, 1955, p. 2.

2. Ibid., pp. 15-17.

3. Memo, CofSA for CofS USAF, 8 Sep 50, subj: Army Organic Aircraft.

4. (1) Ltr, OCAFF to DA ACofS G-3, 9 Aug 50, subj: Report of Study of Requirements of Army Field Forces for Rotary Wing Aircraft, AFF Board No. 1. (2) Memo, ACofS G-3 to DA ACofS G-4, 29 Aug 50, subj: Report of Study of Requirements of Army Field Forces Board No. 1. (3) Ltr, DA ACofS G-3 to OCAFF, 23 Oct 50, subj: Army Organic Air Transport and incl, Study on Army Organic Air Transport, 8 Oct 50.

5. Ltr G-3 580 TS (12 Oct 50), DA to CAFF, 22 Jan 51, subj: Army Organic Air Transport.

6. Bykofsky, pp. 17-18.

7. (1) Ltr, General J. Lawton Collins to General Mark W. Clark, undated, with incl, Memo for CofSA, 13 Dec 50, subj: Army Organic Aircraft (Helicopter). (2) Bykofsky, p. 19.

8. MFR, DA G-3 O&T Div Orgn Br, 30 Dec 50, subj: General Clark's Recommendations on Army Aircraft and Transportation Corps Helicopter Companies.

9. McClendon, pp. 21-22.

10. (1) AFF Bd No. 1, Report of Study of Project No. AD 1250, Tables of Equipment Governing Army Aircraft, with Appendixes A-F, 14 Mar 51. (2) Ltr ATTNG 452.1, CAFF to DA ACofS G-3, 19 Jun 51, subj; Army Field Forces Board Report with 1 incl, subj: Proposed Aircraft Requirements by Type with 1st Ind AGADS 452.1 (19 Jun 51) G-3, DA AGO to CAFF, 26 Jul 51, same subj.

11. (1) McClendon, pp. 22-23. (2) Ltr, General J.E. Hull, VCofS to CAFF, 8 Oct 51, subj: Memorandum of Understanding Between the Secretary of the Army and the Secretary of the Air Force, with incl.

12. Bykofsky, p. 20.

13. Memo, DA G-3 O&T Div for CofS, 31 Mar 52, subj: Requirements for Cargo Type Helicopters, TABs C and G.

14. (1) Summary Sheet G-3 452 (4 Mar 52), DA G-3 O&T Div Orgn R&D Br, 28 Apr 52, subj: Requirements for Cargo Type Helicopters. (2) Bykofsky, pp. 22-23.

15. (1) DF (13 Nov 51), DA ACofS G-3 to Chief of Transportation, 19 Nov 51, subj: Requirements for Cargo Helicopters. (2) Ltr, Chief of Transportation to DA ACofS G-3, 4 Dec 51, subj: Army Helicopter Program, with 1st Ind ATTNG-22 452 (4 Dec 51), CAFF to DA ACofS G-3, 29 Jan 52.

Chapter III

THE FORMATIVE YEARS

Army aviation in 1952 entered on a period of rapid expansion and change. After numerous delays and difficulties, the first helicopter companies were organized, trained, and deployed. At the same time, the entire aviation program underwent extensive review which resulted in a significant expansion of the program. By the end of 1954, the aviation program had taken the form which it was to retain until the development of the airmobility concept in the 1960s.

Helicopter Units

Unit Activations

The Army Field Forces in June 1952 revised its plan for the activation of twelve helicopter ambulance detachments. Two units, the 37th and the 53d, were activated in July, earlier than planned, in order to establish requirements for personnel and equipment. The remaining ten detachments also were to be activated sooner than scheduled. Only the 53d was to remain in the continental United States for general use.[1]

Early in 1952, the XVIII Airborne Corps recommended to OCAFF that a helicopter company be activated at Fort Bragg and attached to the corps. It was the opinion of the corps that the establishment of tactics, techniques, and doctrine concerning the tactical employment of the helicopter could be accomplished only by placing a helicopter unit at the disposal of tactical field units. Despite the recommendations of XVIII Airborne Corps and Third Army, OCAFF recommended that for the time being all transportation helicopter companies should be activated and initially trained at Fort Sill or a helicopter training school. Units would then be moved to a division station to complete their unit training. The Fort Bragg—Camp Mackall area was, in the opinion of OCAFF, a suitable station because of the presence of a division and also the availability of suitable facilities. The Department of the Army in May 1952 approved the recommendation of OCAFF that all transportation helicopter companies be activated at Fort Sill. A total of three companies in addition to the 6th and 13th Transportation Helicopter Companies had been programed for activation at Fort Sill during fiscal year 1953. The Department of the Army anticipated that the 6th Transportation Helicopter Company would be deployed overseas upon completion of unit training, which it hoped would be under a tactical unit. In order to accomplish this training, the 6th Transportation Helicopter Company was transferred to Fort Bragg in mid-1952.

Late in October, the Chief of Transportation rejected the Army Field Forces proposal to use Fort Bragg, Fort Benning, Camp Cooke, Fort Lewis, Fort Riley, and Camp Polk, as training stations for transportation helicopter companies. Fort Bragg was at that time the only post equipped to conduct unit training, both from a personnel and equipment viewpoint. Establishment of other training areas, in the opinion of the Chief of Transportation, would necessitate use of personnel entirely unfamiliar with the concept of employment or the problems involved in the training of such companies. The Chief of Transportation considered it inadvisable to attempt undirected unit training at locations lacking established facilities and personnel qualified by experience. Field manuals on concept of employment were then under study and were unavailable to the field. He also recommended that careful consideration be given to the use of a unit in close proximity to the manufacturers of presently contracted aircraft to facilitate the ferrying of the aircraft to the using unit. The configuration of the H-19 and H-21 was such that movement by rail or truck was impossible unless the aircraft were completely disassembled. The problem of supply had to be considered, as each additional training center would require additional supply channels, storage facilities for spares, and increased personnel to maintain and account for these supplies. By using one unit training center, the supply problem would be held at a minimum.

The Chief of Transportation therefore recommended that Fort Bragg be established as the training center for all transportation helicopter units. The units would undergo unit training at that station prior to assignment to overseas commands or to stations in the continental United States. He further recommended that the ten helicopter companies scheduled for activation be trained and committed as follows:

6th Co	Fort Bragg	Far East Command
13th Co	Fort Bragg	Far East Command
506th Co	Fort Bragg	Fort Benning
509th Co	Fort Bragg	European Command
522d Co	Fort Bragg	Far East Command
527th Co	Fort Bragg	Fort Eustis
530th Co	Fort Bragg	European Command
532d Co	Fort Bragg	European Command
a	Fort Bragg	Fort Bragg
a	Fort Bragg	Far East Command

a = These companies had not been assigned a number.

Army Field Forces did not favorably consider the recommendation for a single Transportation Helicopter Company Unit Training Center at Fort Bragg. It believed that the additional experience gained by army, corps, and division personnel in supervising and observing the training program in each of the army areas would far outweigh the slightly more efficient unit training which might be obtained at a single center. In addition, OCAFF stated that experience gained at these stations would contribute to early development of sound doctrine and tactics and would establish a basis for unit training in the event of a rapid expansion of the helicopter program. In the light of the transportation and supply problems, OCAFF concluded that the two companies recommended for training at Fort Lewis could be more economically trained at Fort Bragg. The companies which would conduct unit training at Forts Benning, Eustis, and Riley and Camp Polk would be permanently stationed at those locations. There might be some sacrifice in efficiency of unit training at these stations, but the experience gained by supervisory personnel would offset the disadvantages. Conduct of unit training at permanent stations was more economical because it eliminated movement of the unit from Fort Bragg to the permanent station. Troops and equipment would be available at those stations for use in conjunction with the unit training program.[2]

The question of a unit training center remained in abeyance while the aviation program as a whole was developed. Late in 1954, the idea was revived and it was decided to establish two such training centers—Fort Sill for activation and training of single rotor helicopter units and Fort Riley for tandem rotor helicopter units. These two Army Aviation Unit Training Commands were programed to begin operation during the first quarter of calendar year 1955.[3]

Field Training

The 6th Transportation Helicopter Company had been organized in late 1950 at Fort Sill. A detachment of the company, consisting of 9 officers, 42 enlisted men, and 7 H-23 helicopters, participated in Exercise SOUTHERN PINE from 13 to 17 August 1951. This was the first major field exercise which included an organized helicopter unit. Exercise SOUTHERN PINE was a joint Army-Air Force exercise in the Fort Bragg-Camp Mackall area. The 6th Transportation Helicopter Company participated in the first phase of the exercise, during which there was an assault by the 82d Airborne Division and a daylight relief of the 82d by the 28th and 43d Infantry Divisions.

The mission of the 6th Transportation Helicopter Company was to provide helicopter medical evacuation, emergency helicopter resupply, and personnel transport. Evacuation requests went direct to the helicopter company from the division surgeon and evacuation hospital and were not coordinated with tactical or logistical personnel prior to commitment. A plan was prepared to perform a helicopter resupply problem to supply a cut-off battalion for one day, but this plan was never implemented.

There was insufficient time for planning for complete integration into the maneuver play. It was quickly discovered that radio equipment of greater range was required in the helicopters. During the maneuver, certain doctrinal considerations were violated because of emergency use of the helicopters for medical evaluation. The supply channels for spare parts proved to be slow

A wounded trooper being evacuated by a helicopter of the 6th Transportation Company during Exercise Southern Pine.

and organizational and field maintenance was inadequate. Radio field maintenance facilities for aircraft signal equipment during the exercise were nonexistent.[4]

The 6th Transportation Helicopter Company next participated in Exercise SNOWFALL at Camp Drum and Pine Camp, New York, from 17 January to 16 February 1952. This exercise was planned to prepare both Army and Air Force units for missions in extremely cold weather areas by providing training in individual survival methods; movement over the snow; and the care and use of equipment, supplies, and weapons. The mission of the helicopter company was to provide transportation for troops and supplies and medical evacuation. Again only a detachment of the company was available, consisting of 4 officers, 28 warrant officers, 52 enlisted men, and 10 H-13s.[5]

Any doubts regarding the capabilities and use of helicopters were quickly laid to rest by the company's performance in supporting the practice air drop of the 11th Airborne Division personnel on 25 and 30 January. Although the division surgeon requested only two helicopters for support on 25 January the transportation officer of the 6th Transportation Helicopter Company put every available aircraft on this mission. Seven helicopters were used and airlifted

Division Support helicopter hovering over tanks of the 4th Tank Battalion (Medium) moving against the enemy forces during Exercise Longhorn in Texas, 1952.

twenty-six actual casualties from the drop zone to the medical collecting station. During the air drop on 30 January, eight helicopters were used in airlifting thirty-two actual casualties.

Maintenance of the helicopters again presented a serious problem. Although a detachment of the 25th Ordnance Light Aircraft Maintenance Company was present, a lack of parts prevented quick repair. The ordnance officer of the maneuver headquarters made arrangements with a Syracuse, New York, firm to purchase parts locally which relieved the situation somewhat. A combination of the extreme cold and the use of an improper grade of fuel caused many of the maintenance problems. The severe weather conditions caused a total of twenty forced landings and auto-rotations. Despite the rough terrain in which these forced landings were made, only one helicopter was damaged. Problems with the communications equipment again were encountered. The actual combat capability of the company could not be determined from information based on the small number of reconnaissance helicopters used. Cold weather operations techniques could not be developed because of the lack of adequate equipment and insufficient maneuver play.[6]

Cargo helicopters were used for the first time in a maneuver during Exercise LONGHORN. Exercise LONGHORN was a joint Army-Air Force field training exercise conducted in the area surrounding Fort Hood, Texas, during the period 25 March to 15 April 1952. The 6th Transportation Helicopter Company provided two H-19s and nine H-13s for the exercise. One of the H-19s belonged to Army Field Forces Board No. 1 at Fort Bragg and was flown approximately 1,300 miles to reach the exercise.

The 6th Transportation Helicopter Company had a mission of moving supplies and casualties, making loud speaker psychological warfare broadcasts, reconnaissance and surveillance, and various administrative duties. Again the maintenance facilities and personnel in the TOE were found to be inadequate. Utilization of only two cargo helicopters in the exercise did not give a complete indication of the capability of a fully equipped company.

The Maneuver Transportation Officer proposed four token exercises to be performed by the Army helicopters. These exercises included the resupply of a surrounded unit, the movement of an infantry company from a reserve to a front line position, the evacuation of an infantry company from an exposed position, and medical evacuation. The Deputy Maneuver Director, an Air Force officer, opposed such exercises on the grounds that they were contrary to Air Force policy. As a result, Army helicopters were used only for medical evacuation from the front lines to division clearing stations where responsibility was transferred to the Air Force. This decision was reached despite the existence of the agreement reached by the Secretaries of the Army and the Air Force in October 1951. The Director of the Joint Airborne Troop Board (Army-Air Force) concluded that an urgent need existed for an interservice decision on the delineation of responsibilities with regard to the administrative air movement of Army troop units, the outloading of combat units for airborne assaults, and aerial supply and resupply. He did not feel that grounds existed for further dispute between the Army and the Air Force concerning the use of Army helicopters in the actual combat zone.[7]

The employment of helicopters in Exercise SNOWSTORM, from 15 February to 19 March 1953 at Camp Drum, was significant in that this was the first time that cargo helicopters in any number were employed in an extended field exercise. The entire move of the 506th Transportation Helicopter Company from Fort Benning to Camp Drum and return was performed with organic aircraft and represented the first Army unit movement of cargo helicopters over a distance greater than 1,000 miles. The 506th Transportation Helicopter Company provided 3 officers, 15 warrant officers, 55 enlisted men, 11 H-19s, and 1 H-23 for the operation. The 53d Medical Helicopter Ambulance Detachment and the 152d Cargo Helicopter Field Maintenance Detachment also participated in Exercise SNOWSTORM.

The mission of the helicopter units was to develop and test Army doctrine, tactics, techniques, and equipment in cold weather operations. The troop movement mission performed by the company consisted of moving a reserve battalion to protect the flanks against an aggressor attack. The mission was considered successful, although the failure of the supported unit to designate helicopter loads for rapid loading and unloading caused some delay. Supplies for the company were adequate, but there was a lack of adequately trained maintenance personnel and special tools.

Air evacuation of casualties was performed according to the Army interpretation of the Army-Air Force agreement of 4 November 1952. The Air Force objected to this and demanded that it be solely responsible for evacuation of all casualties by air, including actual injuries as well as simulated casualties. The Army contended that for humanitarian reasons the evacuation of actual casualties should be accomplished by the quickest means.[8]

The 506th Transportation Helicopter Company and the 152d Cargo Helicopter Field Maintenance Detachment also participated during 1953 in the DESERT ROCK exercises held in Nevada. Upon receipt of the mission order, the 506th Transportation Helicopter Company immediately began planning for the required spare parts and equipment necessary to support the operation. These spare parts were dispatched by rail from Fort Benning to Nevada, but the car with the supplies did not arrive at its destination until two days after the unit had headed for home. The delay in dispatching the spare parts from Fort Benning resulted from the company's recent return from Exercise SNOWSTORM. Prior to the departure of the company for Nevada, the 152d Cargo Helicopter Field Maintenance Detachment performed fourteen major inspections and four engine changes.

The flight from Fort Benning to Nellis Air Force Base took eight days and the return trip eleven. The 4,400-mile round trip proved that cargo helicopter units could undertake long-distance cross country flights and satisfactorily accomplish missions at their destination. The thirteen H-19s encountered no problems en route, but the H-23 was damaged by high winds while on the ground. The company participated in several aerial support movements during the exercise.[9]

Exercise FLASHBURN, the only large-scale maneuver held during fiscal year 1954, took place in the Carolina Maneuver Area during April and May. An airborne corps and an aggressor force participated in offensive and defensive operations, supplied with tactical air support and atomic weapons support. FLASHBURN witnessed the largest commitment of helicopter units to date in an exercise—the 506th and 509th Transportation Helicopter Companies, the 152d and 153d Cargo Helicopter Field Maintenance Detachments, the 25th Army Aircraft Maintenance Company, and the 98th Army Aircraft Repair Detachment.

The fifteen helicopters available for tactical employment took part in two lifts. In the first, two rifle companies were lifted approximately eleven miles to seize critical terrain features in conjunction with the armored task force attack to link-up with the airhead. In the second, after the link-up, helicopters were used by the XVIII Airborne Corps to lift three reinforced rifle platoons to seize critical defiles along a route of advance. The lift capacity of the helicopters employed in these operations was inadequate for a tactical mission. When employed, the Maneuver Director felt the tactics were unrealistic in the face of an aggressive enemy.[10]

Materiel Requirements Review Panel

The Air Force continued to maintain that the Army's helicopter companies were intended to perform only limited functions which were secondary to the Air Force's mission of supplying the Army with its required airlift. The Air Force argued that it must first provide for this

Helicopters of the 509th Transportation Company used to airlift troops into the battle zone of the Carolina Maneuver Area during Exercise Flashburn, 1954.

responsibility before making available identical critical equipment to the Army for the performance of a limited function. It also notified the Army of its intent to provide an Air Force helicopter unit for Exercise LONGHORN.

Considering the Air Force actions as an "abrogation" rather than an "interpretation" of the 1951 Memorandum of Understanding, the Secretary of the Army concluded in June 1952 that the Army should no longer be bound by its provisions. He thereupon called for an Army review of its concepts of the place of the helicopter in land combat. No outstanding agreement, the Secretary declared, should be permitted to hamper the helicopter research and development program or those relating to the procurement and utilization of helicopters. The Secretary directed that he be furnished a reconsidered Army program by 8 August 1952.[11]

On 30 June, the Chief of Staff of the Army directed that the Materiel Requirements Review Panel review the Army helicopter program and submit recommendations by 1 August. Some of the problems to be clarified included the current procurement and utilization programs, the determination of actual requirements, and the proper implementation of the overall program—especially research and development, service testing, procurement, maintenance, and organization and training. The panel was also to determine if the present program was in consonance with the Army's interpretation of the October 1951 Memorandum of Understanding. Also to be considered was whether the Air Force support of the Army helicopter program—training personnel, accomplishing procurement, research and development, and depot maintenance and supply—was the most efficient, economical, and effective means of accomplishing these facets of the program. In addition, the panel was to determine if any duplication existed in the planned utilization of Army and Air Force helicopter units and in what fields there were requirements for the Air Force to provide helicopter units for support of the Army.[12]

Army Field Forces informed the Materiel Requirements Review Panel on 14 July that the existing method of determining actual TOE requirements was basically sound. The existing programing for transportation helicopter units for the type field army, however, was not sound. Army Field Forces recommended to the panel that transportation helicopter companies should be organized into battalions of two to five companies and that each field army should include ten helicopter battalions each averaging three companies. It also recommended that the Memorandum of Understanding be modified to assure Army responsibility for its helicopter transportation within the combat zone.

Army Field Forces reported that the research and development program for Army aviation was being properly implemented, but could be improved by closer integration with Navy and Air Force programs and the establishment of a new system of assigning development priorities on Army aviation projects being conducted by other services. It recommended that the Army initiate design competitions in fiscal years 1953 and 1954 for development of a 1,000 pound payload utility helicopter and a 6,000 pound payload cargo helicopter. Army Field Forces also recommended that Army representation be increased on boards which inspected or considered aircraft of primary interest to the Army.

Relative to service testing of Army helicopters, OCAFF recommended that an "on call" contract be established with manufacturers in order to expedite delivery of spare parts during the user test period; that Army Field Forces Board No. 1 and other user test agencies be given a higher requisition priority; that, as an established policy, two early production models be allocated to Army Field Forces for testing; that user test procurement should be sped up so that testing could be completed prior to full scale production; and, on selected user test items, a troop test quantity should be bought for testing concurrently with the user test. In addition, OCAFF felt that prior to delivery of production aircraft overseas a user test aircraft should be sent over for use in pilot and mechanic orientation and transition training.

In the important area of training of Army aviation personnel, OCAFF concluded that the overall Army helicopter training program was, for the most part, being properly implemented, but recommended to the panel that in order to correct certain deficiencies an Army Aviation School be established and sufficient personnel spaces, funds, facilities, and equipment provided to implement an expanding training program. In conjunction with the establishment of the school, the Army would assume all aviation training then being conducted by the Air Force for the Army. Finally, OCAFF recommended that action then in progress to revise unit ATPs, instrument flight training, and ordnance training of aircraft maintenance personnel continue.

In answer to the question of the need for the Air Force to provide helicopter units for support of the Army, OCAFF concluded that, except for missions appropriate for rotary wing aircraft of the flying crane type, the Army helicopter program provided adequate rotary wing transport aircraft to meet requirements of the type field army. It recommended that Transportation Corps requirements for operation of rotary wing aircraft of the flying crane type outside the type field army be determined by study, and that, based on the recommended study, requirements for helicopter support by other services be determined.[13]

The Transportation Corps, in the study which it prepared for the panel, pointed out that only 224 transport type helicopters had been budgeted for procurement, and only a handful had actually been delivered. Believing this to be completely inadequate, the Transportation Corps proposed a 5-year program which would provide 1,200 transport helicopters to equip fifteen battalions. The Transportation Corps believed that the cargo helicopter program should be separated from the rest of the Army aviation program of which it had been an integral part. Since cargo helicopters functioned more like vehicular rather than air transport, the Transportation Corps felt that they should be integrated into the transportation complex. It therefore recommended that Army responsibilities pertaining to cargo helicopters be assigned to the Transportation Corps, under the general direction of G-3 and G-4.[14]

The Materiel Requirements Review Panel, chaired by Brig. Gen. G. J. Higgins, met on 24 and 25 July 1952 to conduct the requested review. During the review, twenty staff studies prepared by various agencies for the use of the panel were examined. The panel reached a number of conclusions regarding the Army Aviation Program. It found the Army's utilization program in consonance with the Army's interpretation of the Memorandum of Understanding. The current procurement and utilization programs for helicopters were also in consonance with the budget guidelines of the Secretary of Defense. No procurement was therefore planned to meet any portion of the requirements of the Mobilization Reserve.

The panel found that procurement was based upon known issue requirements existing at the time that the fiscal year 1953 budget estimates were prepared, but did not cover some additional requirements for utility helicopters authorized since that time. Programed procurement of utility helicopters, including fiscal year 1953, would leave the Army about 25 percent short of its total requirements through fiscal year 1954, assuming the war continued in Korea. Planned procurement of cargo helicopters would meet all but approximately 15 to 20 percent of the requirements for ten transportation helicopter companies through fiscal year 1954.

The panel believed that the programed twelve ambulance helicopter units were adequate, but that the programed ten transportation helicopter companies would not meet current requirements.

As a result of its study, the panel made several recommendations regarding the future development of the aviation program. It recommended that clear coordination of the Army and Navy helicopter programs should be affected. The panel believed that the Army could obtain greater effectiveness in the research and development programs by having the authority to place projects with commercial concerns or government agencies best qualified to conduct a particular project. The research and development program could be improved by close integration with the Navy and Air Force programs to avoid waste of money and time, duplication of effort, and to permit maximum interservice utilization of the helicopters developed and the engineering staffs and facilities available. In the interest of economy, the panel recommended that the Army should utilize to the maximum extent helicopters under development by other services, while at the same time devoting the bulk of its research and development money to the development of a ship-to-shore helicopter, an optimum cargo helicopter, and improved rotor systems and helicopter power plants.

The panel did not accept the Transportation Corps' proposal for separating the cargo helicopter program from the rest of Army aviation. It did propose a realignment of the overall logistical support responsibilities. Most activities pertaining to the funding, procurement, and research and development of Army aircraft at that time were handled by the Ordnance Corps. The Ordnance Corps had acted generally as an agent for G-3 and OCAFF. The small staffs handling these functions were submerged in the overall Ordnance procurement and research and development programs. The panel recommended that responsibilities for all logistical functions involved in the aircraft program be assigned to one technical service, under the staff direction of a single agency set up in the General Staff.

In the area of supply and maintenance, the panel found that the Army's present organization and field maintenance program, if properly implemented, would support the utility helicopter but not the cargo helicopter program. Depot supply and maintenance, as performed by the Air Force for Army aircraft, was neither the most efficient nor most effective system.

The panel found fault with the entire procurement system. The internal procedure in the Army for the procurement of aircraft was unnecessarily cumbersome. The existing procurement procedures in the purchase of aircraft through the Air Force was cumbersome and inefficient and required radical change.

Of particular interest to OCAFF was the recommendation that the Army assume responsibility for all aviation training then being conducted by the Air Force for the Army. The panel found that the overall Army helicopter program was being properly implemented by the appropriate Department of the Army agencies pertaining to organization and service testing.

The requirement remained for support of the Army by the Air Force in providing airlift from exterior points to points within the combat zone, airlift for joint assault airborne operations, and other airlift beyond the capabilities of Army aircraft. The panel found, however, that there was a serious duplication in the planned utilization of Army and Air Force helicopter units in the fields of transportation of Army supplies, equipment, and small units within the combat zone and medical air evacuation within the combat zone.

The panel believed that further negotiations with the Air Force would be time consuming and would, at best, result in another document restricting Army aviation rather than delineating functions. It felt that the requirement for joint regulations and memorandums of understanding on the subject of Army aviation no longer existed any more than a requirement existed for similar publications on Naval or Marine aviation.

The Materiel Requirements Review Panel recommended that a 5-year cargo helicopter procurement program be established to provide 15 transportation battalions to support a 20-division force. Three of these battalions would be utilized in the Zone of the Interior for experimental projects, training, and development of doctrine, tactics, and techniques. The cost of such a program over a 5-year period was estimated to be $1,000,000,000 and 9,000 personnel spaces. To support this proposed program, the panel recommended that the Army initiate a 5-year research and development program. The cost of this program would possibly amount to an average expenditure of $15,000,000 per year over the next five years. For mobilization planning purposes, the panel recommended that a division slice of thirty-nine helicopters be established. This would provide 7 transportation helicopter battalions per type field army in the ratio of 3 light, 3 medium, and 1 heavy.

Finally, the panel recommended that the Assistant Chiefs of Staff, G-1, G-3 and G-4, and the Offices of the Chief of Army Field Forces, Chief of Transportation, Chief Signal Officer, Chief of Engineers, and Surgeon General be directed to establish within their offices an identifiable agency with responsibility for the overall supervision and coordination of functions of that office relating to Army aviation. To provide overall supervision and coordination for the program, the panel recommended that the Office, Assistant Chief of Staff, G-3, be designated as the General Staff Agency charged with these responsibilities and that this agency be headed by a general officer with an adequate staff.[15]

On 21 August 1952, the Chief of Staff of the Army, following his review of the recommendations on the Materiel Requirements Review Panel, approved the establishment of a modified cargo helicopter program based on twelve transportation helicopter battalions funded over the next five years at a cost of approximately $688,000,000 and 6,000 personnel spaces. Based on a tentative procurement schedule, $138,000,000 was added to the fiscal year 1954 budget. A sum of $2,720,000 was included in the fiscal year 1954 research and development program for helicopters, and the feasibility of reprograming approximately $5,000,000 of the fiscal year 1953 research and development funds was considered. The Chief of Staff approved the panel's recommendations regarding Army assumption of depot supply and maintenance of Army aircraft, procurement of aircraft directly from the manufacturers, and responsibility for all aviation training. Funding for Army aviation training for fiscal year 1954 was approved with the assumption that the Army would conduct all of its own training. The recommendations of the panel and the Chief of Staff were approved by the Secretary of the Army in October. And so began an expanding Army aviation program.[16]

Memorandum of Understanding of 1952

Following approval of the 5-year program to provide the Army twelve transportation helicopter battalions and twelve helicopter ambulance units by 1956, the Chief of Staff invited the attention of the Joint Chiefs of Staff to the fact that the Air Force was programing assault groups in duplication of these Army units. The Chief of Staff of the Air Force replied that the Army helicopter program was completely unacceptable to the Air Force. Maintaining that the units the

Air Force was providing for joint assault operations should be used for logistic operations in the combat zone, he requested the JCS to direct the Army to cease programing air evacuation units and to limit the transportation helicopter program to five experimental companies.

The JCS directed the suspension of the activation of the evacuation units until the two services could settle the matter. A conference was held on 13 October with the Secretary of the Army, the Secretary of the Air Force, the Chiefs of Staff, and the Deputy Secretary of Defense in attendance. On 4 November, the Army and the Air Force concluded a second Memorandum of Understanding on Army aviation which superseded the agreement of 1951. Its changes favored the Army point of view, especially as related to the helicopter.[17]

This memorandum imposed a weight restriction on Army fixed-wing aircraft of 5,000 pounds. This limitation was subject to review by the Secretary of Defense, upon the request of either of the service secretaries, to keep such limitation realistic in the light of "technical developments and assigned missions." The helicopter was defined solely in terms of performance of functions.

The transportation by air of Army supplies, equipment, personnel, and small units within the combat zone became a primary rather than a limited or emergency function of Army aviation. The combat zone was redefined so as to extend normally from 50 to 100 miles in depth. Other primary functions included aerial observation; control of Army forces; command, liaison, and courier missions; and aerial wire laying within the combat zone. Two other types of activity not previously included also were added—artillery and topographic survey and aeromedical evacuation within the combat zone. Evacuation was to include battlefield pickup of casualties, their air transport to the initial point of treatment, and any subsequent move to hospital facilities within the combat zone.

Primary functions of the Air Force in support of ground forces were restricted to the following: (1) airlift of Army supplies, equipment, personnel, and units from the outside to points within the combat zone; (2) airlift for the air movement of troops, supplies, and equipment in the assault and subsequent phases of airborne operations; (3) airlift for the evacuation of personnel and materiel from the combat zone; and (4) aeromedical evacuation of casualties from the initial points of treatment or subsequent hospitalization to points outside the combat zone. In the case of airborne operations, the Air Force was responsible for the evacuation of casualties from the objective area until such time as a ground link-up was attained.[18]

OCAFF Review of the Army Aviation Program

Between July 1952, when the Materiel Requirements Review Panel reviewed the Army Aviation Program, and June 1953, Army Field Forces conducted follow-up studies on various phases of Army aviation. By June 1953, the recommendations of the Materiel Requirements Review Panel and various OCAFF studies had been reviewed by the Secretary of the Army, who used some of them as guidance for the Army aviation program of fiscal year 1954. Early in June 1953, the Department of the Army concluded that a further detailed study of the Army aviation program was needed in order to ascertain the progress made in implementing the recommendations approved by the Secretary of the Army.

Army Field Forces completed its portion of the review by the end of August. A conference composed of representatives of the OCAFF schools and boards, major overseas commands, and appropriate technical services prepared a staff study on the organization of Army aviation. Basically, OCAFF found the existing program to be sound. It recommended that the ratio of helicopters within the twelve programed battalions and within a mobilization procurement program should be two light battalions to one medium battalion to one heavy battalion. In addition to the twelve helicopter ambulance detachments in the current program, OCAFF recommended one detachment per two divisions mobilized.

At this time, OCAFF was of the opinion that there was no continuing requirement for a heavy lift helicopter within the field army. Unless designs would be radically improved, the size, weight, and complexity of the heavy lift helicopter would make its employment in the combat zone impracticable except for special operations. There was, however, a requirement for a heavy lift helicopter for employment by the Transportation Corps. Field testing of current types of fixed and rotary wing aircraft to be conducted during 1953 and 1954 might develop a requirement for a fixed wing cargo aircraft to supplement cargo helicopters.

On the question of what helicopter lift capability should be given to a field army, OCAFF stated that air lift of major forces—divisions or larger for considerable distances—became a joint operation with the Air Force and should not be attempted on a unilateral basis with helicopters. On the other hand, the field army should be able to rapidly shift balanced combat forces within the zone of operation to fill a gap or exploit a success. OCAFF considered the movement in one lift of a battalion combat team to be the minimum capability which should be given the field army. With this capability, a regimental combat team could be moved in three or four lifts. In addition, the minimum lift capability should provide for continuous supply of at least one infantry division.

OCAFF observed that the efficiency of the larger helicopters increased as the round trip distance increased. At average maximum range, the relative efficiency was of the same order as the relative payloads. For short hauls, however, the light helicopter had a high efficiency because of lower turn around time and lower maintenance requirements.

Army Field Forces emphasized that a balance had to be reached as to the numbers of cargo helicopters by type required for the field army. The heavier helicopter, though more efficient in moving tonnage, was costly, complex, and vulnerable and had to be used with caution in forward areas. The light helicopter was tactically versatile, easier to replace and service, but limited in payload. OCAFF surmised that some high payload aircraft would have to be included to move such essential items as the 105-mm. howitzer and the 3/4-ton truck. A force of four helicopter battalions, including one medium and one heavy, would meet the lift requirements and provided adequate helicopters of each type to carry out the numerous and varied missions required.

Army Field Forces recommended no changes in its organization relating to aviation. It concluded that the organization of Army aviation for the Army as a whole, though sound, would be strengthened by the assignment of a general officer to command the principal field agency (school or center), and that this officer should be the principal advisor to the Chief of Staff and the Chief of Army Field Forces on Army aviation. OCAFF recommended that the organization for Army aviation at the Department of the Army would be improved and staff action facilitated by establishing the action office within G-3 at branch level and headed by a senior officer who should be an Army aviator.[19]

According to OCAFF, current organization of Army aviation was weakened by lack of operational facilities, lack of administrative support, lack of provision for adequate maintenance supervision, and lack of operational supervision to prevent duplication of missions and to ensure the best utilization of aircraft. It was the opinion of OCAFF that the establishment of a TOE aviation company would be a workable solution for divisional Army aviation, but one which would involve many administrative, operational, and logistical problems when applied to non-divisional units. By assigning Army aircraft to using units within the division, the Army would assure unit commanders of operational control of the required aircraft.

Army Field Forces concluded that Army aviation in all arms and services except Transportation Corps and Medical Service Corps should be organic to the using unit. The centralization of logistical support and operational facilities should be accomplished to assure the optimum efficiency and use of personnel and equipment without sacrificing the operational control and immediate availability of Army aircraft to using unit commanders. In the opinion of OCAFF, Army aviation support units and aviation in the Transportation Corps should be organized as army troops to provide logistical support for aircraft and to furnish transportation helicopter units. Army aviation in the Medical Service Corps should also be organized as army troops in the form of helicopter ambulance detachments.

OCAFF recommended the establishment of an aviation special staff section at division, corps, and army levels. This section would exercise staff supervision over all Army aviation activities, provide a single source of information concerning Army aviation for the commander and his staff, and provide staff supervision over technical and flight aspects of administration, training, and operations.

The study was forwarded to the Department of the Army, which approved it on 25 September.[20]

This study by OCAFF resulted in a complete revamping of the aircraft procurement program. In order to meet the equipment objectives established in the study, it proved necessary to extend procurement over three additional years. In October 1953, the Transportation Corps drew up an 8-year plan—covering fiscal years 1954 to 1961—costing approximately $1.7 billion. Assuming no further increase in basic requirements, subsequent procurement would be limited to aircraft needed to replace annual losses caused by attrition.[21]

Army Aviation Plan

On 4 September 1954, the Deputy Chief of Staff for Plans and Research of the Army directed a review of the entire aviation program and the development of a comprehensive program to provide long range guidance for the future operation and administration of Army aviation. The Army General Staff, under the monitorship of the Assistant Chief of Staff, G-3, reviewed the

Army aviation program. A plan was developed with the assistance of the major zone of interior commands and agencies.

On 9 November, the Department of the Army G-3 requested that OCAFF, along with all major overseas and CONUS army commands and the commandants of the service schools, submit comments on this plan by 1 December.

The Department of the Army aviation plan contained the conclusion that the organization of aviation within the Army had failed to meet requirements. The organization denied satisfactory career opportunities for Army aviators and failed to provide the leadership and control essential to development and growth. It also failed to assure that development and procurement of aircraft were thoroughly coordinated with procurement and training of personnel. There was a duplication of effort among Army agencies in the fields of training, testing, and development of doctrine and there was competition for personnel and aircraft between the seven branches having organic aircraft. There was inefficiency and ineffectiveness in testing of aircraft, publication of technical information, training of personnel, and formulation of doctrine.

In its Aviation Plan, the Department of the Army emphasized the expansion of aviation in the Army required to provide tactical mobility and logistical support. To accomplish these ends, it proposed the immediate establishment of an Army Aviation Branch through a 3-phase program. First, an Army Aviation Branch of the Career Management Division, the Adjutant General's Office, would be established and would assume control of all Army aviators. An Army Aviation Division also would be established in the Office of the Assistant Chief of Staff, G-3.

In the second phase, all rotary and fixed wing aircraft units in the Army would be redesignated Army aviation units. The technical maintenance and supply units would remain a part of the technical services. No change would be made in responsibilities for logistical support of Army aviation. An Army Aviation Center would be established under the Continental Army Command (CONARC), which would train all pilots, aircraft maintenance personnel at organization and field maintenance level, and air traffic control specialists.[22] The center also would be responsible for the testing of Army aircraft and aviation equipment, excluding development testing accomplished by the other services and the technical services. The center would develop Army aviation tactics, techniques, doctrine, and combat developments in coordination with other service schools.

In the third and final phase, a Chief of Army Aviation would be appointed. He would be responsible for career control of Army aviation personnel, primary logistical support for Army aircraft research and development functions in connection with Army aircraft, and the Army Aviation Center. Finally, all Army aviation personnel and units would be transferred to the Army Aviation Branch.[23]

In distributing the plan for comment, the Chief of Army Field Forces advised that he did not look with favor on the centralization of Army aviation in a new arm or service and that he had emphasized the combat nature of Army aviation's mission. Comments received by OCAFF from the service schools reflected a wide variety of reactions to the plan. The suggestion to establish an Army Aviation Branch received the greatest reaction. Among the schools, the Command and

General Staff College, the Infantry School, the Armor School, and the staff of the Army Aviation School approved of the concept. It was opposed by the commandant of the Army Aviation School and by the Artillery School and the Transportation School. The commandant of the Army War College recommended that decision in this matter be deferred pending completion of scheduled tests and of studies relating to future logistical support concepts.

Army Field Forces recommended on 1 December that the plan not be presented to the Chief of Staff. Pending the resolution of a number of basic issues which it raised, OCAFF recommended several actions. These actions included the monitorship of the assignment of rated aviators and of aviation specialists, necessary expansion of training facilities, approval of procurement planning, changes in procurement procedures, assumption from the Air Force of responsibilities for depot maintenance and supply functions, a statement of research and development objectives, action to minimize the length of the development procurement cycle, installation construction, the establishment of an Army Aviation Center, and the improvement of management. Army Field Forces also recommended that no action should be taken which would alter the control that the Continental Army Command would exercise over Army aviation activities to make it different from the control exercised over the combat arms. OCAFF maintained that CONARC must be responsible for training, combat developments, developing and testing, and related matters just as it was responsible for these subjects for the infantry, artillery, or armor.[24]

On 18 December 1954, OCAFF received from the Department of the Army a draft summary sheet prepared by G-3 for the Chief of Staff of the Army which summarized the planned expansion of Army aviation during the period 1955 to 1959 and the Army Aviation Plan and comments received on it, and recommended several courses of action for approval and implementation. These actions included the centralized control over aviation personnel by the Department of the Army G-1 in order to obtain efficient use of available qualified personnel in branch immaterial flight assignments while ensuring maintenance of branch qualifications. The establishment of an Aviation Center and an Aviation Board at Camp Rucker, Alabama, was recommended. The Office of the Assistant Chief of Staff, G-3, Department of the Army, would be augmented by one general officer and approximately seven of other ranks in order to provide an adequate staff for discharging the responsibilities assigned G-3 for overall supervision of the Army Aviation Program and coordination of Army functions relating to Army aviation.

In regard to OCAFF, the draft summary sheet's recommendations provided that the Chief of Army Field Forces would be charged with conducting all aviation flight and technical training of Army aviation personnel in the zone of the interior. He also would be charged with making appropriate recommendations to the Department of the Army concerning all aspects of the combat or service development of aviation to be used by the Army in the field to include organizational matters, integration of aviation into units, tactical and logistical employment of aviation, and recommending the types, characteristics, and capabilities of aircraft considered best suited for use by the Army in the field.

The Department of the Army also recommended that the Army assume responsibility for depot supply and maintenance as soon as budget and organization requirements would permit. It recommended that planning studies and tests be initiated by appropriate agencies leading to specific recommendations to the Chief of Staff resolving the basic problems of Army aviation as related to personnel, organization, developments, construction, procurement, supply and maintenance, and command.[25]

Although this Army Aviation Plan was never to be implemented in its entirety, it did provide the basis for the development of Army aviation for the remainder of the decade. Army aviation was about to become of age and to begin to play a significant role in the activities of the Army.

Endnotes
Chapter III

1. (1) MFR, Maj H.I. Lukens, OCAFF G-3, 24 Jun 52, subj: Activation of Medical Helicopter Ambulance Detachments. (2) MFR, Maj H.I. Lukens, OCAFF G-3, 9 Jun 52, subj: Activation and Stationing of Medical Helicopter Ambulance Detachments.

2. (1) 3d Ind ATTNG 51 322, OCAFF to DA, 18 Apr 52. (2) 4th Ind AGAO-I 322 (28 Jan 52), DA to OCAFF, 16 May 52, subj: Activation and Attachment of Helicopter Company to XVIII Airborne Corps. (3) Ltr TCATST, Chief of Transportation to CAFF, 31 Oct 52, subj: Transportation Helicopter Company Unit Training Center, and 1st Ind.

3. (1) Ltr ATTNG-45 322 (Units), CAFF to CG Fourth Army, subj: Helicopter Unit Stationing. (2) "The Controversial Fifties," *Army Aviation,* Sep 60, p. 485.

4. Jean R. Moenk, *A History of Large-Scale Army Maneuvers in the United States, 1935-1964,* HQ CONARC, 1969, p. 153.

5. Moenk, *A History of Large-Scale Army Maneuvers,* p. 163.

6. (1) Ltr, Mvr Dir Exer SNOWFALL to CAFF and CG TAC, 29 Feb 52, subj: Final Report, Exercise SNOWFALL, w/incls. (2) Army Helicopters, Transport and Cargo.

7. (1) Moenk, *A History of Large-Scale Maneuvers,* pp. 170, 178- 179. (2) Army Helicopters, Transport and Cargo.

8. (1) Moenk, *A History of Large-Scale Maneuvers,* pp. 184, 187- 188. (2) Army Helicopters, Transport and Cargo.

9. Ibid.

10. (1) Final Report, Exercise FLASHBURN, April-May 1954, Ft Bragg—Camp Mackall, NC, pp. 15, 36, 80. (2) Moenk, *A History of Large-Scale Maneuvers,* pp. 196, 200.

11. Bykofsky, pp. 24-25.

12. Memo CS 452.1 (30 Jun 52), SGS to Chmn, Materiel Requirements Review Panel, 30 Jun 52, subj: Army Helicopter Program.

13. Memo ATTNG-22 452.1, OCAFF to Chmn, Materiel Requirements Review Panel, 14 Jul 52, subj: Army Helicopter Program.

14. Bykofsky, pp. 26-27.

15. Memo G-3 452 (30 Jun 52), Brig Gen G.J. Higgins for CofSA, 31 Jul 52, subj: Materiel Requirements Review Panel Review of the Army Helicopter Program.

16. (1) Memo, General J. Lawton Collins for the Secretary of the Army, 28 Aug 52, subj: Army Helicopter Program. (2) Memo, SA Frank Pace, Jr., for CofSA, 2 Oct 52, subj: Army Helicopter Program.

17. (1) Summary Sheet G-3 452 (4 Mar 52), DA G-3 O&T Div Orgn, R&D Br, 31 Mar 52, subj: Requirements for Cargo Type Helicopters. (2) McClendon, pp. 24-26.

18. DA SR 95-400-5, 19 Nov 52.

19. Detailed information on the organization of Army aviation within OCAFF, and divisions, corps, and armies will be found below.

20. (1) Ltr G-3 360 (10 Jun 53), DA ACofS G-3 to CAFF, 10 Jun 53, subj: Review of Army Aviation Program and Incl 4. (2) Ltr ATTNG-J2360, CAFF to DA ACofS G-3, 29 Aug 53, subj: Review of Army Aviation Program with 6 incls.

21. Bykofsky, p. 55

22. The Office of the Chief of Army Field Forces was scheduled to be reorganized as Headquarters, Continental Army Command, on 1 February 1955.

23. (1) Ltr G-3 OT AV-2, DA ACofS G-3 to distr, 9 Nov 54, subj: Army Aviation Plan. (2) Memo for CAFF, 25 Nov 54, subj: Army Aviation Plan FY 55.

24. Ltr ATSWC-G 360(S), OCAFF to DA ACofS G-3, 1 Dec 54, subj: Army Aviation Plan.

25. (1) Ltr G3-2, DA OACofS G-3 to OCAFF, undated, subj: Army Aviation Problems, Programs, and Estimates, with 1st Ind. (2) Memo for General Dahlquist, 20 Dec 54, subj: Army Aviation Plan.

Chapter IV

RESEARCH, DEVELOPMENT, AND PROCUREMENT

During the 1950s, research and development efforts and the resulting procurement programs had a major impact on the Army Aviation Program. The fixed wing aircraft industry was well established and had an extensive research and development background. The Army therefore was able to rely principally on user tests and modifications of commercial types to meet its requirements. Helicopters, however, were still in a relatively primitive state of development and lacked a significant civilian market. For this reason, helicopter development, particularly of the larger transport types, was heavily dependent on military sponsorship. Prior to 1952 most of this support had been provided by the Air Force and the Navy. Army financial support to rotary wing development had been limited to convertiplanes, small reconnaissance helicopters, and certain power plant and supporting research projects. With the rapid expansion of requirements during the Korean conflict, the Army had procured the best available helicopters, relying on future developments to provide more suitable types.[1]

Early Procurement Activities

The 5-year period between the end of World War II and the beginning of the war in Korea was a time of recession for Army aviation. The number of aircraft organic to the Army dwindled considerably by 1948 and many of those aircraft which remained were obsolete. Plans to completely replace the L-4 and the L-5 with the L-16 and the L-17 liaison aircraft were held in abeyance and a number of the obsolete aircraft were stored at Fort Sill and not declared surplus to the needs of the Army in view of possible future requirements.

At the beginning of the war in Korea, the Army had over 500 2-place fixed wing aircraft, 143 multiple passenger fixed wing aircraft, and 57 utility helicopters; by the end of the first year of the war the overall strength of the Army's air arm had increased by one-fourth. The most notable expansion occurred with the introduction of the utility helicopter. The growth in the number of Army aircraft is as follows:[2]

TYPE	6/50	6/51	6/52	12/52
Two-place fixed wing	525	843	1451	1534
Multi-passenger fixed wing	143	165	271	320
Utility helicopter	57	86	320	647
Cargo Helicopter	0	0	1	72
TOTAL	725	1094	2043	2573

Only 481 aircraft had been procured by the Army in fiscal years 1949 and 1950, but with the outbreak of the war in Korea, a sharp rise occurred in the number and type of aircraft ordered by the Army. A total of 3,637 aircraft were ordered in fiscal year 1951, and 702 were ordered in fiscal year 1952. Most were modified commercial, fixed wing aircraft and small reconnaissance utility helicopters. A limited number of H-19 and H-21 helicopters also had been ordered under the experimental helicopter program. A need for a fleet of large and more complex cargo helicopters under the twelve battalion program resulted in the Transportation Corps developing a long range production program that could be readily modified to meet budgetary limitations, difficulties, and the impact of the cargo helicopter requirement. By November 1952, the Transportation Corps had drawn up a 5-year program, covering both fixed and rotary wing aircraft. Production schedules had to be spread over a number of years because of limited production capability and cost. The total aircraft budget had to be kept within prescribed expenditure ceilings. The relative inexperience in helicopter design and production impeded efforts to attain simplification and standardization.

Information regarding the major types of fixed wing and rotary wing aircraft acquired by the Army from 1942 to 1962 is shown in Tables 1 and 2.

Army Observation Aircraft

The Army realized by 1949 that the L-5 and the L-16, cheap, interim aircraft which were never considered satisfactory, were becoming uneconomical to continue in operation. The L-18, although unsuitable for extensive combat, was satisfactorily used as a training aircraft after being rented on a limited basis from Piper Aircraft Corporation. OCAFF in January 1951 recommended the purchase of 120 L-18s for use at the Artillery School as training aircraft. The Department of the Army approved the recommendation of Army Field Forces and announced that delivery of the L-18s was scheduled for May 1951. The aircraft never proved completely satisfactory and were sold to Turkey or turned over to Army flying clubs.

In order to select an adequate replacement for those obsolete aircraft from commercial sources, the Army held a competition among commercial aircraft during the period of April through June 1950. As a result of the competition, the Cessna Model 305 was chosen and was subsequently designated the L-19. The Cessna entry in the competition actually exceeded the specifications set forth for the new observation aircraft. The L-19 was powered by a 213 horsepower Continental engine which provided performance superior to any of the other entries. Army Field Forces Board No. 1 received one L-19 in December 1950 for user tests which would determine whether or not the aircraft would meet the military characteristics for which it was developed, whether or not the aircraft would be suitable for extended use in combat as an observation-reconnaissance aircraft, and what modifications or changes would be incorporated in future production. Also examined were the suitability of the aircraft for use for aerial drop of emergency supplies, aerial wire laying, aerial photography operations in extreme heat and cold, float operations, and use as a trainer. The suitability of its communications and navigation radio equipment was also scrutinized.

Production of the L-19 was scheduled to begin in December 1950, with a rate of 25 to 30 per month for about 15 months. Long range plans called for the L-19 to replace all 2-place airplanes in the Army. The immediate need in Korea and the increased requirements of the Artillery School caused an accelerated L-19 production schedule.

After passing its user tests, the L-19 was utilized successfully in Korea for battlefield observation. The all-around good visibility with a minimum of blind spots and its good maneuverability were the strong points of the aircraft. Battlefield experience did indicate, however, a need for improved short range performance. A higher rate of climb, greater endurance at higher cruising speeds, and higher ratio of useful load to the gross weight also were needed. The L-19 participated in photo reconnaissance despite having unsatisfactory camera mounts, poor stability, and lack of proper sighting devices.[3]

The last observation type aircraft acquired by the Army during this period was the Piper L-21 Super Cub. This Piper aircraft had been entered in the 1950 competition and had met all of the specifications, but it had been passed over in favor of the superior Cessna L-19. Piper protested this action, with the result that the Army finally did purchase a small quantity of the L-21s. Army Field Forces procured 150 L-21As in 1951 which were mostly utilized as trainers. These were followed by 568 similar L-21Bs which saw extensive service in the Far East. The L-21 was phased out of the inventory in 1953.[4]

Fixed Wing Utility Aircraft

At the outset of the Korean War, the Ryan L-17 was being used extensively for command transportation. However, it lacked the necessary size and adaptability for use in combat. In January 1951, Army Field Forces Board No. 1 conducted a competition at Fort Bragg to choose a multi-place, fixed wing aircraft most suitable to perform utility missions for the Army. As a result of this competition, the Army selected the deHavilland BEAVER for field utility duty and the Beechcraft Twin Bonanza Model 50 for the command mission in higher headquarters. The BEAVER, a rugged aircraft with an exceptionally short takeoff and landing performance and ability to operate from floats and skis, could perform the missions of medical evacuation, resupply, front line photography, and staff transport.

Early in 1951, OCAFF recommended to the Army Field Forces Board No. 1 that it test the deHavilland BEAVER—the XL-20—to determine the degree to which it could satisfy current military characteristics for that type of aircraft which had a capacity of 6 and a cruising speed of 135 miles per hour. The adaptability of the aircraft for extended use by Army units as utility aircraft, its suitability for use in emergency resupply, and its reliability in taking aerial photos and in aerial wire laying also were to be considered.

In order to test it for conditions of extreme heat and cold, one of the XL-20s was assigned to the Desert Testing Center in the summer of 1951 and another was sent to the Arctic Test Branch during the winter of 1951-52. The latter was equipped with a set of wheel skis and floats. The suitability of the communication and navigational radio and adaptability for instrument flying was tested. The L-20 successfully passed all tests and the Army planned to purchase a large number of the aircraft.

During the spring of 1951, the Air Force held up the procurement program for the L-20 because its 2,800 pounds exceeded the allowable empty weight limit by 300 pounds. The Air Force was rapidly organizing assault helicopter squadrons and was reactivating their liaison squadrons. This produced an unfortunate situation as the Air Force tied up commercial production facilities by duplicating Army contracts. Unless the funds for procurement of Army aircraft were used by 30 June these funds would revert to the Treasury. The Army Field Forces, therefore, requested that procurement of the L-20 by the Air Force be expedited.

The Chief, Army Field Forces, recommended to the Department of the Army in June 1951 that the Department of the Air Force be informed that the Department of the Army had no requirement for support by Air Force liaison squadrons. He also recommended that the Department of the Air Force be told that the Department of the Army proposed to equip its Army aviation sections with suitable airplanes, helicopters, and equipment to perform all liaison missions without qualification as described in previous regulations.

The L-20 was more practicable than the L-19 for evacuation of wounded requiring medical attention enroute to the hospital. When using the L-20, the patients were flown directly from the battlefield to an evacuation hospital rather than to an intermediate stop at a mobile army surgical hospital. However, the L-20 was found difficult to load because of its extremely small doors and the limited maneuvering area inside.[5]

Early in the Korean conflict, the Army Field Forces request for the purchase of four Beechcraft Model 50 airplanes for field testing was turned down by the Assistant Chief of Staff, G-4, Department of the Army, as it did not resolve the question of actual need for an airplane with more than one engine. Army Field Forces Board No. 1 tested several aircraft to replace the L-17 and the LC-126 in January 1951. The outstanding performance of the Beechcraft Model 50 confirmed that it was a superior airplane—one which would be suitable for command liaison transportation at higher staff levels. The very fact that the Beechcraft had two engines made it a safer aircraft, and its capacity of six passengers and crew gave it a distinct advantage over either the L-17 or the LC-126, each with a capacity of four. Because of its short field performance, the Beechcraft was superior to any Air Force or commercial twin-engine plane. The reliability of the aircraft, along with its equipment for instrument flying, permitted rigid scheduling for flight in bad weather. The Army Field Forces stated that Air Force multi-engine aircraft not only lacked the short field characteristics of Army aircraft but were not always available. OCAFF recommended that a requirement for multi-engine aircraft be established and that the Beechcraft Model 50 airplane constitute one-third of all multi-place fixed wing aircraft procured and distributed to corps and higher headquarters. Unreasonable delays developed in the procurement processing of the Beechcraft, as had been the case of the L-20 BEAVER, when the Air Force withheld procurement action because the Beechcraft exceeded the allowable empty weight limit of 2,500 pounds. The first model 50s were purchased in January 1952 and were designated the L-23.

OCAFF planned user tests for fiscal year 1952 which were designed to test twin-engine reliability, single engine performance, suitability for instrument and night flight, and short field performance. In addition, tests would be performed to measure general staff transport flight performance and the suitability of the communication and navigational radio package. Modification or change would be incorporated in future production aircraft and a history of failures, deficiencies, and maintenance difficulties encountered—as well as any other constructive criticism—would be duly noted.

At the request of the Assistant Chief of Staff, G-3, Department of the Army, OCAFF prepared a distribution list for the L-23 aircraft in December 1952 in order that plans could be formulated and school quotas allocated for the necessary multi-engine transition training for the pilots. The LC-126 aircraft with units were reassigned to the Army Aviation School for use in the instrument training program.[6]

Rotary Wing Aircraft

The H-13, SIOUX

The first helicopter used by the Army in Korea was the Bell H-13, which carried a pilot and one passenger and was equipped with two baskets or pods for litter patients. The H-13 was first obtained as the YR-13 in December 1946 and by June 1949 the Army had fifty-nine H-13Bs in its inventory. Shortly after the onset of war in Korea, purchase of twenty H-13s was contemplated by the Department of the Army from uncommitted funds.

In order to meet Far East Command requirements, the Department of the Army had by late November delivered three H-13B helicopters to the Far East. Sixteen H-13Bs were furnished for early shipment to that theater, and ten more were returned from Alaska to the Sixth Army area and were rehabilitated for shipment to FECOM by 14 December. Finally, eight H-13D helicopters were airlifted from the manufacturer to the theater. These H-13s proved to be a real asset in the early days of the war in Korea as a means of medical evacuation.[7]

Development and procurement of the H-13 continued throughout the remainder of the Korean conflict and for many years thereafter. By 30 June 1954, the Army had acquired 790 H-13s of various models. The majority of these were H-13E and H-13G aircraft obtained during 1952 and 1953.[8]

The H-23 RAVEN

A Hiller 360 helicopter was purchased for Army evaluation in 1950 and designated YH-23. Successful trials with this aircraft led to an order for 100 two-seat H-23As in the fiscal year 1951 budget, this being the largest Army contract for helicopters up to that time. The majority of the H-23As were delivered in air ambulance configuration with two external, totally enclosed panniers for stretchers mounted on the fuselage sides. The H-23B followed in 1952 and differed in having a larger engine, a changed undercarriage, and detail refinements. By 30 June 1954, 373 H-23s had been accepted by the Army.[9]

The H-19 CHICKASAW

The H-19C CHICKASAW, which originally served with Military Air Transport Service air rescue squadrons, was obtained by the Army early in 1952. Army Field Forces Board No. 1 tested this aircraft for suitability for medical evacuation, hoisting and rescue work, cargo movement by sling, and suitability for troop transportation. In these user tests the board carefully examined the reliability of the aircraft, considering especially a comparison of hours of maintenance and hours of operation. The board also examined the preferability of Air Force radio equipment in the aircraft rather than existing Army aviation navigational radio equipment. Following successful user tests, the Army obtained ninety-seven H-19s by 30 June 1954. The versatility of these aircraft became evident in Korea, where they were used to transport neutral nations' inspection teams, fly resupply missions for isolated troop units, provide medical evacuation, transport military assistance group personnel and VIP's, and provide transportation for training missions held in coordination with United Nations forces widely dispersed throughout the country. Toward the end of the Korean conflict, two Transportation Corps helicopter companies, the 6th and the 13th, were operational, each with twenty-one H-19 helicopters.[10]

Studies prepared in 1954 by Army Field Forces and G-3, Department of the Army, indicated a greater proportionate increase in the requirement for utility helicopters than for any other type aircraft. The Department of the Army urged OCAFF to develop a plan to assure meeting increased requirements at the earliest practicable date with the most suitable aircraft.

Some of the missions of the 800-pound utility helicopter were advanced training of cargo helicopter pilots; special operations of the Transportation Corps, Signal Corps, and Corps of Engineers; aerial movement of casualties; and missions performed by the proposed division, corps, and Army aviation companies as proposed by G-3, Department of the Army. All missions were to be examined to determine the optimum helicopter for each mission. If one type of helicopter was not suitable for all of the missions, could the missions for which the utility helicopter was not suitable be performed by the reconnaissance or light cargo helicopter?

In order to develop a plan for meeting the Army's requirement for utility helicopters, OCAFF would have to analyze the missions planned for the utility helicopter to determine the qualitative requirements for each mission; determine if any changes should be made in the current characteristics of the utility helicopter; determine if the reconnaissance or the light cargo helicopter should be substituted for the utility helicopter in current or planned authorization; compute the phased requirements for utility type helicopters; and determine the extent to which current utility helicopters should be procured against requirements pending development and procurement of a new utility helicopter.

The Department of the Army requested that Army Field Forces make recommendations regarding the ability of any single type utility helicopter to perform all the required missions and whether any changes should be made in the Army Equipment Development Guide. If no single helicopter could perform the required missions, the Department of the Army wanted OCAFF to recommend those helicopters that would be required to perform the missions and also recommend necessary changes that would have to be made to the Army Equipment Development Guide. The Department also wanted to know if any additional utility helicopters should be procured against present and future requirements.

OCAFF computed utility helicopter requirements for the second half of fiscal year 1955 at 154 increasing to 165 in fiscal year 1956 and 177 in fiscal year 1957. Orders had been placed for 182 H-19 utility helicopters of which 112 had been received, with a balance of 70 to be delivered at 5 per month each in January, February, and March 1955, and 28 in the first and 27 in the second half of calendar year 1956. A review indicated that past and planned procurement of the H-19 was sufficient to meet computed requirements for that aircraft by the first half of fiscal year 1957.

Tables of organization for the new experimental Atomic Field Army (ATFA) organizations provided for a substantial increase in the authorizations of utility helicopters within the field army. Utility helicopters were authorized within the division, in corps and Army aviation companies, and in other units. There were indications that the requirement for this aircraft would expand substantially within the field army during the period 1955-1960, for the performance of missions which would include those of command and staff transportation; liaison and courier; aeromedical evacuation; transportation of small groups of personnel and limited amounts of materiel, supplies, and equipment; and transition instrument training.

OCAFF believed that during the period 1955-1960, the requirement for utility aircraft should be met by both helicopter and fixed wing aircraft. The decision as to whether this requirement should be met by both types of aircraft or by a fixed wing aircraft with a good short field performance, a convertiplane, or other configuration should be based on technical developments and the existing state of the aviation art.

Concerning the procurement of additional helicopters against present and future requirements, OCAFF recommended that proposals be obtained from the Bell Aircraft Corporation relative to production and delivery of a modified H-13 that would incorporate a new engine and a cabin configuration permitting internal carriage of four persons seated and two litter patients. OCAFF further recommended that procurement of the H-19 helicopter be limited to the completion of delivery of the thirty funded for fiscal year 1954 and the fifty-five funded for 1955. The H-19 aircraft of transportation helicopter companies should be taken as a substitute for the H-21 or H-34 and be applied against the utility helicopter requirement as soon as the current shortage of one and one-half ton helicopters would permit.

Finally, OCAFF recommended that, assuming that aircraft selected under the utility helicopter design competition would not become available in quantities until 1959 or 1960, requirements be met by the H-19s then on hand and under procurement, supplemented by later procurement of the modified H-13.[11]

Development of the Cargo Helicopter

Among the requirements for Army helicopters, Army Field Forces in mid-1951 expressed a need for a helicopter with a payload of 3,400 pounds and a range of 200 miles. In addition to the H-19, the Army had under procurement the Piasecki H-21, which carried fifteen to twenty passengers. At that time, Army Field Forces ordered the Army Field Forces Board No. 1 to review the requirement for a light cargo helicopter. The H-21 was adopted by the Army, but the first aircraft was not delivered until August 1954. Consequently, plans to equip the 509th Transportation Helicopter Company with H-21s in late 1952 were deferred in favor of the H-25 helicopter which had been procured from the Navy during the year.[12]

It will be recalled that in 1952 the Materiel Requirements Review Panel recommended that there be three sizes of cargo helicopter in the Army: light cargo with a 2,000-4,000 pound payload; medium cargo with a 4,000-8,000 pound payload; and heavy cargo with an 8,000 pound and higher payload. Prior to 1952, the system for processing military characteristics of aircraft through OCAFF and the Department of the Army had been slow, mainly because each organization involved might make changes which required coordination with OCAFF. To reduce to the minimum the time loss incurred in transmission of correspondence, OCAFF already had directed the Senior Army Field Forces Liaison Officer at Wright-Patterson Air Force Base to coordinate informally the military characteristics with the Wright Air Development Center and to submit any comments or recommendations obtained to the Army Field Forces.

Funds were available in fiscal years 1953 and 1954 to initiate development of the Army medium helicopter. In order to accomplish this as soon as possible, OCAFF recommended that after the military characteristics were reviewed that a conference be called by G-3 Research and Development Branch of the Department of the Army prior to 13 October 1952 to consider comments and recommendations received from Wright-Patterson Air Force Base and others. The conference would be empowered to select the agency, if any, to initiate development of the medium cargo helicopter. The military characteristics, as amended, were to be published by the Department of the Army and forwarded, along with fund authorization, to the agency selected as developer with the request that a design competition be initiated to obtain helicopters to satisfy the revised characteristics.

OCAFF commented that the requirement of a ferry range of 750 nautical miles precluded the use of a jet power plant with the accruing advantages of simplicity, producibility, and lower initial cost. It recommended a ferry range of 400 nautical miles be used. OCAFF considered it of the utmost importance that the proposed helicopter be as simple and as inexpensive as possible. The Department of the Army replied in May 1953 that it had reviewed the military characteristics for the Army medium cargo helicopter for applicability to the 3-ton cargo helicopter requirement. The Department of the Army recommended that the review be conducted as part of the overall project then in progress pertaining to military characteristics for all Army aircraft listed in the Army Equipment Development Guide. The department, among its many comments, stated that a requirement for a ferry range of 750 nautical miles was not justifiable in view of the time required to fly this distance and the pilot fatigue which would be involved in extended helicopter flights. A study of the probable needs for ferry range might produce a different figure.

In January 1953, OCAFF directed Army Field Forces Board No. 1 to prepare new military characteristics on all Army aircraft listed in the latest edition of the Army Equipment Development Guide. The board was advised to review past actions for the 3-ton payload helicopter and revise them as needed to reflect any advances in the state of the art or changes in the latest issue of the guide.[13]

Army Field Forces held a conference on 6 November 1953 to review and expedite the military characteristics for the utility and the 5-ton payload helicopters. The conference participants concluded that a requirement existed for a 5-ton payload helicopter for movement of troops and equipment within the combat zone. As envisioned, the helicopter at overload gross weight would have a 7-ton payload capability at full operational radius. It should have facilities and equipment for carrying full passenger and cargo capacity internally, or full cargo capacity externally, and be capable of being quickly converted to carry a maximum number of standard litters. The helicopter would normally be employed in platoon-, company-, or battalion-size units with a capability of operating at night and during instrument flight conditions. The 5-ton payload helicopter would have a mission to transport troops and equipment in the combat zone. The helicopter would have a cruising speed at sea level of 100 knots and an operating radius of 100 nautical miles. It should be able to hover at 6,000 feet and climb at a rate of 1,000 feet per minute. Its single engine service ceiling should be 5,000 feet.

Army Field Forces also established the required armor, armament, protection, and design for the aircraft. Emphasis was to be placed on simplicity of design, mass production, and ease of maintenance. Capability of operating on standard Army fuel and lubricants normally available in the combat zone was desired.[14]

In mid-February 1954, the Army Field Forces prepared and submitted proposed military characteristics for a one and one-half ton payload helicopter. This helicopter, which would also be used for the movement of troops, cargo, and equipment within the combat zone, would have facilities and equipment for carrying full passenger or cargo capacity internally or full cargo capacity externally. Capability of quick conversion to carry a maximum number of standard litters also would be provided. These helicopters would normally be employed in platoons, companies, or battalions.

The helicopter envisioned by Army Field Forces would have a payload of 3,000 pounds—not including the pilot and co-pilot. The cruising speed would be 100 knots, and it would have an operating radius of 100 nautical miles. The helicopter could climb at the rate of 1,000 feet per minute and would have safe autorotation in case of power or transmission failure. The center of gravity location and landing gear would be designed to facilitate return to an upright position when, resting or moving on landing surfaces, the vertical axis would be tipped away from the vertical.[15]

Army Field Forces in early 1954 also prepared military characteristics for a 3-ton payload helicopter based on those prepared by Army Field Forces Board No. 1 in December 1953. The 3-ton helicopter would be used to move troops and equipment within the combat zone, would normally be employed by platoons, companies, or battalions, and would be capable of operating at night and in instrument flight conditions. In contrast to the 5-ton helicopter, the 3-ton helicopter would have a gross weight of 6,000 pounds, but would have the same cruising speed of 100 knots and operating radius of 100 nautical miles. All other characteristics were also the same as the 5-ton helicopter, except for the single axle loading which was 5,000 pounds for the 3-ton helicopter in contrast with 6,000 pounds for the 5-ton aircraft.[16]

Procurement Planning

The establishment in 1952 of the twelve helicopter battalion program resulted in Transportation Corps plans for equipping the battalions. These plans were integrated into the overall aircraft procurement and production picture. Although the twelve battalion program had been approved in principle in August 1952, the requirement had been based on the estimated production time, rather than on the current troop basis. To facilitate budgetary planning, the Transportation Corps was directed to fit the requirements to the troop basis and to prepare a recommended procurement program. In December 1952, the Transportation Corps presented requirements for 299 light and 614 medium cargo helicopters and a $670,000,000 program for their procurement from fiscal year 1953 through fiscal year 1957. It recommended procurement of H-21s and H-34s in the first three years and proposed that H-16 and H-37 helicopters be procured in prototype quantities in fiscal year 1954 and in increasing numbers in subsequent years, as production capacity permitted.

The Secretary of the Army approved the proposed Transportation Corps helicopter procurement program in January 1953. Eighty H-34s were ordered in fiscal year 1953. The recommended quantities of cargo helicopters were included in the fiscal year 1954 budget, and the amounts and types for subsequent years were approved for planning purposes.

The Transportation Corps soon developed an ambitious but tentative program calling for the funding of $736,230,000 over a 5-year period. Most of this sum, about $684,000,000, was to be spent on cargo helicopters. The remainder would be used to procure reconnaissance helicopters and fixed wing aircraft of the observation, utility, and command types. This program soon required important modifications. Changes in Air Force and Navy procurement planning left the Army as the sole buyer of H-21s and H-16s with fiscal year 1954 funds; and resulted in the Army deferring its production planning for H-16s by one year and providing orders for H-21s to sustain the Piasecki facility until it could begin producing the H-16s. Moreover, fiscal year 1954 funds, initially programed for reconnaissance helicopters, were to be used to procure H-19s which could be used for the utility mission.

The Army Field Forces study of aircraft requirements in the summer of 1953 resulted in a complete revamping of the procurement program. The new 8-year Transportation Corps procurement program, which cost approximately $1,700,000,000, placed major emphasis on cargo helicopters. Few serious technical problems were anticipated in meeting the requirement for fixed wing or smaller rotary wing aircraft. With the exception of the L-20, which was replacing the obsolete L-17, fixed wing aircraft requirements were being met by assets on hand or previous year funding. Initial procurement was limited to the L-20, and subsequent orders were delayed until fiscal years 1956 and 1957 in order to take advantage of improvements coming out of the development program. New procurement of reconnaissance helicopters also was held off until fiscal year 1956 to allow for the determination of the suitability of the XH-32 and XH-26. To meet the utility helicopter requirement, the H-19 was procured in fiscal year 1954, and provision was made in the fiscal years 1956 and 1957 budgets for the procurement of a new model.

The Army Field Forces review demonstrated an initial requirement for 475 light, 224 medium, and 214 heavy cargo helicopters. The light cargo needs would be met by previous orders and by additional procurement of H-21s and H-34s. The medium cargo helicopter, the H-37, was scheduled to enter production in calendar year 1955. The heavy cargo helicopter, the H-16, was still in the development stage.

Because of Army Field Forces objections that funds for specific aircraft should not be committed until it had undergone service testing, G-4 directed that action be held up on H-21s and H-34s recommended for fiscal year 1954 procurement. The Transportation Corps protested this action and was supported by the Chief of Staff of the Army who approved the Transportation Corps procurement program for fiscal year 1954 and for subsequent planning. Steps were taken, however, to spread out future spending for reconnaissance and cargo helicopters over the 8-year period to keep within expenditure ceilings.

In the latter part of fiscal year 1954, design difficulties resulted in the cancellation of the fiscal year 1954 order for fifty-six H-21 helicopters. To compensate for this slippage, action was taken to increase the fiscal year 1955 procurement of H-34s by a corresponding number. The procurement of additional H-21s was deferred pending corrective action by the contractor. Delays in approving and committing research and development funds for the H-16 resulted in the phasing back of an additional year of its pre-production financing and initial production.[17]

At the close of fiscal year 1954, the H-19 utility helicopters were in short supply, a shortage in part attributable to the need to employ these aircraft as interim cargo helicopters. The Army expected that their release from the cargo mission as new, larger helicopters became available, plus new procurement, would materially ease the shortage by fiscal year 1956. The H-25 had been scheduled for delivery beginning in June 1951. Production difficulties delayed initial deliveries until October 1952. The aircraft proved unsuitable for the utility mission and production was halted in 1953. The H-25s already accepted or on order were used as trainers. Thus, the Army's cargo helicopter requirement was still to be met at the end of fiscal year 1954. All cargo helicopter units were equipped with smaller, interim types of aircraft.[18]

Endnotes
Chapter IV

1. Bykofsky, pp. 37-38.
2. McClendon, p. 29.
3. (1) Ltr ATTNG-27 452.1, OCAFF to DA ACofS G-3, 3 Jan 51, subj: Procurement of Liaison Type Aircraft. (2) Annual History, OCAFF 1 Jan-31 Dec 50, pp. 9-10. (3) Ltr ATDEV-7 452.1, OCAFF to AFF Bd No. 1, 1 Mar 51, subj: User Test of L-19 Aircraft. (4) MFR, Personal Experiences of Capt Richard D. Kisling, undated.
4. (1) F.G. Swanborough, *United States Military Aircraft Since 1909* (New York: Putnam, 1963), p. 402. (2) Brig Gen John J. Tolson, "Aircraft Hardware: Aviation Milestones," *Army Aviation*, Feb-Mar 1964, p. 19.
5. (1) Ltr, OCAFF to CofSA, 16 Jul 51, subj: Aircraft Most Suitable to Perform Utility Missions. (2) Ltr ATDEV-7-452.1, OCAFF to Pres AFF Bd No. 1, 1 Mar 51, subj: User Test of L-20 deHavilland BEAVER. (3) DF, ACofS G-3 DA to OCAFF, 11 Apr 51, subj: Procurement of L-20 Aircraft. (4) 1st Ind ATDEV-7 (10 Mar 51), OCAFF to ACofS G3 DA, 5 Jun 51, subj: Operational Suitability Test of L-20 Aircraft. (5) Kisling MFR.
6. (1) DF ATTNG-27, G3 OCAFF to CofS OCAFF, 26 Feb 51, subj: Army Requirements for Command Transportation Aircraft. (2) Ltr, OCAFF to DA ACofS G3, undated, subj: Army Requirements for Command Transportation Aircraft. (3) Ltr, General Mark W. Clark to General J. Lawton Collins, 14 Jul 51, subj: Aircraft Most Suitable to Perform Utility Missions. (4) Memo, OCAFF for DA, 13 Mar 52, subj: User Test of the Beechcraft L-23. (5) Memo, DA ACofS G4 for OCAFF, 23 Dec 52, subj: Distribution Plan for L-23 Aircraft.
7. (1) Tierney and Montgomery, *The Army Aviation Story*, pp. 208-210. (2) Ltr OPS 452.1 (12 Sep 50), ACofS G3 to OCAFF, 12 Sep 50, subj: Procurement of Army Helicopters. (3) Ltr G4 D558521, DA ACofS G4 to DA ACofS G3, subj: Shipment of Helicopters to the Far East Command, 20 Nov 50.
8. (1) Tierney and Montgomery, *The Army Aviation Story*, pp. 256-257. (2) Bykofsky, p. 50.
9. Swanborough, p. 274.
10. (1) Tierney and Montgomery, *The Army Aviation Story*, pp. 213, 249. (2) Memo, ATDEV-7, OCAFF to AFF Bd No. 1, 13 Feb 52, subj: User Test of the H-19C (Sikorsky) Helicopter. (3) Swanborough, pp. 432-433.
11. Ltr G3 452, DA ACofS G-3 to CAFF, 8 Oct 54, subj: Requirement for Utility Type Helicopters, with 1st Ind.
12. (1) Memo ATDEV-7, OCAFF for AFF Board No. 1, 25 Jun 51, subj: Military Characteristics for an Army Light Cargo Helicopter. (2) Memo, CAFF for Chief of Transportation, 21 Nov 52, subj: Assignment of Aircraft to the 509th Transportation Helicopter Co.
13. Ltrs ATDEV-7452.1/83 (C), OCAFF to DA, 19 Sep 52, subj: Military Characteristics for an Army Medium Cargo Helicopter, with 1st Ind, G-3 452 (19 Sep 52), DA G-3 to OCAFF, 20 May 53, same subj, and 2nd Ind ATDEV-7452 (C) (19 Sep 52), CAFF to President, AFF Board No. 1, 11 Jun 53, same subj.
14. Ltr ATDEV-7452.1/426 (24 Nov 53), OCAFF to DA ACofS G-3, 24 Nov 53, subj: Military Characteristics for a 5-ton Helicopter.
15. Ltr ATDEV-7452.1/2 (C) (18 Feb 54), CAFF to DA ACofS G-3, 18 Feb 54, subj: Military Characteristics of a One and One-Half Ton Payload Helicopter.
16. Ltr ATDEV 452.1/1 (21 Jan 54), CAFF to DA ACofS G-3, 21 Jan 54, subj: Military Characteristics for a 3-ton Helicopter.
17. (1) Bykofsky, pp. 50-57. (2) Ltr ATSWC-G 452.1 (C), CAFF to DA ACofS G-3, 14 Jul 54, subj: Procurement of Light Cargo Aircraft.
18. Bykofsky, p. 59.

Chapter V

THE ORGANIZATION OF ARMY AVIATION

Following World War II, Army aviation, which up to that time had consisted only of organic air observation for field artillery, was expanded to various other arms. In some cases, as in separate battalions and regiments, the aircraft and men were made organic to the unit. In the infantry and armored divisions, all aircraft and crews serving units other than artillery were included in the division headquarters company. From 1945 to 1950, the allotment of Army aircraft changed very little. With the outbreak of war in Korea, the expansion of aviation organization at every level of command, from the Army Field Forces down to the smallest medical service helicopter ambulance detachment, occurred very rapidly, causing constant study, review, and change in the allotment of equipment and personnel.

Army Field Forces, the General Staff, and the Transportation Corps worked closely in the planning and monitoring of the activation, training, and employment of the experimental cargo helicopter companies. This work increased in importance with the adoption of the twelve cargo helicopter battalion program. The Transportation Corps assumed similar functions pertaining to the Army aircraft maintenance units transferred to it from the Ordnance Corps.

Army Field Forces

The Chief of Army Field Forces had overall responsibility for the organization and training of Army aviation as it pertained to the Army in the field. Early in 1950, the G-3 Section of Army Field Forces was the operating agency having general staff responsibility for training, with the G-4 Section responsible for those matters pertaining to logistics. Within the G-3 Section, responsibility for aviation training at the end of calendar year 1950 was divided between the Air and Airborne Branch of the Joint Training Maneuvers and Special Projects Division and the Army Aviation Branch of the Combined Arms Training Division.

Virtually no change occurred in the aviation organization within Army Field Forces from 1950 to 1952. On 20 March 1952, a revised version of Army Regulations 95-5, governing Army aviation, was issued. Through the provisions of this regulation the Chief of Army Field Forces exercised general direction, supervision, and coordination over matters pertaining to the training of Army aviation personnel, Army Aviation Sections, and Army aviation units utilized by the

Army in the field. He also was responsible for developing and preparing doctrine pertaining to the tactical and technical employment of Army Aviation Sections and units utilized by the Army in the field and for the materiel and equipment necessary in the performance of their missions.

The Chief of Army Field Forces conducted inspections of Army aviation activities and units, keeping the Chief of Staff of the Army informed of the state of training and operational readiness of units. Among his technical responsibilities were the preparation, coodination, and revision of flight regulations for Army aircraft operated in the continental limits of the United States. He also prepared, coordinated, and revised regulations necessary for the control of Army aircraft used in disaster operations.

In the area of research and development, the Chief of Army Field Forces prepared and coordinated proposed military characteristics for Army aircraft and related items of equipment used in a type field Army. He initiated qualitative requirements for items of Army aviation equipment for which units in the Army in the field had a primary need and directed and controlled appropriate Army Field Forces agencies to ensure continued research, development, and testing of this equipment from the point of view of user interest.[1]

To carry out these many responsibilities, the component elements of the Office of the Chief of Army Field Forces were delegated specific areas of interest. The Deputy Chief of Army Field Forces for Combat Developments had the responsibility for the overall supervision and coordination of the Army aviation program in OCAFF. He coordinated OCAFF efforts in research and development of both doctrine and materiel for the Army in the field. Included on his executive staff was a senior officer charged with monitorship of the program. The G-1, Personnel and Administration, advised the Chief of Army Field Forces and furnished guidance to the staff on all personnel matters pertaining to Army aviation, determined the spaces, and reviewed personnel requirements for Army aviation personnel in boards and schools. The G-2, Intelligence, advised the Chief of Army Field Forces and furnished guidance to the staff on matters pertaining to the employment of aviation in intelligence activities.

The G-3 Training provided advice and guidance on all matters pertaining to the organization, composition, and training of Army aviation sections and units utilized by the Army in the field, developed and supervised a training program for Army aviation personnel, conducted inspections of Army aviation activities and units, and determined the state of training and operational readiness of Army aviation units. The G-3 Section also developed and prepared doctrine pertaining to the tactical employment of Army aviation sections and units utilized by the Army in the field and for the materiel and equipment necessary in the performance of their missions. It prepared, coordinated, and revised flight regulations for Army aircraft operating in the United States and in disaster operations. In addition, G-3 developed and stated military requirements for items of Army aviation equipment for units of the Army in the field, evaluated the impact of new scientific achievements on development of equipment for field units of the Army, and reviewed all Army aircraft accidents involving fatalities or those which would reflect inadequacies of training, doctrines, regulations, or equipment.

Within the G-3 Section, the Army Aviation Branch, Combined Arms Training Division, initiated and coordinated actions on all general training matters and specifically on matters pertaining to Army aviation. The division reviewed aviation accident reports, recommended safety doctrine, and coordinated with the G-3 Schools Division on matters pertaining to aviation training of Army personnel. This division also coordinated with the Organization and Equipment Division on the preparation and modification of tables of organization and equipment, tables of allowances, and tables of distribution for Army aviation units.

The Schools Division of G-3 was responsible for courses, curricula, and instruction for the Army Aviation School as well as for recommending policy and administrative quotas governing attendance at the school. The Joint Training Division of G-3 determined the requirements for modification of existing materiel required for Army aviation operations and the development of doctrine and techniques. Additional duties included analysis of accident reports and the subsequent recommendations concerning aviation safety doctrine.

During fiscal year 1954, the G-3 Joint Training Division assumed from the Combined Arms Training Division the responsibility for the determination of requirements for the modification of existing materiel required for Army aviation. It also revised existing organization, doctrine, and techniques pertaining to aviation. In addition, the Joint Training Division determined requirements for the development of new materiel for aviation operations.

The Combat Developments Division of G-3, organized effective 1 October 1952, supervised the G-3 portion of the combat developments program and specifically was responsible for materiel requirements and development of organization and doctrine. Its staff included an Army aviator for full time work on aviation matters.

The G-4 Logistics advised the Chief of Army Field Forces and furnished guidance to the OCAFF staff on all matters pertaining to logistical support of research and development and operational requirements of Army aviation. He developed and prepared doctrine pertaining to the logistical employment of Army aviation units utilized by the Army in the field. He also provided functional guidance to the staff on matters pertaining to logistical activities as they related to the training of Army aviation personnel, sections, and units.

The Air and Airborne Division, one of the nine operating divisions of the Development and Test Section, was responsible for development of military characteristics and for coordination and control of appropriate Army Field Forces agencies engaged in user tests of aircraft and allied equipment. The Transportation Section of the Special Staff included an Army aviator to advise the section chief and to take action on aviation matters.[2]

Army Field Forces Board No. 1

In the latter part of 1945, Army Ground Forces consolidated the former branch boards into four Army Ground Forces Boards under the supervision of its Developments Section. Each board was assigned definite responsibilities for equipment testing in accordance with designated types and classes. Army Field Forces Board No. 1 at Fort Bragg eventually became responsible for tests relating to Army aviation, airborne items, communications and electronics, and field artillery. The Army Aviation Service Test Section of the board was responsible for user service tests, preparation of military characteristics, and conduct of studies and investigations associated with fixed and rotary wing aircraft.

The conduct of user service tests to ensure that development equipment met the requirements established for it and that the equipment would do the required job called for broad knowledge and thorough appreciation of the problems of the field forces as well as constant coordination and cooperation with other agencies. To ensure that test plans were complete and thorough from the user viewpoint, continual coordination and liaison was maintained with all Army Field Forces schools, certain tactical units, and other interested agencies in the conduct of service tests on equipment. Whenever possible, tests and demonstrations took place at stations other than Fort Bragg so that opinions and recommendations of other agencies could be secured.

A similar procedure was followed in the preparation of military characteristics and in the conduct of studies and investigations. In the preparation of military characteristics for the development of new items of equipment, the board had to know the needs of the field forces. Moreover, the capabilities of science and industry had to be considered. Toward this end, liaison was maintained with the technical services and with the civilian research and development agencies.[3]

The rapid improvement of Army aircraft in late 1950 led Army Field Forces Board No. 1 to suggest that the existing equipment tables might be out of balance as to numbers and types of aircraft assigned. The board therefore recommended to the Chief of Army Field Forces that it reevaluate the need for aircraft in the various Army units and revise the bases of issue. On 21 November 1950, Army Field Forces concurred in this recommendation. The study directed by OCAFF was to reevaluate the needs for Army aircraft in the various types of units and headquarters in order to determine types and quantities recommended for future inclusion in tables of organization and equipment. The study was to include a reevaluation of existing allotments as well as desirable new assignments, to include special organizations.[4]

Army Field Forces Board No. 1 circulated a questionnaire late in 1950 to interested agencies for comment, and the entire scope of the study was discussed at an Army Aviation Conference, held 8-10 January 1951, and attended by representatives of the Department of the Army, Army Field Forces, the CONUS armies, the principal schools, and the board. The conclusions and recommendations of the board represented the consensus of both the questionnaires and the conference. Although the board report reviewed the types of aircraft available or likely to be available—both rotary and fixed wing—its most significant findings were in the area of organization.

The board believed that it would be uneconomical to decentralize Army aviation, a change which would require more equipment and personnel than a centralized organization would need for the same job. The board also felt that decentralized organization was inefficient because it would not provide adequate technical command supervision over training, maintenance, and operations; could not afford to provide all the technical skills needed; would make it difficult to take up the slack in maintenance when mechanics were in short supply; and would not conform to common use of necessary base field equipment.

The board concluded that the formation of an Army Aviation Corps was desirable in order to provide an adequate structure for the proper management of a highly technical Army, ensure proper standards of training, provide qualified supervision, promote flight safety, provide a career outlook for officers comparable to that in other arms and services, and provide a suitable agency for planning and for monitoring new developments. Such a corps also would furnish an agency for making recommendations regarding expenditure of the large sums of money then budgeted for Army aviation. The proposed Army Aviation Corps would be organized to include aviators and mechanics of the organic air sections, the field maintenance units then designated as ordnance light aircraft maintenance companies, the transportation helicopter companies, and any aviation elements which might be added in the future.

Finally, the board recommended that Army aviation in each division be organized into a single unit of squadron type and that a similar unit be provided in each of the corps and army headquarters. The assignment of organic Army aircraft to nondivisional organizations was to be continued, but these were to be limited to the 2-place observer aircraft. No action was taken on these recommendations at this time.[5]

Staff Organization

A rapid expansion of Army aviation occurred following the implementation of the Materiel Requirements Review Panel study and the adoption of the Army-Air Force Memorandum of Understanding in November 1952. The Department of the Army directed Army Field Forces to conduct a study to determine the most suitable aviation organization on army, corps, and division level. The OCAFF study, initiated in March 1953, was conducted in coordination with the Infantry School, the Artillery School, the Command and General Staff College, and the Chief of Transportation.

In its approach to the problem of suitable aviation organization, the OCAFF group examined the command and staff functions involved in the administration and control of Army aviation in order to determine their appropriate place in the organizational structure of the Army. In the opinion of the study group, consolidation of existing personnel to carry out Army aviation functions in the division headquarters would bring about the formation of a suitable staff section. At corps and army headquarters, those people could be integrated into existing staff agencies.

The study group pointed out the advantages accruing from the placement of staff responsibility in a single agency. A single agency would handle all functions and would integrate all the many facets of the program then being separately handled by several agencies. About half of the pertinent functions relating to Army aviation had already been assigned to a single agency, the Transportation Corps, while others were being loosely monitored on an uncoordinated basis by many general and special staff officers as the problem arose. This arrangement prohibited any real integrity or responsibility for the program. For this reason, and because of the rapid growth of the complexity of operations, the study group felt that all elements should be drawn into a single responsible agency that would provide technical supervision over aviation training, operations, supply, and maintenance. The Transportation Corps seemed to be the most logical agency in which to centralize these responsibilities.

At the time of the study, transportation activities in a division were being performed by Transportation Corps officers and enlisted men assigned to the G-4 section, an unsound arrangement that required the section to perform the duties of a special staff section at the expense of its own function. In addition to responsibilities regarding rail and highway movement, the new Army helicopter activities had been superimposed upon the division transportation officer along with all logistical functions of all Army aviation. The study group recommended that the division transportation officer be assigned to the special staff. Existing personnel scattered among the various staff sections would then be consolidated in a suitable staff section to carry out aviation functions at division headquarters. The need for centralized maintenance, supply, and logistical support for divisional aviation had long been recognized. The requirements for pilots to be well trained in their basic arm or service and to be under the command and control of their individual organizational commanders could be met by leaving the pilots assigned to units and pooling the aircraft and maintenance personnel. Unit commanders would continue to assign missions to their pilots and control them during the missions. The transportation officer would assign the pilot the proper aircraft and relieve the unit commanders of the responsibility for organizational maintenance of aircraft. He would provide the logistical support required to operate the common facilities, would constitute the agency to exercise centralized control when so directed by the division commander, and would provide for uniform and supervised technical training of aviation personnel.

There were transportation officers on the special staff at the corps and army levels where Army aviation functions had not been consolidated and specifically assigned to a single staff section. The study group therefore recommended that the staff function of Army aviation be assigned to the transportation officer of the corps and army, a move which would involve some readjustment in the personnel assigned to the staff sections.[6]

Organization in the Field Army

In another Army aviation study, this one conducted in August 1953, OCAFF concluded that the transportation staff section at army level should include qualified personnel to exercise technical staff supervision of Army aircraft maintenance and supply and an Army aviator to advise the Army transportation officer on employment of transportation helicopter units. The study group felt that the medical staff section at army level should include one Medical Service Corps major qualified as an Army aviator to advise the Army surgeon on aeromedical evacuation and employment of medical service helicopter ambulance units. Finally, the OCAFF group concluded that the signal section at army level should include one signal officer also qualified as an Army aviator to advise the Army Signal officer on aviation electronics, communications, and aerial photography.[7]

Corps Aviation Organization

In its August 1953 review, Army Field Forces concluded that Army aviation at the corps level needed reorganization. The proposed reorganized corps aviation section would have a lieutenant colonel as Army aviation officer, two assistant Army aviation officers, and one operations sergeant assigned to corps headquarters. The corps signal battalion would have six Army aviators, one aircraft maintenance supervisor, and seven enlisted maintenance personnel assigned. Nine Army aviators and eleven enlisted men would be assigned to the aviation section of the corps headquarters company. The Army aviation section of headquarters battery, corps artillery, would have three Army aviators and five enlisted men assigned.

The Army airfield operative unit, which would be assigned to corps, army, or other major Army airfield installation in a combat zone, overseas command, or the zone of the interior, had the mission to provide air traffic control, radio aids for air navigation, flight planning data, and coordination as required for day, night, and instrument flight operations service. This unit, composed of 7 operating teams, would consist of 11 officers, 1 warrant officer, and 71 enlisted men.[8]

Army Aviation within the Division

The staff organization on the division level for Army aviation had evolved from World War II when aircraft were authorized only in artillery battalions and in artillery group and division artillery headquarters batteries. During the war in Korea, this division organization, in the opinion of Army Field Forces, was weakened by lack of operational facilities, administrative support, adequate maintenance supervision, and operational supervision to prevent duplication of missions. This situation was unfortunate because the organization of Army aviation within the division provided the key to the organization of Army aviation within the Army. Thus, the same principle of assignment of aircraft to using units or centralization of aircraft in a TOE aviation unit should be applied to both divisional and nondivisional units. Since using units were organic to the division, establishment of a TOE aviation company would be a workable solution in the division. Many administrative, operational, and logistical problems would occur, however, if this solution were applied to nondivisional units.

OCAFF believed that any reorganization which would reduce the effectiveness of the Army aviation team, or introduce delaying administrative procedures in obtaining Army aviation support, would reduce the capability of Army aviation to perform its assigned function. The assignment of Army aviation to using units within the division was the best means of assuring unit commanders operational control of the required aviation. The Army Field Forces study group which reviewed organization on the division, corps, and army level in August 1953 concluded that Army aviation officers should be included in the G-3 section at division level in order to provide supervision over Army aviation activities and to provide a source of information concerning Army aviation for the commander and other staff sections. The implementation of these recommendations had to wait until the development of new division organizations in 1956.[9]

Tactical Aviation Units

The war in Korea proved to be a major factor in initiating the concept of close unit aviation medical support rather than relying solely on the Air Force's area medical coverage. In Korea, Army aviation units were located in forward areas with major tactical commands and were separated from Air Force facilities. These units thus were organized to provide medical evacuation support for the Army. The helicopter detachment—later designated the medical detachment, helicopter ambulance—operated early in the war, while the transportation helicopter company finally became operational in Korea toward the end of the war after the solution of a number of organizational problems. During 1954, OCAFF began planning for the formation of a light cargo fixed wing aircraft company and a division combat aviation company.

Medical Service Helicopter Ambulance Detachments

In June 1950, Army Field Forces recommended to the Department of the Army that a helicopter organization be provided for each division and field army for the purpose of providing aerial vehicles for medical evacuation. OCAFF suggested that in a division this organization be placed under the control of the division surgeon, be operated by Army medical personnel, and be considered in the same category as a Medical Department ambulance unit.

The evacuation of wounded personnel was handled early in the war in Korea by the Air Force as a secondary assignment, but the Army, which was quick to notice the advantages of helicopter evacuation, organized a helicopter detachment composed of four pilots and placed under the operational control of the Eighth Army surgeon.

By the early months of 1952, H-13 helicopters, with casualties carried on externally mounted pods, were being used in Korea for medical evacuation. Seventy H-25s were under procurement to be used for the same mission. Plans for equipping and training twelve helicopter ambulance detachments were dependent upon the availability of personnel spaces for instructors. Army air evacuation units, each of which consisted of five utility helicopters flown by medical service officers, were attached to medical units according to the dictates of terrain and battle conditions. Normally, one unit would be assigned to each division medical battalion. The units would be used for forward air evacuation of seriously wounded casualties to Mobile Army Surgical Hospitals located in the vicinity of the division medical battalion or to evacuation hospitals located farther to the rear. Casualties would be picked up where wounded, if possible, or picked up at the battalion aid station if the terrain or battle conditions prohibited normal evacuation.

In August 1952, after four helicopter detachments had arrived in Korea and operated with considerable success, the Department of the Army authorized the activation of helicopter ambulance units, redesignated medical detachments, helicopter ambulance. Requirements for medical service helicopter ambulance detachments recommended by the Materiel Requirements Review Panel on 31 July 1952 were approved by the Army Chief of Staff on 28 August 1952.

With the ever increasing tempo of the war, the Department of the Army granted authority to the Far East Command to organize six medical helicopter ambulance detachments, each having a strength of seven officers and twenty-one enlisted men. These air evacuation units, equipped with H-13 helicopters and flown by other than medically trained pilots, were provided for the same purpose as the ambulance company and were attached to the division. These units were not restricted to the division area. By evacuating seriously wounded casualties directly to evacuation hospitals, the load on the Mobile Army Surgical Hospitals would be reduced, as would be the requirement for medical personnel and installations in the forward areas.[10]

In August 1953, OCAFF recommended the organization of helicopter ambulance detachments equipped with five utility helicopters and manned by seven pilots with appropriate supporting personnel and equipment. OCAFF also recommended a mobilization program for helicopter ambulance detachments on a ratio of one unit per two divisions and a plan for twelve detachments to support the fiscal year 1954 troop program. These twelve detachments, in addition to meeting operational requirements of the troop program, would provide training personnel for the Medical Field Service School, the schools of the arms and services, and for participation in field exercises in the continental United States.[11]

Light Cargo Fixed Wing Aircraft Company

Because of difficulties in the procurement of H-21 helicopters to equip transportation helicopter companies, OCAFF recommended to the Department of the Army in July 1954 that the deHavilland OTTER be adopted as substitute standard for the one and one-half-ton payload cargo helicopter. The OTTER was a fixed wing aircraft which compared favorably with the H-21 on an initial cost, spare parts cost, man-hour maintenance, payload, operational radius, POL consumption, and general performance basis. OCAFF recommended that approximately 100 OTTERS be procured for equipping one battalion of transportation cargo aircraft companies (light) in lieu of one programed battalion of transportation helicopter companies (light).

The Department of the Army on 30 September 1954 approved the early activation of three light cargo fixed wing aircraft companies and directed Army Field Forces to prepare a TOE for this organization. OCAFF established a tactical mission for fixed wing cargo aircraft of directly supporting forces in the combat zone by providing tactical air mobility and tactical aerial supply. The unit was assigned a TOE designator in the 1 series—aviation—instead of the 55 series—transportation—and was given the title, Army aviation transport company (airplane). The organization of this company was a significant step in the development of Army transport aviation and constituted the first recognition of the airplane as a major element of Army tactical transport aviation.[12]

Division Combat Aviation Company

As part of the planning for an experimental new type field army—known as the ATFA (Atomic Field Army)—OCAFF in 1954 began the development of a TOE for a division combat aviation company. The mission of the company was to support the division and its elements through day and night aerial observation, reconnaissance, and surveillance. The company also was to be capable of limited air movement of troops, supplies, and equipment. Other missions included battlefield illumination, aeromedical evacuation, wire laying, radio relay and propaganda leaflet dissemination, artillery survey, courier and messenger service, and aerial transportation of commanders and staffs.

The division aviation officer would serve both as a commander and a staff officer. In addition to commanding the division combat aviation company, he would be a special staff officer and provide advice to the division commander and coordination with the division and subordinate unit staffs. Both the division aviation officer and aviation detachment commanders would be responsible for organization and operation of the air installation, reconnaissance, conduct of displacement, security, air defense, maintenance, discipline, and training. Staff responsibilities of the division aviation officer and aviation detachment commanders included advising the division commander and subordinate staffs concerning the planning, employment, and establishment of operational policies with respect to Army aviation.

The division combat aviation company was organized for operation in one or more combat elements in order to permit support of the division and its subordinate units from one or several locations as the tactical situation dictated. The organization was designed for maximum flexibility in order to meet changing tactical requirements. The company would be fully mobile and capable of supporting itself and detached combat elements with specialized aviation logistic functions. Its proposed TOE called for 143 officers and men.

The company headquarters was to be divided into four sections. The headquarters section would include the company commander (division aviation officer), who was to be concerned with overall planning, staff coordination, and command liaison activities; and the company executive (assistant division aviation officer) who was to have command supervision of the company.

The operations section, responsible for operational planning for the company and its elements, would consist of the operations officer who would be responsible for overall supervision of operational planning and aircraft utilization within the company; the assistant operations officer (combat) who would conduct the planning and supervise the operations of the combat platoon, as well as being the unit intelligence officer; the assistant operations officer (combat support) who would conduct the planning and supervise the operations of the combat support platoon; and the assistant operations officer (special missions) who would conduct the planning and supervise the operations of the special missions platoon and would be the unit communications officer. The communications section would contain the men and equipment necessary for installation and operation of wire, radio, and teletype communications for the company and for specialized aviation navigation devices. It also would perform second echelon maintenance on specialized aviation signal equipment. The technical inspection section would perform technical inspections of aircraft to determine serviceability and compliance with technical orders. The combat platoon of the division combat aviation company would consist of three identical flights, each consisting of four L-19 aircraft and one H-13 helicopter, with men and equipment for sustained operations when detached from the company.

The combat support platoon would consist of two flights. A light cargo fixed wing flight would have seven L-20 aircraft capable of aerial resupply by air landing, paradrop, and freefall drop of three and one-half tons of equipment or supplies in one sortie, or movement of a platoon of combat troops. A light cargo helicopter flight would be equipped with seven H-19 helicopters and would be capable of resupply or movement of specialist teams and equipment as well as movement of a platoon of combat troops. Both flights would be capable of supplementing the special mission platoon in aeromedical evacuation and administrative aerial transportation.

The special mission platoon would consist of a light helicopter flight of twelve H-13 helicopters and a fixed wing flight of three L-19s. The helicopter flight would provide command liaison transportation for the division commander, assistant division commander, division artillery commander, and their staffs. Six of the helicopters would have the primary mission of providing battlefield aeromedical evacuation for the division and, in addition, would provide a means for engineer and other specialized reconnaissance, signal courier and message service, and artillery survey. The fixed wing flight would provide photo reconnaissance by hand held and mounted cameras for the division as a supplement to photo reconnaissance of the other services and that provided by the combat platoon elements when detached with combat commands. In addition, the fixed wing flight would provide combat reconnaissance specifically for the division staff.

The aviation service platoon would consist of three sections—the aviation maintenance section, the aviation supply section, and the refueling section. The aviation maintenance section would perform second echelon aircraft maintenance, including adjustments, minor repairs, and replacement of components, second echelon periodic inspections, and component calendar inspections of all aircraft assigned to the company. The aviation supply section would accomplish receipt, issue, storage, and turn-in of aircraft parts, components expendables, and accessories. The refueling section would draw, transport, store, and dispense the various aviation petroleum, oil, and lubricants required by the company.[13]

Cargo Helicopter Units

Concepts for the employment of cargo helicopter units were developed in an evolutionary fashion. Early Army planning had envisioned the assignment of helicopter companies directly to divisions and helicopter battalions to corps. In view of the high cost and scarcity of helicopters, the lack of experience regarding their employment, and their small unit capacity, it was determined subsequently to assign cargo helicopter units to field armies.

Early in August 1950, the Department of the Army requested that Army Field Forces submit recommendations regarding the organization, activation, and stationing for four of the five transportation helicopter companies which had been approved by the Joint Chiefs of Staff and the Secretary of Defense for fiscal year 1951. Approximately 500 spaces had been included in the augmented fiscal year 1951 Troop Basis which had been approved by the Joint Chiefs of Staff. In July 1950, the Department of the Army G-3 had approved the purchase of H-19 helicopters to equip the four companies. The success of the first four companies would be a controlling factor in the organization of the proposed fifth company. The Department of the

Army requested that OCAFF prepare a TOE and plan to arrange procurement by the end of fiscal year 1951 for the largest and best available aircraft to equip the fifth helicopter company.

Tentative doctrine, issued in December 1950, contemplated that the field armies would attach helicopter companies to corps, divisions, or smaller tactical units for specific operations. Used to augment existing transportation facilities, the companies would greatly enhance the speed and flexibility of ground combat units and make possible operations in areas where terrain and operating conditions rendered impracticable the use of other means of transportation.

On 24 October 1950, a tentative TOE had been issued for the transportation helicopter company. In the absence of a prototype helicopter suitable to the proposed mission, an organization was created to utilize a type of helicopter which the Army did not possess and could plan on procuring at some future date. Reflecting great credit on the foresight of the planning officers, this original TOE was virtually unchanged when the first transportation helicopter company was deployed to Korea late in 1952. The TOE called for 7 commissioned officers, 28 warrant officers, and 76 enlisted men. The company was composed of three helicopter platoons, with nine pilots per platoon. The company had twenty-one light cargo helicopters—H-19s or H-21s—and two H-13 utility helicopters. One utility helicopter was in the maintenance and service section and the other in the operations section. On 1 November 1950, the first helicopter company—the 1st Transportation Helicopter Company, Army—was activated at Fort Sill.[14]

As a result of experience, the TOE was revised in August 1952. The new TOE called for a unit with 131 officers, warrant officers, and enlisted men and 21 cargo and 2 utility helicopters. Since helicopters were unusually complex and existing aircraft maintenance units were equipped largely to care for fixed wing aircraft, it proved necessary to provide for Transportation Corps field maintenance detachments for each cargo helicopter unit. Such detachments were activated beginning in late 1952, and two accompanied the cargo helicopter companies assigned to Korea.[15]

One of the most significant changes in the new TOE was the substitution of commissioned officer pilots for warrant officer pilots. The Transportation Corps strongly objected to this change. In order to provide for the recruitment and retention of cargo helicopter pilots, the Transportation Corps recommended that they be given the grade of warrant officer, and that an appropriate career field be established. It had been determined, however, that it was impracticable to set up a definite grade or rank for cargo helicopter pilots. In practice, the Transportation Corps used both officers and warrant officers as helicopter pilots, with the latter flying cargo helicopters as their primary duty. After studies had shown that the twelve battalion program would require 2,000 pilots, recommendations for the approval of the warrant officer grade for cargo helicopter pilots were renewed. These proposals were under consideration at the end of 1954.[16]

The next logical step was the development of an organization to control and administer cargo helicopter companies assigned to the field armies. Army Field Forces did not accept the Transportation Corps idea of establishing a fixed battalion organization with a predetermined number of assigned companies. Because of the limited availability of cargo helicopters and the early stage of the testing of their use, it appeared that their employment in operations would be limited to separate company rather than battalion-size organizations for some time. Army Field Forces favored the establishment of an interim flexible battalion headquarters to direct a varying number of helicopter companies, each of which would be capable of separate operations if required in an active theater.

In line with this reasoning, an interim TOE was published in June 1953 providing for a battalion headquarters to direct two to four helicopter companies and accompanying field maintenance detachments. The detachments were subsequently reorganized as teams, and provision was made for grouping them in those cases where parent helicopter companies were brought under a battalion. Steps also were taken to augment helicopter companies with cellular helicopter teams in order to provide short haul liaison and cargo and personnel movements.

As of 30 June 1954, there were three cargo helicopter battalion headquarters, seven companies, and an equal number of field maintenance detachments in CONUS and overseas. This number was still considerably short of the goal of twelve battalion headquarters and thirty-six cargo helicopter companies approved by the Chief of Staff of the Army in August 1952. In large part, this was due to the need for scheduling activations in accordance with the availability of equipment. Another limiting factor was the shortage of pilots. Despite the efforts at intensified recruiting and publicity, the Army-wide shortage persisted.

Transportation Corps efforts in the development of doctrine and organization for Army aircraft maintenance units began with its assumption of the logistical support mission in August 1952. At that time, the only TOE aircraft maintenance units were field maintenance companies and repair teams brought into the Transportation Corps from Ordnance. No formal provision had been made for the administration and back-up support of such units at the field army level. In Korea, however, an improvised battalion organization had been developed, providing valuable guidance to the Transportation Corps in formulating concepts for the organization and utilization of maintenance units.

By the end of 1953, the Transportation Corps had developed a suitable organization and published TOE's for a battalion consisting of a headquarters detachment, three transportation Army aircraft maintenance (TAAM) companies, and a heavy maintenance and supply company. The headquarters would exercise command, staff planning, and administrative functions for the assigned units. The TAAM companies, reorganized with additional personnel and equipment and set up to handle rotary wing as well as fixed wing aircraft, would each handle the field maintenance and recovery of the aircraft of an army corps. They also would furnish supplies and spare parts for organizational and third echelon maintenance. When necessary, these units would be augmented by transportation Army aircraft repair (TAAR) teams. Back-up (fourth echelon) support for the TAAM companies and repair teams and the evacuation of salvageable and repairable materials to the Air Force depot maintenance facilities were to be accomplished by the heavy maintenance and supply company. As of 30 June 1954, there were 2 battalion headquarters, 7 TAAM companies, and 8 TAAR teams at various locations in CONUS and overseas. Orders had been issued for the activation of the first heavy maintenance and supply company at Fort Eustis.[17]

Supply Support

Division of Responsibility

Early in 1950, supply and maintenance support for Army aircraft cut across service lines. The Air Force handled purchase and depot storage and issue of spare parts, tools, and other equipment for Army aircraft and performed the necessary depot maintenance. The Army determined requirements for those air items needed for operation and maintenance of aircraft, made funding arrangements, placed cross-service orders for their procurement, and performed storage, issue, and maintenance at organization and field levels. Responsibility for supply support of Army aircraft below the depot level and for coordination with the Air Force regarding depot support initially was assigned to the Ordnance Corps in June 1949. Following the assumption of the logistical support mission by the Transportation Corps in 1952, the Transportation Corps Army Aviation Field Service Office (TCAAFSO) became responsible for the procurement, supply control, and maintenance tasks.[18]

Expansion of Responsibility

With the outbreak of the war in Korea and the sudden expansion of requirements, it became necessary to provide for support of new helicopters coming into the system on the basis of limited experimental data. Limited production capacity, long lead time, and continuing design changes further complicated the supply support problem. The program tended to outgrow the personnel and facilities provided. The establishment of Transportation Corps liaison officers at Air Force depots resulted in expedited supply action on requisitions from the field and closer cognizance of Army stocks. Procedures were set up for joint Army-Air Force action in determining the range and quantity of spare parts and equipment required for concurrent delivery with the aircraft, and in developing supporting technical data. This provided a sound basis for the supply and maintenance support of aircraft during their initial phase of operation. Measures also were taken to step up procurement of air items required for the replenishment of stocks for aircraft already in the system.[19]

Shortage of Parts

A chronic shortage of spare parts for aircraft was precipitated by delays in providing sufficient funds for replenishment of parts, long production lead times, and difficulties inherent in an interservice system. While the spare parts shortage was world-wide, it was especially critical in the Far East, where aircraft were operated and maintained under extremely rugged conditions.

The spare parts problem in Korea was symptomatic of various difficulties encountered by the Transportation Corps in the supply support area. Initial purchases of spare parts for helicopters based on limited experience and a low estimate of flying time proved inadequate for expansion of helicopter employment following the outbreak of war. As a result of the buildup of parts required for support, the TCAAFSO had to recompute supply requirements and arrange for additional procurement to compensate for previous deficiencies. The supply shortage was aggravated by delays in providing adequate funds for the follow-up procurement of spare parts. The $10,000,000 budgeted for fiscal year 1954 by the Ordnance Corps for replenishment spare parts was less than one-half the amount required to support the operating program in effect. Efforts to obtain additional funds were not immediately successful. Restrictions on the release of funds limited the amount that could be obligated quarterly during the first half of fiscal year 1954. The necessary funds finally were made available in December 1953, and purchasing action was instituted. Because of the long production lead time, however, it was anticipated that material relief of existing shortages would be delayed six to eighteen months.[20]

Incompatibility of Army and Air Force Supply Structures

Adequate logistical support of Army aircraft was further complicated by the incompatibility of the Army and Air Force supply structures. The Air Force's distribution and accounting systems were not responsive to Army requirements. The Air Force failed to supply the Army with timely and accurate information regarding the status of Army stocks in Air Force depots. This situation resulted in impairment of supply control, budgetary planning, and procurement action by the Transportation Corps and serious losses of Army equities due to absorption in Air Force stocks or diversions to Air Force use.

Late in 1953, agreement was reached regarding the refining and improvement of Air Force stock position reports. Provision was made for the advance notice to the Army of withdrawals from its equities and for improved reimbursement procedures. These measures did not materially improve the situation. Stock status data furnished by the Air Force continued to be untimely, incorrect, and lacking in uniformity. Army report requirements were basically incompatible with Air Force requirements and procedures. Remedial action proposed by the TCAAFSO included the placement of records of Army equities of secondary transportation air items at Air Force CONUS depots under TCAAFSO control; the designations of Army-Air Force audit teams to investigate and correct discrepancies relating to stock status of Army equities; and the conduct of negotiations for segregation of Army stocks in Air Force depots until such time as the Army assumed full responsibility for supply and maintenance of Army aviation.

By the end of fiscal year 1954, the Air Force depot support of the Army had not worked out. The problem appeared to be the inability of the Army to perform the supply control and budgeting functions with the record keeping and depot reporting system employed by the Air Force. A total of $3,000,000 in parts that had been diverted from Army equity were recovered in fiscal year 1954, alone. The Army would either have to assume control of stocks in Air Force depots or perform the depot function itself.[21]

Depot Transfer

By the latter part of fiscal year 1954, it was obvious that action should be taken to transfer depot responsibilities. Negotiations with the Air Force for the transfer of the responsibility had been undertaken by the Chief of Ordnance in 1951, and regulations published by the Army had announced its intent to take over the depot functions. The Materiel Requirements Review Panel

Study of July 1952 found the interservice system of depot support neither efficient nor economical and recommended the transfer of the responsibility. Upon the transfer of the logistical support mission to the Transportation Corps, however, it was decided to hold the project in abeyance until the latter had absorbed the functions assigned. The Chief of Transportation drew up new plans for the assumption by the Army of the depot support function, but these plans were deferred because of personnel and budgetary limitations.

Continuing problems with the depot support brought the matter up for reconsideration. By the latter part of fiscal year 1954, it was obvious at the highest Army levels that action should be taken to effect the transfer. The Air Force, which earlier had indicated some opposition, now appeared willing to go along with such a transfer of functions. At the close of the fiscal year, joint Army-Air Force negotiations looking toward assumption by the Army of the depot support responsibility were in progress.

In the interim, the Transportation Corps took various actions in an attempt to improve the situation. It attempted to eliminate backlogged orders, develop more accurate demand and usage data, and establish interim and long range programs to place support on a sound basis. The war initiated a program to facilitate supply and maintenance through the standardization of aircraft by geographical locations wherever possible. Steps were taken to develop flying hour programs that would assure effective utilization of assigned aircraft and permit more accurate planning for their supply and maintenance. Provision was made for development and periodic revision of flying hour quotas for various types of aircraft. The Transportation Corps proposed that army area commanders be responsible for monitoring aircraft utilization in their areas in order to assure that established quotas were met and to take corrective action in the event of deficient utilization. Consistent failure to obtain the minimum criteria for use of equipment would result in the redistribution or withdrawal of aircraft. These proposals were expected to provide a standard provisioning and budgeting guide for all Army technical services involved in supplying air items and for the Air Force in budgeting for and programing depot maintenance activities.[22]

Endnotes
Chapter V

1. AR No. 95-5, Flying, Army Aviation—General Provisions, 20 Mar 52.

2. (1) Functions Pertaining to Army Aviation, 27 Oct 52. (2) OCAFF Summary of Major Events and Problems, FY 1953, Part B. (3) OCAFF Summary of Major Events and Problems, FY 1954, Part B. (4) Ltr ATTNG-52 360(S), Acting CAFF to DA ACofS G-3, 29 Aug 53, Incl 3 to Incl 2, 10 Aug 53, subj: Review of Organization of Army Aviation.

3. AFF Bd No. 1, Fort Bragg, North Carolina, undated (c 1950).

4. Ltrs GNBA-8 400.34, AFF Bd No. 1 to OCAFF, 14 Nov 50, subj: Tables of Equipment Governing Army Aircraft, with 1st Ind; OCAFF to Pres AFF Bd No. 1, 21 Nov 50, same subj.

5. Report of Study of Project AC1250, AFF Bd No. 1, 14 Mar 51.

6. (1) Ltr G-3 360 (23 Dec 52), DA ACofS G-3 to CAFF, 23 Dec 52, subj: Organization for Army Aviation. (2) Staff Study, Organization for Army Aviation, undated.

7. (1) OCAFF Staff Study, 10 Aug 53, subj: Organization for Army Aviation within Division, Corps, and Armies. (2) Revision of OCAFF Staff Study, 15 Sep 53, same subj., Annex J, Appendixes I, II, and III.

8. OCAFF Staff Study, 15 Sep 53, Annex II, Appendixes I, II, and III.

9. (1) OCAFF Staff Study, 15 Sep 53, Annex II, Appendices I, II, III. (2) Interview, Hist Ofc with Col W. R. Mathews, ODCSOPS Avn Div, 2 Jun 71.

10. Msg AGAO-I-M-332 (20 Nov 52), DA to CINCFE, 26 Nov 52, subj: Activation of Certain Medical Detachments.

11. (1) Tierney and Montgomery, *The Army Aviation Story*, p. 189. (2) Fact Sheet, OCAFF G-3 Section, 10 Aug 53, subj: Requirements for Medical Service Helicopter Ambulance Detachments.

12. (1) OCAFF Summary of Major Events and Problems, FY 1955, Vol. I, Part B, pp. 29-30. (2) Semiannual Hist Rept, G-3 Section Doctrine and Requirements Div, 1 Jul - 31 Dec 54, p. 8. (3) Ltr G-3 DA 451 (21 Sep 54), DA to OCAFF, 20 Sep 54, subj: Preparation of TOE for Light Cargo Fixed Wing Company.

13. (1) Ltr 322 AKPSIAS-CS, Army Aviation School to OCAFF, 28 Jun 54, subj: Deviation for Guidance for Division Combat Aviation Company, ATFA-1, w/1st Ind, OCAFF to Aviation School, 8 Jul 54, and w/incl, Division Combat Aviation Company, ATFA-1.

14. In 1951, the 1st Transportation Helicopter Company was redesignated as the 6th Transportation Helicopter Company.

15. (1) Bykofsky, pp. 81-83. (2) Annual History, OCAFF, 1950, Vol. II, Chap. 16, pp. 5-6.

16. Bykofsky, pp. 86-87.

17. (1) Bykofsky, pp. 83-86, 87-88. (2) OCAFF Staff Study, 10 Aug 53, Appendix III to Annex J to Incl 2.

18. Bykofsky, pp. 60-61.

19. Ibid., pp. 61-63.

20. Ibid., pp. 63-66.

21. Ibid., pp. 66-68.

22. Ibid., pp. 68-71.

Chapter VI

EARLY AVIATION TRAINING

The outbreak of the war in Korea imposed an immediate requirement for the expansion of aviator and mechanic training. The Department of the Army increased the authorized overstrength of Army aviators from 50 to 100 percent, began the activation of helicopter transportation companies, and started calling up Reserve Component units. In addition, a standing requirement for twelve replacement pilots each month was established for the Far East Command. The recent transfer of 200 airplane and engine mechanics to light maintenance units had left tactical units short of qualified mechanics. The activation of the helicopter transportation companies and other new units would further increase the requirements for mechanics.

The Impact of the Korean Conflict

Even before the Korean conflict, the Department of the Army had asked the Air Force to increase the class capacity of the Army liaison pilot course from forty to sixty students, but the Air Force stated that no aircraft were available to meet that requirement. Possible solutions to the training problem included the purchase of Piper PA-19 aircraft for training and utilization of civilian contractors, as had been done during World War II. The utilization of civilian contractors seemed to be the best solution to the OCAFF G-3, as it would eliminate problems of men and equipment.

The general feeling within the Department of the Army was that the Army could handle its own training program. In August 1950, the OCAFF G-3 Section recommended that the Army begin conducting all aviation personnel training and phase out Air Force training as early as practicable. An Army training plan would be developed, the Air Force would be advised of the proposed action, and plans would be made to phase out Air Force training and to withdraw Army equipment then being used by the Air Force.[1]

The OCAFF G-3 calculated that at that time there was an immediate requirement for training approximately 919 Army aviators to meet Regular Army needs alone—a 144 annual requirement in the Far East Command, 200 for helicopter transportation companies, and 575 to build up to authorized strength. In addition, the National Guard Bureau had a requirement for 200 Army aviators per year, and the Organized Reserve Corps was short aviators. Although personnel reports indicated a surplus of airplane and engine mechanics, G-3 did not believe there was an actual surplus. Plans for training would have to be sufficiently flexible to permit expansion on short notice. Also, the rotary wing mechanic training program had to be expanded to meet the needs of the helicopter transportation companies.

The Artillery School reported that it could train the Army's aviators and airplane and engine mechanics. It also reported that it could expand to a maximum annual output of 480 Army aviators, and, if additional expansion were required, civilian Civil Aeronautics Administration approved schools could be used for the basic phase of the Army aviator course and also airplane and engine mechanics training.

The proposal of the Artillery School reflected a 157 percent increase in the capacity of the Army fixed wing aviator course, although there would be very little change in the capacity of the helicopter pilot, airplane and engine mechanic, and rotary wing mechanic courses. The expansion required a 147 percent increase in personnel and a 50 percent increase in aircraft. In addition to aircraft, necessary additional equipment, facilities, training aids, and $20,000 for rehabilitation of class rooms would be required.

The OCAFF G-3 reported that training could be implemented with an Army aviator course nine weeks after receipt of the directive; a helicopter pilot course ten days after receipt, if additional personnel were available; and an Army airplane and engine mechanic course and an Army rotary wing mechanic course four weeks after the rehabilitation of class rooms.[2]

As a result of these recommendations, on 24 August 1950, General Mark W. Clark proposed that the Army conduct all training of Army aviation personnel and that the Army Field Forces be authorized to take the necessary action to implement such a program. These recommendations found considerable support at Department of the Army level and resulted in the establishment of the Joint Ad Hoc Committee on Evaluation of the Current System of Training Army Aviators and Mechanics in January 1951. The committee, composed of representatives from the Army and the Air Force, was to determine whether or not the current system satisfied qualitative and quantitative requirements for trained personnel and whether or not it achieved optimum utilization of committed resources. Matters considered by the committee included the accomplishment of the training objective, maximum use of available facilities and manpower, provision of a continuing source of men in the event of mobilization, and improvement of training procedures. The qualification of instructors, flying techniques for combat missions, and the reduction of the number of washouts also were considered.

The Air Force continued to voice strong objections to the transfer of the entire training mission to the Army. As a result of the failure to reach a satisfactory agreement between the two services, the transfer of responsibilities had to await the final approval of the entire Army aviation program. No basic changes in the training system were therefore made until the establishment of the Army Aviation School.[3]

Helicopter Pilot Training

While the Army and the Air Force continued their dispute over the control of training, the existing training programs steadily expanded. Reflecting the growing Army interest in helicopters, the number of graduates from the tactical helicopter course increased from eight in the first class on 8 December 1948 to 274 by fiscal year 1953. Early in 1951, the enrollment of the Army Field Forces Helicopter Pilot Course had jumped to 18 students, while the class capacity for helicopter pilots trained by the Air Force was raised from 6 to 11 students. The overall program stayed at one class every two weeks.

In November 1950, Army Field Forces asked the Artillery School to provide requirements for training pilots and mechanics for helicopter transportation companies. OCAFF anticipated that personnel and equipment previously requested in October, except light cargo helicopters, would be available by February, with the starting date of each class approximately 1 March. The class capacity for both pilots and mechanics was set at fifty, with the duration of the courses not to exceed nineteen weeks. Each of the classes was scheduled to terminate at an appropriate time for the activation of the respective helicopter transportation companies in accordance with the anticipated delivery schedule of cargo helicopters from the manufacturer. The Artillery School scheduled the Army Helicopter Transport Class to be twelve weeks long, since it expected that students would be selected from among trained Army aviators. All remaining pilot classes would be nineteen weeks. Since the students for the first Army Helicopter Transport Mechanics Class were to be trained automobile mechanics, that class would be thirteen weeks long, with subsequent classes being sixteen weeks.

The Artillery School noted that in order to conduct the training, it would be necessary to augment the proposed tables of distribution for the staff and faculty of the Air Training Department by 41 officers, 1 warrant officer, 109 enlisted men, and 1 civilian. Most of the enlisted men were mechanics, the requirement for which was based on a ratio of one and one half mechanics per utility helicopter and three per cargo helicopter. Thirty-two of the forty-one officers had to be qualified helicopter flight instructors. The bulk of the requested officers would be trained as fixed wing instructors, replacing some instructors then assigned to the Air Training Department who were to be trained as helicopter instructors. At least ten additional utility helicopters would be required for instructor training and would have to be provided no later than 11 December. In order to conduct the transport helicopter class, it would be necessary to provide thirty-five utility helicopters and twelve cargo helicopters. The mechanics for the maintenance of those helicopters were to be provided concurrently with the delivery of the helicopters.

The necessity of factory training for instructor personnel would arise only for cargo helicopters. The Artillery School therefore requested that it be authorized to send one officer and two enlisted instructors to the appropriate factory for a course in the erection and maintenance of cargo helicopters.[4]

The expansion of training activities at the Artillery School placed a strain upon the facilities at Fort Sill. Early in April 1951, Army Field Forces began studying the feasibility of moving a portion of the helicopter training to Fort Riley. Prohibitive costs, however, kept all of the training at Fort Sill until the founding of the Aviation School at Fort Rucker in 1953.[5]

Expansion of Courses

Changes in the Army helicopter program in the summer of 1952 required a major revision of the training program. The Department of the Army changed all warrant officer pilot spaces in the new transportation helicopter companies to officer pilot spaces. In addition, the Department approved a TOE for medical evacuation helicopter detachments which included officer helicopter pilots. The increase in personnel resulting from these actions and the proposed activation schedule of new units necessitated a revision in the course being conducted at the Artillery School for transport helicopter pilots.

Army Field Forces considered that the most desirable and economical method for training Medical Service Corps pilots would be to integrate them into the pilot course then being conducted for Transportation Corps personnel. That course could be revised to provide training for any service requiring only transport helicopter type training.

Army Field Forces informed the Artillery School in late July that in order to provide personnel to fill both transportation and medical units on the dates required, it would be necessary to graduate 196 pilots—an increase of 46 over the number planned for fiscal year 1953. Future planning indicated that there would be a requirement for 235 Transportation Corps helicopter pilots by October 1954. It would therefore be necessary to enter approximately 250 students to produce the 196 required by August 1953 and 300 students to obtain the 235 required by October 1954.

Army Field Forces anticipated that personnel for all future Transportation and Medical Service pilot classes would be officers. It would be necessary at first to assume that all students would meet the existing fixed wing flight time requirements required for the Transportation Helicopter Pilot Course. OCAFF pointed out to the Artillery School that it might be necessary to arrange classes so as to graduate part of the personnel for certain units prior to the unit ready date. Classes were to start no later than the scheduled transportation helicopter class in September 1952.

The expansion in the number of helicopter units naturally led to an increased demand for mechanics. Army Field Forces believed that the most efficient method of meeting this requirement would be to expand the existing Transportation Helicopter Mechanic Course. In order to meet the requirements for transport helicopter mechanics, it was necessary to graduate 266—116 more than the number which had been planned for fiscal year 1953. In addition, future requirements for Transportation Corps helicopter mechanics were 430. Therefore, 360 students would have to be entered to obtain the 266 required by August 1953, and approximately 580 students to get the 430 needed by October 1954.

The Artillery School reported that the men and equipment were available to start both the pilot and mechanic courses in September. There was sufficient time to train pilot instructors prior to the expansion in the sizes of the classes in January 1953. The most expeditious manner of obtaining flight instructors was to authorize the retention of approximately 20 percent of each of the first four classes. The Artillery School proposed a class capacity of 25 mechanics each two weeks, beginning in September, and building up to a resident load of 175 mechanic students by 12 January 1953. This solution reduced the requirements for classrooms and training aids, and resulted in the maximum use of assistant enlisted instructor personnel.[6]

Liaison Pilot Training

Early in 1950, the training of liaison pilots for the Army was still being conducted in two increments—the Air Force Liaison Pilot Course at Connally Air Force Base, and the Light Aviation Officer Course at the Artillery School. In November 1949, the Army Field Forces had requested that the Air Force expand the quota for the liaison pilot training program from thirty-five to forty students per class. At the same time, the attrition factor was adjusted from 40 to 26 percent, a change which was expected to meet the requirement to fill existing pilot vacancies. Army Field Forces also requested that there be some flexibility in class capacity to allow for unexpected changes in National Guard input.

The Air Training Command agreed to the changes in class quotas and attrition rate, but refused the request for flexibility in class entrance rates. As a possible solution to the problem, the Air Training Command suggested that the number of Regular Army students be increased or decreased to adjust for any problems encountered with the National Guard quota. Army Field Forces replied that this was not a satisfactory solution since the Regular Army students were assigned on a permanent change of station, and it would be injurious to morale to make last minute changes. The Air Training Command finally agreed to permit small overloads in the class capacity of forty as long as this was compensated by a reduction in the size of subsequent classes. The Army furnished three additional L-16s for the expanded training program.[7]

In May, the Department of the Army informed Army Field Forces that the output of trained aviation officers from the Artillery School had only moderately exceeded the normal attrition rate. With the recent reduction in the number of reserve officers on extended active duty, the need for an additional input into the aviation program was imperative. The Department of the Army recommended that the class quota for Regular Army and reserve officers on extended active duty be doubled from twenty to forty. At the same time, the quota for Reserve and National Guard officers in the classes would remain the same, requiring a class input of sixty.

The Air Force informed the Army that this proposed increase could be met provided additional resources were available. The Department of the Army informed the Army Field Forces in August that the aircraft required were not available because of operational commitments. It requested that other means be considered to accelerate training to meet current and projected requirements. It had suggested to the Chief of Staff of the Air Force that the curriculum be revised to eliminate nonessential elements and that the work week be increased to forty-four hours. Apparently the question of expanding pilot training was related to the increased requirements resulting from the war, rather than the original personnel problems.

In September, the Department of the Air Force agreed to expand the training classes from forty to forty-eight students, an increase of 20 percent. Army Field Forces advised the Artillery School that this increase at Connally Air Force Base could be expected to result in a corresponding increase in the tactical phase of training.[8]

The need for trained pilots soon led to another increase in the fixed wing training program. On 7 February 1951, the Department of the Army directed Army Field Forces to expand the class capacity to fifty students effective 2 April. The frequency of the class also was changed to one class every six weeks. The Army would furnish the Air Force with thirty-six L-16s and seven L-5s to conduct this expanded training program. This expansion raised the annual output of this course to 300 pilots per year.[9]

The Department of the Army submitted its training requirements for fiscal year 1952 in April 1951. At first estimate, the Army stated that it would need 624 light aviation officers, a requirement which increased to 1,542 by the time a conference was held on 22 May. At the conference, the Air Force representatives stated that they would be able to train the necessary number of pilots, but requested that they be given a day to study the requirement and to compute the number of training aircraft to be furnished. On 24 May, the Air Force furnished a plan for a 17-week course for fixed wing pilots which would begin on 27 August 1951 with a class capacity of 255 and an attrition rate of 25 percent. The student load varied from 131 in July to 867 in late November. The Air Force estimated that it would need 388 L-19s and 136 L-5s by November to conduct the training. These aircraft would be furnished on a phased schedule as the student load expanded.

On 25 May, the Department of the Army requested that OCAFF study the Air Force training proposal to determine if the Army could accept the trainees from the Air Force at the proposed rate and phase them into tactical training at Fort Sill. Consideration was to be given to aircraft production schedules and availability of housing and classroom facilities and instructor personnel. Shortly thereafter, the Department of the Army questioned the Artillery School concerning the capabilities of the Air Training Department. The School prepared a preliminary plan in which it would receive student aviators from San Marcos Air Force Base beginning on 15 December 1951 at a rate of 200 per month. OCAFF also asked the Air Training Department for a preliminary estimate of what additional instructor personnel, aircraft, and facilities would be required. The Artillery School felt it could handle the proposed load, but would need 14 additional flight instructors—one-third of whom could be civilians, 13 officers and 4 enlisted ground school instructors, 255 2-place training aircraft (preferably L-19s), an additional stage field, and two expandable hangars.[10]

Fixed Wing and Helicopter Mechanic Training

During World War II, student aircraft mechanics were selected from members of the ground forces who had considerable mechanical experience. These men received extensive training in maintenance and repair of aircraft and engines in an enlisted Field Artillery Air Mechanic Course. Course graduates were capable of performing all first and second echelon maintenance.

After World War II, the Army fixed wing mechanic and the Army and Air Force rotary wing mechanic programs were conducted at Sheppard Air Force Base, Texas. This training was shifted to Gary Air Force Base when that installation was reactivated early in 1951.[11]

Early in November 1949, the Department of the Army directed the Chief of Ordnance to hold a conference to determine the adequacy of the Airplane and Engine Mechanic Course conducted by the Air Force. When this course had been given at Fort Sill, it covered only the L-4 and L-5 aircraft. The length of the course was then 520 hours, conducted during thirteen weeks. After the transfer of the training to the Air Force, 130 academic hours were eliminated due to the change from a 40- to a 30-academic hour week. At the same time, L-17 instruction was added to the course.

The conference reported that although the course was basically sound, insufficient time was devoted to many subjects and the course was therefore inadequate for training either organizational or field maintenance mechanics. Accordingly, the course syllabus was reviewed and changes were prepared at the conference. As a result of the conference, the Department of the Army requested that the Air Force increase the academic week to thirty-five hours.[12]

Early in 1950, the Department of the Army began to consider a proposal to discontinue training of maintenance personnel by the Air Force and to train the men at Fort Sill. In response to a request from Army Field Forces, the Artillery Center reported in June 1950 that additional overhead would be required at the Artillery School in order to train Army aircraft maintenance personnel. Along with costs for machinery, supplies, transportation, utilities, and miscellaneous items, the cost per student would be $517.32. These overhead costs were based on an airplane and engine mechanic class of sixteen beginning every month and a rotary wing mechanic class of eight starting every two months. If classes were scheduled every two weeks for liaison aircraft and engine mechanics and every four weeks for rotary wing mechanics, six additional sergeants would be required in the personnel overhead and the cost would be increased approximately 13 percent. Classroom facilities were available at the Artillery School, but an estimated $20,000 would be required to cover rehabilitation. Training aids would be transferred from Sheppard Air Force Base to Fort Sill by Army trailer. By moving to Fort Sill, mechanics would get better integrated tactical training and would work on the type of aircraft which they would have to maintain in the field. Instruction could be given covering the day-to-day difficulties experienced by the Artillery School in the maintenance of aircraft peculiar to the Army. No further action was taken on this proposal as the Army raised the question of assuming all training of Army aviation personnel.[13]

Army Field Forces continued to urge that the Department of the Army take action to transfer maintenance training. Late in 1950, the Chief of Ordnance recommended that he be authorized to establish the necessary maintenance training program for aircraft and engine mechanics on a contract basis at CAA licensed civilian aircraft maintenance schools. In January 1951, the Department of the Army informed the Chief of Ordnance that the entire problem of supply and maintenance of liaison and helicopter aircraft was under study and no action would be taken on the Ordnance recommendation.

The Department of the Army established a course for training Army helicopter mechanics at the Artillery School in January. The 19-week course, which began on 15 March, was designed to assist the Chief of Transportation in meeting requirements for helicopter mechanics in Transportation Corps units. The Chief of Ordnance protested to the Department of the Army that this course had been established without coordination with his office, maintaining that he had the responsibility for providing trained ordnance field maintenance personnel to support the using units.[14]

In February 1951, the Department of the Army informed the Air Force of the revised training requirements for fiscal year 1951. While the requirement for fixed wing mechanics remained at 200, the requirement for helicopter mechanics was increased from 250 to 425. The Department of the Army agreed to furnish nine additional helicopters to the Air Force to conduct this training.[15]

The expansion in the number of helicopter units during 1952 led to an expanded training program for helicopter mechanics which took place at the same time that helicopter pilot training was increased.

Development of Instrument Training

It was often necessary for Army pilots to fly in all types of weather in order to accomplish their mission. Experience gained in World War II indicated that Army pilots had to fly under adverse conditions in combat, and a number of pilots were killed because they lacked instrument flight training. Early in fiscal year 1949, emphasis on arctic operations made it even more essential that Army pilots be able to fly under instrument conditions.

Army Field Forces initiated an experimental instrument flight training course for selected aviation officers in 1949. There were several types of combat flying situations in which instrument training would be of decided value: marginal weather flying, night flying, arctic flying, and extended overwater flying. OCAFF believed that instrument proficiency would add a considerable factor of safety and success to all these flying conditions. Marginal weather and night flying were required in almost every combat operation.[16]

The Liaison Pilot Training Course conducted by the Air Force was designed to qualify Army officers as liaison pilots proficient in flying under contact, marginal weather, and night flying conditions. The course included fifteen hours of instrument flying instruction and ten hours of instrument trainer instruction.

In late 1949, the Department of the Army suggested that Army Field Forces conduct another test of instrument training. OCAFF replied that in its opinion the Air Force training was inadequate to meet current requirements. It had discovered that only twelve and one-half actual flying hours of instrument training were being received. OCAFF believed that the instrument training course as originally agreed upon with the Air Force would be adequate for student Army aviators if conducted for the full fifteen hours. There were approximately 500 Army aviators on active duty who graduated from flight school prior to the inclusion of instrument training, only four of whom were found to have current instrument ratings. It was therefore not feasible for the

Army to undertake the instrument training proposed by the Department of the Army. OCAFF suggested that the Air Force train sufficient Army instructors who could then train Army personnel.[17]

The Air Force made an effort to improve instrument training in the Liaison Pilot Training Course, but no satisfactory solution was found for training aviators who had completed the course. In early June 1951, OCAFF requested that the Department of the Army provide funds for training aviators as instrument pilots in civilian schools. The Department of the Army approved this request on 19 June, and directed OCAFF to submit recommendations for a permanent program designed to meet requirements for instrument training.[18]

In July, OCAFF contacted both the Air Force and the Artillery School to determine their ability to provide the required instrument training. The plan proposed by OCAFF provided not only for instrument training of student officers enrolled in a regular course of flight training, but also for those aviators who had already graduated and could not receive instrument training under the recently initiated civilian program.

OCAFF envisioned the students in the Liaison Pilot Course at San Marcos Air Force Base receiving the maximum amount of instruction in instrument flying and related academic subjects which their level of flying experience would enable them to absorb. Then during the tactical phase of training at Fort Sill, the students would receive the remainder of the instruction necessary to qualify them as instrument pilots. Students entering the aviation courses at Fort Sill without having attended the Liaison Pilot Course at San Marcos would receive at Fort Sill all instruction necessary for qualification as instrument pilots. Army aviators who did not attend a civilian instrument pilot training school under the interim program would attend an instrument course at Fort Sill.[19]

In July, the Joint Standardization Board approved an integrated program of instruction for the Liaison Pilot Course and the Army Aviation Tactics Course which would graduate students from Fort Sill with a Civil Aeronautics Administration instrument card. Two months later, the Artillery School submitted to OCAFF the requirements for additional men and equipment necessary to conduct this expanded training program. The instrument phase of the course was to be four weeks in length, with twenty-five students reporting each week.

OCAFF prepared an instrument training program based on recommendations of the Joint Standardization Board and the Artillery School. In addition to these programs, OCAFF recommended to the Department of the Army that Army instrument certificates be established incorporating the best features of the Air Force, Navy, and CAA instrument requirements. The proposed plan was based on a two card system—Army instrument certificate (standard) and Army instrument certificate (special). The standard certificate incorporated the requirements outlined in the training circular prepared by the Artillery School, while the special certificate included the requirements for the standard certificate in addition to experience requirements.

The inclusion of instrument training in the military aviation courses would take place at such time as the necessary equipment became available. OCAFF had initiated procurement requests for LC-126 aircraft for use by the Artillery School as an instrument trainer and C-8 synthetic instrument trainers. It expected the instrument phase of the flight courses to be implemented some time after 1 July 1952. Civilian contract schools would continue to operate until that time. The Air Training Department at Fort Sill took the necessary action to qualify instrument instructors to implement the program when equipment became available. The source of students for instructor training was from within the Air Training Department, but this would not provide enough instructors to meet the requirement.[20]

Continued shortages of equipment and a shortage of instructor personnel delayed the implementation of the full instrument training program. In April 1952, the Artillery School submitted a proposed program of instruction for an Army Aviation Instrument Course. OCAFF directed in November that the Army Aviation Instrument Course be fully implemented by 1 July 1953. It also directed that a program of instruction be prepared for an instrument flight examiner course which was not to exceed four weeks.

Army Field Forces informed the Artillery School that it was essential that instrument flight training be phased into the fixed wing pilot course as soon as practicable. Delivery of L-19 basic instrument trainers to San Marcos Air Force Base would begin in January 1953. The San Marcos phase of the course would be integrated as soon as sufficient L-19 instrument trainers became available to augment the L-5 trainers on hand. The Artillery School would integrate its portion of instrument training into the Army Aviation Tactics Course, phasing it with the implementation of the San Marcos course. Integration of this training was coordinated with San Marcos Air Force Base through the Joint Standardization Board.

The shortage of personnel continued to delay full implementation of the courses. In January 1953, the instrument course was organized and placed under the supervision of the Department of Flight of the Army Aviation School at Fort Sill. Army Field Forces informed Fourth Army that full implementation of the courses would not be scheduled until fiscal year 1954. In August 1953, the Instrument Flight Examiner's Course finally was initiated to teach pilots to conduct and grade the Army's annual instrument flight examinations. The students received about forty hours of instrument time during the 4-week course.[21]

Endnotes
Chapter VI

1. DF Cmt 1, OCAFF G-3 to CofS, 4 Aug 50, subj: Training of Army Aviation Personnel.
2. Df Cmt 3, G-3 to CAFF, 19 Aug 50, subj: Training of Aviation Personnel.
3. (1) Df Cmt 2, Ord Sec to G-3 Sec, 5 Feb 51, subj: Aircraft and Engine Mechanic Training (MOS 0747). (2) Report of Ad Hoc Committee on Evaluation of the Current System of Training Army Aviators and Mechanics, undated.
4. (1) History of the US Army Artillery and Missile School, Vol. III, p. 237. (2) Ltr AGAO-S 353 (1 Feb 51), DA G-3 to CAFF, 7 Feb 51, subj: Training of Army Aviation Personnel. (3) Ltr ATTNG-27 353, CAFF to CG, The Artillery Center, 8 Nov 50, w/1st Ind, AG 353.11 AKPSIAT (9 Nov 50), Cmdt, The Artillery School, to CAFF, 26 Nov 50, subj: Training of Army Aviation Personnel.
5. Msg, OCAFF to Fifth Army, 101500Z Apr 51, subj: Feasibility of Moving Light Aviation Helicopter Training.
6. (1) Ltr ATTNG-32 353 OCAFF to Artillery School, 21 Jul 52, subj: Transport Helicopter Pilot Training, w/2d Ind AG 352.11 AKPSIRI-AT (21 Jul 52), Artillery School to OCAFF, 28 Aug 52. (2) Ltr ATTNG-32 353, OCAFF to Artillery School, 28 Aug 52, subj: Transport Helicopter Mechanic Training, w/2d Ind AG 352.11 AKP- SIRI-AT (28 Jul 52), Artillery School to OCAFF, 28 Aug 52.
7. (1) Ltr 353 Fly, CG Air Training Command to CAFF, 10 Oct 49, subj: Liaison Pilot Training Program, w/1st Ind ATTNG-27 353 (10 Oct 49), CAFF to CG Air Training Command. (2) Ltr 353 Fly, CG Air Training Command to CAFF, 18 Jan 50, subj: Increased Entrance Rate in Liaison Pilot Training Program, w/1st Ind ATTNG-27 353 (18 Jan 50), CAFF to CG Air Training Command, 8 Feb 50, and 2d Ind 353 Fly, CG Air Training Command to CAFF, 17 Apr 50.
8. (1) Ltr AGPA-UT 210.63 (11 Apr 50) CSGPA-O-CA, DA to CAFF, 9 May 50, subj: Increase in Student Officer Quota for Army Aviation Training. (2) Ltr AGAO-C 353 Aviation (21 Jun 50), DA G-3 to CAFF, 17 Aug 50, subj: Expansion of the Liaison Flying Training Program. (3) Ltr AGAO-S 353 (15 Sep 50), DA G-3 to CAFF, 22 Sep 50, subj: Expansion of Liaison Flying Training Program. (4) Ltr ATTNG-27 353.01, CAFF to CG Artillery Center, 2 Oct 50, subj: Expansion of Liaison Flying Training Program.
9. Ltr AGAO-S 353 (1 Feb 51), DA G-3 to CAFF, 7 Feb 51, subj: Training of Army Aviation Personnel.
10. (1) Ltr AGAO-S 363, DA to OCAFF, 17 Apr 51, subj: FY 1952 Requirements for Training of Army Aviation Personnel, w/1st Ind ATPER 353 (17 Apr 51), OCAFF to DA, 11 May 51. (2) MFR, 1 Jun 51, subj: Fiscal Year 1952 Army Aviation Training Requirements.
11. Tierney and Montgomery, *The Army Aviation Story*, p. 80.
12. (1) Ltr CSGOT 353 (15 Jul 49), Dir of O&T to CAFF, 29 Nov 49, subj: Requirements for Training of Aircraft Maintenance Specialists, w/Inds. (2) DF 353 (29 Nov 49), AG to G-3, 29 Nov 49, subj: Requirements for Training of Aircraft Maintenance Specialists, Cmt 2, G-3 to CofS, 15 Dec 49.
13. Ltr ATTNG-27 353, OCAFF to ACofS G-3, 30 Mar 50, subj: Training of Army Aircraft Maintenance Personnel, w/3d Ind AKPSIAT (30 Mar 50), CG The Artillery Center to OCAFF, 2 Jun 50.
14. (1) Msg, OCAFF to CofSA, 181433Z Aug 50. (2) Memo, Maj Gen E.L. Ford, CofOrd, for Lt Gen T.B. Larkin, ACofS G-4, 1 Mar 51, subj: Army Aircraft Maintenance Training.
15. Ltr AGAO-S 353 (1 Feb 51) GS, DA to CAFF, 7 Feb 51, subj: Training of Army Aviation Personnel.
16. (1) Msg, CAFF to CG Arty Cen, 131650 Jan 49. (2) 4th Ind ATTNG-27 211(LnO) (17 Mar 49), CAFF to Dir of O&T GS, 4 Jun 49, to ltr AF100S 211-1, CG Tenth Air Force to CG Continental Air Cmd, 17 Mar 49, subj: Instrument Ratings for Liaison Pilots.
17. MFR and 8th Ind ATTNG-27 211 (LnO) (17 Mar 49), OCAFF to ACofS G-3, 17 Mar 50, to ltr AF100S 211-1, CG Tenth Air Force to CG Continental Air Command, 17 Mar 49.
18. DF ATTNG-22 352 (Arty Sch), OCAFF G-3 to CofS, 3 Jul 51, subj: Instrument Training for Army Aviators.
19. (1) Ltr ATTNG-22 352 (Arty Sch), OCAFF to Artillery School, 10 Jul 51, subj: Instrument Training for Army Aviation Personnel. (2) Ltr ATTNG-22 352 (Arty Sch), OCAFF to Air Training Command, 10 Jul 51, subj: Instrument Training for Army Aviation Personnel.
20. Ltr AG 352.11 AKPSIRI-AT, Artillery School to OCAFF, 19 Sep 51, subj: Instrument Training for Army Aviation Personnel, w/inds.
21. (1) Ltr ATTNG-32 352, OCAFF to Artillery School, 14 Nov 52, subj: Instrument Training for Army Aviation Personnel, 2/inds. (2) Tierney and Montgomery, *The Army Aviation Story*, p. 81.

Chapter VII

THE FOUNDATION OF THE ARMY AVIATION SCHOOL

Army Field Forces had proposed even before the outbreak of the Korean conflict that the Army assume the complete training of Army aviators. In late July 1950, OCAFF broadened its proposal to include the training of aviators, helicopter pilots, airplane and engine mechanics, and rotary wing mechanics at the Artillery School.

In August, General Clark wrote to the Chief of Staff of the Army regarding the necessity for immediate expansion of training facilities for Army aviation personnel. He pointed out that the Department of the Army was responsible for training which was peculiar to the Army, but did not have direct control over the primary flight training and mechanic training then being conducted for it by the Air Force. The training of Army personnel was of primary importance to the Army, but was only of tertiary importance to the Air Force. The best training equipment and facilities and the best instructors were utilized within the Air Force for other purposes. General Clark pointed out the savings which would result from the consolidation of all training under Army jurisdiction and requested that the phasing out of Air Force training be studied. The opposition of the Air Force to any plan to expand Army aviation prevented action from being taken on this this proposal at the time.[1]

Planning for Expansion

Despite the Air Force opposition, the Army continued to consider the question of consolidating all aviation training. In the following months, the rapid expansion of Army aviation in response to the requirements of the war emphasized the need for such a consolidation. In October 1951, the Army Field Forces prepared a study to determine the best method to expand existing facilities for the training of aviation personnel to meet current and anticipated requirements. It pointed out that in the past few months the student load in aviation courses at the Artillery School had increased from a peak of 45 in residence to 378—a jump of 800 percent. This load was designed to provide an output of approximately 1,200 per year. If fiscal year 1952 requirements proposed by the Department of the Army were to be met, the output would be doubled, and the student load would increase accordingly. Transfer of training responsibilities from the Air Force, as had been proposed in August 1950, would more than triple the training load for fiscal year 1952. With the formation of helicopter medical evacuation units the training load would soar still higher. Assuming an attrition rate as low as 10 percent, the requirements for the Active Army, plus Reserve Components, should not fall below 1,000 per year.

Maximum conservation of facilities, OCAFF believed, would be realized only if all courses in aviation were closely related to one another. Fixed wing and rotary wing mechanic training should be conducted where pilot training was conducted which would allow the same aircraft to be used in both programs. Classes could be integrated in common subjects and overhead requirements for maintenance reduced. OCAFF stated that the facilities at Fort Sill already were overtaxed and proposed the transfer of a portion of the aviation courses to Fort Riley. It therefore recommended that an Army Aviation School be established at Fort Sill with a helicopter branch at Fort Riley. On 14 December 1951, OCAFF submitted this proposal to the Assistant Chief of Staff, G-3, Department of the Army, and recommended the steps necessary to implement the establishment of the Army Aviation School.[2]

On 23 January 1952, the Deputy Chief of Staff for Operations and Administration, Department of the Army, approved for planning purposes the establishment of an Army Aviation School. During the period, 18-20 March, the Department of the Army held a conference, which included representatives of all interested Army agencies, on the training of aviation personnel.

The objectives of the Army aviation program, as presented by the Department of the Army G-3 to the conference, were 3,000 fixed wing pilots, 1,053 helicopter pilots, and 340 Transportation Corps helicopter pilots for the ten transportation helicopter companies. There also was a requirement for 2,400 fixed wing mechanics, 912 rotary wing mechanics, and 490 Transportation Corps mechanics for the helicopter companies. Fort Sill at that time was producing 66 fixed wing pilots per month, 20 helicopter pilots per month, 40 Transportation Corps pilots every five months, and 50 Transportation Corps mechanics every four months. The Air Force primary flight training was producing 75 fixed wing and 22 rotary wing pilots per month and 36 fixed wing and 8 helicopter mechanics per week. The Department of the Army placed the numbers of aviation personnel required to be trained above those estimated to be on hand on 1 July 1952 as 1,764 fixed wing and helicopter pilots, 104 cargo helicopter pilots, 2,076 fixed wing mechanics, 384 utility helicopter mechanics, and 75 cargo helicopter mechanics.

Having defined the problem, the Department of the Army G-3 then discussed the organization of an Army Aviation School which would train the pilots and mechanics for all of the branches authorized aviation, with all branches represented on the staff, faculty, and academic board. The representatives from Fort Sill and Fort Riley were requested to comment on the command relationships and administrative channels of an Army Aviation School as proposed by Army Field Forces. It quickly became apparent that everyone agreed that the Army should assume all aviation training and that the establishment of a school was desirable, but there was considerable divergence of opinion as to the location and command relations of the school.

The representatives of the Commanding General of the Artillery Center stated that the location of the school was incidental, but the artillery as a primary user should retain a strong influence over the programs. There was no objection to moving helicopter training to Fort Riley provided some helicopters remained at Fort Sill for tactical use, training, and development of doctrine. The representatives from Fort Riley and Fifth Army believed that Fort Riley was suitable for helicopter training, but did not believe that it should be a branch of a school at Fort Sill. They proposed that a helicopter school be established at Fort Riley under the commandant of the Army General School, also located at that post. The administrative problems resulting from the split in the school between Fourth and Fifth Armies also were indicated.

The representatives of the Chief of Ordnance stated that the Ordnance Corps desired to maintain operational control of Ordnance aircraft maintenance training whether it was established as a branch of the Army Aviation School or not. The Department of the Army G-1 representative stated that additional officer and civilian space authorizations were not available, and if training rates were increased adjustments within Fourth Army authorizations would be required.

A proposed plan for the transfer of training from the Air Force to the Army was presented. There were no objections to this plan provided personnel, facilities, and funds were made available. The representatives were requested to present requirements under six alternative plans.[3]

The Artillery School submitted its recommendations for personnel, materiel, facilities, and funds to OCAFF on 17 June. It recommended that the Army Aviation School be established at Fort Sill, or at some other single appropriate post, and that no further consideration be given to the establishment of a separate helicopter branch. On 9 July, OCAFF forwarded to the Department of the Army detailed data showing requirements for personnel, materiel, facilities, and funds for an Army Aviation School to handle the combined Army and Air Force training load.

The information supplied by OCAFF applied to three alternatives: a school located partly at Fort Sill and partly at Fort Riley; a single school located at Fort Sill; and a single school at a location other than Fort Sill. A single school located at Fort Sill would require some 200 fewer people than a school at two locations, and from 200 to 1,100 fewer personnel than a combined school at a location other than Fort Sill. A single school at Fort Sill would require $879,600 for construction; a single school at another location would require in excess of $2,500,000; and a school split between Forts Sill and Riley would require $1,033,500. Other costs—conversion of buildings, training aids, annual operating costs, and civilian personnel—would be about the same for each plan.[4]

The planning conducted during the early part of 1952 gave principal emphasis to plans based on the existing division of responsibility for Army aviation training. During the summer of 1952, however, it was realized that budgetary requests for construction or conversion of facilities, or the activation of installations, were difficult to justify if the long range training loads were not known.

The Department of the Army generally recognized that considerable overlapping and unnecessary expense was involved in conducting preliminary training of Army pilots and mechanics by the Air Force at San Marcos, followed by additional training by the Army at Fort Sill. The Army was still desirous of having all Army aviation training conducted by the Army.

By August 1952, designation of Fort Riley as a location for part of the activities of an Army Aviation School based on Fort Sill was no longer seriously considered. It was realized that a split school with elements in two different army areas would result in command and administrative difficulties. The principal merit in consideration of Fort Riley was that it met the requirement that an Army installation already in being must be named for budgetary planning purposes. For tentative budgetary planning, it was necessary to identify construction or building conversion items that would be needed for an Army Aviation School with an existing Army installation.

At this time, OCAFF was giving serious consideration to a plan under which Frederick Airfield, at Frederick, Oklahoma, located some forty miles from Fort Sill, would be acquired from the Air Force and operated as a subpost of Fort Sill to accommodate part of the activities of the Army Aviation School under Department of the Army policy, a request for activation of Frederick Airfield would have to be presented before funds for its rehabilitation and for necessary construction could be requested of Congress.

On 19 June, the Chief of Staff of the Army recommended to the Secretary of the Army that all training of Army aviation personnel be transferred to the Army. The Materiel Requirements Review Panel, which included among its deliberations the equipment requirements for Army aviation training, also recommended the training of all Army aviation personnel by the Army. The recommendations of the Materiel Requirements Review Panel were approved by Secretary of the Army on 26 October 1952.[5]

On 26 September, as a fresh approach to the problem of the most suitable location for the proposed school, a Site Committee for the Army Aviation School was appointed by the Chief of Army Field Forces.[6] The mission of this committee was to develop a plan, and one or more alternate plans, for the location of the Army Aviation School. The committee also was directed to study training requirements of the school and make a ground survey of potential sites.

After conducting an on-site survey of seventeen installations ranging across the southern part of the United States, the committee prepared three plans for establishment of the school. Plan I called for the location of the main part of the school at Fort Sill and a part at Frederick. This plan proposed the acquisition by the Army of Frederick Airfield, a former World War II installation of the Army Air Forces but currently under municipal operation, and the conduct of rotary wing training at that location. Plan II called for the acquisition of San Marcos Air Force Base and its auxiliary fields for Army use, with all pilot and mechanic training to be conducted there. Plan III called for location of the school in its entirety at Fort Sill which would be the site of all Army aviation training. The committee recommended approval of Plan I.

The Army Field Forces forwarded the report of the Site Committee to the Department of the Army on 6 October with a recommendation to adopt Plan I. Acquisition of Frederick was at this time felt to be mandatory for the handling of the expected fiscal year 1954 training load, whether or not the Army took over that part of the training conducted by the Air Force.[7]

Little of further significance with reference to establishment of the school developed at the OCAFF level during the remaining weeks of 1952. During the latter part of December, in response to a request from the Organization and Training Division, G-3, Department of the

Army, OCAFF developed a phased plan for implementing the assumption by the Army of responsibility for the training of all Army aviation personnel. OCAFF's plan consisted principally of a timetable for the transfer of Army aviation courses conducted by the Air Force to the proposed Army Aviation School. OCAFF estimated that the integration of this training into the Army Aviation School programs could begin four months after the school received the required spaces and personnel and could be completed within twelve months.[8]

Establishment of the Army Aviation School

The Army Aviation School was established on 16 January 1953 at Fort Sill by Department of the Army General Order Number 9. The mission of the school was to instruct and train officers, warrant officers, and enlisted men of all components of the Army in the duties of Army aviation personnel and in the employment of Army aviation by the various branches in which it was authorized. The school was to develop and standardize the instruction and training of officers, warrant officers, and enlisted men in techniques and tactics relating to Army aviation. It also was to develop and prepare Army aviation doctrine, techniques, and tactics for dissemination to the Armed Forces. The school would assist in the development of Army aviation extension literature and other special training publications. In addition, the school would maintain liaison with other military schools and agencies and disseminate information pertaining to instruction and training methods and materials developed at the Army Aviation School to the Armed Forces.

In order that the school would have the appropriate proportions of representatives of all branches authorized Army aircraft, Army Field Forces had recommended in July 1952 that the branch representation on the staff and faculty be 33 percent for artillery, 25 percent for infantry, 12 percent for armor, 9 percent for transportation, 8 percent for ordnance, 6 percent for engineers and signal, and 1 percent for medical.

The proposed table of distribution (TD) for the Army Aviation School submitted in March 1953 amounted to 294 officers, 5 warrant officers, 535 enlisted men, and 150 civilians. In approving the proposed TD and authorization for additional spaces, Army Field Forces recommended that, in view of the relatively short time remaining before the beginning of fiscal year 1954 and because many of the classes would begin on or about 1 July, authority be granted to Fourth Army to begin requisitioning personnel against the proposed document up to 75 percent of the recommended strength prior to review and approval of the TD.

The Department of the Army on 19 June advised OCAFF that the requested increase in Fourth Army's space authorization to fill the Army Aviation School TD had been approved, except for the space for an aide to the school commandant. And under the existing strict limitations on the number of authorized general officers, the grade of brigadier general for the commandant could not be supported, and the position had been downgraded to colonel.

The Army Aviation School during the initial months of its operation was, for all practical purposes, a separate school in name only. Courses already in progress or scheduled for presentation in the early months of 1953 by the Air Training Department of the Artillery School were continued as scheduled. The school began operation with the 69 officers, 128 enlisted men, and 1 civilian allotted to the Air Training Department of the Artillery School.

Authority for complete separation of the Army Aviation School from the Artillery School was granted by the Department of the Army on 1 June 1953, to become effective on 1 July. Separation was accomplished in accordance with a detailed plan submitted to Fourth Army by the Artillery Center on 27 March. This plan included provision for transfer of all responsibilities for the training of Army aviation personnel for the Artillery School to the Army Aviation School, discontinuance of the Artillery School's Department of Air Training, submission of academic reports on Army aviation students by the Army Aviation School, separation of fiscal matters as of the beginning of fiscal year 1954, and operation of the Army Aviation School under its own table of distribution and table of allowances. Budget estimates pending before Congress at the end of fiscal year 1953 provided for funds in the amount of $699,000 for operation of the school during the coming fiscal year.[9]

Organization of the School

The organization of the Army Aviation School was to be prescribed by the Commandant pursuant to policies established by the Department of the Army, Army Field Forces, and Fourth Army. The Assistant Commandant was in charge of the administration of instruction of the school and had general charge of the preparation and publication of text and reference books. The Secretary supervised correspondence and other administrative matters pertaining to the school, was custodian of the school records, acted as agent officer for disbursement of school funds, and served as executive officer for the Commandant and Assistant Commandant.

Responsibilities of the Materiel and Services Staff Section included the operation of the school supply, supervision of aircraft maintenance performed by civilian contract personnel, supervision of operation and maintenance of motor vehicular transportation and parachute maintenance coordination, assistance to the post engineer in maintenance of airfields and landing strips, and coordination with the post engineer in maintenance of buildings and utilities of the school.

The Operations Staff Section operated Post Field and supervised the operation of stage fields, as well as preparing, planning, and scheduling all programs of instruction. It also coordinated courses of instruction with school facilities and transportation, revised aviation procedures and courses of instruction, and coordinated and evaluated the grading plan and academic evaluation programs. The Flight Surgeon of the Army Aviation School was directly responsible to the Commandant for enforcement of all flight regulations and prepared literature on flying safety, conducted accident reports, and reviewed all reports of accident boards.

All flight training was to be conducted by the Department of Flight which also conducted a flight course for instructors to standardize methods and instruction. The instruction pertaining to the maintenance of all types of aircraft was conducted by the Department of Aviation Maintenance, while the Department of Tactics and General Subjects conducted instruction in the tactics and employment of all types of Army aircraft and also conducted administrative instruction pertaining to employment of Army aviation. It was responsible for the coordination of the study of doctrine and procedures as they affected tactics, techniques, organization, logistics, and equipment in Army aviation and the maintenance of liaison between the school and other agencies. The Department of Tactics and General Subjects also edited material prepared for publication by various departments and staff sections of the school.

The First Year of Operation

Class Schedules

During its first six months of operation, the Army Aviation School graduated 478 officers and warrant officers and 259 enlisted men. Courses and their length and output were as follows:

Officer and WO Courses	Length	Graduates
Army Aviation Tactics	12 wks	285
Army Helicopter Aviation Tactics	5 wks	136
Twin Engine Transition Flight Training	2 wks	49
Helicopter Transport Pilot Training	19 wks	8
Enlisted Courses		
Army Helicopter Transport Maintenance	16 wks	128
Helicopter Mechanic, Transition	1 wk	30
Twin Engine Transition Maintenance	2 wks	76
Helicopter Transport Pilot Training	19 wks	25

In addition to the personnel completing various types of training at the Army Aviation School, several hundred individuals received training in courses conducted by the Air Force at San Marcos. These courses, which were prerequisites for training of similar types at Fort Sill, were: Army Field Forces Helicopter Pilot Training, Officer—5 weeks; Liaison Pilot Training—18 weeks; Liaison Airplane and Engine Maintenance—15 weeks; and Rotary Wing Mechanic, H-13—6 weeks. Additional Army aviation personnel received training in officer aircraft maintenance and airframe mechanics conducted under contract by the Spartan School of Aeronautics.[10]

In addition to the previously mentioned courses, certain short-term special purpose courses were given during fiscal year 1953 which included a Twin Engine Transition Flight Training—a 2-week course with 114 enrolled; Twin Engine Transition Maintenance Training—a 2-week course with 117 enrolled; Army Helicopter Mechanic Transition Maintenance Training, H-23—1-week in duration with 130 enrolled; and Army Helicopter Mechanic Transition Maintenance Training—2 weeks in length with 130 in attendance.

As a result of an Army decision to qualify its pilots for instrument flying by a military course instead of through instruction provided under contract by civilian agencies, an Army Aviation Instrument Training Course of eight weeks with an input of 140 students was scheduled for presentation during fiscal year 1954. Also scheduled was a 4-week Army Instrument Examiner Course which had a student input of sixty-five.

During FY 1954, the Air Force would conduct the 17-week Army Primary Flight Training Course for 1,300 men, the 5-week Army Field Forces Helicopter Pilot Training Course for 460 men, the 12-week Army Helicopter Mechanic Course for 1,440 men, and the 11-week Army Airplane Mechanic Course for 2,160 men—all at Gary Air Force Base. The input of 1,300 students to the Army Primary Flight Training Course was based on the requirement of the Army to train 975 Army aviators with an allowance for a 25 percent attrition during the training period. The Army Field Forces had expanded the Army Helicopter Mechanic Course for FY 1954 from seven to twelve weeks. Originally, it had been intended to qualify airplane mechanics as helicopter mechanics; the revised course was to be a complete maintenance course not requiring prior training as an airplane or engine mechanic.[11]

Estimated Training Requirements

In late October 1952, the Army Field Forces submitted estimated training requirements for Army aviation personnel at San Marcos and the Artillery School for fiscal years 1953 through 1957. Computation of the fiscal year 1954 Instrument Flight Course requirements was based on the 657 trained under civilian contract during fiscal year 1952 and 1,000 programed to be trained for fiscal year 1953—a total of 1,657. The estimated requirement for the Instrument Flight Examiner Course was ninety-six. The requirement for the Cargo Helicopter Pilot Course, which would provide pilots for the transportation helicopter companies and the medical service helicopter evacuation detachments, was fixed at 384. The requirement for the Utility Helicopter Pilot Course was set at thirty-two, while the requirement for the Airframe Mechanic Course was seventy. For the Cargo Helicopter Mechanic Course, which provided helicopter mechanics for transportation helicopter companies, medical service evacuation detachments, and helicopter repair detachments, the requirement was set at 501.

The Department of the Army on 19 January 1953 approved these requirements with certain exceptions. It insisted that the input of fixed wing pilots remain at 100 per month through fiscal year 1955, but could be reduced to the figures indicated for fiscal years 1956 and 1957. Because of the critical shortage the training of airplane and engine mechanics should remain at 144 per month through fiscal year 1955.

The Department of the Army announced that procurement plans for cargo helicopters were then being formulated for submission to the Chief of Staff of the Army. The training rates for cargo helicopter pilots and mechanics would have to be based on the delivery dates for cargo helicopters. When firm procurement plans were approved, the forecast production schedule for cargo helicopters would be forwarded to Army Field Forces to permit the computation of more accurate training requirements. According to the Department of the Army, a review of procurement plans and production schedules indicated that the proposed training rates would be more than adequate to fill requirements.

The Department of the Army also was considering a request for additional MOSs for aviation maintenance personnel. No funds were included in the fiscal year 1954 budget for a continuation of the training of aircraft maintenance officers and airframe mechanics in civilian schools. Upon receipt of decisions on MOSs and transfer of training from the Air Force, maintenance courses would have to be reviewed to determine the number and type of course to be conducted by the Army Aviation School. In order that the required revision of courses and adjustments in training rates could be accomplished, the Army Field Forces was to be advised when decisions would be made on MOSs and transfer of training from the Air Force to the Army.[12]

The Department of the Army called a conference on 29 December 1952 to discuss the effect of the mechanic shortage on the training program for Army aviation and the integration of Air Force training of Army personnel into an Army Aviation School program. A shortage of helicopter mechanics caused the postponement of a transportation helicopter pilot class from 5 December 1952 to 5 January 1953, which disrupted the sequence of classes for the remainder of the fiscal year. In order to meet the scheduled training requirements, 120 helicopter mechanics would be required for January, 220 in February, and 325 in March. Fourth Army advised the Department of Air Training that ten additional mechanics would be assigned in January and thirty in February. The Assistant Chief of Staff, G-1, Department of the Army, indicated that no action would be taken to freeze personnel then assigned to the Army Aviation School. Forecast losses would equal the additional mechanics promised, and there was no source which could furnish military helicopter mechanics in the number needed. The Assistant Chief of Staff, G-4, Department of the Army, sent representatives to Fort Sill in early January 1953 to confer with the school and Fourth Army representatives and determine a solution to the maintenance problem. Utilization of civilian mechanics or a contract with a civilian firm for maintenance of the helicopters was thought to be the best solution, and the G-4 estimated that civilian maintenance assistance could be made available in February. The G-3 informally accepted the concept that some reduction in training during calendar year 1954 should be made to ease the problems of Army assumption of present Air Force training.[13]

Suspension of Transfer of Air Force Training

Student load forecasts for fiscal year 1954 at both the Army Aviation School and San Marcos indicated substantial increases in the training requirements for Army aviation personnel over the previous year. Army Field Forces planning to meet these needs was hampered by the unwarranted assumptions that the Army would assume responsibility for all training of Army aviation personnel by January 1954, that Frederick Airfield would be released to the Army by the Air Force by 15 March 1953, and that the Army Aviation School at Fort Sill would utilize Frederick, with its satellite fields, as a sub-post.

The Army Field Forces on 12 March emphasized the need for acquisition of Frederick Airfield, but received word from the Department of the Army a few days later that Frederick would not be available for Army use in the immediate future. Then on 19 May, the Department advised OCAFF that, because of budget limitations, plans to reactivate Frederick Airfield as an Air Force base had been suspended. This decision necessitated the suspension of any immediate plans for the Army to assume responsibility for the training of Army aviation personnel then being conducted by the Air Force. In addition to the financial problems, the Air Force in

February had reversed its position regarding the transfer of training, and the entire problem was unsettled.[14]

Duplication of Training Activities

Maj. Gen. Charles E. Hart, commanding general of the Artillery Center, reported to Army Field Forces in February 1954 that there was a duplication of training activities between the Helicopter Mechanic Course being conducted by the Army Aviation School and a similar course being conducted exclusively for Army personnel by the Air Force at Gary Air Force Base. Attempts to resolve the duplication had been made at all levels to no avail. General Hart also complained that the fixed wing aircraft mechanics were being trained at Gary Air Force Base instead of Fort Sill. Division of responsibility, according to General Hart, produced difficulty in coordination, control, and direction of effort. The introduction of any changes in the curriculum or equipment in the basic training portion required approval at several levels within each service up to and including departmental headquarters. The compartmentalized nature of the two phases of the training program precluded concurrent and integrated training in both the technical and tactical aspects. If the two phases were merged, an actual saving of training time could be realized. General Hart recommended that the full responsibility for the training of all Army aviation personnel be assigned to the Department of the Army, a move which would result in a more effective, more efficient, and better coordinated training program; improve the quality of instruction and its direct application to Army needs; eliminate unnecessary duplication in facilities and service support; and assure a more effective and broader mobilization base for Army aviator training.[15]

Lt. Gen. John E. Dahlquist, the Chief of Army Field Forces, concurred that the Army should control this training and had made his feelings known to the Department of the Army in August and December 1953. The G-3, Department of the Army, had recommended to the Secretary of the Army that this training be transferred starting in fiscal year 1956, but by the end of 1954 the problem was still unresolved.[16]

Shortage of Fixed Wing Pilots

In May 1954, the Department of the Army completed a study on the status of Army aviators which showed that there were 2,282 aviators on active duty, 867 of whom were on assignments not involving the piloting of aircraft as a primary duty. This meant that there were 1,415 pilots to fly 2,300 aircraft issued against TOE and TA authorizations. The critical shortage of Army aviators had to be alleviated at the earliest practicable date. A study by the Office of the Comptroller of the Army had indicated that the gain in pilot strength during the period of June 1953 through February 1954 was less than 100. The actual pilot strength did not follow the anticipated pilot strength because the elimination rate during primary training was nearer 40 percent than the projected 25 percent. Moreover, classes did not begin training at full strength and more pilots were released from active duty than anticipated. The input for fixed wing pilot training had to be increased to 200 per month if Army requirements for pilots were to be met by fiscal year 1958.

To alleviate this problem, the Department of the Army requested that OCAFF submit recommendations on the means of doubling the current output of the Army Aviation Tactics Course at Fort Sill. It also queried the Air Force concerning its capability to increase the capacity of the Army Primary Flight Course. In view of the critical shortage of aviation training personnel and facilities, consideration was to be given to the utilization of L-19 aircraft in primary flight training and to reducing by half the length of the Army Aviation Tactics Course.

On 19 July, Army Field Forces reported to the Department of the Army that the shortage of Army aviators could be eliminated in three years by an increase of 1,230 for the first year, which would be less than double the present yearly output of the Army Aviation Tactics Course. This could be accomplished by utilizing the L-19 in primary flight training, reducing the Army Aviation Tactics Course by two weeks, and reducing the Army Cargo Helicopter Pilot Course by one week.[17]

Training of Mechanics

At a conference on facilities for Army aviation held on 14 May 1954, the G-3, Department of the Army, announced that he was recommending that all Army aviation maintenance instruction be conducted at the Transportation School at Fort Eustis. At this time, OCAFF informed the Department of the Army that it believed organizational aircraft maintenance instruction should be conducted by the Army Aviation School and that field and depot aircraft maintenance instruction should be conducted by the Transportation School. In the following months, the exact position of the Department of the Army regarding the location of the training of aircraft maintenance personnel became unclear. Late in July, the commandant of the Aviation School strongly recommended that organizational aircraft maintenance training continue to be conducted by his school. OCAFF requested a clarification of Department of the Army policy and was informed that the entire Army aviation program was under examination. Until the completion of this examination late in the year, there would be no changes made in planning for the conduct of organizational aircraft maintenance instruction at the Army Aviation School and field maintenance instruction at the Transportation School.[18]

The Transportation Corps obtained an increase in the number of MOSs for Army aircraft maintenance and developed a program for the specialist training at the Transportation School. Under this program, one officer and six enlisted courses were set up, five of which were in specialties new to Army maintenance. Provision was made for specialist training in the repair of major components or systems of aircraft such as rotors and propellors, engines and power trains, airframes, and instruments and electrical systems. Instruction at the Transportation School began in June 1954, and previous arrangements for maintenance training at a civilian institution were discontinued. It was planned to train approximately 1,300 field maintenance personnel in fiscal year 1955.[19]

Movement of the Army Aviation School

The rapid growth of the Army Aviation School placed a severe strain on the facilities available at Fort Sill. By August 1954, the staff and faculty of the school had grown to almost 300 members. There were also at Fort Sill approximately 800 students and about 500 aircraft. Such rapid growth resulted in numerous problems and crowded conditions which began to hamper the school's ability to perform its mission. Inadequate hangar space, dispersal of activities, and submarginal facilities resulted in excessive costs and inefficient operations. Insufficient parking hardstands meant that about 80 percent of the aircraft had to be parked on the sod and continuously operated under extremely poor conditions. The sod became a sea of mud when it rained and was dusty when it was dry. Dust circulating through the engines resulted in excessive deterioration and frequent engine replacements. In addition, a lack of hangar space made the aircraft extremely vulnerable to the frequent and severe storms. Over an 11-year period, ending in 1953, storm damage amounted to $2,161,730 and 39,505 training hours lost. The location of the heliport also posed a problem, due to its encroachment on other training activities at the Artillery School and its proximity to fixed wing traffic at Post Field.

A number of possibilities were considered to relieve the Army Aviation School's problem. The possibility of expanding activities at Fort Sill and utilizing Frederick Airfield as a subpost was explored. Other facilities considered were at Shawnee and El Reno, Oklahoma; Gary Air Force Base; DeRidder Army Field Forces Base, Camp Polk, Louisiana; Stewart Field at Savannah, Georgia; Camp Mackall, North Carolina; Fort Riley, Kansas; Camp Rucker, Alabama; and an abandoned Air Force installation at Childress, Texas. Camp Rucker was chosen primarily because Ozark Army Air Field had three 5,000-foot runways. Buildings had just been renovated at a cost of $8,000,000. Huge truck stands on the reservation would serve as good heliports, and the large buildings used for truck repair would serve as good rotary wing maintenance hangars.

On 20 July 1954, the Chief of Staff of the Army approved transfer of the Army Aviation School from Fort Sill to Camp Rucker. Three days later, the commandant of the school was directed to work with the commanding generals of Third and Fourth Armies to prepare movement plans by 1 September.

An advance party of fifty men departed for Camp Rucker in late August. Brig. Gen. Carl I. Hutton, who had been commandant of the Army Aviation School since July, departed Fort Sill on 1 September and assumed command of Camp Rucker. The assistant commandant of the school remained at Fort Sill until early in November when he, too, left for Camp Rucker. The move took place with a minimum cancellation of classes, although some smaller courses, which were scheduled consecutively (twin-engine, instrument, and some mechanic classes) were cancelled. The school also was forced to cancel some helicopter courses after problems developed during the move. The first course to get under way at Camp Rucker was a combined Army Aviation Tactics Course. This combined class began training on 18 October and graduated 120 officers on 29 January 1955.[20]

The Army Aviation School was organized in five departments—Fixed Wing Training, Rotary Wing Training, Aviation Maintenance, Tactics and General Subjects, and Publications and Non-Resident Instruction. Also included were the Army Aviation School Regiment, Combat Development Office, Office of the School Secretary, and Office of the Director of Instruction.

During the first few months of operations at Camp Rucker, flight training began to fall behind schedule. With only Ozark Army Air Field located on post, training was moved to municipal airports near the neighboring towns. Many valuable hours were lost traveling to and from training sites—one was located almost 100 miles away. Soon tactical landing sites were selected on post and flying began from unimproved strips. Within a few weeks the dust created by the prop wash had forced training back to the improved airfields.

On 1 October 1954, 16 of the 250 helicopters used for rotary wing training arrived at Camp Rucker from Fort Sill. The trip took three days with twelve fuel stops along the 855-mile course. It was late October when the first mass movement of helicopters came over the same route. Accompanying each flight was one L-20 airplane and one H-19 or H-25 helicopter which acted as control aircraft and carried extra fuel and maintenance personnel. By mid-October, the newly formed Department of Rotary Wing Training became operational at Camp Rucker.

The Department of Aviation Maintenance began the move on 20 November, and six days later the first maintenance instruction at Camp Rucker began. At this time, the department conducted two courses—the Army Helicopter Maintenance Course and the Twin-Engine Maintenance Course. The move was conducted in phases and completed on 17 December. During the move, one class from each course was cancelled and the first Helicopter Maintenance Course class was scheduled for graduation on 8 January 1955. Due to the enthusiasm of the instructors and students the class was accelerated and graduated before Christmas. Like all segments of the Army Aviation School, the department suffered with inadequate facilities. An old vehicle shop building was used as a classroom, furniture was scarce, heating systems consisted of pot belly stoves, and the department's physical location in relation to classrooms presented transportation problems.

The Department of Tactics and General Subjects began moving from Fort Sill on 9 October. As classes graduated at Fort Sill, the remaining instructors moved to Camp Rucker. Three former classroom buildings provided instructional space. Even though these facilities were inadequate by normal standards, they were the finest the school could offer. The first few months at Camp Rucker were spent selecting training areas for field problems and modifying facilities to meet existing needs.[21]

Endnotes
Chapter VII

1. (1) Ltr AKPSIAT 352.11, Artillery School to CAFF, 26 Jul 50, subj: Flight Training for Army Aviators. (2) Ltr AKPSIAT 352.11, Artillery School to CAFF, 2 Aug 50, subj: Training of Army Aviators and Airplane and Engine Mechanics. (3) Ltr ATTNG-27 353, CAFF to CofSA, 19 Aug 50, subj: Training of Army Aviation Personnel.

2. (1) OCAFF Staff Study, 30 Oct 51. (2) Ltr ATTNG-22 352, OCAFF to DA ACofS G-3, 14 Dec 51, subj: Establishment of the Army Aviation School.

3. (1) Ltr AGAO-CC 337 The Pentagon (21 Feb 52) G-3, DA to CAFF, 26 Feb 52, subj: Conference on Training of Army Aviation Personnel. (2) Ltr ATTNG-22 352, OCAFF to Artillery School, 25 Apr 52, subj: Establishment of Army Aviation School.

4. 1st Ind ATTNG-22 352, OCAFF to DA ACofS G-3, 9 Jul 52, to ltr G-3 352 (11 Apr 52), DA ACofS G-3 to CAFF, 11 Apr 52, subj: Establishment of Army Aviation School.

5. OCAFF Summary of Major Events and Problems, FY 53, chapter 7.

6. OCAFF LO No. 9-138, 26 Sep 52, subj: Orders.

7. Ltr ATTNG-22 352, OCAFF to DA ACofS G-3, 6 Oct 52, subj: Location of Army Aviation School.

8. OCAFF Summary of Major Events and Problems, FY 53, chapter 7.

9. Ibid., pp. 10-14.

10. OCAFF Summary of Major Events and Problems, FY 53, chapter 7.

11. (1) Ltr ATTNG-32-352, OCAFF to Artillery Center, 17 Feb 53, subj: Integration of Present Air Force Training. (2) Ltr ATTNG 352/14, OCAFF to distr, 8 Apr 53, subj: Army Aviation Instrument Training.

12. Ltr ATTNG-22-353(C), OCAFF to DA ACofS G-3, 27 Oct 52, subj: Training Requirements for Army Aviation, w/1st Ind.

13. Memo, OCAFF G-3 for General Conley, 30 Dec 52, subj: Report of Conference on Army Aviation, 29 Dec 52.

14. (1) Ltr ATTNG-32-352, OCAFF to Artillery Center, 17 Feb 53, subj: Integration of Present Air Force Training into the Army Aviation School. (2) Ltr ATTNG-32-352, OCAFF to DA ACofS G-3, 12 Mar 53, subj: Army Aviation Training. (3) Ltr ATTNG-32-342 (Army Avn Sch), OCAFF to Artillery Center, 17 Mar 53, subj: Army Aviation Training Program, FY 54, w/1st Ind, DA ACofS G-3 to OCAFF, 19 May 53. (4) Ltr ATTNG-32-352, OCAFF to distr, 1 Jun 53, subj: Schedule of Classes for Instruction, Army Aviation. (5) DF CofS OCAFF to OCAFF G-3, 23 Feb 54, subj: Ltr to Gen Dahlquist, 16 Feb 54, from Maj Gen Charles E. Hart, CG, The Artillery Center, re/ Training Duplication in Aviation Mechanic Courses, Cmt 2, G-3 to CofS, 24 Feb 54.

15. Ltr, Maj Gen Charles E. Hart to Lt Gen John E. Dahlquist, 26 Feb 54.

16. Ltr, Lt Gen John E. Dahlquist to Maj Gen Charles E. Hart, 3 Mar 54.

17. Ltr GS 360 (1 Apr 54), DA ACofS G-3 to CAFF, 6 May 54, subj: Increase in Training of Army Fixed Wing Pilots, w/1st Ind, OCAFF to DA ACofS G-3, 19 Jul 54.

18. Ltr 353 AKPSIAS-OP, Brig Gen Carl I. Hutton to CAFF, 26 Jul 54, subj: Training of Organizational Aircraft Mechanic Personnel.

19. Bykofsky, p. 89.

20. (1) Tierney and Montgomery, *The Army Aviation Story*, pp. 82-86. (2) History of the U.S. Army Aviation Center, Ft Rucker, AL, 1954-1964, pp. 2-3. (3) OCAFF Summary of Major Events and Problems, FY 55, Vol. II, Plans and Operations Div, G-3 Sec., p. 8.

21. U.S. Army Aviation Center History, 1954-1964, pp. 3, 6, 10, 14, 15.

Chapter VIII

PLANS AND PROGRAMS

The development of Army aviation between 1955 and 1962 must be viewed against the general background of national defense policy during that period. The late 1950s were in many ways a time of uncertainty and difficulty for the Army. Following the end of the Korean conflict came a series of strategic decisions known collectively as the New Look. The basic premise of this new strategic policy was defined by Secretary of State John Foster Dulles in his massive retaliation speech in January 1954.

The keystone of this doctrine was the threat of the use of nuclear force and the selected use of weapons tailored to United States strategy rather than to moves or presumed intent of the enemy. This strategy was based on the belief that the threat of the use of nuclear weapons against an enemy's homeland or his armed forces could substitute for military manpower. Working from this hypothesis, the United States placed greater reliance on strategic nuclear air power and de-emphasized land, naval, and tactical air forces. For the Army, this policy meant that both men and money would be hard to come by for the development of any new missions or tactical concepts.

General Matthew B. Ridgway, the Chief of Staff of the Army, strongly opposed the New Look. He believed that whether nuclear weapons were used or not, it was the ground soldier who must finally achieve victory. General Ridgway realized, however, that the Army which had fought in World War II and Korea could not meet the challenge of the prospective nuclear battlefield. One solution for the Army to the problem created by the atomic age appeared to be a greater use of air power.

General Ridgway believed that if the Army was to become a streamlined, hard-hitting force, as many elements as possible must be transportable by air, both between continents and on the battlefield. Fixed land lines of communication and huge supply dumps would probably no longer be possible. More than ever before, aircraft would have to provide the means of troop transport, resupply, evacuation, and communications.

Of great concern to General Ridgway was the failure of the United States Air Force to make adequate provision for the future requirements of the Army. With the New Look, the Air Force devoted most of its attention to the formation of a strategic bomber force supported by high performance jet interceptors. Little interest was shown in the development of close air support or in "low and slow" type aircraft needed by the Army. The Army required what amounted to aerial trucks and jeeps and combat aircraft which could serve as flying gun platforms. The Air Force made no effort to develop such aircraft. General Ridgway maintained that if the Air Force would not undertake such projects, the Army would have to in order to survive on the battlefield. He therefore determined that Army aviation would have to undergo an extensive reorganization to prepare it for the future. In order to provide adequate guidance for future developments, General Ridgway directed that a comprehensive Army aviation plan be developed.[1]

Army Aviation Plan

On 4 September 1954, General Ridgway directed that a comprehensive review of the Army aviation program be undertaken as a first step in the preparation of the comprehensive Army aviation plan which he had called for. Thus, for the first time the Army attempted to prepare a long range program for aviation. In response to a Department of the Army request for input to the overall plan, OCAFF developed separate plans for Army aviation training, combat developments, and testing and development of Army aviation equipment.[2] These plans were forwarded to the Department of the Army on 30 September. The training plan provided separate courses, course locations, and student inputs for instruction through 1960. The combat developments plan outlined the role of OCAFF in the combat developments function, including the relationship with the Army Aviation School. The testing and development plan provided for the establishment of an Army Aviation Board, located at the Army Aviation School, to assume the responsibility and missions performed by the Army Aviation Service Test Division of OCAFF Board No. 6, Camp Rucker; the Aviation Branch, Aviation and Metro Division, Army Electronic Proving Ground, Fort Huachuca; and the Air Transportation Division, Transportation Research and Development Command, Fort Eustis.[3]

On 9 November, the Department of the Army forwarded to OCAFF for review and comment the proposed Army Aviation Plan, FY 1955-FY 1959, which was designed to provide long range Department of the Army guidance on the development of Army aviation. OCAFF, in turn, asked the service schools concerned, the Command and General Staff College, and the Army War College for comments and recommendations. Responding to the Department of the Army, OCAFF pointed out on 1 December two basic issues which had to be resolved prior to acceptance or rejection of the proposed Army Aviation Plan. First, definition was needed of what aviation missions were to be performed by the Army and the Air Force. Second, a decision then had to be made as to how Army aviation was to be organized to perform those missions. Until these issues could be resolved, OCAFF recommended that the plan not be presented to the Chief of Staff of the Army.

The Army Field Forces took this opportunity to make a number of specific recommendations regarding Army aviation. These included the establishment of a career management program for aviators, the expansion of training facilities, the establishment of an Army Aviation Center, and the assumption by the Army of the responsibility for depot supply and maintenance.

OCAFF also recommended that aircraft requirements be considered as tentative and valid for short range planning only pending the completion of OCAFF studies. Also needed was authority, together with appropriate agencies at the Department of the Army level, to investigate means of shortening the aircraft development-procurement cycle.

On 7 December, a conference was held on the Army Aviation Plan attended by General John E. Dahlquist, the Chief of Army Field Forces, Maj. Gen. Paul D. Adams, the Deputy Assistant Chief of Staff, G-3, Department of the Army. At this conference, OCAFF once again recommended the establishment of an Army Aviation Center and that the Department of the Army should proceed immediately to solve the career problems of Army aviators that had arisen. OCAFF also recommended that training should be emphasized and that the Department of the Army should initiate action to take over depot maintenance and supply. Conference discussions also included the Army's maximum use of Air Force and Navy procurement facilities. OCAFF wanted assurances that the proposed expansion of the Department of the Army G-3 Army aviation functions would not duplicated those of OCAFF.

On 18 December, the Department of the Army asked OCAFF for concurrence and comment on a draft summary sheet for the Chief of Staff of the Army. This document summarized the planned expansion of Army aviation and the proposed Army Aviation Plan. It also included comments from the field and recommended courses of action. These actions included the centralized control over aviation personnel by the Department of the Army, G-1, and the establishment of an Army Aviation Center and Army Aviation Board at Camp Rucker. Moreover, a general officer with the responsibility for overall supervision and coordination of the Army aviation program should be added to the Office of the Assistant Chief of Staff, G-3, Department of the Army.

The Chief of Army Field Forces would be charged with conducting all flight and technical training of Army aviation personnel in the zone of the interior. He also would be charged with making recommendations to the Department of the Army concerning all aspects of the combat and services development of aviation used by the Army in the field to include organizational matters, integration of aviation into units, tactical and logistical employment of aviation, and recommending the types, characteristics, and capabilities of aircraft to be used. The Department of the Army recommended the Army assumption of depot supply and maintenance responsibilities and the implementation of planning studies and tests to resolve the basic problems of Army aviation as related to personnel, organization, developments, construction, procurement, supply, maintenance, and command. OCAFF, with most of its previous objections satisfied, concurred in the content of the summary sheet on 22 December 1954.[4]

While the comments from the field on the proposed Army Aviation Plan were generally favorable, they were not unanimously so. For this reason, G-3 submitted specific recommendations relating to Army aviation to the Chief of Staff of the Army rather than the complete plan. On 11 January 1955, the Army Policy Council approved these Army aviation recommendations, including those relating to OCAFF. As a result of this decision, the Department of the Army directed the Commanding General, Continental Army Command (CONARC) to recommend the mission and organization for the Army Aviation Center and the Army Aviation Board.[5] The Army Aviation Center had been officially established at Camp Rucker on 1 February. CONARC Board No. 6 was also established at Camp Rucker to replace the Army Aviation Test Division of CONARC Board No. 5. The Department of the Army requested CONARC to provide plans under which it would execute its responsibilities for all aviation flight and technical training of Army aviation personnel in the zone of the interior.[6]

On 12 April the Department of the Army requested that CONARC prepare detailed plans for training sufficient aviators in FY 1956 to meet all aviator requirements Army-wide by the end of fiscal years 1956-1957. CONARC recommended on 29 April a means of reaching the objectives by the end of FY 1957. The Department of the Army revised the desired requirements and recommended a plan which was approved by the Army Aviation School on 11 May and by CONARC three days later. The FY 1956 Fixed Wing Training Plan was published by the Department of the Army on 13 June and was forwarded by CONARC to the Army Aviation School for implementation on 27 June.[7]

Despite the failure of the original Army Aviation Plan to gain approval, the Army Aviation Division of G-3 still strongly believed that a document was required which would outline official guidance for the development of the Army aviation program. On 17 September 1955, therefore, the Department of the Army forwarded to CONARC for comments a draft plan for Army aviation for fiscal years 1956 to 1960. The plan outlined seven primary functions of Army aviation and discussed required aircraft, personnel, training, installations, and research and development programs. In comments submitted on 11 October, CONARC nonconcurred with the Army assumption of a function of close air support within the time frame of the plan and recommended that a requirement for optimum close support aircraft be placed on the Air Force.

After seeing the revised Army Aviation Plan, General Dahlquist on 30 December again voiced strong objections to the Department of the Army G-3 about Army plans for procuring and testing currently available aircraft in the close support role. He pointed out that CONARC's comments on Project ABLE BUSTER, submitted earlier that month, had also included this recommendation.[8] General Dahlquist stated that he was not aware of any reductions which could be made in the field army as the result of adding organic light attack aircraft to perform the close support role. If the Army were to assume this new function, it should first determine the most advanced weapon system it could attain by the early part of the 1960-1970 decade and then concentrate on the development of an optimum weapon system which would meet the requirements of warfare during that period. He charged that the plan overlooked the urgent necessity of placing a firm requirement on the Air Force for the development of an optimum close support aircraft. General Dahlquist therefore recommended again that this requirement be placed on the Air Force while the Army simultaneously initiated a comprehensive study of weapons systems, which might include aircraft, to undertake the missions being performed by close support aircraft. He did not consider that the procurement and testing of currently available light aircraft and munitions would contribute toward that goal.[9]

Because controversy continued regarding various aspects of the Army Aviation Plan, the Department of the Army convened a conference in Washington on 24 January 1956 to settle on the recommendations to be made to the Chief of Staff of the Army. Attending the conference were General Dahlquist, Lt. Gen. Willard G. Wyman, the CONARC Deputy Commanding General who was to succeed General Dahlquist in March, and, from the Department of Army, the DCSPER, DCSLOG, DCSOPS, Director of Army Aviation, and the Director of Development and Chief of Aircraft and Electronics from the Office of the Chief of Research and Development. The purpose of the conference was to agree on a position for the Army's requirement for direct support aviation, National Guard and Army Reserve aviation units, the need for a heavy helicopter, and the requirement for a fixed wing cargo aircraft of greater than 5,000 pounds empty weight.

The conferees agreed that the Army should proceed without delay in the development of aircraft to control the trajectory of ground launched missiles against point targets. They recommended that the Army request the Air Force to develop an aircraft specifically designed for the close support mission. The Army would participate in all phases of the development, but use Air Force funds. In combat, these aircraft were to be placed under the operational control of the Army. This recommendation was later modified by the Chief of Staff of the Army; he simply dispatched a memorandum to the Chief of Staff of the Air Force stating the Army's requirement for close air support and asking how the Air Force intended to meet that requirement. The Army Aviation Plan, as originally presented to the conference, had included a provision that unless the Air Force met the request for a close air support aircraft, the Army would sue for revision of support functions to allow it to assume responsibility for development of such aircraft. But neither the majority of the members of the conference nor the Army Chief of Staff was willing to go that far in this controversial area.

The conference recommended that the twenty-seven National Guard divisions be provided aircraft for their organic aviation. Army procurement was limited to a 40-division force, nineteen of which were Regular Army. The six National Guard divisions with the highest mobilization priority would receive 100 percent of authorization. Total aircraft for fifteen divisions would then be distributed among the remaining twenty-one National Guard divisions. No aircraft would be authorized to Army Reserve divisional units, and only such support units in the Army Reserve necessary for the support of the first forty divisions should receive organic aircraft. The conference also recommended that no pure aviation units should be activated in the National Guard. Separate aviation units should be activated in the Army Reserve, as necessary, to provide required support for the forty division force, but the level of equipment would be subject to the availability of funds.

The conferees concurred in the requirement contained in the plan for a heavy helicopter to provide an interior 5-ton lift and to operate a crane with a capacity of eleven tons for short hauls. They believed that successful development of the H-16 helicopter would meet both these requirements. The conference also supported the requirement for a fixed wing cargo aircraft of greater than 5,000 pounds empty weight. This support was based on the belief that this probably would be the largest fixed wing aircraft capable of operation in forward areas and that it would be an economical and essential complement to the helicopter for troop movement and logistical support within the combat zone.

Maj. Gen. Hamilton H. Howze, who had become the first Director of Army Aviation on 1 January 1956, presented the recommendations of the conference to General Maxwell D. Taylor, the Chief of Staff of the Army, later the same day. The latter approved all of the recommendations on 5 March, with the exception noted above regarding close air support. The Army Aviation Plan, FY 1956-1960, was then revised and approved for publication on 16 March.[10]

As a result of a presentation on the status of the Army Aviation Program made by the Director of Army Aviation to the Commanding General, CONARC, on 12 September 1956, six days later CONARC provided the Department of the Army with recommendations on the scope and content of the program. CONARC pointed out that many of the controversial aspects of the Army Aviation Program which were mentioned during the Director of Army Aviation's presentation possessed such far-reaching implications that CONARC could not furnish definitive answers to the problems without considerable study, testing, and detailed evaluation.

On 18 September, CONARC also furnished a summary of aircraft required in proposed TOEs for the ROCAD (armored), ROTAD (airborne), and ROCID (infantry) divisions and for the experimental helicopter reconnaissance unit scheduled for testing in the SKY CAV II troop test during Exercise SLEDGE HAMMER.[11] This summary indicated that 60 or 70 aircraft would be required to perform the normal missions of a division aviation company plus SKY CAV missions and about 26 aircraft would be required in SKY CAV type units.

CONARC still felt that the division commander had a continuing day-to-day need for light cargo helicopters for tactical movements of small units, for SKY CAV roles, and for emergency resupply. CONARC also felt that the program for twelve aviation battalions should not be revised downward from a required lift point of view. CONARC advised that the program be reviewed in light of industry's ability to support it, the capacity of the training establishment and manpower resources to provide the qualified personnel to man the units, and also the advisability of transferring a portion of the program to the Reserve Components.

CONARC's position on maintenance within the twelve battalion program was that maintenance should be at battalion level rather than decentralized to companies. As regards the advisability of a part of the twelve helicopter battalion program being transferred to the Reserve Components, CONARC stated that this could be determined only after an exhaustive investigation of the sources of qualified active Army personnel to man the units and provide maintenance. Other considerations were the availability of sufficient interested reserve component aviation personnel in the proper grades and ranks, and the ability of the active Army training establishment to provide necessary training support.

Another matter which had been discussed at CONARC on 12 September was an aero-reconnaissance concept, under which a special type unit equipped with Army aircraft would, in addition to the three principle elements found in a SKY CAV type unit possess a fourth element equipped with helicopters armed for offensive operations. On 18 September, CONARC pointed out that the aero-reconnaissance concept differed from the SKY CAV concept in tactics and techniques. CONARC felt that a light cargo helicopter was needed to transport ground vehicles along with ground reconnaissance elements. In addition, the larger helicopter was of greater value than the utility helicopter in tactical movements of small units and in emergency resupply operations. The employment of armed helicopters offered interesting prospects worthy of further development and tests.[12]

Late in 1956, the Army Aviation Directorate undertook the first revision of the Army Aviation Plan. The title was changed to "The Army Aviation Guidelines for the Development of Doctrine and Organization through FY 1961," which more accurately reflected the purpose and the contents of the document. In December, the Department of the Army forwarded this document to CONARC for comment and concurrence. While this plan was not to be considered inflexible, it was regarded as firm guidance to agencies and commands concerned with Army aviation matters, subject to annual revision.

On 8 January 1957, CONARC forwarded to the Department of the Army its views on the proposed document after consulting the CONUS armies, selected units, and certain of the combat arms service schools. One of the matters of major policy significance was whether the Army or the Air Force had primary interest in the conduct of battlefield surveillance which indicated that, "The basic responsibility for aerial surveillance will be that of the Air Force," with the Army using its observation aircraft and surveillance helicopters to "thicken Air Force coverage over the immediate battle area."

CONARC's comments to the Department of the Army pointed out that the policy decision of the Secretary of Defense on 26 November 1956 had stated in part that, "The Army Aviation Program will consist of those types of aircraft required to carry out the following Army functions envisaged within the combat zone: ...observation, visual and photographic, reconnaissance, fire adjustment, and topographical survey." In view of this Department of Defense policy statement, CONARC recommended to the Department of the Army that the definition of battlefield surveillance be amended to include the following: "The Army has a primary interest in the conduct of battlefield surveillance in the combat zone. Air Force tactical reconnaissance will assist the Army in this function. Aerial surveillance beyond the combat zone is the responsibility of the Air Force." The Department of the Army accepted this amendment, and the Chief of Staff approved the revised plan on 14 February 1957.[13]

Department of Defense Policies

Controversy regarding the interpretation of their aerial missions, as they related directly to ground combat, had existed between the Army and the Air Force ever since the National Security Act of 1947. Attempts had been made to clarify these missions with the Key West agreement of 1948 and two memoranda of understanding signed by Secretary of the Army Frank Pace, Jr., and Secretary of the Air Force Thomas K. Finletter on 2 October 1951 and 4 November 1952. The latter memorandum placed a weight restriction of 5,000 pounds on Army fixed wing aircraft.

This limitation was subject to review by the Secretary of Defense upon the request of either service secretary.

The air transportation of Army supplies, equipment, personnel, and small units within the combat zone became a primary rather than a limited or emergency function of Army aviation. The combat zone was redefined so as to extend from 50 to 100 miles in depth. Other primary functions included aerial observation; control of Army forces; command, liaison, and courier missions; and aerial wire laying within the combat zone. Two activities, not previously included, were added at this time—artillery and topographic survey and aeromedical evacuation within the combat zone. Evacuation was to include battlefield pickup of casualties, air transport to the initial point of treatment, and any subsequent move to hospital facilities within the combat zone.

Primary functions of the Air Force in support of ground operations were restricted to the following: airlift of Army supplies, equipment, personnel, and units from the outside to points within the combat zone; airlift for the movement of troops, supplies, and equipment in the assault and subsequent phases of airborne operations; airlift for the evacuation of personnel and materiel from the combat zone; and aeromedical evacuation of casualties to points outside the combat zone.[14]

The reorganization of Army aviation and the initiation of a long range Army aviation program by General Ridgway led to growing concern on the part of the Air Force. General Nathan Twining, the Chief of Staff of the Air Force, charged that the proposed expansion of Army aviation could bring duplication and waste. This charge resulted from the proposal in the Army Aviation Plan to increase aircraft from 3,516 to 8,486 by 1959, while at the same time increasing personnel from 13,024 to 48,479. Another source of concern to the Air Force was the Army's interest in the T-37 jet reconnaissance airplane.

In January 1956, Secretary of the Army Wilber M. Brucker decided to request the removal of the 5,000 pound limit on fixed wing aircraft contained in the 1952 Memorandum of Understanding. General Taylor, Frank G. Millard, the Army General Counsel, and the Military Council all cautioned against making such a proposal because of the adverse impact it might have on the pending Joint Chiefs of Staff decision of the T-37 question.

Secretary Brucker waited until September before he broached the subject of removing the weight restriction to Secretary of Defense Charles E. Wilson. Negotiations between Brucker and Wilson continued through October into November. Wilson indicated he might agree to an amendment of the weight restriction rather than its complete removal. Brucker then proposed a maximum payload radius capacity of 1,200 ton-miles to permit development of an airplane capable of operating from forward landing areas less than 600 feet in length and carrying a 4-ton cargo for a mission radius of 300 nautical miles. Secretary Wilson on 20 November, however, informed the Armed Forces Policy Council that he wanted to retain the weight restriction, but would consider making exceptions for specific aircraft. In response to this statement, Secretary Brucker asked for procurement authority for five new 3-ton transports which exceeded the weight restriction. Secretary Wilson approved the transport procurement exception.

On 26 November 1956, Secretary Wilson issued a memorandum which attempted to clarify the previous service agreement and again defined the missions of the services. The Wilson memorandum retained the 5,000 pound limit on fixed wing aircraft and imposed a 20,000 pound weight limit on helicopters. Secretary Wilson did permit the Army to request specific exceptions to these limitations. A significant change made by the Defense Secretary was the redefinition of the combat zone as an area not more than 100 miles forward of the general line of contact. The extension of the combat zone to the rear of the line of contact was to be designated by the appropriate field commander, but normally would also be 100 miles. Within this 200 mile combat zone, it was proper for the Army to use organic aircraft.

In his attempt to define missions, Secretary Wilson forbade Army aircraft from strategic and tactical airlift during airborne operations, airlift and medical evacuation from points within the combat zone to points without, medical evacuation from an airhead where the airborne operation included air-landed logistical support by the Air Force, tactical reconnaissance, interdiction of the battlefield, and close combat air support.

Despite the apparent restrictiveness of the 26 November memorandum, the door was left open for the continued expansion of Army aviation. The provision for exceptions to the weight limitations permitted the Army to develop larger aircraft. The memorandum did not limit the performance of Army aircraft in the combat zone, although the weight limitation did affect performances. The new definition of the combat zone gave Army aircraft twice the operational distance than did the Pace-Finletter memorandum of 1952.[15]

On 18 March 1957, Department of Defense Directive 5160.22 was issued reaffirming the previous provisions of the Pace-Finletter agreement and the modifications made by Secretary Wilson. The directive reconfirmed the Air Force roles in strategic and tactical airlift, tactical reconnaissance, interdiction, and close air support. It also stipulated that there should be no unnecessary duplication or overlapping among the services, a proviso that would lead to continuing controversy.[16]

In October 1959, the Army tested the use of divisional combat reconnaissance companies equipped with armed helicopters. The decision prompted Air Force speculation that his might be the first move toward eventual Army assumption of the functions of battlefield interdiction and close combat air support. In the field of tactical surveillance, the Army had made considerable progress in the use of electronically equipped fast drones to monitor enemy movements, acquire target information, and report on the results of missile firings. Another significant increase in battlefield surveillance had been made with the mounting of side-looking airborne radar on aircraft, which flew parallel to the area being scanned instead of traversing hostile territory.

Despite the limitations imposed by the Department of Defense, the Army intended to take full advantage of the air for travel, observation, and communication to ensure the success of the land battle. The Army asked private industry for assistance in developing some major technological improvements in aircraft design to tailor aircraft to the jobs they must perform instead of tailoring battle missions to the capabilities of existing aircraft.[17]

Personnel Policies

All the planning and policy directives relative to Army aviation would be meaningless unless the necessary number of aviators could be obtained and given the career incentive to remain in the program. Army aviation had its own peculiar personnel problems. Since Army aviation was a specialty and not a branch, problems arose in providing an adequate number of pilots while ensuring proper career development and progression for aviators. The grade distribution of aviators also caused concern early in the period. The use of a greater number of warrant officer pilots and the training of senior officers as aviators helped to solve this problem. Despite difficulties, the Army during this period continued to develop a corps of highly trained and motivated pilots to meet the needs of the expanding program.

Review of Officer Grades for Army Aviators

An Army Aviation Officer Career Program had been formulated by the Department of the Army G-1 in 1950, but had been suspended the following year until the rapid Korean conflict personnel expansion was over. General Ridgway's directive in 1955 reorganizing Army aviation reinstituted this program. Studies made by the Department of the Army G-1 indicated that the existing grade spread for Army aviators was greatly at variance with the overall grade structure of the Army. The bulk of Army aviators by May 1955 were predominantly in the lower officer grades, only 4 percent being above the grade of major.

On 6 July 1955, G-3, Department of the Army, requested the assistance of CONARC in the solution of the problems with the grade structure of Army aviation officer personnel. Correction of this situation, G-3 pointed out, was necessary in the interest of developing an Army Aviation Officer Career Program which would attract and retain capable officers.

A related problem cited by G-3 resulted from the requirement for keeping a sufficient number of these officers assigned to higher command and staff positions in other types of activity, over and above the number actually needed to fill positions requiring rated aviators. This measure was necessary in order to keep officers from becoming overspecialized; it also ensured enough technically trained personnel for the expansion of Army aviation activities during mobilization. Under existing TOE and TD grade authorizations, however, most Army aviators were in the grade of captain or lower, whereas many of the higher command and staff positions through which it was desirable to rotate these officers called for field grade officers.

As an immediate and partial solution to these problems, G-3 proposed three measures. First, the maintenance of authorized overages of Army aviation officers in the higher grades. Second, a review of current TOE to determine whether the Army aviation grade authorizations were realistic and equitable. Third, a careful scrutiny of the experimental TOE being tested in the ATFA project to assure the grade authorizations for Army aviation positions were commensurate with the duties and responsibilities of such positions.[18] CONARC was requested to recommend the desired percentage of overage in each grade, and review the Army aviation space authorizations in current TOEs and recommend revisions where appropriate. They were also to carefully scrutinize the grade authorizations in the experimental TOE for suitability of the grades authorized.

CONARC concluded that it was undesirable to remedy defects of the grade structure by authorizing overages in certain grades. Authorization of grade overages for Army aviation officers would result in proportional reductions in other branches in order for the Army to stay within its overall officer grade ceilings. Moreover, the projected expansion of Army aviation would absorb some of the excess of company grade aviators and thus bring the grade distribution more nearly in line with the Army-wide distribution. CONARC determined that the number of Army aviators authorized for the current year provided an adequate base for expansion during mobilization. The Army aviators authorized as of 1 September 1955 would be adequate to support an Army expansion of approximately four times its current strength.

CONARC replied to the Department of the Army on 1 September, suggesting that a better way to strengthen the Army aviation mobilization base would be to procure more aviators in the reserve components. The headquarters pointed out that, in the current National Guard troop basis, approximately 1,000 TOE spaces were authorized for aviators, but as of 1 June 1955, only 810, or 73 percent, of these spaces were filled. The current Army reserve troop basis contained 2,821 aviator spaces, but as of 30 June 1955, only 1,018, or approximately 36 percent, were filled.

As requested by the Department of the Army, CONARC reviewed all current TOE which contained spaces for rated aviators. A study of the grade spread of aviation officers authorized in the type field army as compared to that of all officers in the type field army disclosed numerous inequities. Accordingly, CONARC recommended upgrading or downgrading aviator spaces in twenty of the TOEs. Thus in the case of the infantry division, which was authorized 1 lieutenant colonel, 5 captains, and 22 lieutenants, CONARC recommended that these 28 spaces be regraded to 1 lieutenant colonel, 1 major, 5 captains, 16 lieutenants, and 5 warrant officers. Because only 4.8 percent of the 919 commissioned officer spaces in the type field army were of field grade, CONARC recommended that this be raised to 5.6 percent.

The most sizable reallocation of grades recommended by CONARC was the conversion of 42.6 percent of the rated aviator spaces in the type field army to warrant officers. This recommendation was based on a previous CONARC view that aviator duty positions requiring tactical or technical knowledge in addition to skill as a pilot should be filled by warrant officers. The analysis of aviator grade authorizations in the ATFA tables was held in abeyance pending completion of Exercises BLUE BOLT II and SAGE BRUSH.

As the result of CONARC's recommendations and its own studies, the Department of the Army G-1 instituted a new Army Aviation Officer Career Program. One solution to the problem of the shortage of senior aviator officers was the sending of senior and general officers to flight training to assignments involving aviation. By July 1959, there were eleven generals on flight status. The Chief of Transportation in 1954 had also proposed the use of warrant officer aviators and during 1955 applications began to be accepted from enlisted men throughout the Army for training at Fort Rucker as warrant officer candidates.[19]

Recommendations for Warrant Officer Aviators

In addition to the 1954 recommendation of the Chief of Transportation, CONARC on 30 March 1955, forwarded to the Department of the Army results of a study concerning the desirability and feasibility of utilizing warrant officer and enlisted pilots (fixed wing) in lieu of officer pilots. The study included information regarding the number of TOE and TD positions in which warrant officer pilot spaces required during fiscal year 1956; the scope of OCS-type training deemed desirable for enlisted men taking flight training for duty as warrant officer pilots; the location; feasible starting date, and required input for such training.

CONARC recommended that enlisted personnel not be used as pilots at that time and that warrant officer pilots be used in the combat arms and technical services where the requirement for command and leadership was not present. As regards requirements for warrant officer pilots, CONARC reported that of the 3,190 aviator spaces that would be required by the Army during fiscal year 1956, 1,227 could be filled by warrant officers and that, of these, 439 should be fixed wing qualified and 778 should be rotary wing qualified only. These figures were exclusive of Transportation Corps requirements, but included the three proposed fixed wing transport aviation companies.

CONARC also recommended that OCS-type training of ten weeks' duration be given at the Army Aviation School prior to flight training. Based on an overall attrition rate of 50 percent, CONARC recommended that the total input to this training be 3,054, but that it be phased over a 3-week period. CONARC estimated that six months lead time would be required for the Army Aviation School to initiate the proposed preflight or OCS-type training and that seventeen officers and fifty-four enlisted men would be required to conduct the training. CONARC's recommendations were accepted for the most part and training of warrant officer candidates began at Camp Wolters in November 1956.[20]

Aviator Requirements

As a result of White House and Congressional interest in reducing the costs involved in proficiency flying, Department of Defense Directive 1340.4, Proficiency Flying Programs, was published on 29 May 1959. This directive required that the services institute a program to review and validate requirements for aviators to ensure that only those with real potential were retained on flying status. Only the minimum flying essential for retention of aeronautical skill was permitted. As a corollary to this directive, AR 600-105, Army Aviation Officer Career Program, was republished on 21 August 1959. This regulation for the first time established four categories of assignment for Army aviators. Category I included positions where the primary duty was pilot, or the direct command of aircraft in a unit below battalion level. Command staff positions where flying was a requisite skill, but not required as the primary duty, were encompassed in Category II. Category III comprised career development assignments necessary to improve the aviator's qualification as an Army officer, provided such assignments did not exceed two consecutive years' duration. Finally, aviators assigned to primary duties other than those described above would be placed in Category IV and be indefinitely suspended from flying status for the period of such duties. If such duties extended for more than three years, the individual would be eliminated for the Army aviation program.[21]

An annual review and validation of requirements for aviators was required by the Department of Defense directive. To accomplish this review, the Deputy Chief of Staff for Personnel, Department of the Army, appointed an ad hoc committee to recommend FY 1961 requirements and authorizations for Army aviators, forecast in general terms the requirements for aviators through FY 1970, and generally review the career development of Army aviators. The committee developed criteria for determining Army aviator positions. It also queried the major field commands as to their requirements for aviators. The committee made an individual review of all field grade positions. Future requirements were computed on the basis of projected aircraft inventories and a continuation of existing organization and employments of Army aviation.

The ad hoc committee determined that the FY 1961 Army aviator authorizations be set at 6,449—5,299 officers and 1,150 warrant officers—and apportioned to the major commands by grade and branch as a ceiling under which assignments would be made. The committee also recommended that a small increase be made in training field grade officers, to include eight colonels, and that the Department of the Army DCSPER consider greater utilization of warrant officers. The existing 20 percent career management factor for officer aviators below the rank of colonel would be retained and branch qualifying assignments for officer aviators would be accorded the highest priorities.[22]

The rapid aviation expansion as a result of the Berlin Crisis negated many of the findings of the committee. The committee's deliberations, however, were a reflection of the Army's continuing efforts to come to grips with its long term aviator requirements.

Planning for Future Development

With the formal adoption of a helicopter weapons system, the successful development of the air cavalry troop, and the plans for the proposed utility tactical transport company, the time had come to formulate a unified airmobile program.[23] During 1960 and 1961, CONARC formed two committees and a board to study the future of Army aviation. The Rogers Board, officially designated as the Army Aircraft Requirements Review Board, met early in 1960 to study to Army's future needs for aircraft. This was followed by the Rogers Committee on Army Aviation which developed a training program to support Army aviation expansion. In 1961, the Ad Hoc Committee to Study Aircraft Armament Systems was convened.

Army Aircraft Requirements Review Board (Rogers Board)

On 15 January 1960, the Chief of Staff of the Army directed the establishment of the Army Aircraft Requirements Review Board. Chaired by Lt. Gen. Gordon B. Rogers, the board was directed to recommend as a matter of first priority the course of action to meet the requirements during the 1960-1970 time period for light observation aircraft and to explore the possible courses of action to improve the Army's capabilities in the areas of surveillance and tactical transport. The Board was to recommend a priority for development to include the specific developments to be initiated with FY 1961 research, development, test, and experimentation funds. Finally, the board was to submit its best estimate of the Army's requirements during the 1960-1970 time period, supported by a proposed procurement program, to include cost and quantities by year, of current and future types of aircraft.

Some steps had already been taken in the development of a long range aircraft program. In October 1959, the Chief of Research and Development had initiated a plan which would develop firm guidance for Army aviation for the period, 1960-1970. Army Study Requirements (ASRs) describing broad development objectives in the area of light observation, manned surveillance, and tactical transport aircraft were prepared and presented to industry on 1 December 1959. The latter submitted 119 design concepts as solutions to the problems presented by the ASRs.

Industry design concepts were evaluated during February 1960 in two phases. During Phase I—1 to 15 February—a technical evaluation was conducted under the direction of the Chief of Transportation. In Phase II—16 to 28 February—an operational evaluation was conducted under the direction of the Chief of Research and Development. The Phase II operational evaluation teams prepared and presented their results to the Rogers Board.

After receiving general background orientation briefings, the Rogers Board received the reports of the three operational evaluation teams. Following each presentation, the members of the teams concerned and consultants from the National Aeronautics and Space Agency, Bureau of Weapons, Marine Corps, Transportation Corps, and Signal Corps were questioned by the Board. The Board's conclusions and recommendations were made against this background and submitted to the Department of the Army on 10 March 1960.

The Rogers Board recommended that a design competition be conducted to develop a light observation aircraft. More than one design should be selected and at least two be developed through flying prototype testing prior to selection of the final production design. The selected design would be procured in FY 1964 to meet the requirement for the light observation aircraft. Existing observation aircraft—the L-19, H-13, and H-23—would be phased out and replaced by the new helicopters. Long range research efforts for the light observation aircraft mission should be continued toward improvement of helicopter performance, economy, and efficiency of operation in the field.

The Board's recommendations regarding surveillance aircraft were dependent on the development of equipment and techniques. It recommended that increased effort be placed in FY 1961 on the development and testing of sensory devices for manned aircraft. Increased emphasis also was needed for the development of secure data link transmission systems capable of transmitting information gathered deep in hostile territory to ground stations with minimum time delay and loss of quality. Equipment and techniques for receiving, processing, and interpreting the data collected by airborne surveillance systems needed to be developed simultaneously and with the same priority as the surveillance systems. The requirement for an organization for processing and interpretation activities should be reviewed by CONARC. The board recommended that a study on survivability should be completed prior to 1 January 1961 for use in the preparation of the military characteristics of a new manned deep penetration surveillance aircraft. Subject to the outcome of studies on aircraft survivability and satisfactory assurance of the availability of suitable surveillance equipment, the Rogers Board recommended that a new manned deep penetration surveillance aircraft be developed beginning with FY 1962 funds, with the objective of providing operational aircraft no later than 1970.

The Rogers Board recommended establishing a policy of replacing each aircraft model at least every ten years, or sooner if warranted by operational requirements or state-of-the-art advances.

The Board recommended that operational studies be made to determine specific requirements for Army airlift of supplies, equipment, and personnel within the combat zone to support contingency plans, with emphasis on the equipment of the Strategic Army Corps (STRAC) in specific operational areas.[24] If these operational studies did not establish a high priority requirement for a larger than 3-ton aircraft, the Board recommended that a program be established with the objective of providing a vertical/short take off and landing (V/STOL) replacement for the HC-1 helicopter and the AC-1 airplane, with initial production deliveries in the early 1970s. These two aircraft were just entering service in 1960, and by the Board's criteria, would be due for replacement in the 1970s. Research and study should continue to determine the technical and operational feasibility of V/STOL aircraft to meet future Army requirements.

The areas of study, research, and development listed below, in order or priority, were those required to support the Board's conclusions and recommendations:

1. Continuation of aircraft under development to include projects in direct support of these aircraft.
2. Development of a new light observation aircraft.
3. Studies and tests on aircraft survivability and operation of aircraft at low altitude and high speed to provide information required prior to initiating development of a manned surveillance deep penetration aircraft.
4. Development and test of sensors, processing, and interpretation equipment, and avionics equipment.
5. Studies on the requirements for airlift to support contingency plans.
6. Development of V/STOL research aircraft for technical and field evaluation.
7. Study and tests on noise level and downwash problems.
8. Long range research to improve helicopter performance.
9. Research on propulsion systems.
10. Research on ground effects machines.

The Board developed a procurement program for the coming decade. The proposed light observation aircraft would be introduced as rapidly as practicable, and, by FY 1970, would nearly meet active Army TOE requirements. The L-19, H-13, and H-23 aircraft were provided as interim substitutes until the higher performance aircraft became available to meet the needs of table of allowance (TA) and Reserve Component units. By about 1973, all requirements were expected to be met with the new aircraft.

The procurement program give first priority support to the UH-1 utility helicopter. By 1970, all foreseen Active Army TOE requirements would be provided, in addition, to some TA. Orderly phase-out of L-20, H-19, H-21, and H-34 aircraft would take place through transfer to the TA and Reserve Forces Training Base as new aircraft became available. The HC-1 transport helicopter and the AC-1 transport airplane were to be introduced at a rate compatible with production capacity and to meet the requirements of planned TOE Active Army units by 1968-1969. Existing U-1A airplanes and H-37 helicopters would be phased out simultaneously into the training base or disposed of. The AO-1 surveillance aircraft would be bought at the most advantageous pace so as to achieve a reasonable Active Army TOE capability by 1965-1966. The quantitative requirement generated by this aircraft would be the subject of restudy by the staff.

The Rogers Board believed that by 1965 the current research and development effort would produce air-to-surface point and area weapons ready for installation in one or more tactical aircraft. The funds earmarked by the Board were an estimate of those required to provide installation of the weapons on Army aircraft. A small fund was also earmarked for limited purchases of essentially commercial model aircraft for training and for augmentation of the L-23 fleet.

Funds also earmarked by the Board in modest amounts late in the 1960s provided for initial procurement of a deep penetration surveillance aircraft, that would be a replacement for the AC-1 and the HC-1, and an aerial crane. The Board could not predict the quality or the timing for these aircraft. The Board's philosophy in submitting these three items was to point out the major problem implicit in these areas. At the same time it wished to indicate the earliest time in which funding support must begin to provide a significant capability by about 1975.

Maj. Gen. Hamilton H. Howze, then serving as Chief, Military Advisory Group, Korea, submitted a memorandum to the Rogers Board which had far reaching implications. He pointed out that the latest studies had assigned combat units additional quantities of light aircraft. While substantial benefits would accrue from this, these assigned and attached aircraft would simply improve the ability of units to execute their conventional missions. The employment of aircraft would be restricted to those missions.

General Howze proposed that the Army proceed at once with the development of fighting units whose mode of tactical employment would take maximum advantage of the unique mobility and flexibility of light aircraft. These aircraft would provide not only mobility for some riflemen and machine gunners, but also direct fire support, artillery and missile fire adjustment, command, communications, security, reconnaissance, and supply benefits.

Missions which General Howze believed to be appropriate for assignment to these airmobile—which he called air cavalry—units were: the seizure of critical terrain in advance of larger forces, delaying action and cover for the withdrawal of larger forces, raids, penetration of shallow enemy positions and the disruption of enemy rear areas, pursuit and exploitation, the protection of a long flank, and wide reconnaissance. He felt that new weapons developments would provide air cavalry units with destructive fire power. Air cavalry would be particularly appropriate in any battle area in which the threat of area weapons forced wide troop dispersion and in brush fire actions against relatively unsophisticated opponents.

To test the concept, General Howze recommended the formation of an experimental air cavalry unit in one of the airborne divisions. Assuming that the concept proved sound, he estimated that one air cavalry regiment consisting of about 175 utility helicopters and 85 light observation helicopters would be needed for each corps of 3 divisions. For the active Army this would mean about 5 regiments totaling about 875 utility and 425 light observation helicopters. General Howze admitted that this concept would be costly, but considered this development a vital requirement in the evolution of a modern Army.

The Rogers Board found that the aircraft acquisition objectives it had developed for the UH-1 and light observation helicopters were compatible with the development of General Howze's concept. Sufficient aircraft could be found in the existing inventory to permit activation of the proposed experimental unit. The Board recommended that DCSOPS, Department of the Army, and CONARC be directed to study the feasibility of the concept of air fighting units and their armament. They also were to look into the desirability of activating an experimental unit to test the feasibility and develop materiel requirements.

The aircraft procurement figures developed by the Rogers Board provided part of the basis for the training program later proposed by the Rogers Committee. Of greater importance, however, was the influence of the Rogers Board on the Howze Board two years later.[25]

Rogers Committee on Army Aviation

Following the completion of the work of the Rogers Board on aircraft requirements, the next logical step was to develop a training plan. On 28 July 1960, General Bruce C. Clarke, the Commanding General, CONARC, directed General Rogers to chair a committee to study the training requirements to support the Army Aviation Program, 1960-1970, developed by the Rogers Board earlier in the year. The Rogers Committee convened at Fort Monroe on 15 August and, in conjunction with working groups, continued in session until 22 December. Information was compiled from trips, special questionnaires, working group meetings, discussions, and interviews with selected individuals.

General Clarke directed the committee to submit appropriate findings and recommendations in the following areas: the degree to which Department of the Army approved operations and training programs for Army aviation were compatible with resources made available to CONARC; the adequacy and suitability of Army aviation construction programs to meet current and projected training requirements; the degree to which the current and projected training programs for Army aviation would provide the correct skills in the proper proportion to meet the requirements of the Department of the Army Aviation Program; and the extent of Army aviation activities that could be consolidated, reduced, or eliminated without significant loss of operational effectiveness.[26]

The committee submitted its final report on 22 December. It found that modifications to the current Army Aviation Training Program—which had been published on 19 September 1958 as part of the Army Aviation Guidelines for the Development of Doctrine and Organization Through Fiscal Year 1963—were necessary in order to provide the correct skills in the proper proportions to meet the requirements of the Department of the Army Aviation Program. The approved FY 1961 operation and training programs for Army aviation were not compatible with the resources made available to CONARC. The Army's current and planned construction programs were not adequate to meet the needs of the Army Aviation Program.

Based on these conclusions, the committee made numerous recommendations. Among the sixteen which the Commanding General, CONARC, could implement were the initiation of helicopter gunnery training in the advanced tactics phase of the observation and utility/transport helicopter course and the revision of the current preflight training program for warrant officer candidates, to include combined arms tactical training similar to that presented in existing officer candidate courses. The committee also recommended that the CONARC commander revise the current applicable programs of instruction of the service schools to provide detailed instruction of officers in duties and responsibilities for exercising command and tactical employment of Army aviation units.

The committee recommended the establishment of the aviation program as a designed program of special interest under an activity monitor to ensure coordination and timely actions in programing and budgeting. Two recommendations related specifically to training facilities. Programing actions were needed to provide additional resources at Camp Wolters, Fort Rucker, Fort Benning, or another suitable site to permit continuation of planned and future tests involving jet aircraft. The committee felt that plans should be developed for providing a long range Army aviation training complex to support the quantitative and qualitative growth potential and mobilization requirements of the expanding program.

In addition to actions which the CONARC commander could take, the committee made twenty recommendations for consideration by the Department of the Army, most of which were related to personnel changes. The committee recommended the establishment of the enlisted, officer, and warrant officer aviator requirements as valid planning objectives for the period through FY 1970 and the modification of the current imposed aviator rated ceilings in order to be in consonance with the recommended personnel planning objective.

A major problem since the beginning of Army aviation had been the maintenance of adequate career development for officer aviators. The committee recommended that officer aviators spend at least one year out of every five on basic branch material assignments in order to maintain branch proficiency and that the policy apply to all officer aviators through the grade of major. Assignments for colonel and lieutenant colonel would be dictated by requirements determined by the career branch. The committee also recommended modification of the grade distribution for officer aviators to provide qualified individuals in the program for the optimum period of time in order to reduce replacement training costs. Warrant officer aviators should be assigned to those branches of the service that had a requirement for them, and regulations pertaining to the current warrant officer career program should be revised to provide for an adequate warrant officer aviator career field. The committee proposed modification of the criteria to permit substitution of warrant officer aviators for certain officer aviator positions in combat and support type units, and the subsequent modification of the TOE to reflect these conversions. Further, the committee recommended a review and adjustment of warrant officer utilization after experience had been obtained and performance and utilization factors analyzed.

Like the findings of the Rogers Board, many of the recommendations of the Rogers Committee on Army Aviation were soon overtaken by events or were modified by the Howze Board in 1962. Nevertheless, the work accomplished by the committee provided the foundation for the rapid expansion of aviation training which was to take place in the 1960s.[27]

The Berlin Crisis

The partial mobilization of reserve forces and the expansion of the active Army in the fall of 1961 as a result of the crisis in Berlin created problems for Army aviation. Although plans were under development for an orderly long range expansion of the aviation program, the Berlin crisis required an immediate and unexpected expansion.

The Berlin crisis, which began to escalate in the summer of 1961, occurred at a most inopportune time for the Army. President John F. Kennedy, who had recently assumed office, directed a thorough reappraisal of strategic plans, force levels, and military programs with a view to determining their adequacy to fulfill commitments. He directed the Secretary of Defense to develop a force structure in harmony with United States military requirements. This structure was to be determined without regard to arbitrary or predetermined budget ceilings. At about the same time, the Army began to take steps to reorganize its tactical division organization as a result of experience with the PENTOMIC organization. The ROAD division would have greatly increased aviation assets.[28] Both the reappraisal of the force structure and the division reorganization would have a significant impact on the form and extent of the aviation program.

The Army build-up which resulted from the Berlin crisis mobilized 119,622 members of the reserve components and an increase of 86,481 in the active Army. Included in the reserve mobilization was the 32d Infantry Division and the 49th Armored Division. Most of the increase in the active Army went to bringing a 6 division STRAF force and the units in USAREUR to full strength. After considerable debate, the Department of Defense agreed to a permanent increase of two divisions in the force structure. This required the activation of the 5th Infantry Division and the 1st Armored Division in early 1962 so they could complete organization and training before the relief of the two National Guard divisions from active duty.

Problems were encountered in equipping the National Guard divisions, including a shortage of helicopters. The helicopter shortage also had a serious effect on several mobilized nondivisional units. One temporary solution was the redistribution of equipment from low priority units to those oriented to reinforcing Europe. For example, on 23 March 1962, the Department of the Army directed withdrawal of fifteen H-19 helicopters from active Army units and the further redistribution of ten H-19 helicopters within CONARC to meet the training requirements of four reserve medical air ambulance companies. The Department of the Army also diverted to those companies six new H-23D helicopters destined for the U.S. Army, Pacific.

An amendment to the FY 1962 budget permitted the Army to procure ten additional AO-1 surveillance aircraft and seventy-six H-23 observation helicopters. These aircraft were scheduled for delivery by 30 June 1962.[29]

Aviator Shortages

The buildup of the Army during 1961, coupled with past and projected shortfalls in programed inputs to the Army Aviation School, resulted in substantial shortages of aviators necessary to fill TOE/TD positions worldwide. The Army's end FY 1961 aviator strength was 6,531 against a requirement of 7,149. This disparity was expected to increase in FY 1962 when the anticipated strength of aviators would be approximately 6,700 versus a requirement for 7,900. Included in aviator requirements, in addition to allowances for training, transients, and patients, was a 20 percent factor which represented those aviators on branch qualifying ground duty. The Army was faced with the problem of meeting flying requirements at the expense of branch tours or vice versa. Long lead time training made it difficult to overcome these difficulties on a short term basis.

This critical shortage of aviators was reflected in CONARC units. To alleviate this shortage, the Department of the Army reemphasized aviator recruiting and provided additional guidance pertaining to applications for aviation duty and effective use of current assets. Another step taken was the training of additional warrant officer aviators and the conversion of certain commissioned officer spaces to warrant officers. CONARC directed the CONUS army commanders personally to encourage qualified lieutenants and enlisted men to volunteer for aviation training. Until increased procurement could ease the situation, effective use of available assets supplemented by exceptions to permanent change of station restrictions to reassign aviators returned to aviator duty afforded some relief. These measures resulted in some improvement in the situation by the end of FY 1962, but increased requirements placed a constant drain on resources.[30]

Mobilization of Reserve Aviation Units

Eight major Army aviation units were called to active duty for a period of one year during the partial mobilization in the fall of 1961. These units were:

Unit	Station
32d Aviation Company	Fort Lewis
32d Infantry Division	
149th Aviation Company	Fort Polk
49th Armored Division	
1063d Aviation Company	Fort Riley
136th Transportation Company	Fort Riley
24th Medical Company	Fort Leonard Wood
132d Medical Company	Fort Bragg
152d Medical Company	Fort Ord
317th Medical Company	Fort Sam Houston

The 136th Transportation Company and the 24th, 152d, and 317th Medical Companies were assigned to the STRAC. The 32d and 149th Aviation Companies, 1063d Transportation Company, and 132d Medical Company were assigned to an additional two-division force consisting of the 32d Infantry Division and the 49th Armored Division.

All of the mobilized aviation units experienced much the same problems. These mainly involved administration, qualification of personnel, lack of training, and shortages of equipment. Much difficulty was experienced in updating personnel records and procuring adequate copies of Army regulations, other administrative publications, and training publications. Flight records were often not forwarded to active duty stations, particularly for filler personnel. Incorrect and incomplete processing of flight physicals for filler personnel resulted in long delays in receiving flight status orders. A number of Army reserve aviators could not meet required medical standards.

A large number of enlisted men and some officers were assigned a duty MOS they were not capable of performing. Many primary MOSs had been awarded based on only two weeks of on-the-job training at a summer camp. A number of aviators who were former Navy or Air Force pilots had not attended the tactical flight training course at the Army Aviation School and did not qualify as Army aviators. Specific details as to service school requirements were not known in most units. As a result, in many cases quotas were available, but requirements were unknown to higher headquarters.

Preparation Overseas Replacement (POR) and Preparation Overseas Movement (POM) training had not been emphasized while in reserve status. A delay in the regular training program resulted after the unit reported for active duty until such required training was complete. Few aviators in helicopter units were qualified in anything but the observation helicopter. Individuals generally were not qualified in their primary MOS. Delays were experienced in sending these people to school. In many cases, unit training was handicapped by the temporary loss of these men while in school. Shortages of equipment, including aircraft, excessively delayed training.

Existing critical shortages of aircraft and support equipment were exacerbated by the call-up. Although aircraft were redistributed within the active Army and large numbers of observation helicopters were withdrawn from the National Guard, it was still impossible to attain full authorizations of aircraft. All aviation units attained a reasonable degree of training readiness despite equipment shortages.[31]

Deployments to Europe

By January 1962, more than 40,000 active Army troops had been sent to Europe as part of the Berlin buildup. Included in these deployments were three Army aviation units, the 90th Transportation Company (medium helicopter) from Fort Knox, the 45th Medical Company (air ambulance) from Fort Bragg, and the 15th Medical Detachment (helicopter ambulance) from Fort Ord.

After lengthy high level discussion, the decision was made to preposition equipment in Europe for two additional divisions and ten nondivisional units rather than actually deploying the units. Full authorizations of H-34 and L-20 aircraft were prepositioned in USAREUR for the 4th Infantry Division and the 2d Armored Division. At the same time, efforts were made to modernize the equipment of the forces permanently stationed in Europe. Despite the serious shortages of aircraft in CONUS, quantities of UH-1 helicopters and AO-1 airplanes were sent to Europe during this period.[32]

With the release of the mobilized reserve component units and individuals in August 1962, the permanent strength of the Active Army was established at 960,000 men. For the force structure, this meant an increase of 90,000 men and two divisions. Except for the aviation units for the two new divisions, there was no immediate impact on the Army aviation program which had been developed before the mobilization. The experience gained during the mobilization, however, would be of use three years later when the rapid expansion for Vietnam began.

Southeast Asia Deployments

Even while attention was focused on Berlin and preparations to reinforce Europe, another major crisis was developing. Organized Communist guerrillas threatened to overthrow the government of the Republic of Vietnam. The United States developed counter-measures to meet this increased Communist threat and gave increasing support in equipment and advisor teams to the established government.

At the same time that the Berlin crisis was causing the deployment of aviation units to Europe, the deteriorating situation in Vietnam led to the deployment of six Army aviation units to Southeast Asia. These units were:

Unit	Station	Date
8th Trans Co	Fort Bragg	20 Nov 61
57th Trans Co	Fort Lewis	8 Nov 61
93d Trans Co	Fort Devens	24 Nov 61
18th Avn Co	Fort Riley	14 Jan 62
HHD, 4th Trans Bn	Fort Sill	8 Jan 62
57th Med Det	Fort Meade	8 Mar 62

These units originally deployed on a temporary change of station basis, a status subsequently changed to permanent change of station. In addition, the 33d Transportation Company at Fort Ord was alerted for movement to USARPAC on 15 March 1962, an order which was canceled a week later.[33]

Accomplishments of the Period

The years from 1954 to 1962 proved to be crucial to the development of Army aviation. Although disputes regarding missions and functions continued with the Air Force, the decision of Secretary Wilson in fact gave the Army authority to form and equip the types of aviation units which suited its needs.

Of key importance was General Ridgway's order to formulate a coherent Army aviation plan. Though the plan encountered obstacles and appeared at various times under various guises, it provided for the first time an overall program for the development, expansion, and use of Army aviation. The program developed during this period was limited by the technical limitations of available aircraft. By 1960, however, greatly improved aircraft were becoming available which increased the capabilities of the Army's air arm. The recommendations of the Rogers Board and Rogers Committee pointed the way to an even more expanded aviation program in the following decade. Even though the Howze Board was to radically change the course of Army aviation, the findings of this board were based upon the foundations established by General Ridgway's aviation plan and the Rogers reports.

The formation and deployment of aviation units during the Berlin crisis and the first year of active United States involvement in Southeast Asia was on a limited scale. Nevertheless, the experience gained in these actions was to prove valuable in the following years during the dramatic expansion of Army aviation to meet requirements in Southeast Asia.

The planning and program development at the Department of Defense, Department of the Army, and CONARC would have been of limited practical value with the organization which existed in 1954. In the following chapter, the organizational changes at Department of the Army, Transportation Corps, and CONARC levels necessary to carry out the expanded Army aviation program will be examined. From the Department of the Army down to company level, significant changes took place to reflect the new doctrine, equipment, and role of Army aviation.

Endnotes
Chapter VIII

1. General Matthew B. Ridgway, *Soldier: The Memoirs of Matthew B. Ridgway* (New York: Harper & Brothers, 1956), pp. 298-299, 312-315.

2. Army Ground Forces was redesignated the Office of the Chief of Army Field Forces on 10 March 1948. OCAFF was the field operating agency of the Department of the Army within CONUS for the general supervision, coordination, and inspection of the training of all units and individuals employed in a field army. OCAFF also retained functions relating to the development of tactical and technical doctrine and the supervision of research and development. The six CONUS armies and the Military District of Washington were made major commands under the direct control of the Chief of Staff of the Army. Jean R. Moenk, *A History of Command and Control of Army Forces in the Continental United States 1919-1972* (CONARC: 15 Aug 72), p. 29 (hereafter cited as Moenk, *Command and Control*).

3. (1) DA ACofS G-3 Army Avn Div Summary of Major Events and Problems, FY 55, p. 1 (TOP SECRET—Info used is UNCLASSIFIED) (2) CONARC Summary of Major Events and Problems, FY 55, G-3 Sec Doc and Req Div, Jul-Dec 54, p. 7.

4. (1) CONARC Summary of Major Events and Problems, FY 55, Vol. IV, Cbt Dev Sec Gen Div, Jul-Dec 54, p. 4. (2) Richard P. Weinert, *A History of Army Aviation, 1950-1962: Phase I: 1950- 1954*, CONARC, Jun 71, pp. 52-55 (hereafter cited as Weinert, *Army Aviation*).

5. The Office of the Chief of Army Field Forces was reorganized and redesignated as Headquarters, Continental Army Command, on 1 February 1955. The command had responsibility over the six armies in the continental United States, the Military District of Washington, and such other units, activities, and installations as were assigned by the Department of the Army. See Moenk, *Command and Control*, pp. 35-36.

6. (1) DA ACofS C-3 Summary of Major Events and Problems, FY 55, Army Avn Div, p. 1 (TOP SECRET—Info used is UNCLASSIFIED). (2) Ltr G-3 AV PO 1, DA G-3 to CG CONARC, 16 Feb 55, subj: Army Aviation Plan. (3) History U.S. Army Aviation Center and Army Aviation School, 1954-1964, pp. 24,50.

7. CONARC Summary of Major Events and Problems, FY 55, Vol. VI, G-3 Sec Tng Div, Jan-Jun 55, p. 15.

8. For a discussion of Project ABLE BUSTER, see below.

9. (1) CONARC Summary of Major Events and Problems, FY 56, Vol. IV, Cbt Dev Sec Div, Jul-Dec 55, p. 6. (2) Ltr ATSWD-G 360(C), CG CONARC to DA ACofS G-3, 10 Dec 55, subj: Army Aviation Plan.

10. (1) MFR, DA DCSOPS, 25 Jun 56, subj: Conference Aviation Plan FY 56-60. (2) CONARC Summary of Major Events and Problems, FY 56, Vol VIII, Cbt Dev Sec Gen Div, Jan-Jun 56, p. 1. (3) DA DCSOPS Summary of Major Events and Problems, FY 56, Army Avn Dir, p. 1. (TOP SECRET—Info used is UNCLASSIFIED).

11. For a description of SKY CAV and Exercise SLEDGE HAMMER, see below.

12. CONARC Summary of Major Events and Problems, FY 57, Vol. II, Army Avn Sec, Oct-Dec 56, pp. 3-5.

13. (1) CONARC Summary of Major Events and Problems, FY 57, Vol. II, Army Avn Sec, Oct-Dec 56, pp. 2-3. (2) DA DCSOPS Summary of Major Events and Problems, FY 57, Army Avn Dir, p. 2 (TOP SECRET—Info used is UNCLASSIFIED).

14. Weinert, *Army Aviation,* pp. 12, 24-26, 48-49.

15. (1) Draft ms, History of Army Aviation, Ch VII, pp. 41-43, in CMH files. (2) DA DCSOPS Army Avn Dir Summary of Major Events and Problems, FY 57, pp. 1-2.

16. (1) A Short History of Close Air Support Issues, HQ USACDC, Jul 68, pp. 44-45. (2) Charles H. Donnelly, *United States Defense Policies Since World War II* (Washington: Government Printing Office, 1957), p. 74. (3) Charles H. Donnelly, *United States Defense Policies in 1957* (Washington: Government Printing Office, 1958), pp. 65-66.

17. *United States Defense Policies in 1960* (Washington: Government Printing Office, 1961), pp. 79-80.

18. For a discussion of ATFA, see below.

19. (1) CONARC Summary of Major Events and Problems, FY 56, Vol. II, G-3 Sec Org & Equip Div, Jul-Dec 55. (2) Draft ms, History of Army Aviation, Ch VIII, pp. 7-9, in CMH files. (3) Camp Rucker was redesignated Fort Rucker and established as a permanent Department of the Army installation on 13 October 1955.

20. CONARC Summary of Major Events and Problems, FY 55, Vol I, Introductory Narrative, Pt B, pp. 33-34; Vol II, G-3 Sec Trn Div Sp Tng Br, p. 6; and Vol VI, G-3 Sec Tng Div, p. 15.

21. AR 600-105, Army Aviation Officer Career Program, 21 Aug 59.

22. DA ODCSPER Summary of Major Events and Problems, FY 60, pp. 142-144.

23. See below.

24. Three of the six divisions that formed the Strategic Army Forces (STRAF) in CONUS were reduced in strength and lacked essential combat support; their main function was training recruits. The other three divisions formed the STRAC, a CONUS-based reserve maintained to meet immediate force development requirements of cold, limited, or general war. At this time it was composed of approximately 115,000 men in the Headquarters, XVIII Airborne Corps, and the 82d Airborne Division, 101st Airborne Division, and 4th Infantry Division. U.S. Army Expansion, 1961-1962, OCMH, 1963, p. 22.

25. (1) Ltr, Lt Gen Gordon B. Rogers to CofSA, 10 Mar 60, subj: Army Aircraft Requirements Review Board. (2) CONARC Summary of Major Events and Problems, FY 60, Vol V, Mat Dev Sec Army Avn & Abn Div, Jan-Jun 60, p. 6. (3) DA DCSOPS Summary of Major Events and Problems, FY 60, pp. C-1 to C-6 (TOP SECRET—Info used is UNCLASSIFIED).

26. (1) CONARC Summary of Major Events and Problems, FY 61, Vol VI, Army Avn Sec, Jul-Dec 60, pp. 12-13. (2) Ltr ATCG, CG CONARC to Lt Gen Gordon B. Rogers, 28 Jul 60, subj: Directive for the Conduct of a Study of Training in Support of the Army Aviation Program of the Department of the Army.

27. Ltr, Lt Gen Gordon B. Rogers to CG CONARC, 22 Dec 60, subj: Requirements for Training in Support of the Army Aviation Program, 1960-1970.

28. For a discussion of the PENTOMIC and ROAD organization, see below.

29. U.S. Army Expansion, 1961-1962, pp. 9, 26, 78-80, 164-165, 223-224, 240-241, 245, 254.

30. (1) CONARC Summary of Major Events and Problems, FY 62, Vol II, DCSPER P&D Div, Jul-Dec 61, pp. 13-14, and Dist Div, Jan-Jun 62, p. 12. (2) DA DCSOPS Dir of Army Avn Summary of Major Events and Problems, FY 61, p. B-III-2 (TOP SECRET—Info used is UNCLASSIFIED).

31. CONARC Summary of Major Events and Problems, FY 62, Vol VI, Army Avn Sec, Jan-May 62, pp. 1-3.

32. (1) U.S. Army Expansion, 1961-1962, pp. 187, 263. (2) CONARC Summary of Major Events and Problems, FY 62, Vol VI, Army Avn Sec, Jan-May 62, p. 4.

33. (1) U.S. Army Expansion, 1961-1962, p. 5. (2) CONARC Summary of Major Events and Problems, FY 62, Vol VI, Army Avn Sec, Jan-May 62, pp. 4-5.

Chapter IX

ORGANIZATIONAL DEVELOPMENT

Since its beginning, organizational responsibility for Army aviation had been badly fragmented at all levels of command. With the rapid growth of Army aviation following the end of the Korean War, a better organizational structure emerged. The key element in this reorganization was the approval by the Chief of Staff of the Army in January 1955 of the establishment of an aviation division in the Department of the Army G-3 for overall staff supervision. The Director of Army Aviation in G-3 became the focal point of all Department of the Army actions relating to the program. Army aviator assignment authority was also centralized in the Department of the Army G-1.

At the CONARC level, most of the functions related to Army aviation were drawn together into an Army Aviation Section in the special staff in October 1956. The Army Aviation Center, including an aviation test board, was established at Fort Rucker in February 1955. Of vital importance to the growth of Army aviation was the assumption by the Army of depot maintenance and supply responsibilities and certain changes in procurement control procedures.[1]

A significant expansion of Transportation Corps activities in regard to Army aviation also took place. The assumption of depot responsibility from the Air Force led to the establishment by the Transportation Corps of an extensive aviation maintenance and supply system. Management of this system was centralized in the Transportation Supply and Maintenance Command at St. Louis. The Transportation Corps also had a number of other field agencies which were devoted to varying degrees to different aspects of aviation transportation.

The expanding tactical use of Army aviation was reflected in the organization of the combat field elements of the Army. As the Army division evolved from the triangular organization of World War II and Korea to the AFTA concept, the PENTOMIC divisions, and finally the ROAD divisions, the aviation component in the division structure steadily increased. In addition to the aviation expansion in division organizations, new separate Army aviation units were developed in response to equipment improvements and new concepts in the employment of aviation.

Organization Changes in the Department of the Army

The Army Aviation Branch, Organization and Training Division, in the Office of the Assistant Chief of Staff, G-3, had been established in the Department of the Army on 21 April 1954. Within the year, the expanded use of aviation, particularly in combat elements, greatly increased the size, scope, and complexity of G-3's responsibilities in relation to Army aviation. General Ridgway in January 1955, as a result of the comprehensive review of the aviation program, directed that Army aviation functions be consolidated in one element of the staff in order to give the program greater visibility and to provide firmer supervision.

As a result of General Ridgway's decision, on 1 February the Army Aviation Branch was discontinued and a separate Army Aviation Division was created in G-3. To indicate the importance of the program and of the Army Aviation Division, it was to be headed by a general officer. The division was established with an authorization of 11 officers, 1 warrant officer, and 5 civilians.

The general officer position was not immediately filled, and on 3 January 1956 the Army Aviation Division was expanded into a Directorate of Army Aviation. Maj. Gen. Hamilton H. Howze was appointed the first Director of Army Aviation. Although not an aviator himself at the time of his appointment, General Howze was to become the key figure in the growth of Army aviation during the next six years. The directorate originally had the same staff as the Army Aviation Division, but in March 1956 a manpower control survey authorized three additional military and two additional civilian spaces.[2]

In addition to the G-3, which became the Deputy Chief of Staff for Operations in 1956, several other elements of the Army staff were concerned with Army aviation. The Chief of Research and Development was directly responsible to the Chief of Staff of the Army for the overall supervision of all Army research and development programs. In this capacity, he assisted and coordinated the many activities of the Transportation Corps and CONARC related to the development of aircraft and equipment for the Army aviation program.

The Assistant Chief of Staff, G-1, who became the Deputy Chief of Staff for Personnel in 1956, had responsibility for the assignment of aviation personnel. The expansion of the aviation personnel program posed problems which had to be resolved at a high staff level. The responsibilities of the Department of the Army G-1 included recruiting new personnel for the program, managing the careers of those in it, and screening records of officers of doubtful future value.[3]

Organization Changes in the Transportation Corps

The Office of the Chief of Transportation had been reorganized early in 1953 when the Transportation Corps assumed logistical responsibility for Army aircraft from the Ordnance Corps. To direct the Transportation Corps' Army aviation activities, including staff and technical control of the field installations involved, and Air Transport Division, monitored by the Assistant Chief of Transportation for Operations, was established.

Because of the newness of the mission and the rapid growth of the program, Army aviation was temporarily excluded from the reorganization of the Transportation Corps in the fall of 1953. In view of the growing program, however, the position of Assistant Chief of Transportation (Army Aviation) was created in March 1954. He directed the activities of the Army Aviation Division (a redesignation of the Air Transport Service Division) and supervised the Transportation Corps Army aviation field installations. The Army Aviation Division consisted of the following components: Plans and Programs Office, Training Branch, Engineering and Development Branch, Procurement and Supply Branch, and Maintenance Branch.

To handle procurement and production, supply control, and maintenance functions of the program in the field, the Transportation Corps established the Transportation Corps Army Aviation Field Service Office (TCAAFSO). This field agency, located at St. Louis, began operations in January 1953.[4]

When the Transportation Corps began planning in 1954 to assume the depot functions from the Air Force, one of its first considerations was the organizational realignment of materiel functions. The separate Army aviation structure had been regarded as a temporary expedient, and one which was fundamentally at variance with the basically functional organization of the Transportation Corps. Action to combine TCAAFSO with the Transportation Materiel Command—which was only concerned with surface materiel—and to consolidate materiel functions in the Office of the Chief of Transportation had been deferred pending the attainment of a greater degree of maturity in the aviation logistic support mission. Since two of the three planned transportation sections at the general depots would soon be handling air as well as surface items, the Transportation Corps deemed essential that the merger of the two field elements be accomplished prior to the scheduled initiation of the interservice transfer of responsibilities on 1 July 1955. Office space limitations and the pressure of time, however, made an immediate physical merger impossible. As an interim measure, a joint skeleton staff, drawn from both field commands, was formed to build and develop the new headquarters and to make detailed plans for the phased integration of the two commands. The Transportation Supply and Maintenance Command (TSMC) was established at St. Louis on 1 March 1955, and was placed in command of TCAAFSO and the Transportation Materiel Command. By 1 July, though the absorption of the commands was still in progress, TSMC had attained operational status.

At the same time, a focal point in the Office of the Chief of Transportation was established for the direction and guidance of the new field agency. In the spring and summer of 1955, responsibilities pertaining to procurement, production, and supply distribution of Transportation Corps air materiel were transferred from the Army Aviation Division to the Supply and Maintenance Division.

Experience after the assumption of depot responsibility pointed to defects in this organization. Along with other responsibilities relating to the Army aviation program, the Army Aviation Division continued to handle end item requirements determination, engineer change proposals, monitoring of aircraft utilization, and the computation of flying hour factors. Although there was some shifting of functions from the Army Aviation Division to materiel elements in the

Office of the Chief of Transportation and TSMC, these problems were not fully resolved until late 1958. At that time, the Army Aviation Division was discontinued, and its remaining materiel functions were turned over to the Supply and Maintenance Division. At the same time, the position of Assistant Chief of Transportation (Army Aviation) was discontinued and functions relating to training and military personnel were given to the Training and Organization and Military Personnel Divisions. Remaining staff functions dealing with overall planning and coordination and systems analysis were brought directly under the Deputy Chief of Transportation for Aviation, a position which had been established in August 1958 to give direction to all phases of the Transportation Corps' Army aviation program.[5]

On 1 July 1959, the Transportation Corps underwent another reorganization. The position of Deputy Chief of Transportation for Aviation was retained to serve as the Chief of Transportation's principal assistant and advisor on Army aviation. The Deputy Chief of Transportation for Aviation continued to be responsible for the execution of approved plans and programs pertaining to all phases of the Transportation Corps Army aviation program. He evaluated overall policies and practices in the light of objectives and progress achieved, making changes in the best interest of the Chief of Transportation. To fulfill this responsibility, he coordinated Transportation Corps activities with the other Army agencies involved in Army aviation.

The Assistant Chief of Transportation (Military Operations) was responsible for development of concept and doctrine, preparation of plans, and supervision of the Transportation Corps portion of the Army Aviation Training Program, and also directed military personnel activities. Aviation activity constituted the major responsibility of the Assistant Chief of Transportation for Materiel. He was responsible for timely and adequate materiel support by the Transportation Corps; for staff and technical supervision over materiel, standardization, requirements, cataloging, procurement, production, supply distribution, storage and depot operations, maintenance, and disposal; and for industrial mobilization activities. The Transportation Supply and Maintenance Command was redesignated as the Transportation Materiel Command in October 1959 and actually performed this mission. The Assistant Chief of Transportation for Research and Development was responsible for the development and execution of the research and development program for all Army aviation.

Following the FY 1959 reorganization, the Chief of Transportation and the Assistant Chief of Transportation for Materiel investigated TSMC and provided suggestions for helping the command control its serious problems. These problems had also led to investigation by the Army Inspector General in March 1959 and the General Accounting Office in September. A Department of the Army DCSLOG team inspected the National Inventory Control Point in October and by the end of 1960, most of these problems had been solved or were well on the way to solution.

The major complaint about organization and management concerned the Procurement and Production Division of the Transportation Materiel Command which had divided its aircraft procurement staffs and lacked quality control and cost analysis offices. These defects were remedied. To shorten the commander's span of control, four deputy commanders were appointed, one to handle administration, another supply management, a third maintenance, and the fourth research, development, and testing. The investigators also noted the lack of maturity and skills among procurement and maintenance personnel, a problem which TSMC had begun to attack during FY 1958. About 500 jobs were reevaluated. An accelerated and intensive recruiting program, with schooling for about 125 individuals in various procurement and maintenance management courses, laid the basis for orderly progress. The publication of a handbook of principles for Transportation Corps commodity managers also helped.

These basic management improvements were essential for better supply effectiveness, procurement, and maintenance, but more important, they were mandatory to the assumption of further responsibilities in Army aviation support.

In addition to the Transportation Materiel Command, the Transportation Corps had several other field agencies devoted to Army aviation. The Transportation Research and Engineering Command at Fort Eustis contained an Aviation Division which conducted research and development related to Army aircraft. The command was subsequently redesignated the Transportation Research Command. The Transportation Army Aviation Coordinating Office at Wright-Patterson Air Force Base, Ohio, provided coordination for the Chief of Transportation and Transportation Corps agencies with certain agencies of the Air Force and the Navy. This office supervised the execution of the Army's research and development program performed for the Army by the Air Force, Navy, and Civil Aeronautics Administration. The Transportation Aircraft Test and Support Activity at Fort Rucker came under the control of the Transportation Materiel Command. Its primary mission was the conduct of phase F (logistical evaluation) tests of new types of aircraft. These tests were conducted to determine service life of components, inspection cycles, improve technical publications, and to develop quick change kits and modifications. The Transportation Training Command and Transportation School located at Fort Eustis were responsible for maintenance training and training in other aspects of Transportation Corps mission relating to aviation.[6]

The 1962 reorganization of the Army abolished the Office of the Chief of Transportation. Transportation Corps functions relating to training were transferred to CONARC, those relating to logistics were transferred to the United States Army Materiel Command, and those involving research and development were split between the United States Army Materiel Command and the United States Army Combat Developments Command.

Organization Changes in CONARC

Establishment of Army Aviation Section

The establishment of the Director of Army Aviation at the Department of the Army level in January 1956 had a direct impact on CONARC. A difference of opinion existed between CONARC and the Department of the Army as to the direction the Army aviation program should take.

On 28 May 1956, General Willard G. Wyman, the CONARC commander, wrote to General W. B. Palmer, the Vice Chief of Staff of the Army, regarding future functions and responsibilities of CONARC. General Howze had recently visited the headquarters to urge that the rapid expansion of Army aviation required a special degree of coordination at each level of command. He felt that the lack of an identifiable coordinating agency at CONARC was a missing link in the structure. While General Wyman did not agree completely with General Howze's views, he took the opportunity to suggest to General Palmer that if the G-3 Aviation Division continued in the operational and training fields it properly belonged at the CONARC level. General Wyman agreed that the procurement and distribution of aircraft, together with worldwide analysis of aircraft utilization, availability of aviation personnel, and correlated matters, belonged at the Department of the Army level. General Wyman believed, however, that action to relieve difficulties that arose in organization and training, establishment and review of training policies, and all other functions pertaining to Army aviation in the United States were CONARC's responsibility, except for broad supervision at the Department of the Army level. Instead of establishing a distinct aviation element in CONARC headquarters, General Wyman urged the transfer of the G-3 Aviation Division to CONARC. He informed General Palmer that this would require no increase in space allocations and might possibly lead to some reductions.

The Department of the Army did not favorably consider General Wyman's suggestion to transfer the Army Aviation Division to CONARC. General Palmer informed the CONARC commander that there were many aspects of the aviation program which would have to be handled by the Department of the Army, even if the division were transferred to CONARC. He recognized CONARC's responsibilities in the indicated areas and told Wyman to establish an Army aviation section at CONARC. But General Palmer made it clear that there would be no transfer of Department of the Army functions relating to Army aviation to CONARC.[7]

The Army Aviation Section of Headquarters, CONARC, was organized on 22 October 1956, consisting of the Training, Operation, Doctrine, and Organization Division; the Materiel, Maintenance, and Supply Division; and the Administrative and Analysis Division. The mission of the section was to advise the commanding general and the staff on matters pertaining to Army aviation activities; within established policies, direct and control courses, curricula, and instruction at Army aviation schools; review and revise existing organization, doctrine, tactics, and techniques; determine the state of training of individuals and units; determine and formulate requirements for product improvement of materiel; and assist appropriate staff sections in the direction, coordination, and inspection of Army aviation activities. The section had an authorized strength of 1 general officer, 2 colonels, 2 lieutenant colonels, 4 majors, 1 master sergeant, and 5 civilians. The general officer space was not filled and CONARC subsequently revised the authorized strength to 4 colonels, 2 lieutenant colonels, 3 majors, 1 warrant officer, and 5 civilians.

On 4 April 1957, Army Regulation 10-7 established new policies, functions, and activities for the organization and functions of CONARC. Basically, the new regulation covered the same aviation activities and functions as before. The scope of the aviation activities, however, was expanded to provide specifically for the direction, supervision, coordination, and inspection of all matters pertaining to organization and training of all Army aviation units and personnel within CONUS, except Army aviation activities directly assigned to the Chief of Transportation.[8]

Prior to the establishment of this section, responsibilities for aviation had been diffused throughout the headquarters. Although the various general and special staff sections retained the same functions and responsibilities for aviation as for other arms, services, and activities, the Army Aviation Section served as the focal point for this rapidly growing, complex, and many-sided field.

During 1961, the Army Aviation Section was reorganized and given a more detailed statement of missions and functions. The number of divisions in the section was increased to four: Program, Safety, and Airspace; Materiel, Facilities, and Armament; Training; and Organization, Plans, and Doctrine.

The mission of the Army Aviation Section was now stated in the following terms: The Army Aviation Officer advises the Commanding General and the staff on Army Aviation and air space matters, provides staff supervision over Army Aviation operations throughout the Command and assists the general staff in actions involving Army Aviation activities and functions.[9]

The Army Aviation Section was responsible for exercising direction, supervision, coordination, and inspection of all matters pertaining to the organization and training of Army aviation units and personnel within the continental United States, except for those Army aviation units and personnel directly associated with field and depot maintenance and supply and those aviation activities directly assigned to the Chief of Transportation. It recommended to the Deputy Chief of Staff for Operations, Plans, and Training appropriate aviation elements for operational, training, and other missions.

The section was responsible for the preparation, review, and revision of current and proposed organization, doctrine, tactics, techniques, and training literature for all Army aviation type units involving the employment of organic manned and unmanned aircraft. It directed and controlled the courses, curricula, and instruction at the Army Aviation School and CONARC aviation courses of instruction to include those operated under civilian contract.

The Army Aviation Section initiated and coordinated qualitative materiel requirements as well as requirements for product improvement for air support operations involving the employment of organic manned and unmanned aircraft. It prepared detailed comments and recommendations on feasibility studies; proposed military characteristics; items under development; plans for user (service and troop) tests; reports of user and engineering tests and classification of materiel as to type; and basis of issue. The section also prepared and supervised tactical troop tests and combined troop tested of units and equipment.

The Army Aviation Officer recommended to the Deputy Chief of Staff for Operations, Plans, and Training priorities for the allocation of critical items of equipment and allocation of equipment and aircraft for training of units and individuals of the active Army, reserve components, and the ROTC. The section ensured that the organization and training program of

Army aviation fixed wing and rotary wing transport units and organic aviation sections and units and the availability of equipment were coordinated.

The section established and implemented the CONARC Army Aviation Safety Program; reviewed accident investigation reports on aircraft under operational control of CONARC; and reviewed aircraft accident report analyses, determining adequacy of corrective action taken and recommending further action. It reviewed plans for the activation, organization, and stationing of Army aviation units and submitted comments and recommendations thereon to the Deputy Chief of Staff for Operations, Plans, and Training.

The growing Army interest in air traffic control was shown by the responsibility for directing, coordinating, reviewing all matters pertaining to and affecting the establishment, utilization, retention, modification, and revocation of Army assigned airspace at all Army installations within the continental United States. The section also exercised direction, review, and revision of flight regulations for Army aircraft operations within the continental United States.

The Army Aviation Section assisted other staff elements in the preparation of personnel and MOS training requirements for training and mobilization; tables of distribution and allotment of personnel required to conduct instruction at schools and training commands; Army extension course programs and extension course material; policy governing attendance of personnel at schools, quotas, and prerequisites for attendance; new concepts of organization, doctrine, tactics, and techniques; mobilization and capabilities plans and primary programs; programs and procedures concerned with supply of units; training and maintenance directives and guidance to include Army training programs and Army training tests; policy, doctrine, and procedures affecting the Reserve Components and ROTC; and logistic actions incident to training or operation of aviation units or schools.

In coordination with the appropriate staff sections, the Army Aviation Section reviewed policies concerning the allocation and assignment of officers, warrant officers, and enlisted men of Army aviation; procedures pertaining to the flow of officers, warrant officers, and enlisted men into, through, and out of the Army aviation training system; instruction pertaining to Army aviation at other schools; Army aviation aspects of the CONARC Human Research and Operations Research Office activities; requests, requirements, and assignment of tasks placed upon the Army Aviation School and courses; and operational and training concepts and requirements to ensure that they were integrated into the systems management programs for Army aircraft.[10]

Although the Army Aviation Section was the CONARC staff element mainly responsible for Army aviation, many other offices were involved with the program to a varying degree. The rapid changes in aviation equipment and organization intimately involved the Organization and Equipment Division and the Doctrine and Requirements Division of the G-3 Section, the General Division of the Combat Developments Section, and the Army Aviation and Airborne Division of the Materiel Developments Section. The G-2 Section and the Transportation Section also became involved in various Army aviation matters. The organization of

Headquarters, CONARC, before the advent of the Army Aviation Section (1955) and at two later dates (1957 and 1959) is shown in charts 1, 2, and 3.

1962 Reorganization

During 1962, a major reorganization of the Army took place which established the United States Army Materiel Command, placed the technical service schools—including the Transportation School—under the command of CONARC, and removed the combat development function from CONARC with the establishment of the United States Army Combat Developments Command. This organization of the Army was to remain unchanged until 1973.

The reorganization eliminated all special staff sections, including the Army Aviation Section, within Headquarters, CONARC. Aviation staff officers were decentralized throughout the headquarters, but there was an Aviation Division in the Office of the Deputy Chief of Staff for Unit Training and Readiness. The Aviation Division consisted of four branches: Training Branch, Plans and Operations Branch, Aviation Safety and Airspace Branch, and Equipment Requirements Branch. The functions of the division remained much the same as in the old Army Aviation Section except for the removal of the responsibility for individual training to the Office of the Deputy Chief of Staff for Individual Training and doctrinal matters to the United States Army Combat Developments Command.[11]

Establishment of the Army Aviation Center

As a result of recommendations submitted by the Chief of Army Field Forces to the Department of the Army in the fall of 1954, an Army Aviation Center was established at Camp Rucker, the site of the Army Aviation School, during the latter half of fiscal year 1955. Establishment of this center was expected to aid materially in the successful conduct of operations of the Army Aviation School in support of the continuing expansion of Army aviation as an element of the Army's field forces.

While the Army Aviation Center was officially established, effective 1 February 1955, by Department of the Army General Orders 17, 2 March 1955, the mission and proposed elements of the center were not officially determined until near the end of the fiscal year. As recommended by CONARC on 18 March and approved by the Department of the Army on 12 April, the Army Aviation Center comprised the following major elements: Army Aviation Center Headquarters; Army Aviation School; school troops; and the Army Aviation Flight Safety Board.[12]

The U.S. Army Aviation Flight Safety Board, consisting of 2 officers, 1 enlisted man, and 2 civilians, had originated at Fort Sill, before the transfer of the school, as the Aircraft Accident Review Board. Until 24 September 1956, the mission for the organization, operation, and support of the Army Aviation Flight Safety Board was vested in the Army Aviation School. The establishment of the responsibility for prescribing and coordinating safe practice and safe operating standards applicable to flight operations of Army aircraft in the Office of the Director of Army Aviation, Department of the Army, resulted in a reevaluation of the mission of the Army Aviation Safety Board.

As a result of this reevaluation, and with the concurrence of CONARC, the board was reorganized and transferred to the Army Aviation Center, effective 24 September 1956. AR 15-76, 3 January 1957, announced the establishment of this board and the mission, composition, tasks, direction, and control and administrative responsibility for its operation. On 25 April 1957, the Army Aviation Safety Board was officially established as a Class II activity at Fort Rucker under the jurisdiction of the Deputy Chief of Staff for Military Operations, Department of the Army, to conduct research and determine what improvements could be made in aviation materiel, operations, supervision, personnel, and training. Based on this research, the board recommended appropriate actions to enhance the durability, reliability, and efficiency of Army aviation, particularly in its combat environment. The board was authorized direct communications with any agency or individual on aircraft accidents, accident investigation, and accident prevention, to accomplish this mission. On 25 July 1957, the board was redesignated as the U.S. Army Board for Aviation Accident Research (USABAAR).[13]

Aircraft Systems Management

On 28 February 1957, the Department of the Army proposed to CONARC the establishment of a coordinating board for new Army aircraft. So it was that during the second half of FY 1957, CONARC assisted the Department of the Army in laying groundwork for the establishment of a system under which all significant actions pertaining to a given type or model of Army aircraft—from the time of introduction into the Army inventory until withdrawal as a result of obsolescence—would be accomplished in accordance with a program developed well in advance of the time at which the various actions were to be taken.

The Department of the Army proposed that the introduction of specific aircraft should be accompanied by a board created to monitor all phases of the introduction of the item, from the time of issuance of development contracts through the cycle of procurement, distribution, and utilization in training and operations. CONARC concurred in the need for coordinating action within the Army to cover all phases of the introduction and utilization of new types of aircraft and allied equipment, but did not favor the creation of an individual board for each item.

Instead, CONARC recommended that a long range committee be established to draw up a phased program applicable to the development of aircraft and associated equipment and for the introduction of these items into the Army inventory. The timing of such a program would be based on backward planning from the date established for initial distribution of production items. The program would set the time such actions as funding, revision of TOEs, development of ground support equipment, changes in doctrine, and arrangement for factory training of mechanics and instructor personnel should be initiated and completed. CONARC also contemplated that the specific responsibility for each such action would be established and the program published as an Army regulation.

A conference, which included representatives from the principal Department of the Army general staff divisions, CONARC, and the Chief of Transportation, was held at DCSOPS, Department of the Army, on 27 March. The conferees determined that the guiding agency, at least for launching the program, should be the Army Aircraft Systems Coordinating Group, composed of representation from the Deputy Chiefs of Staff for Personnel and Logistics, Department of the Army, CONARC, and the Chief of Transportation, and chaired by a DCSOPS, Department of the Army, representative.

At the suggestion of CONARC, it was agreed that a draft Army regulation should be prepared to identify the types of actions which would be taken under an Aircraft Systems Management Program and to determine the proponency for and timing of the required actions. As a framework within which the Aircraft Systems Management Program would operate, it was decided that a master schedule for phasing out and replacing all current aircraft types should be prepared. The Chief of Transportation was given the tasks of preparing the draft regulation and the aircraft replacement schedule, with such assistance as he might require from other agencies. On 4 June, CONARC officially concurred in the establishment of the proposed Aircraft Systems Coordinating Group and designated a principal and alternate member.[14]

Doctrine on Employment of Army Transport Aviation

On 9 July 1954, the Department of the Army requested OCAFF to prepare training literature for the employment of helicopter companies as tactical combat units. As an initial step toward meeting the requirement for training literature which reflected concepts on the employment of Army transport aviation, OCAFF/CONARC during fiscal year 1955 prepared a new training circular on this subject. Published by the Department of the Army as TC 1-7, Employment of Army Transport Aviation, on 29 March 1955, the new circular replaced Department of the Army TC 19, 1950, Transport Helicopter Company (Army) TT/O&E 55-17).

The new circular was based on the concept that the primary function of Army transport aviation was combat support, with service support as an additional function. In accomplishment of the primary function, Army transport aviation units were to have the specific mission of moving Army combat units operationally by air. Heretofore, employment of Army transport aviation had been envisaged principally as having a service support role, including such missions as delivery of supplies and replacement personnel and units and aeromedical evacuation. While rotary wing aircraft, organized in helicopter companies and battalions, constituted the existing structure of Army transport aviation at the time of the circular's preparation, it was contemplated that fixed wing transport aircraft companies and battalions would be incorporated into the structure.

In support of the new doctrine contained in the circular, CONARC in May 1955 announced a long range plan for the preparation of field manuals by various Army service schools. The Infantry School would prepare, coordinate, and submit to CONARC the manuscript for a new field manual in the 57-series entitled Army Transport Aviation—Combat Operations. This manual would provide interim guidance until such time as the subject matter was sufficiently firm to be included in branch manuals.

The Command and General Staff College was directed to prepare two publications. The first, a change to FM 100-5, Operations, would provide the general concept of employment contained in both TC 1-7 and the manual prepared by the Infantry School. The second, a new field manual in the 100-series, would cover the employment of Army transport aviation in logistical support of Army operations. The Army Aviation School was responsible for a new field manual in the 1-series covering the organization and operation of Army aviation transport units. The Chief of Transportation was to prepare a manual covering the organization and operation of maintenance and supply units in support of Army aviation.[15]

Army Aviation in the New Division Organizations

The Army began the development of a new divisional organization immediately following the Korean War. Rapid advances in technology and the implications of tactical nuclear weapons required a more flexible organization than was possible with the triangular divisions which had been used in World War II and Korea. A primary consideration in the design of the new divisions was that any massing of troops or units during atomic operations would be disastrous. Units would have to be small, powerful, and self-sustaining. Success would depend on a high degree of mobility, rapid and efficient communications, and devastating fire power.[16]

AFTA and PENTANA

Only slight organizational changes had been made to the triangular divisions of World War II. In April 1954, at the direction of General Ridgway, a study began to improve the combat-to-service manpower ratio in the divisions and the ultimate reorganization of units. The problem was to develop organizational concepts which would permit formation of combat units with greater mobility and less vulnerability to atomic attack. The study which eventually emerged was known as the Atomic Field Army-1 1956 (AFTA-1). The ATFA study derived many of its concepts from the organization of the World War II armored division. The division structure envisioned in AFTA-1 was to be made of three independent tactical headquarters (combat commands) to which independent battalions and other organic divisional units could be attached or detached as required. Logistical support for the division would be provided by a Divisional, Logistical, or Support Command. At the same time as the ATFA study, the Operations Research Office of Johns Hopkins University proposed a radically new organization. This study recommended a break with the triangular tactical grouping by using a five-figured tactical structure. Five battalions would be grouped to form a combat command. The combat command would be solely a tactical headquarters. A corps would be formed of five combat commands, the division being eliminated.[17]

During FY 1955, a major portion of OCAFF/CONARC's effort was devoted to preparation of TOEs for new infantry and armored divisions and for the accompanying combat and service support units to make up the experimental field army called for by Project AFTA-1. The proposed infantry division was evaluated during Exercise FOLLOW ME and the armored division during Exercise BLUE BOLT.[18]

The Operations Research Office study was one of many prepared under CONARC's direction that assisted in the preparation of the Pentagonal Atomic-Nonatomic Army (PENTANA) study. This study, begun by CONARC in September 1955, developed the organizational and doctrinal concepts for the field army in the decade 1960-1970. The PENTANA study proposed a field army with the capability of conducting sustained operations with or without the use of nuclear weapons. The field army envisioned by PENTANA was to contain five corps and an army support command. Each of the corps was to contain five divisions and two tank brigades. The universal-type PENTANA division would contain five integrated combat groups, a general support artillery battalion, and other combat and service support units. Operations of the PENTANA army would be in greater depth and involve greater dispersion of units than before.[19]

Aviation in the Pentomic Divisions

The PENTOMIC organization was derived from the PENTANA studies. General Maxwell D. Taylor, the Chief of Staff of the Army, apparently assumed that as long as the strategy of massive retaliation remained the national military policy any future war would be fought with nuclear weapons. He therefore saw that the Army would have to make an interim adjustment to the environment of the nuclear battlefield. To this end, the Army would have to create a single fixed standard division organization built around tactical nuclear weapons.

The new PENTOMIC organization was basically the same as that proposed in the PENTANA study. The 101st Airborne Division was the first unit organized under this concept. The program under which this reorganization took place was designated Reorganization of the Airborne Division (ROTAD). Field testing of the organization began in November 1956 when the 101st Airborne Division participated in Exercise JUMP LIGHT. Further testing of the PENTOMIC concept took place in the spring of 1957 with more than 20,000 troops from the 1st Infantry Division. The 1st Armored Division and the 101st Airborne Division, together with troops from III Corps, XVIII Airborne Corps, 3d Infantry Division, and 82d Airborne Division participated in Exercise KING COLE in Louisiana.

Increases in combat infantry strength were achieved in the infantry battle group—the PENTOMIC division's primary fighting element—while reducing the size of the unit. This gave the ROCID (Reorganized Combat Infantry Division) a small, more self-sufficient combat unit, somewhat larger than a battalion. Through increased firepower, mobility, and communications, the PENTOMIC organization enabled the division to operate with greater dispersion among the five battle groups.[20]

During the Korean conflict, divisions had found it necessary to consolidate their separate aviation sections into provisional aviation companies. These provisional units provided adequate supervision and control of aircraft maintenance and supply, developed and implemented an effective integrated retraining program, and coordinated and controlled aircraft utilization. The division structure devised under Project ATFA-1 included many of the changes that had been battle tested in Korea and carried forward in the PENTANA study and the PENTOMIC organization. Army aviation elements were consolidated into company-size units at division, corps, and army levels. The introduction of the combat aviation company into each division increased the organic aircraft in an infantry division from 26 to 50, in an armored division from 28 to 50, and in an airborne division from 26 to 53.[21]

Advanced plans for the TOEs of Army aviation organizations for the revised type corps and field army were prepared by the Army Aviation School. CONARC reviewed these plans, established a command position, and submitted them to the Department of the Army G-3 for placement in final advance plan format and for submission to the Department of the Army for concept approval. The TOEs for the Fixed Wing Aviation Company (Light) were given priority because certain aviation units were scheduled for reorganization under these tables in the second quarter of FY 1958. The TOEs were published for the new PENTOMIC infantry, armored, and airborne division aviation companies during the second quarter of FY 1957. Reorganization of the various divisional aviation companies under these TOEs was initiated in the third quarter of that year. Plans were completed during the year to provide additional personnel, equipment, and facilities required to support the reorganization. Minor revisions of the TOEs resulted from troop tests and field exercises. An example of the revisions was the consolidation of all aircraft into the ROTAD (airborne) division aviation company from the airborne division reconnaissance troop and consolidation of first and second echelon aircraft maintenance. These changes resulted in moving 18 additional aircraft and approximately 107 personnel into the airborne division aviation company.[22]

The consolidation of Army aviation into company-sized units improved maintenance and logistical support. This reorganization permitted the attainment of a high degree of training and technical proficiency. Although it greatly improved the use of Army aviation, problems were soon evident with the new organization. It did not always provide the immediate aviation support enjoyed previously by certain subordinate elements of the division. To a great extent this problem was aggravated by inadequate allocations of aviation support and excessive maintenance requirements. The need for continuous aviation support quickly outstripped the resources of the approximately fifty aircraft in the aviation company. Fresh studies indicated that divisions could fully utilize from 90 to 100 aircraft, and that at least 20 organic transport helicopters should be included in the total.[23]

The following units containing Army aviation were included in the organizational structure of the field army under the PENTOMIC concept:

- **Army Aviation Company, Headquarters Field Army** provided the army headquarters and its elements with aerial observation, reconnaissance, transportation, and other aerial missions within it capabilities.
- **Signal Battalion, Army** had an organic aviation section within the headquarters and headquarters company.
- **Aerial Reconnaissance Support Battalion** had a signal air photo reproduction and delivery company which provided finished aerial photo materiel down to division levels.
- **Headquarters, Air Defense Artillery Brigade** had a small organic aviation section within the brigade headquarters which contained two reconnaissance helicopters and one observation airplane.
- **Air Defense Artillery Group** contained an aviation section equipped with one observation airplane and one reconnaissance helicopter.

- **Artillery Battalion, 280-mm. Gun** had two observation airplanes within its organic aviation section.
- **Aviation Company, Armored Cavalry Regiment** increased the combat effectiveness of the regiment by providing the regiment and its elements with immediately responsive aviation support.
- **Sky Cavalry Squadron, U.S. Army Missile Command (Medium)** performed reconnaissance through the use of a combination of ground and air reconnaissance elements over wide fronts and extended distances. The sky cavalry troop of the squadron also provided security by surveillance and by the air transport of the airborne reconnaissance platoon to critical areas.
- **Army Ambulance Company (Rotary Wing)** had thirty-eight utility helicopters which were allocated and controlled by the field army surgeon to provide normal aeromedical evacuation support.
- **Army Aviation Operating Detachment** provided flight information and planning data; coordinated day, night, and instrument flights; provided enroute navigational aids; provided air traffic control; and provided operations service for Army aviation units.
- **Headquarters and Headquarters Detachment, Aviation Group** provided command, control, staff planning, and administrative supervision to assigned or attached Army aviation units.
- **Headquarters and Headquarters Detachment, Transportation and Transport Aircraft Battalion** provided command, control, staff planning, and administrative supervision for two to seven transport aircraft companies.
- **Aviation Fixed Wing Light Transport Company** provided air transport to expedite tactical operations and logistical support in the combat area.
- **Transportation Company, Light Helicopter, and Transportation Company, Medium Helicopter** both provided air transport to expedite tactical operations and logistical support within the combat zone.
- **Corps Aviation Company** provided corps headquarters and its element with aerial observation, photography, reconnaissance, tactical transport, and other aerial missions within its capabilities.
- **Corps Artillery Aviation Company** provided corps artillery units with immediately available and responsive aviation support.
- **Corps Signal Battalion** contained a 2-aircraft aviation section.

The PENTOMIC division Army aviation organizations consisted of the following units:

- **Armored Division Aviation Company** increased the combat effectiveness of the armored division by providing the division and its elements with immediately responsive Army aviation support.
- **Infantry Division Aviation Company** increased the combat effectiveness of the infantry division and its elements with on call aviation support.

- **Airborne Division Aviation Company** provided the airborne division and its elements with aerial observation, reconnaissance, resupply, and transportation.[24]

Fixed Wing Light Transport Companies

A significant event in the development of Army transport aviation had been the development in OCAFF of a type transportation light aircraft company, and the activation of one of these companies by the Department of the Army.

Because of difficulties in the procurement of H-21 helicopters to equip transportation helicopter companies, and in light of the highly favorable comparison of the OTTER fixed wing aircraft on an initial costs, man-hour maintenance, payload, operational radius, POL consumption, and general performance basis, OCAFF in July 1954 had recommended to the Department of the Army that the OTTER be adopted as substitute standard for the one and one-half ton payload helicopter and that approximately 100 of these aircraft be procured to equip one battalion of transportation cargo aircraft companies (light) in lieu of one programmed battalion of transportation helicopter companies (light).

The Department of the Army approved these recommendations on 30 September 1954 and directed OCAFF to prepare a TOE for a light cargo fixed wing company. The early activation of these fixed wing transport companies was approved at this time. To meet this requirement, CONARC prepared and forwarded to the Department of the Army on 19 March 1955 TOE 55-107, Transportation Light Airplane Company. This table, published on 15 April as TOE 1-107 (Tentative), Army Aviation Company (Fixed Wing-Tactical Transport), called for a unit equipped with twenty-one OTTER type aircraft. The Department of the Army on 5 May directed the activation of the first of these companies—the 14th Aviation Company—at Fort Riley. The second company was activated during FY 1956 and the final company in August 1956.[25]

The Department of the Army advised CONARC that only officer aviators would be assigned to the 14th Aviation Company since the fixed wing training program for warrant officers had not yet been approved. The Army Aviation Unit Training Command at Fort Riley was responsible for supervision of the activation and for unit training. The 14th Aviation Company received the OTTER aircraft beginning in August.[26]

Medium Helicopter Aviation Company

During the fall of 1955, CONARC formulated a concept for an Army aviation medium helicopter company to be equipped with 6,000-pound payload twin-engine helicopters, forwarding in December the concept and a proposed TOE to the Department of the Army for review and concept approval. The proposed company was to be equipped with sixteen H-37 MOJAVE helicopters, delivery of which was expected to begin during February 1956. These aircraft were at that time the largest helicopters in production in the United States. CONARC considered that four of these companies, operating together, would have a capability of airlifting 192 tons—the weight of the assault echelon of an infantry battalion. The internal organization of the company was to consist of a company headquarters, four flights of four aircraft each, and a maintenance element and twenty-eight pilots. Subject to Department of the Army concept approval, CONARC foresaw the activation of the first of these companies during 1956.[27]

Critical shortages of special tools and instructional equipment in FY 1958 delayed H-37 pilot and mechanic training courses. During April 1957, the Army Aviation School had requested supply action to provide special tools and equipment for the conduct of pilot and mechanic training for the H-37. Delivery of helicopters to the school began in January 1958, with concurrent delivery of special tools.

On 1 February 1958, the 4th Transportation Company (Medium Helicopter) became the first company to be equipped with the H-37. CONARC advised the Deputy Chief of Staff for Logistics, Department of the Army, that mechanic training could not be initiated without minimum quantities of special tools, the conversion of H-34 companies to H-37s could not be accomplished until trained mechanics were available, and that delivery of new production H-37s could not be accepted until trained operating and maintenance personnel were available at the receiving unit. The Chief of Transportation agreed to place new production helicopters in limited storage at a depot pending verification of the availability of tools necessary to initiate crew transition training and development of a balanced capability at receiving units to operate the aircraft.

On 8 April 1958, the Chief of Transportation indicated that tools critical to the initiation of crew transition training would be available at Fort Rucker by 30 April. Training courses were started at the Army Aviation School on 5 May, with four complete crews being graduated during the latter part of June. Conversion of the 54th Transportation Company at Fort Sill started on 1 July and a second company, the 64th at Fort Knox, converted late in the second quarter of FY 1959.[28]

Army Aviation in the ROAD Organization

The PENTOMIC structure had never been intended as more than an interim solution to the Army's organizational problems. Field tests of the PENTOMIC organization continued after its adoption in 1956 and revealed significant weaknesses. A major problem was the marked imbalance between the PENTOMIC division's nuclear and nonnuclear capabilities. In the PENTOMIC division, tactical nuclear weapons had become the mainstay of the ground forces.

Experience had shown the PENTOMIC divisions to be relatively inflexible, fixed organizations. They had only a single echelon between the division commander and the company commander, giving the division commander a span of control that included sixteen units. Field tests had shown that this span of control was much too large.[29]

Development of the ROAD Concept

During 1959, CONARC prepared an organization study entitled the Modern Mobile Army 1965-1970 (MOMAR I). The purpose of the study was to supply a common, unifying long range objective to focus Army-wide efforts aimed at modernization of equipment, organization, doctrine, techniques, and procedures. The MOMAR I study was published in February 1960.

The MOMAR I study assumed that limited, rather than general, war was the most likely. Such a war would be characterized by limited objectives, restricted geographical areas of combat, restrictions upon types of weapons employed, limitations upon the forces participating, and restrictions on the phasing and timing of operations. The forces employed by the Army would require a capability to employ both conventional and special weapons in a graduated and selective mix best suited to the immediate situation.

The MOMAR I division would be composed of five combined arms combat commands, each capable of semi-independent operations. The division could be tailored to fit particular environmental or mission requirements by the attachment or detachment of combat commands in any combination. The MOMAR I field army would also have air transportable combat brigades for rapid reaction in cold or limited war situations. These brigades would be multi-capable, fighting organizations which could be transported by a minimum of strategic aircraft to any point in a matter of hours or a few days. There would also be fire support brigades composed of air-transportable composite fire support units, designed to provide multi-capability (nuclear, chemical, biological, and conventional) and multi-purpose support for local indigenous forces.[30]

By the end of 1960, the Army had decided that the MOMAR I organization lacked the necessary flexibility to meet the Army's needs. Drawing heavily upon MOMAR I, CONARC published in September 1960 a new study—Field Army-75 (FA-75). This study extended the field army portion of MOMAR I into the 1970-1975 time frame. In FA-75, a universal type division would have to have sufficient flexibility to enable it to be tailored readily to the requirements of the traditional infantry, armor, or airborne roles under a wide range of strategic and tactical conditions. FA-75 assumed that two-thirds or more of the units attached to a division would form a nucleus which would remain relatively stable, while additional units would be added or removed as required for specific conditions.[31]

The decision during the spring of 1961 to shift emphasis within the Department of Defense from nuclear to nonnuclear warfare led to the abandonment of the PENTOMIC organization. CONARC had been directed in December 1960 to undertake yet another study to develop an optimum infantry, mechanized, armored vision organization—this time for the period 1961-1965. The new study—Reorganization Objective Army Division (ROAD) 1965—was submitted by CONARC to the Department of the Army on 1 March 1961 and approved by General George H. Decker, the Army Chief of Staff, a month later. Shortly thereafter Secretary of the Army Elvis J. Stahr, Jr., recommended the abandonment of the PENTOMIC organization and adoption of the new concept. Following approval by the President, the conversion from PENTOMIC to ROAD began in early 1962.

The ROAD division had three brigades and each brigade could control from two to five maneuver battalions. An integral aspect of the ROAD division was its high degree of flexibility, achieved by rapid tailoring of the number and type of combat units. The division base contained the elements required by all divisions, regardless of type. It had the command and control elements, including the three brigade headquarters, the division artillery, and division support command, composed of administrative and service support units. Divisions of various types were formed by combining varying mixes and numbers of combat maneuver battalions—infantry, airborne infantry, mechanized infantry, and armor—with the division base.[32]

Basic Concept for Assignment of Aircraft

As depicted in the TOEs, each ROAD division contained 103 organic aircraft, approximately twice the number in the PENTOMIC division organization. Forty-five of these aircraft were in the division aviation battalion, which replaced the company-size unit found in the PENTOMIC divisions, 25 were in an airmobilie company, and 20 were in a general support company. The remaining 58 aircraft were allocated as follows: 18 in the brigade headquarters and headquarters companies (6 in each); 27 in the air cavalry troop of the reconnaissance squadron; 12 in the division artillery headquarters and headquarters battery; and 1 in the aircraft maintenance company of the maintenance battalion.

Aircraft in the ROAD divisions were centralized in the aviation battalion when their utilization elsewhere in the division was not full-time. Aircraft assigned to units other than the aviation battalion were assigned on the basis that full-time support of the unit was required. This arrangement did not preclude temporary attachment of aircraft between organizations as dictated by operational requirements. Distribution of aviation assets in the ROAD division is shown in Chart 4.

The Army Aviation Battalalion

The mission of the division Army Aviation Battalion was to provide aviation support for division headquarters, division support command, and other divisional units which did not have organic aircraft. The battalion staff supplemented the division aviation special staff section. The forty-five aircraft in the battalion were available for surveillance, logistical support, command liaison, and the support of small airmobile operations. The battalion also operated the division surveillance drone system, as directed by the division intelligence officer. The battalion included a headquarters and headquarters company, an airmobile company, and an aviation general support company. A total of 51 officers, 26 warrant officers, and 373 enlisted men made up the battalion.

The aviation battalion in airborne divisions differed slightly in organization from the others in that a flight operations center was provided for operations outside of the field army or corps air traffic system. Moreover, the airborne battalion did not contain a drone section. The battalion staff had an additional major who was the assistant division aviation officer.

The headquarters and headquarters company was composed of 13 officers, 1 warrant officer, and 62 enlisted men. The company included a battalion headquarters, company headquarters, and communications, maintenance, and medical sections.

The aviation general support company, commanded by a major, had 26 officers, 6 warrant officers, and 125 enlisted men. The company was composed of a general support, an aerial surveillance, and a service platoon. The general support, an aerial surveillance, and a service platoon. The general support platoon had a tactical support section with ten light observation helicopters and a utility section with six UH-1Bs. In the aerial surveillance platoon, the aerial radar section had two AO-1s, the aerial infrared section two AO-1s, and the drone section contained twelve drones. The service platoon provided maintenance for aircraft, drones, and communications, as well as airfield service.

The mission of the aviation general support company was to provide support for the division headquarters, support command, and other divisional units without organic aircraft. In addition, the company provided medium range aerial surveillance to acquire combat intelligence and target information and limited general support and reinforcement to units with organic aircraft. The company had the capability of aerial observation, reconnaissance, and surveillance of enemy areas for the purpose of locating, verifying, and evaluating targets, studying terrain, and adjusting fire. It could provide rapid spot aerial photography and night vertical photography from piloted and drone aircraft, radar and infrared surveillance, and radiological survey. The company had the capability for command control, liaison, reconnaissance, and augmentaion of aeromedical evacuation from the immediate battlefield.

Commanded by a major, the airmobile company contained 13 officers, 19 warrant officers, and 86 enlisted men. Its components were company headquarters, three airlift platoons, and service platoon. The company's twenty-four UH-1s were in the airlift platoons, while the one UH-1 in the service platoon was primarily for emergency transport of critical parts and maintenance personnel. Each of the airlift platoons was subdivided into two airlift sections of four aircraft each for more effective control.

The airmobile company provided tactical air movement for combat troops in airmobile operations and of combat supplies and equipment within the division area. The company provided supplemental fire support to maneuver elements of the division. It had a continuous operations capability during visual weather conditions and limited operations during instrument weather conditions. It furnished airlift, in a single lift, for one infantry company or one dismounted mechanized infantry company. The airmobile company also was capable of aerial fire support, utilizing organic detachable weapons, and it could augment aeromedical evacuation.[33]

Aviation in Separate Brigades

Since the divisional brigades were not designed for permanent independent operations, separate brigades were developed to fill the need for brigade-sized forces. The same organizational concept for aircraft used in the division was applied in the development of the separate brigades. Fifty-five aircraft were organic to each infantry, armored, and mechanized brigade, twenty-seven of which were in the brigade aviation company. The air cavalry troop of the reconnaissance squadron had twenty-seven aircraft, and the maintenance company of the brigade support battalion had one.[34]

Army Organization for the Period 1965-1970

In June 1961, the Command and General Staff College submitted the preliminary report on CONARC combat developments study requirement, "Army Organization for the Period

1965-1970 (RODAC-70)". In this study, which concentrated on corps and field army organization, all transport aviation units for the field army were assigned to an aviation group at field army. Surveillance aircraft and drones were organized in a company at corps and surveillance squadron at field army. An Army air traffic regulation and identification (AATRI) company was assigned to the field army air defense brigade.

Internal staffing of the report at CONARC resulted in several changes. One corps tactical aviation battalion was added, consisting of a headquarters and headquarters company, corps aviation company, and a surveillance airplane company. Also added was one corps airmobile battalion with its headquarters and headquarters company, airmobile company (UH-1), airmobile company (HC-1), and airmobile company (AC-1). These units were drawn from the field army aviation group to provide the corps with an organic airmobile capability. A corps artillery aviation company (battery) was assigned to the corps artillery. A tactical aviation battalion, consisting of the army aviation company, AATRI company, drone surveillance company, and surveillance airplane company, was assigned to the army headquarters. The aviation group, minus the units assigned to each corps, was placed in the field army support command (FASCOM).

The Vice Chief of Staff of the Army was briefed on the preliminary report, as changed, in July 1961. Although several modifications were directed at the completion of the briefing, the aviation organization was not affected. On 12 August, the Command and General Staff College received guidance for preparation of the final report on this study which it submitted to CONARC on 3 November.

Staffing at CONARC produced two additional changes to aviation organizations. An airmobile battalion was withdrawn from the aviation airlift group in the FASCOM and assigned to the army headquarters. An aerial weapons company was placed in the tactical aviation battalion in each corps. This unit, in concept only, had been undergoing wargaming at CONARC and appeared worthy of consideration for this overall army organizational concept. CONARC forwarded this final study to the Department of the Army on 5 February 1962.

Composite Aviation Battalion

On 7 December 1961, the Department of the Army directed CONARC to develop specific tactics, procedures, and techniques for operations against irregular forces. CONARC was also to ascertain the augmentation in units and equipment required by a brigade of a ROAD division to conduct such operations. This augmentation, to include both divisional and nondivisional support requirements, was to address three levels: minimum brigade air mobility; complete brigade air mobility; and complete division air mobility.[35]

Special Warfare Aviation Detachment

A proposed organization, and plan of implementation, for an Army aviation unit to support counterinsurgency operations was submitted by CONARC to the Department of the Army on 28 November 1961. The concept was approved on 31 January 1962 with certain modifications, including the substitution of UH-1B for H-34 helicopters. The Department of the Army did not look favorably on the inclusion of MOHAWK surveillance aircraft, believing that necessary long range reconnaissance would be accomplished by the Air Force.

The Department of the Army forwarded to CONARC the approved advance plan for a Special Warfare Aviation Detachment, Light Aviation Special Support Operations (LASSO), on 27 February. This plan consisted of cellular organizations for performance and operation of specific missions, functions, activities, and equipment. A tentative TOE was prepared on a high priority basis and published by CONARC on 14 March.

This concept permitted flexibility in organization for requirements of varying conditions in connection with training teams and operational teams and provided a capability to operate as a unit with primary missions assigned to one or more teams composed of aerial reconnaissance, aerial assault, and airmobile elements. The flexibility of the organization permitted rapid organization of platoon teams specifically tailored to accomplish the mission assigned. When a mission did not require the entire unit, only those essential elements were committed.

The 22d Special Warfare Aviation Detachment was activated at Fort Bragg on 21 March 1962 and began training on 16 April. The detachment had an authorized strength of 19 officers, 80 warrant officers, and 123 enlisted men.[36]

Army Aviation Air Traffic Operations

Army Aviation Operating Detachments

In December 1956, CONARC recommended that implementation of an interim air traffic control system be completed in the field at the earliest possible date by activating Army aviation operating detachments (AAOD). On 17 January 1957, the Department of the Army recommended to CONARC that a proposed schedule of activation of AAODs be submitted by CONARC for consideration for inclusion in the Strategic Reserve troop basis. The Department of the Army further recommended that, upon activation, the detachments be assigned to tactical units and undergo intensive training to enable them, within the limits of available equipment, to handle the traffic load expected to be imposed by combat.

On 1 February, CONARC recommended that two AAODs be activated 1 September 1957 and assigned to Third Army and that two additional detachments be activated at the same time and assigned to Fourth Army. Consideration should also be given to activating four more AAODs for assignment to the other CONUS armies. This program was subsequently modified so that CONARC on 18 March proposed activation of the first AAOD at Fort Benning on or about 1 September, with the second unit to be activated in the third quarter of fiscal year 1958 at Fort Bragg, with assignment to the XVIII Airborne Corps. Activation for eventual overseas deployment of one AAOD in each quarter during fiscal years 1959 and 1960 until unit overseas requirements were satisfied was also suggested. The Department of the Army approved the proposed activation schedule and, at the request of the Third Army, CONARC activated the first detachment at Fort Bragg and the second at Fort Benning.

The mission of the Army aviation operating detachment was to provide assistance to Army aviation elements in the combat and communications zones to enable these elements to operate at night and in adverse weather conditions. In accomplishing this function, the AAOD provided flight information and planning data; navigational facilities at major Army airfields; airfield lighting and instrument approach facilities at major airfields; air traffic coordination and control under all flight conditions; a means of integrating Army flight operations with existing air defense systems; airfield service at major Army airfields; weather services by means of an attached weather cell; warning and in-flight assistance for Army aircraft; and communications incident to the performance of the above functions. Normal assignment was one detachment per corps, army, and major Army airfield in the communications zone. These units were not self-sufficient and were attached to other units for administration, mess, and supply. The detachment was 25 percent mobile utilizing organic automotive transportation.

Each detachment had 4 officers, 2 warrant officers, and 26 enlisted men. The operating elements of the AAOD were the flight operations section, air traffic control team, approach control team, and airfield service section. An airfield augmentation team, added when handling a daily average of over 50 aircraft, provided services for up to 200 aircraft. The first detachments were organized under TOE 1-207C of 15 September 1957.[37]

The 6th Aviation Operating Detachment (Army), the first of the new units, was activated at Fort Bragg on 4 September 1957. In November, a revised TOE for AAODs prepared by CONARC was approved and published by the Department of the Army as TOE 1- 207D, 4 October 1957. The revised table provided additional communications and control equipment.

The Department of the Army and CONARC completed an inspection of the flight operations center (FOC) van and a mock-up of a portable control tower on 20 November 1957. At that time, CONARC took action to ensure delivery of the FOC van to the 6th Aviation Operating Detachment and the U.S. Army Aviation Board at an early date. The U.S. Army Signal Engineering Laboratories, Fort Monmouth, in conjunction with a contractor, developed the portable control tower. The first FOC van was delivered to the 6th Aviation Operating Detachment on 1 December, and a second unit went to the U.S. Army Aviation Board at Fort Rucker on 30 December. Both would undergo a two month service test.

The 6th Aviation Operating Detachment began unit training under its Army Training Program on 19 December and began performing its support mission after completing its training test in May 1958. CONARC recommended to the Department of the Army that the activation of the second AAOD—the 70th Aviation Operating Detachment (Army)—take place at Fort Benning on 1 March 1958.[38]

During the first half of fiscal year 1959, CONARC reviewed the results of a troop test of Army aviation air traffic operations. It was concluded that the detachment organized under TOE 1-207D was adequate to control the safe and orderly flow of traffic for a limited time only, that supplemental radio communication was necessary when aircraft were beyond range or radio line of sight, that authorized equipment was not completely adequate, and that the air traffic control system was compatible with air defense at such times as they were functioning as a team.

To correct the deficiencies, CONARC proposed that a second AAOD van with an operating crew be provided as an alternate means of control during displacement. Procedures for aircraft radio relay of control instructions were incorporated in the Army Aviation Air Traffic Operating Manual. CONARC requested that the Chief Signal Officer correct deficiencies in the FOC van and recommend TOE revisions for generators.

Observations by CONARC during Exercise ROCKY SHOALS indicated that the 6th Aviation Operating Detachment was capable of controlling air traffic after landing on shore and that Army and Navy air traffic control systems were compatible.[39]

Army organizational and operational air traffic regulation doctrine continued to develop. A study on the subject, covering 1959 to 1965, prepared jointly by the Army Aviation School and the Air Defense School and reviewed by other CONARC field agencies, was received in late December 1959. After review and modification, CONARC returned the study to the Army Aviation School on 18 June 1960 for the development of an advanced plan TOE.

The conclusions of this study were that the existing organization, concepts, and procedures for Army air traffic control were inadequate. Undesirable restrictions on air defense reaction time and Army aviation freedom of action were inherent in the existing system and both procedures and organization were inadequate for high traffic densities. The study recommended that an Army air traffic regulation and identification (AATR&I) group be organized at field army level and that the Signal Corps be responsible for the activation, training, and operation of the AATR&I system.

Modification to this study, made by CONARC, including reducing the AATR&I group to an AATR&I company and designating responsibility for the system to Army aviation instead of the Signal Corps. The reduction in the size of the AATR&I unit was made to save men and to retain air traffic control of airfields and ground control approach radar responsibility within the subordinate units. This action was in consonance with the principle of maximum freedom of utilization of Army aviation by subordinate units and maximum responsiveness to the ground commander. Assignment of responsibility for the AATR&I system to Army aviation was based on the mission of the system which was to regulate the flight of aircraft—a function of Army aviation.[40]

The AATR&I company was to replace the existing TOE 1-207D Army aviation operating detachment, which required revision for greater efficiency. The AATR&I company TOE advance plan was staffed at CONARC during the first half of fiscal year 1961 prior to submission to the Department of the Army for advance plan approval.[41]

Use of Restricted Airspace

The Federal Aviation Act of 1958 authorized and directed the Administrator, Federal Aviation Administration (FAA), to develop plans and formulate policy with reference to the navigable airspace and to assign by rule the terms, conditions, and limitations necessary for the safe use of the airspace. Accordingly, the FAA Administrator notified all agencies of his intention to assume the airspace responsibility. He recommended abolition of the Airspace Division of the Air Coordinating Committee. This resulted in discontinuance of Army representation on the Regional Subcommittees, the pertinent portions of AR 15-95 no longer being applicable. Procedures for airspace assignment and utilization were to be accomplished in accordance with FAA regulations.

The Department of the Army requested comments from CONARC on a proposal to provide full-time assignment of qualified field grade Army aviators as Army liaison officers to the FAA Regional Offices and designation of a qualified officer from each CONUS army headquarters to serve as the army commander's representative, on a part-time basis, in coordinating airspace and air traffic control matters of direct interest to the field army. This action was eventually initiated.

Authorization was given for an increase of one officer space to establish an Army liaison officer from CONARC with the FAA Regional Offices at New York, Fort Worth, Kansas City, and Los Angeles. These officers were assigned to the CONUS armies in which the regional offices were located. Each CONUS army and the U.S. Army, Caribbean, continued to retain a qualified officer on the army staff to coordinate airspace and air traffic control matters within the army area. Since CONARC had an overall interest in airspace allocation and utilization, it was kept informed of all negotiations.[42]

The FAA took numerous actions pertaining to modification and revocation of special use airspace designated used by Army agencies. The FAA in many cases initiated action as the result of Army reports on utilization of airspace. Because it was clear that the FAA would continue aggressive action to reduce the amount of special use airspace, it became incumbent upon Army agencies to prepare and process airspace actions carefully to preclude loss of required special use airspace.

CONARC was represented at a meeting at the Department of the Army in March 1960 which was held for the purpose of discussing airspace problems and to provide guidance for handling airspace actions. The meeting was attended by representatives of all CONUS armies as well as U.S. Army, Alaska, and U.S. Army, Pacific. Verbal guidance given at the meeting was the basis for handling the majority of airspace actions due to the obsolescence of AR 15-95.[43]

To meet the new FAA requirements, ODCSOPS, Department of the Army, with CONARC help, rewrote AR 15-95 to clarify and update special use airspace responsibilities, methods, and time of reporting, and established airspace officers and airspace officers and airspace liaison officers. It placed CONARC in the reporting chain, charged it with the logistical support of the four Department of the Army airspace representatives, and put most airspace actions through the Army Aviation Sections in the CONUS army headquarters.[44]

U.S. Army Tactical Air Navigation and Landing Aids System

During FY 1955, the Office of the Chief Signal Officer planned to test and evaluate the OCAFF proposed Tactical Air Navigation and Landing Aids System as well as an air traffic control system proposed by the Army Aviation School.[45]

An interim system for air traffic control and navigation of Army aircraft was approved by the Department of the Army and published as Training Circular 1-8, 12 October 1955, Army Aviation Operating Detachment. The same system was included in the AFTA type field army organization and doctrine. A study of Army aviation electronic equipment was initiated by CONARC for the period through 1965.[46]

A report on the Army Aviation Electronics Program was completed in draft form on 30 August 1956 and coordinated with CONARC and with external agencies. This report was, in effect, an overall summary of the Army aviation electronics program, including equipment and related optional concepts for the period through 1965.

On 21 December, CONARC recommended to the Department of the Army that the implementation of an interim Army air traffic control system be completed in the army in the field at the earliest possible date. This was to be done by the activation of additional Army aviation operating detachments utilizing the latest equipment on the basis of one per corps and field army, both in CONUS and overseas.[47]

The existing systems utilizing ground based nondirectional radio beacons, marker beacons, terminal radar, and airborne automatic directions finders were known to be incompatible with advanced concepts of tactics. The long range CONARC concept envisioned air navigation independent of ground aids. Major elements of the proposed system were self-contained navigators, pictorial terrain and air navigation viewers, and absolute altimeters, which combined with a secure IFF system, would permit Army aircraft to navigate without reference to ground beacons, or air defense agencies. Qualitative materiel requirements were expressed and development was started on all items of the air traffic control, communication, and navigation system. Schedules indicated, however, that an operational capability could not be reached before 1965. The concern of the Commanding General, CONARC, over this situation was expressed on 29 April 1958 in a letter to Lt. Gen. Arthur Trudeau, the Chief of Research and Development, Department of the Army. General Trudeau replied on 19 May that increased funding and effort was being directed to the solution of these requirements and further indicated that the major problems were technical and required advances in the state-of-the-art for solution.

A series of joint CONARC/Department of the Army conferences on the expedited development program were scheduled. The first of these conferences was held at CONARC on 1 and 2 July 1957 to establish agreements with regard to specific equipment and the engineering and service test plans for this equipment. A second conference, on 6 and 7 January 1958, established separate working committees to study communication, combat surveillance, and avionics. The conclusions and recommendations of these committees formed the basis for the 1958 Research, Development, and Testing Program. A similar meeting was held at Fort Monroe, 5-6 August, to consider items of signal equipment which should be accorded expedited development procedures in the 1959 program.[48]

Common TA for Army Airfields

On 1 August 1955, the Department of the Army requested CONARC comments and recommendations relative to a study conducted by the Office of the Chief of Signal Officer to place Signal Corps equipment requirements for Army airfields in tables of allowances (TA) rather than to provide such support by the special projects system. CONARC on 27 August concurred in the concept, but stated that such TAs should include all equipment for Army airfields as well as Signal Corps items. The Department of the Army agreed with this position and requested that CONARC prepare a common type TA for CONUS Army airfields. CONARC requested the Army Aviation School on 6 October to prepare a draft of a proposed type TA in which all equipment requirements would be provided for Army airfields operating within CONUS. It was also recommended that a type table of distribution be submitted for each class of airfield authorized equipment by this table. CONARC felt that there was sufficient similarity of requirements by all CONUS airfields to permit their grouping in representative categories or classes, based upon the volume and type of operations. The Army Aviation School submitted the proposed TA on 21 March 1956 and CONARC forwarded it to the Department of the Army on 25 September.[49]

Organizational Progress

Progress in the development of Army aviation was assured by organizational changes which took place at both staff and tactical levels. The establishment of the Directorate of Army Aviation in the Department of the Army and its counterpart, the Army Aviation Section, at CONARC were essential to manage the growing aviation assets and to plan for the future development of Army aviation. The increasing importance of organic aviation was recognized in the expanded number of aircraft in the PENTOMIC division which was to double with the conversion to the ROAD organization. At the same time, new aircraft and new doctrine for their employment dictated the formation of new types of aviation organizations. By the end of the period under review, Army aviation had become an integral part of the ground combat army.

At the same time that these organizational changes were taking place, the concept of airmobility was born and was rapidly taking form. The next two chapters will deal first with the adoption of armed aircraft by the Army and then with the doctrinal and organizational developments that took place relating to airmobility, once the necessary armament and aircraft were available.

Endnotes

Chapter IX

1. "The Controversial Fifties," *Army Aviation,* Vol. 8, No. 9 (Sep 60), p. 485.

2. (1) DA ACofS G-3, Summary of Major Events and Problems, FY 55, p. 5; and Army Avn Div, p. 1. (2) DA DCSOPS Summary of Major Events and Problems, FY 56, Army Avn Dir, p. 1 (Both TOP SECRET—Info used is UNCLASSIFIED).

3. *The Army Almanac* (Harrisburg: The Stackpole Company, 1959), p. 301.

4. (1) Joseph Bykofsky, *The Support of Army Aviation 1950-1954,* TC in the Current National Emergency, Historical Report No. 4, 1 Jun 55, pp. 31-33. (2) Report of the Chief of Transportation, 1 Apr 53 - 31 Jan 58, p. 2.

5. *The Army Aviation Depot System: Its Origins and Development,* DA OCofT, 15 Oct 59, pp. 5, 7-8, and 13.

6. (1) OCofT Summary of Major Events and Problems, FY 60, pp. 4, 59, 61. (2) "Responsibilities of the TC with Respect to Army Aviation," FY 1960, pp. 1-5.

7. (1) Ltr, General W.G. Wyman to General W.B. Palmer, 28 May 56. (2) FONECON, Palmer and Wyman, 6 Jul 56.

8. CONARC Summary of Major Events and Problems, FY 57, Vol. II, Army Avn Sec, Oct-Dec 56, p. 1, and Jan-Jun 57, p. 1.

9. Organization and Functions Manual, HQ CONARC, 1 Jan 59, Change 21, 10 Oct 61.

10. Ibid.

11. (1) Organization and Functions Manual, HQ CONARC, 1 Jul 62. (2) Maj Kenneth D. Mertel, "USCONARC Report," *Army Aviation,* Vol. II, Jul 62, pp. 365-368. (2) For a detailed description of the reorganization, see CONARC Summary of Major Events and Problems, FY 1962.

12. CONARC Summary of Major Events and Problems, FY 55, Vol. I, Introductory Narrative, Pt B, pp. 35-36, and Vol. VI, G-3 Sec Tng Div, Jan-Jun 55, pp. 14-15.

13. (1) Ibid., FY 57, Vol. II, Army Avn Sec, Oct-Dec 56, p. 10. (2) U.S. Army Aviation Center and Army Aviation School History, 1954-1964, p. 51.

14. CONARC Summary of Major Events and Problems, FY 57, Vol. II, Army Avn Sec, Jan-Jun 57, pp. 7-9.

15. Ibid., FY 55, Vol. I, Introductory Narrative, Pt B, pp. 17- 28; Vol. II, G-3 Sec Doc & Req Div, Jul-Dec 54, p. 4; and Vol. VI, G-3 Sec Doc & Req Div, Jan-Jun 55, pp. 21-22.

16. (1) Virgil Ney, *Evolution of the US Army Division 1939-1968,* CORG, Jan 69, pp. 71-75. (2) Myles G. Marken, Sr., "The Atomic Age Divisions," *Army Information Digest,* Vol. 20, No. 9 (Sep 65), pp. 58-59.

17. E.F. Fisher, Jr., *Relationships of the ROAD Concept to Moral Considerations in Strategic Planning,* OCMH, 28 Oct 64, pp. 42-48 (hereafter cited as Fisher, *ROAD Concept*).

18. CONARC Summary of Major Events and Problems, FY 55, Vol. I, Introductory Narrative, Pt B, pp. 22-25.

19. Fisher, *ROAD Concept,* pp. 48-50.

20. (1) Army Aviation Handbook, US Army Armor School, Aug 59, pp. 3-4. (2) *Evolution of Army Aviation within the Division (A Limited Study), 1940-1965,* Army Avn School, 1 Jun 66.

21. (1) Army Aviation Handbook, US Army Armor School, Aug 59, pp. 3-4. (2) *Evolution of Army Aviation within the Division (A Limited Study), 1940-1965,* Army Avn School, 1 Jun 66.

22. CONARC Summary of Major Events and Problems, FY 57, Vol. II, Army Avn Sec, Jan-Jun 57, pp. 10-11.

23. Army Aviation Handbook, p. 4.

24. Army Aviation Handbook, pp. 65-85.

25. (1) CONARC Summary of Major Events and Problems, FY 55, Vol. I, Introductory Narrative, Pt B, pp. 29-30; and Vol. II, G-3 Sec Doc & Req Div, Jul-Dec 54, p. 8. (2) DA ACofS G-3 Army Avn Div,

Summary of Major Events and Problems, FY 55, p. 3. (3) DA DCSOPS Army Avn Dir, Summary of Major Events and Problems, FY 56, p. 1 (Both TOP SECRET—Info used is UNCLASSIFIED).

26. CONARC Summary of Major Events and Problems, FY 55, Vol. VI, G-3 Sec Tng Div Sp Tng Br, pp. 16-17.

27. Ibid., FY 56, Vol. II, G-3 Sec Doc & Req Div, Jul-Dec 55, supplement.

28. (1) Ibid., FY 58, Vol. II, Army Avn Sec, Jan-Jun 58, pp. 10-11. (2) Ltr OPS AV OR-7, DA DCSOPS to CONARC, 5 Aug 57, subj: Allocation of and Training in Medium Helicopters.

29. (1) Fisher, *ROAD Concept,* pp. 57-58. (2) US Army Expansion, 1961-1962, p. 26.

30. Fisher, *ROAD Concept,* pp. 58-63.

31. Ibid., pp. 63-68.

32. (1) US Army Expansion, 1961-1962, pp. 29, 135. (2) Fisher, *ROAD Concept,* pp. 74-83.

33. Lt Col Morris G. Rawlings, "Army Aviation and the Reorganized Army Division," *United States Army Aviation Digest,* Vol. 8, No. 2 (Feb 62), pp. 1-4.

34. CONARC Summary of Major Events and Problems, FY 62, Vol. VI, Army Avn Sec, Jul-Dec 61, pp. 6-10.

35. Ibid., FY 62, Vol. III, DCSOPS Doc & Req Div, Jul-Dec 61, p. 23.

36. (1) Ltr OPS CD DC, Brig Gen Walter B. Richardson, Dir of CD, DA DCSOPS, to CG CONARC, 31 Jan 62, subj: Development of Army Aviation Capability for Support of Counterinsurgency Operations. (2) CONARC Summary of Major Events and Problems, FY 62, Vol. III, DCSOPS Doc & Req Div, Jul-Dec 61, p. 8; Vol. IV, DCSOPS SWCA Div, Jan-May 62, p. 3, and Org & Equip Div, Jan-May 62, pp. 7-8. (3) CONARC GO 16, 19 Mar 62. (4) TOE 31-500T, 14 Mar 62.

37. CONARC Summary of Major Events and Problems, FY 57, Vol. II, Army Avn Sec, Jan-Jun 57, pp. 3-6.

38. Ibid., FY 58, Vol. II, Avn Sec, Jul-Dec 57, pp. 3-4.

39. Ibid., FY 59, Vol. III, Avn Sec, Jul-Dec 58, p. 16.

40. Ibid., FY 60, Vol. V, Avn Sec, Jul-Dec 59, p. 4; and Jan-Jun 60, pp. 8-9.

41. Ibid., FY 61, Vol. VI, Avn Sec, Jul-Dec 60, p. 8.

42. Ibid., FY 60, Vol. V, Avn Sec, Jul-Dec 59, pp. 8-9.

43. Ibid., FY 60, Vol. V, Avn Sec, Jan-Jun 60, pp. 16-17.

44. Ibid., FY 61, Vol. VI, Avn Sec, Jul-Dec 60, p. 10 (CONFIDENTIAL—Info used is UNCLASSIFIED).

45. Ibid., FY 55, Vol. IV, Cbt Dev Sec Gen Div, Jul-Dec 54, p. 4.

46. Ibid., FY 56, Vol. IV, Cbt Dev Sec Gen Div, Jul-Dec 55, p. 3.

47. Ibid., FY 57, Vol. VI, Cbt Dev Sec Sp Div, Jul-Dec 56, p. 1.

48. Ibid., FY 58, Vol. II, Avn Sec, Jan-Jun 58, pp. 8-9.

49. Ibid., FY 56, Vol. II, G-3 Sec Org & Equip Div, Jul-Dec 55, and Vol. VI, G-3 Sec Org & Equip Div, Jan-Jun 56, pp. 23-24; FY 57, Vol. III, G-3 Sec Org & Equip Div, Jul-Dec 56, p. 31.

CHAPTER X

DEVELOPMENT OF AIRCRAFT ARMAMENT

The potential of the helicopter to provide the ground combat soldier additional mobility had long been recognized. During the Korean War the first attempts to use airmobility had been made mainly by the Marines, but the limited number of helicopters and their technical limitations had prevented any conclusive demonstration. As helicopter units became available to the Army, their use was included in field exercises. The first attempts to move units as such were made during Exercises SNOWSTORM in March 1953 and FLASHBURN in April and May 1954.[1]

These exercises proved inconclusive. Strong Air Force opposition to troop transport by Army aircraft further delayed the development of airmobile doctrine. It was apparent that successful airmobile operations required the use of armed helicopters. The arming of helicopters had been proposed in World War II and various attempts had been made during the Korean conflict. The development of a suitable helicopter—the UH-1—and the successful efforts to develop an aerial weapons system laid the foundation of Army airmobility.

Weapons System Development

Project ABLE BUSTER

The Army's interest in arming helicopters and other light aircraft after the Korean War was originally limited to the development of a flying tank destroyer. On 1 February 1955, the Department of the Army requested that CONARC conduct necessary tests to determine the desirability and the feasibility of employing Army aircraft as tank destroyers. The tests were to establish requirements, doctrine, tactics, and techniques which, on confirmation of requirements and feasibility, would lead to the establishment of military characteristics for aircraft more suitable than those presently available to the Army. It was envisioned that these armed light aircraft would be organized into Army Aviation Attack Companies operating in direct support of regimental combat teams and combat commands. Operating against enemy armor, the attack companies were to deliver aerial armaments in a minimum time following a request for support.

CONARC, on 15 April, directed the Army Aviation School to conduct tests, designated Project ABLE BUSTER, during the period 15 April-1 July, to determine the desirability and practicability of the concept so that a decision as to the requirement for subsequent testing could be reached by 1 July. The Army Aviation School was to make preparations for combined troop testing to be conducted during the period 1 July to 1 September provided the requirement was established by the first phase testing.

The Army Aviation School, utilizing civilian off-the-shelf and Army aircraft to fire munitions including small arms, rockets, and chemicals, conducted tests during May and June and submitted a first interim report on 15 June. For testing, the school had been assigned one T-34 trainer, Fletcher FD-25 and TEMCO M-33 light aircraft in addition to L-19s, L-20s, and L-23s. Helicopters were briefly evaluated, but were rated as poor performers. One of the first problems encountered concerned ordnance. No appropriate aerial rockets were available from Army Ordnance Corps sources. Modern aerial rockets had been designed to be released from aircraft traveling several hundred miles an hour, while the Army's aircraft flew much slower. This problem was never completely overcome, however numerous rockets were tested and it was determined that a fixed fin rocket was the most suitable for this type of launch platform. The Army Aviation School concluded that no aircraft assigned to the Army or any of the special aircraft tested were suitable for the antitank role. The Army use of Air Force or Navy fixed wing aircraft was proposed, but this suggestion was never pursued. The Army Aviation School recommended that a separate project designed to determine requirements and characteristics of an optimum close support aircraft was required.[2]

On 25 October, the Army Aviation School submitted its final report on the feasibility test. The school concluded that employment of light aircraft of types organic to the Army in the antitank role was feasible and recommended the conduct of troop tests with modified civilian aircraft to be procured by the Army. It also recommended that an efficient aerial weapons platform be developed for this one particular mission and not be expected to carry cargo or fly command liaison missions. CONARC nonconcurred with the Army Aviation School recommendations on 7 December, and recommended to the Department of the Army that no further tests be conducted using currently available aircraft and munitions.[3]

Army Aviation School Experiments

The failure of Project ABLE BUSTER and the unfavorable report on the SKY CAV experiment conducted during Exercise SAGE BRUSH resulted in a serious setback to the development of an armed helicopter and of airmobile doctrine. Brig. Gen. Carl I. Hutton, the Commandant of the Army Aviation School, was a firm believer in the future of the armed helicopter. General Hutton's opportunity to proceed on his own with the development of the armed helicopter came in June 1956. On 4 June, CONARC issued Training Memorandum No. 13, Organization and Training for Mobile Task Force-Type Operations, which emphasized the need for new concepts in mobility and flexible organization and required commanders to conduct experiments in this area.

Upon receipt of Training Memorandum No. 13, General Hutton immediately took two actions. First, he asked Col. Jay D. Vanderpool, Chief of the Combat Developments Office of the school to undertake the fabrication and testing of weapons systems to be used on Army helicopters. Secondly, General Hutton on 27 June wrote to General Wyman that the mobility of task forces was still no greater than it had been during World War II. He believed that the only solution to the problem was putting the soldier into aerial vehicles. At that time, the Army only had aircraft designed as transports, but General Hutton believed that the development of fighting aerial vehicles was necessary. General Hutton requested approval to experiment with existing helicopters, organized into tactical formations, and to run some problems similar to those contained in Training Memorandum No. 13. As far as he had been able to determine there was nothing in the regulations to prohibit this testing, and it was only a question of policy and whether the Army Aviation School should conduct the experiments.

General Wyman agreed on 13 July that air vehicles were a promising means of increasing mobility. He pointed out that the scope of Army aviation in the PENTANA Army represented a great stride forward. Although the quantity and types of aircraft in that army were considered to be state-of-the-art, he felt that no opportunity should be missed to improve on the PENTANA concept. He therefore approved General Hutton's plan and requested that details be submitted to CONARC by 24 August. The plan was to include a statement of the purpose, the objective, and an outline of the method of accomplishment. General Wyman directed that coordination should be made with the Infantry School. He also approved experimentation with existing helicopters to run problems similar to those in Training Memorandum No. 13, providing this effort was coordinated with the Infantry School and that it would in no way retard the accomplishment of the primary mission of the Army Aviation School. General Wyman did not tell General Hutton to use armed helicopters, nor did he tell him not to use them.[4]

On 23 August, the Army Aviation School published its proposal, entitled The Armed Helicopter Mobile Task Force. This proposal expanded earlier Army Aviation School and Infantry School studies of airmobile doctrine to include the tactical use of armed Army aircraft. The school stressed that these weapons were intended only to provide suppressive fires during the assault. At that time, the concept envisioned the use of existing Army aircraft equipped with standard weapons.

The primary objective of the Army Aviation School study was to determine the effectiveness of existing aircraft and weapons in this new role. Following the full evaluation of these concepts, the development of requirements for new or modified equipment and recommendations to higher staff offices would follow. The Army Aviation School was responsible for the details of organization and the methods of employing men and equipment during the evaluation. The Infantry School provided assistance in forming this special force, test problems for inclusion in the program, and observers/umpires to evaluate the tactical feasibility of the concepts.

The 351st Regimental Combat Team, a school troop unit at Fort Rucker, furnished the nucleus of the experimental unit. Aircraft and operating and maintenance personnel were taken from existing resources of the Army Aviation School. The establishment of the composite unit assisted in determining the logistical support demands of this type of unit. Believing it had adequate funds to organize and test the unit, the Army Aviation School made no request for additional money.[5]

The first problem was determining whether existing helicopters could be successfully armed. Colonel Vanderpool, starting work on the project with a cadre of five people, selected the H-13 helicopter as the first test vehicle. The cadre originally had been assigned to Project ABLE BUSTER, and they used armament remaining from the project. By early July, without awaiting General Wyman's formal approval, the first live fire test was conducted using a kit consisting of two .50-caliber machine guns and four Oerlikon 8-cm. rockets.

The tests were conducted with extreme caution since no one knew exactly what would happen when rockets and machine guns were fired from a helicopter. The H-13 was first securely anchored to an elevated wooden platform. The machine guns were fired singly and then in pairs with increasingly long bursts. Inspection revealed that there was no structural damage to the helicopter. The rockets were then fired by remote signal. Test firings both singly and in ripple revealed a much smaller dispersion pattern than had been expected and again no damage to the aircraft. The weapons were then fired while the helicopter hovered and when it was in forward flight at an altitude of approximately 100 feet. Having proven that weapons could be fired successfully from a helicopter, the testers turned their attention to the fabrication and improvement of the armament system.

First attempt to fire rockets from H-13 helicopter.

The Army Aviation School was now ready to study armed airmobile tactical organizations and formations. General Hutton directed Colonel Vanderpool on a Friday afternoon to develop a conceptual sky cavalry—an airmobile tactical force of company size; determine the aircraft requirements; determine troop and pilot requirements; sketch a troop maneuver scenario; assemble the pilots, troops, and aircraft on the parade ground Sunday morning for briefings; and conduct a maneuver Sunday afternoon. Using helicopters taken from the school training fleet, selected instructor pilots were picked and infantrymen were drawn from the school troops. This first exercise demonstrated the potentialities of the concept and during the remainder of 1956 and early 1957, Colonel Vanderpool's group worked on experimental weapons systems during weekdays and experimented with tactics and techniques on weekends when the school was closed. Since funds were not available, these tests were conducted with volunteer pilots from the school.[6]

Aerial Combat Reconnaissance Company

The success of the experiments and tests conducted in 1956 and early 1957 led to the approval of the Army Aviation School recommendation to continue testing of the doctrine, techniques, and tactics of the airmobile concept. On 5 March 1957, the Army Aviation Center directed the organization of a Sky Cavalry Platoon (Provisional) to continue the testing of the concept. On 8 July, this unit, consisting of 11 officers, 16 enlisted men, and 10 helicopters, was placed under the operational control of the Department of Tactics of the Army Aviation School. These people were assigned on special duty, and the equipment was provided on a temporary loan basis.

The Sky Cavalry Platoon was divided into four flights, equivalent to squads. The reconnaissance flight consisted of seven officers and seven aircraft. Six of the aircraft were helicopters, while the seventh was a fixed wing observation plane. The infantry flight was equipped with a cargo helicopter to carry the integral infantry squad. The weapons flight had one officer and one armed utility helicopter. The maintenance section contained five enlisted men and a test engineer. The new platoon, including the experimental armed helicopter, was officially unveiled on 6 June at Fort Rucker before an industrial-military symposium sponsored by the Association of the United States Army.[7]

In order to eliminate the confusion that existed over different types of air cavalry, the unit was redesignated in November 1957 the Aerial Combat Reconnaissance Platoon, Provisional (Experimental). Then, on 24 March 1958, the platoon was expanded to full company size and redesignated the 7292d Aerial Combat Reconnaissance Company (Provisional). The company was organized under TD 92-7292 and assigned the following mission: "To support the Army Aviation School with 100 percent of its personnel and equipment in the conduct of approved training programs and in the development of tactical doctrine, organizational data, operational concepts, materiel requirements, tactics, techniques, and procedures for employment of a completely airmobile combat force." After its reorganization, the unit was placed under the 2d Battle Group, 31st Infantry, as part of the school troops at Fort Rucker. The company was subsequently redesignated on 25 March 1959 as the 8305th Aerial Combat Reconnaissance Company.[8]

Concurrent with the tactical tests and weapons experimentation, the platoon and later the company held demonstrations before several military and civilian groups. On 27 March 1957, two teams gave the first off-post demonstrations of emerging airmobile tactics before the U.S. Armor Association at Fort Knox and an industrial symposium at Fort Benning. By mid-1957, the platoon had acquired 6 OH-13s, 2 CH-21s, 1 H-25, and 1 UH-19. As mentioned above, an impressive display of experimental weapon systems was presented at the Army Aviation-Industry Symposium conducted at Fort Rucker on 6 June 1957. The demonstration was repeated with some change in armament on 10 June for the Ordnance Association Conference at Redstone Arsenal. Additional demonstrations were conducted during the Joint Civilian Operations Conference at Fort Benning in October 1957 and again in 1958 and at Fort Bliss in July 1958. All of these exercises generated a great deal of command interest in the armed helicopter.[9]

Formal Armament Program

In March 1957, the Chief of Research and Development, Department of the Army, directed the Chief of Ordnance to implement recommendations of the Deputy Chief of Staff for

An H-25 Army Mule helicopter firing a 1.5-inch rocket at Fort Rucker, July 1957.

Operations, Department of the Army, for development of a single machine gun installation on the H-13, H-21, and H-34 helicopters and a 4-gun kit for the YH-40. This represented the first formal program for the development of helicopter armament. Because the helicopter armament program crossed responsibility lines of several agencies, a 3-member steering committee was formed to coordinate and exchange information among the agencies concerned. The committee consisted of representatives from the Office of the Deputy Chief of Staff for Operations, the Chief of Transportation, and the Chief of Ordnance.

This formal adoption of an armament program not only caused concern within the Air Force, but it also met strong objections in the Army staff. The Deputy Chief of Staff for Logistics, Department of the Army, nonconcurred in arming helicopters for tactical use against enemy soldiers and positions. He had no objections, however, to the passive use of helicopter armament to retaliate against enemy ground fire that interfered with the accomplishment of the helicopter's mission. Much of the opposition of the Department of the Army staff was based on the desire not to aggravate the Air Force. Development of an Army attack helicopter would appear to infringe on the Air Force mission of close air support. Theoretically, any armament on Army aircraft was to be for defensive purposes only. Another factor causing a lack of enthusiasm for armed helicopters in certain quarters was the Transportation Corps' view that helicopters should be primarily used for transportation purposes under its control and not as a weapons system in the combat arms. The Chief of Research and Development, Lt. Gen. Arthur Trudeau, and Lt. Gen. Carter B. Magruder, the Deputy Chief of Staff for Logistics, reached a compromise by formally stating that the helicopter was too vulnerable to attack enemy ground forces and that because of its normal low level flying techniques would be unable to locate or hit targets.

By the terms of an agreement reached in July 1957, the Transportation Corps received prime responsibility for the helicopter while the Ordnance Corps was delegated responsibility for the weapons and the weapons systems. The Transportation Corps would handle budgeting and funding, transferring funds to the Ordnance Corps as necessary. The Ordnance Corps would contract for the necessary modifications to the helicopters and for all attachments and mounts that were to be a permanent part of the aircraft. Upon completion of testing, the operational evaluation of the weapons system would be accomplished at Fort Rucker. After the completion of this phase, disposition of the equipment would be made upon instructions from the Deputy Chief of Staff for Research and Development.[10]

In 1958, the Department of the Army directed the development of the single flexible machine gun system. The contract for this first funded project was awarded to the Townsend Company and was supervised by Springfield Armory. The contract resulted in the Townsend fire suppression kit. Another program was begun with the General Electric Company, again supervised by the Springfield Armory, to install a 40-mm. grenade launcher on the H-34A helicopter.[11]

In April 1958, the Ordnance Weapons Command outlined in detail and recommended a series of potential projects in support of Army aviation. Since the Ordnance Weapons Command had furnished liaison officers to Fort Rucker since 1957, it was acquainted with the projects under development concerning the aerial combat reconnaissance company. Fort Rucker had requested

An H-34 armed with 2 20-mm. machine guns, 3 50-caliber machine guns, 6 30-caliber machine guns, 2 pods of 20 2.75-inch rockets, and 2 5-inch rockets.

the Ordnance Corps install two 20-mm. M39 guns on a helicopter for the Army Aviation School and had also made various requests to test rocket launchers. The Ordnance Weapons Command realized that the character of this work and its relationship with Fort Rucker would be greatly improved by providing a formal research and development project with adequate funds.

Areas of great interest at this time were the use of rockets on Army aircraft in an antitank role and upgrading the stability of the gun and rocket platforms. Work in the latter area would provide valuable information for the whole program of improving the accuracy of aerial armament kits. The basic need at the moment, however, was to have an available research and development category where user input could be evaluated and prototypes could be developed.

The Ordnance Weapons Command outlined ten categories to be examined: the fabrication of mounting structures required for installing standard ordnance on Army aircraft; the modification of the aircraft as needed; the simple modifications to the ordnance as required by the installation; the purchase of commercially available ancillary equipment; the fabrication of components to complete the system; the purchase of test quantities of nonstandard munitions not otherwise available; functional testing to determine that the system operated as intended and was safe for further testing; the conducting of design studies on aircraft armament installations; the conducting of tests of aircraft installations to obtain data for use in systems refinement, for systems effectiveness studies, and to establish parameters of design of complete systems; and the preparation of system performance specifications. The Ordnance Weapons Command sought the appropriation of moderate funds to finance work requested in support of projects at Fort Rucker.[12]

Airborne Troop Test of the SS-10 Missile System

A major area of interest in arming helicopters continued to be the search for a flying antitank weapons system. Testing of various types of ordnance to meet this requirement continued under CONARC direction. In August 1958, the CONARC commander directed the Commanding General, Third Army, the Commandant of the Army Aviation School, and the President of the Army Aviation Board to conduct a troop test for the airborne launching and guidance system for the SS-10 missile.[13] The test was to be conducted at the Army Aviation Center at Fort Rucker and was to be a combined organization and tactical test. Firing demonstrations were also to be conducted at the Armor School and the Infantry School. Equipment required to conduct the test was to be furnished by the Army Aviation Center, except a minimum of two H-13 helicopters to be furnished to the Army Aviation School by the Army Aviation Board. Airborne guidance and launching equipment for the SS-10 missile was to be installed on both helicopters.

The troop test had several objectives. First, it would test doctrine, tactics, techniques and procedures, and concepts for the organization and employment of the airborne-launched SS-10 in support of infantry and armor. Tactics were to include aerial maneuvers used in the attack of a target, to include a comparison between the tactics for the SS-10 and those used with free rockets. Additional modifications desired for the installation of airborne guidance and launching systems on the reconnaissance type helicopter which were not reported during the ordnance safety test and the CONARC Board user service test were to be determined. Information was also needed for the preparation and revision of training literature, technical manuals, and supply bulletins and to ascertain the maintenance support required for the airborne missiles and launching and guidance system. Any reorganization required in the ROCID, ROCAD, and ROTAD divisional aviation company to provide for ground handling and loading of the missile was to be determined, as were training requirements for firing crew and organizational maintenance personnel.

On 10 November 1958, the interim report of the troop test was submitted to CONARC. The content of the report was general in nature, outlining what had been done, what remained to be done, and deficiencies noted in the early phases of the troop test.[14]

CONARC had forwarded to the Department of the Army on 18 July 1958 a proposed qualitative materiel requirement for an armed aircraft weapons system. On 19 December, the Department of the Army stated that action was deferred in view of the Department of Defense policy limiting Army aircraft armament to suppressive fire systems for helicopters.[15]

Adoption of the Armed Helicopter

On 22 July 1959, CONARC sent the Army Aviation School a study directive for Army Aerial Vehicle Weapons System Requirements. The headquarters needed a study that would determine weapon systems requirements for use on Army aerial vehicles. The increasing emphasis placed on these vehicles in support of the field army dictated that they have weapon systems capable of delivering suppressive antitank fires and providing defense against low performance aircraft.

The study was to determine requirements for weapons systems for use on Army aerial vehicles in the 1960-1965 period. The following types of missions were to be considered: aerial combat reconnaissance, aerial tactical troop movement, anti-personnel, antitank, anti-materiel, and defense against low performance aircraft. The systems to be examined included, but were not limited to, automatic weapons, recoilless rifles, guided and ballistic rockets and missiles, electronic control of air and ground launched devices, and infrared, microwave, or other target seeking systems. The system would consider various types of warheads to include those of fractional atomic yield.[16]

On 4 February 1960, CONARC submitted to the Department of the Army a study, which had been held in a deferred status, on the Armed Helicopter Weapon System. The Department of the Army had established a requirement for a system of armament capable of rapid mounting and dismounting on utility helicopters. The armament system could consist of weapons and ammunition from current weapons systems of advanced design, nuclear and nonnuclear, together with synchronized sighting, mounting, and firing devices providing for elevation, depression, and transverse where required. A mounting system would be provided to permit attachment of various combinations of weapons to fit the mission. The system would be employed as an elevated firing platform to support offensive and defensive ground combat operations and provide for full utilization of new weapons and ammunition and the maneuverability of Army helicopters.[17]

On 15 March 1960, the Chief of Research and Development, Department of the Army, assigned to the Transportation Corps the responsibility for coordinating all work of the technical services in developing helicopter weapons for suppressive fire, armor for both aircraft and crew, and equipment for smoke laying, missile guidance, and aircraft stabilization. By the end of FY 1960, the Chief of Research and Development accepted a 10-year program proposed by the Office of the Chief of Transportation as an official guide for future developments. Weapons to be considered for suppressive fire included machine guns, rockets, and missiles.

The first qualitative materiel requirement for armed helicopter weapons systems was approved by the Department of the Army on 16 May 1960 and disseminated by CONARC to interested agencies on 8 June. This qualitative materiel requirement had undergone extensive staffing in CONARC during 1959 and had been forwarded to the Department of the Army on 4 February 1960.[18]

On 21 November 1960, CONARC submitted to the Department of the Army a basis of issue for kits arming the H-13 helicopter with dual machine guns. The following list was approved on 23 December:

Unit	Quantity
Infantry division	10
Armored division	8
Airborne division	10
Armored cavalry regiment	7
Air cavalry troop	14
Infantry brigade, separate	6
Transportation light helicopter company	2
8305th Aerial Combat Reconnaissance Co	15

This marked the first approval for standard armament on Army helicopters. Also in November, a tentative basis of issue for armament of utility and transport helicopters was submitted to the Department of the Army. The XM138 grenade launcher was proposed to be issued on the basis of one per UH-1 helicopter armed with a wire-guided antitank missile and one per platoon of UH-1 helicopters in the proposed utility tactical transport company. The M153 7.62-mm machine gun kit would be issued one per platoon in the transportation light helicopter company, transportation medium helicopter company, and utility tactical transport company. A procurement order was placed for 150 .30-caliber machine gun kits for the H-13 helicopter and 16 SS-11 missile kits for the UH-1B helicopter. The SS-11 kits were to be delivered to CONARC for the conduct of troop evaluations beginning in January 1962.[19]

CDEC Experiments

A major concern in the development of Army aviation was the vulnerability of low flying aircraft to forward area ground fires. To a great extent, the practicality of the entire emerging airmobile concept depended on the ability of Army aircraft to survive in the forward battle area. The first attempt to answer the vulnerability question was an experiment scheduled to begin at the Combat Development Experimentation Center (CDEC) at Fort Ord on 26 August 1957. The experiment required the use of a considerable number of helicopters. Since Fort Ord could not fill the requirement, it was forwarded to CONARC. As a result, the 33d Transportation Company (Light Helicopter, H-21), augmented by the 573d Transportation Detachment, was moved from Fort Riley to Fort Ord to support this experiment. These units arrived at Fort Ord on 29 June.[20]

Experimentation conducted during FY 1958 was but a prelude to the major work to be conducted in FY 1959. Training of aircraft pilots, umpire troops, and aggressor forces began on 29 July 1957, but owing to the lack of special photographic equipment and a shortage of personnel, the main experiment was postponed until the next fiscal year. A platoon-size experiment was conducted between 17 and 25 September.

UH-1 helicopter armed with SS-11 antitank rockets.

CONARC boards and the Army Ballistics Research Laboratories had already compiled considerable data on the probability of hits and kills, but not on the likelihood that ground troops could detect and react in time to fire. Information on the reaction of ground troops was required to make better judgments about such questions as aircraft armor, suppressive fire, and flight tactics. The experimenters set up trails employing the M-1 rifle, the automatic rifle, the M-42 twin 40-mm. gun, and the M16 dual .50-caliber antiaircraft machine gun. Cameras mounted on the weapons recorded sighting pictures of the target L-19 airplanes and H-21 helicopters at the instant of simulated firing. Results of the experiment were limited by the partial failure of the gun cameras.[21]

In related activity, CDEC assisted the Army Aviation School in preparing an outline plan for tests of a helicopter suppressive fire experiment which was begun on 26 May 1958 and was scheduled for completion on 26 August. A CDEC team of one officer and one scientist participated in the conduct of the experiment. Cameras were used to determine their feasibility as a substitute for the guns on aircraft to determine hits. Concurrently, the Engineer Research and Development Laboratories at Fort Belvoir, Virginia, were investigating the feasibility of developing infrared devices which could be used to simulate ground-to-air and air-to-ground fire.[22]

As a result of the limited accomplishments of the 1957 experiment at CDEC, CONARC directed a second experiment addressing the same question in broader terms. The latter was to investigate the vulnerability of several types of low flying aircraft, expected to be available to the Army in 1965, to ground fires from aggressor forward battle area weapons during the same period. Types of aircraft employed during the experiment included Army fixed wing and rotary wing, Army experimental jet models, and Air Force F-100Cs. Record runs were conducted at Hunter Liggett Military Reservation between 8 October and 29 November 1958. Low, medium, and high performance aircraft flew at speeds of 75, 200, 325, and 450 knots and at altitudes of contour and 300 feet, in formation of 1, 3, and 9 aircraft, over tactical ground dispositions of representative forward area troops and weapons. Fifty-nine gun cameras mounted on automatic weapons and M-1 rifles exposed some 17,000,000 frames of 16-mm. movie film and 18,000 frames of 35-mm. film, respectively. Also, fifty-nine recorders operated during the record runs to collect time data.

A preliminary report based on a partial analysis was published on 15 June 1959 and distributed in July. The final report was published on 30 November, with distribution in December.

Aircraft participating in the experiment encountered a higher kill probability when operating over areas defended by the REDEYE missile than when operating over areas defended by other types of weapons tested.[23] During periods of good visibility, 75 and 200 knot aircraft operating over open areas in the airspace immediately above the forward edge of the battle area experienced prohibitively high kill probabilities from REDEYE-type weapons. At speeds of 75 and 200 knots, aircraft flying over wooded areas were less vulnerable to REDEYE-type weapons than were aircraft flying over open areas. Only half as many rounds were fired by these missiles in wooded areas as by the same weapon in open areas. Generally, the REDEYE did not have time to fire effectively at aircraft flying at speeds of 325 and 450 knots over wooded areas.

Aircraft flying at 75 knots at both contour and 300-foot altitudes were highly vulnerable to VIGILANTE-type weapons within engagement ranges of 1,200 yards.[24] Vulnerability to these weapons for 200 knot aircraft was less than for the 75 knot aircraft, but was still high. Vulnerability to VIGILANTE-type weapons for 75 and 200 knot aircraft flying at contour altitudes decreased sharply at ranges beyond 1,200 yards.

The capability of conventional hand held weapons to track aircraft was low. Their best performance was achieved against 75 knot aircraft flying at contour altitude and overhead flight paths. In more than 75 percent of the cases in which aggressor gunners were confronted with a sequential combination of aircraft targets, they did not switch or change targets during the course of that run, even when the second aircraft proved to be a more lucrative target.[25]

Based on the above conclusions, the CDEC experimenters recommended the development of effective countermeasures against weapons of the REDEYE and VIGILANTE type and urged more testing with more variables controlled. The basic conclusion of the report was that low flying aircraft were highly vulnerable to ground weapons.

The CONARC position on the evaluation report was forwarded to the Department of the Army on 16 April 1960. The command had rejected the major conclusion of the report, that low flying aircraft were highly vulnerable to ground weapons, pointing out that criteria of vulnerability such as operating techniques, evasive air tactics, and suppressive fire had not been considered in the experiment. The command concurred in the recommendations of the report with the exception of one which said that Army aircraft should have a speed of 200 knots or better. It was not feasible that all Army aircraft be required to have the capability to fly at speeds in excess of 200 knots, especially light observation aircraft. CONARC recommended that the conclusions of the report not be accepted as final until additional study and experimentation were completed. The report was valuable as a source of data for use by agencies developing future air vehicles. It also provided a measure of the vulnerability problem, thereby furnishing a basis for further study and evaluation.[26]

During the last half of FY 1960, the Combat Operations Research Group (CORG) undertook an unprogrammed study of the survivability of surveillance aircraft in combat use during the 1965-1970 period. Several previous studies had investigated specialized portions of the aircraft survivability problem. In addition, many studies on the subject of survivability of aircraft in a hostile environment had been conducted for the Air Force and the Navy by industry. To the extent possible, existing studies and military judgment were to provide the basic information for the successful completion of the CORG study. Using this information, aircraft performing missions over a hostile environment would be studied to estimate survivability as a function of altitude-speed-terrain parameters. The completed study, forwarded to the Department of the Army on 3 October 1960, supplied planners with estimates of performance characteristics and mission profiles required to produce high survivability rates.[27] It also provided survivability estimates to determine the feasibility of the development of a manned deep penetration aircraft. In addition, the study indicated a plan of future research to fulfill the long range aircraft survivability requirements.

Following CONARC direction, CDEC conducted further experimentation with the REDEYE during April and May 1960. Vulnerability and kill probabilities were not considered. The experiment concentrated on the REDEYE's actual operation performance against aircraft under varied combat conditions. This was followed by an experiment in May and June 1961 at CDEC to determine the capabilities of Army aircraft using evasive tactics to survive in forward areas in which units equipped with REDEYE air defense weapons were operating. The field exercises of the troops were designed to provide a tactical background and realistic battlefield environment for the employment of aircraft and the REDEYE air defense weapons. The combat situations included attack, defense, advance, and rear guard actions; retrograde movements; and bivouac and assembly. The exercises were controlled in accordance with prepared scenarios to the extent necessary to provide the situations for realistic missions of the organic and supporting aircraft. The assigned aircraft missions included reconnaissance, surveillance, resupply and evacuation, suppressive fires, and airmobile operations. The aviation units and pilots were allowed maximum latitude in selection of routes, use of suppressive fires, evasive tactics and other means to accomplish successfully the assigned missions. The REDEYE teams were employed in accordance with the latest doctrine. They were controlled by their organic or support unit commanders and were subjected as realistically as possible to the normal confusion and distraction of the battlefield.

Once again the air defense weapons scored a high percentage of kills. But it had become increasingly apparent that the findings of the succession of experiments conducted by CDEC since 1957 were considerably biased. The survival of aircraft depended on several factors, and the idealized conditions of these experiments left many of these factors uncontrolled. The aircraft for the most part were not permitted to take the evasive actions which would be expected in combat, and they did not have the opportunity to use suppressive fire. While valid in the context of the stated experimental assumptions, the findings could not be projected to general tactical situations.[28]

During the last half of FY 1961, CDEC conducted an experiment to obtain basic data to be used by Ordnance Corps agencies in feasibility studies of weapons for Army aircraft, weapon design, and fire control equipment requirements. The objective of Phase I of the experiment was to determine the capability to detect ground targets and the types of ground targets most likely to be detected and identified. Also, it was to measure the accuracy of range estimation by an observer without the aid of mechanical ranging devices. Phase II of the experiment measured the ability of the pilot to select from a map the most desirable nap-of-the-earth route to a specific target, to fly a given route, and to identify and attack a specific target. It also measured the accuracy of range estimation by the pilot without the aid of mechanical range finders and the capability of an observer to locate, identify, and report location while flying nap-of-the-earth.

Within an area of eight square kilometers, various types of equipment were placed in defensive positions. The targets were located on preselected positions and utilized natural cover and camouflage to avoid detection from project aircraft. During Phase I of the experiment, helicopters entered the target area from eight different points and flew an S-shaped pattern across the target area on a predetermined flight path. During the course of the flight, a photographic aircraft flew above the project helicopter. Upon notification of a target detection and identification by the observer, a photo was taken recording the helicopter's position at the time. Radio communication from the pilot, and by the control agencies, were taped and time recorded. During Phase II of the experiment, each pilot was given a mission of locating and destroying a specific target while flying a given course at nap-of-the-earth level. Again, a photo aircraft took pictures of the project helicopter during the entire flight and a pen scriber and tape recorder at the control center recorded times and actions during the flight. Firing on the specific target was simulated and recorded by gun-type camera activated by the pilot. The project aircraft did not attack targets of opportunity, but an observer in the aircraft recorded the location of such targets as the pilot pointed them out. All data collected in this experiment were released to the Ballistic

Research Laboratories, Aberdeen Proving Ground, for subsequent analysis and submission of a final report.[29]

During the fall of 1961, the Combat Developments Experimentation Center conducted a helicopter armament range estimation experiment. This experiment represented an extension of the previous helicopter armament experiment and was to obtain basic data on the capability of air observers to estimate range. Data accumulated were used by Ordnance Corps agencies in subsequent feasibility studies of weapons and fire control equipment for Army aircraft.

The experiment had three objectives. First, to determine the accuracy with which an observer or pilot using the "pop-up" technique could estimate the slant range from a helicopter to a ground target from three different altitudes. Second, to determine the accuracy with which an observer could initially estimate the slant range to a target while in forward flight at three different altitudes. Finally, to determine the accuracy of sequential range estimates made while closing on a target, again at three different altitudes.

The Human Engineering Laboratories, Aberdeen Proving Ground, provided Ordnance Corps personnel for project coordination and guidance during planning, training, and field experimentation and established the data collection requirements. This organization also analyzed the data collected. The Commanding General, CDEC, was responsible for the design and conduct of the experiment.

On three different record courses, panels were placed at varying distances from targets to a maximum range of 2,200 meters. Eighteen pilots acting as observers were flown over each record course twice, once using pop-up technique and once on a straight run to target. Each observer estimated from a prescribed altitude the range to the target as he passed over the panels along each of the courses. An after action report was forwarded to CONARC on 12 October 1961.[30]

Army Aircraft Armament Ad Hoc Committee

At the conclusion of a briefing on 26 April 1961, Lt. Gen. Gordon B. Rogers, the acting Commanding General, CONARC, requested that the CONARC DCSOPS provide him with the current status of Army aircraft armament systems and recommended actions to expedite procurement and issue of these systems to troops. On the following day, General Herbert B. Powell, the Commanding General, CONARC, directed the formation of a CONARC Ad Hoc Committee to Study the Army Aircraft Armament Program. General Powell recommended to the Chief of Staff of the Army action to expedite procurement and issue of required armament kits and ammunition and the establishment of an early Department of the Army/CONARC conference to resolve these problems. On 10 and 12 May, a preliminary committee developed terms of reference and a draft directive to establish an ad hoc committee. On 13 June, Maj. Gen. Louis W. Truman, the CONARC Deputy Chief of Staff for Operations, Plans, and Training presented CONARC recommendations at a Department of the Army/CONARC conference in the Pentagon. The directive establishing the Army Aircraft Armament Ad Hoc Committee was approved by the commanding general on 16 June. Definitive CONARC quantitative requirements for Army aircraft armament systems and ammunition were presented at the second Department of the Army/CONARC conference by General Truman on 27 June, and the ad hoc committee convened for the first time on 29 June at Fort Monroe.[31]

During the period, July through August, Maj. Gen. T.F. Van Natta, the CONARC Deputy Chief of Staff for Combat Developments, chaired an ad hoc committee which was to determine requirements and establish implementing procedures for Army aircraft armament systems for the period 1961 to 1970. The following areas were considered: missions of armed aircraft; type and number of aircraft to be armed; caliber and type of armament for each aircraft recommended; personnel, materiel, and facility support requirements for testing, operations, and training; and ways and means of expediting the development, testing, procurement, and issue to troops of the present armament systems.

The final report was submitted to the commanding general on 26 August. General Powell submitted it to the Department of the Army on 1 September, recommending approval. Among other things, the report recommended machinegun, antitank guided missile, rocket, and grenade launcher armament for helicopters within the Army's combat divisions and armored cavalry regiments, as they were reorganized under the ROAD concept, and certain armament for the MOHAWK fixed wing aircraft.[32]

Chief among the CONARC revisions was the deletion of the antitank guided missile and rocket-armed helicopters from the reorganized divisions in favor of an armed helicopter unit at the corps level. CONARC also recommended the reduction in the weight of the armed observation helicopter by use of a one-gun system as a follow-on to the dual machinegun system currently in production.

The Department of the Army approved the modified report for planning on 1 December. On 29 December, the Department of the Army decisions and comments on the report were presented in a briefing to General Powell. Subsequently distributed by CONARC to the CONUS army commanders and selected Department of the Army agencies in the form of a memorandum for record, the briefing represented a consolidation of the Department of the Army/CONARC position on the requirements for Army aircraft armament.

The committee's report dealt with requirements for three time frames. The briefing for General Powell on 29 December dealt in some detail with the requirements for FY 1961 through FY 1963 and discussed only in general terms the requirements for FY 1964-1966 and FY 1967 and beyond. For FY 1961-1963, four weapons systems were discussed, including appropriate Department of the Army production and procurement plans.

The basis of issue of the XM-1 machinegun system for the observation helicopter within the reorganized combat divisions was 6 for the aviation battalion, 10 for division artillery, 10 per cavalry squadron, and 6 for each of the three brigades. Issue of 150 of the XM-1 machinegun kits was to take place between January and June 1962. In addition, CONARC recommended procurement of 200 kits with FY 1962 funds and 168 with FY 1963 funds. This quantity, allowing for anticipated helicopter shortages, was described as sufficient to equip 14 divisions, 2 brigades, and 5 armored cavalry regiments while satisfying school training requirements for the armed observation helicopter by FY 1964.

The basis of issue of the SS-11 antitank guided missile mounted on the UH-1B helicopter was three per general support company of the aviation battalion and four per air cavalry troop. Sixteen limited production SS-11 systems were to be issued for troop evaluation during March and April 1962. CONARC recommended the purchase of an additional 84 systems and 14,000 missiles during FY 1962 and FY 1963.

The basis of issue of the 2.75-inch rocket mounted on the UH-1B helicopter was the same as the SS-11 system. Complete development and production of the 2.75-inch rocket system could not be accomplished prior to March 1963. To meet immediate high priority requirements, however, limited production 2.75-inch rockets mounted on H-34 helicopters could be made available in June 1962. CONARC recommended procurement of 100 2.75-inch rocket systems for FY 1962 and FY 1963.

The basis of issue of the XM-153 quad machinegun system mounted on the UH-1B helicopter was nine per air cavalry troop. This system was still under development with 125 systems programed and funded through FY 1963.

CONARC noted that if the various follow-on procurement plans were affected in fiscal years 1962 and 1963, in accordance with its recommendations, the Army would progressively have sufficient armed helicopters to support requirements of the Special Warfare Center, equip ten combat divisions and four non-divisional air cavalry troops, and satisfy CDEC and school requirements.

In addition to the four weapons systems discussed above, the ad hoc committee's recommendations for arming the MOHAWK airplane were under consideration by the Department of the Army and would be handled as a separate action. In this connection, since October 1960 the Army Aviation Board at Fort Rucker had accumulated sufficient information to begin testing the MOHAWK with the armament proposed in the ad hoc committee report. Testing would begin upon receipt of the Department of the Army approval.

The briefing of General Powell concluded with a summarization of the actions which CONARC was currently taking, or proposed to take at an early date, for implementing those portions of the Army Aircraft Requirements report which had been approved by the Department of the Army. TOEs were to be revised to reflect changes in quantities of aircraft armament prior to submission of the final reorganized (ROAD) division TOEs to the Department of the Army. A concept for an aerial weapons unit at corps level had been developed and was to be tested in war games. Revisions of qualitative materiel requirements and military characteristics to reflect concept changes stemming from the recommendations of the ad hoc committee report would have to be made. In coordination with the Chief Chemical Officer, further development of requirements for aircraft-mounted CBR weapons was necessary.

At the conclusion of the briefing, General Powell stated that CONARC should recommend sufficient quantities of aircraft armament to the Department of the Army to equip sixteen divisions. He also stated that CONARC should reopen, with the Department of the Army, the need for further procurement of H-34 helicopters to alleviate serious shortages.[33]

The report of the ad hoc committee provided a firm basis for establishment of a comprehensive program for arming Army aircraft. It served as a guide to Department of the Army agencies for preparing research and development plans and distribution schedules of aircraft armament systems. The published working papers of the committee provided a compilation of data pertinent to the subject of arming Army aircraft. The report of the CONARC Ad Hoc Committee to Study Army Aircraft Armament Systems, along with the report of the Rogers Committee on Army Aviation, provided the basis on which the Howze Board in 1962 was to revolutionize Army aviation.

Department of the Army approval of the recommendations of General Powell in regard to a program for arming Army aircraft provided a firm basis for development of qualitative materiel requirements for Army aircraft armament systems. Accordingly, CONARC directed on 26 December that qualitative materiel requirements be prepared by the Army Aviation School with the assistance of the Army Aviation Board. Five distinct qualitative materiel requirements (QMR), were to be developed for the following armament systems: light weapons, area weapons, point weapons, air-to-air weapons, and a target marking system. These QMRs were to replace the existing ones for an Army helicopter weapons system.

As finally developed, the air-to-air weapons system was dropped and the Army helicopter weapons system was revised. The five qualitative materiel requirements were forwarded to the Chief of Research and Development, Department of the Army, on 21 May 1962. The revised QMR for the armed helicopter weapons system was an updating of the existing version to include the weapons which were currently programmed. An area weapons system was proposed to be mounted on Army utility helicopters and used in support of ground combat operations to deliver area fires against such targets as groups of men and vehicles and supply installations. This system was to be a follow-on to the existing 2.75-inch rocket. The proposed light weapons system provided for a reliable, lightweight armament for installation on selected Army aircraft would be used for marking tactical targets for air strikes and other fire support means. Finally, the proposed QMR for point weapons systems provided two distinct, reliable, light-weight armament systems for installation on Army utility helicopters for the mission of destruction of such point targets as armored vehicles, unarmored vehicles, and fixed emplacements. These would be an anti-heavy armor and an anti-light armor system. These systems were to be a follow-on for the SS-11 missile and 20-mm. gun.[34]

Armament and Airmobility

The development of aircraft armament by the Army was to change the orientation of Army aviation completely. Until the successful mounting of weapons on helicopters and light airplanes took place, Army aviation had been limited to a role of logistical support and aerial observation. The emphasis on transport aircraft had naturally led to a dominant position in the aviation field of the Transportation Corps. With the acceptance of the armed helicopter and the shift toward combat operations, CONARC became the focal point of aviation developments.

Many Army officers had long envisioned a much broader mission for Army aviation. General Matthew Ridgway, Maj. Gen. James Gavin, and Maj. Gen. Hamilton Howze all put forth concepts for the use of light aviation directly in combat operations. The realization of these concepts depended on two things—the provision of proper aircraft and the arming of Army aircraft.

Experiments with armament actually began before the new aircraft entered service. The speed with which a successful helicopter armament system was developed resulted from the imagination and dedication of such officers as Brig. Gen. Carl Hutton and Colonel Jay Vanderpool rather than of a concerted Army directed development program.

At about the same time that development of aircraft armament began, a new doctrine and organization for Army aviation began to evolve. In the following chapter we will trace the growth of the airmobility concept. The introduction of the aircraft needed to implement this concept will be covered in a later chapter.

Endnotes
Chapter X

1. Weinert, *Army Aviation*, pp. 39-40, 42.

2. (1) Leonard C. Weston and Clifford W. Stephens, *The Development, Adoption, and Production of Armament for Army Helicopters, 1957-1963*, HQ US Army Armament Command, Pt I, pp. 22-30 (hereafter cited as Weston and Stephens, *Helicopter Armament*). (2) CONARC Summary of Major Events and Problems, FY 55, Vol. VIII, Cbt Dev Sec Gen Div, Jan-Jun 55, pp. 7-8. (3) History of US Army Aviation Center and Army Aviation School, 1954-1964, pp. 52-53.

3. CONARC Summary of Major Events and Problems, FY 56, Vol. IV, Cbt Dev Sec Gen Div, Jul-Dec 55, pp. 3-4.

4. (1) CONARC Summary of Major Events and Problems, FY 56, Vol. VI, G-3 Sec Tng Div Gen Tng Br, Jan-Jun 56, p. 7. (2) Lt Col Charles O. Griminger, "The Armed Helicopter Story," *United States Army Aviation Digest*, Pt I, Jul 71, pp. 15-17. (3) Col Jay D. Vanderpool, "We Armed the Helicopter," *United States Army Aviation Digest*, Jun 71, p. 4. (4) Lt Gen John J. Tolson III, *Airmobility, 1961-1971* (Washington: Department of the Army, 1973), p. 6. (5) Ltr, Brig Gen Carl I. Hutton, Cmdt Army Avn School, to General W. G. Wyman, CG CONARC, 27 Jun 56. (6) Ltr, Wyman to Hutton, 13 Jul 56. (7) Weston and Stephens, *Helicopter Armament*, Pt I, pp. 3-5.

5. Weston and Stephens, *Helicopter Armament*, Pt I, pp. 5-8.

6. (1) US Army Aviation Center History, 1954-1964, p. 53. (2) Vanderpool, "We Armed the Helicopter," pp. 4-6. (3) Griminger, "The Armed Helicopter Story," Pt I, pp. 16-17. (4) Weston and Stephens, *Helicopter Armament*, Pt I, pp. 8-17.

7. Weston and Stephens, *Helicopter Armament*, Pt I, pp. 18-19.

8. (1) Vanderpool, "We Armed the Helicopter," pp. 27-28. (2) Griminger, "The Armed Helicopter Story," Pt II, *United States Army Aviation Digest*, Aug 71, p. 15. (3) Army Aviation Center History, pp. 16, 53.

9. (1) Griminger, "The Armed Helicopter Story," Pt II, pp. 17-18. (2) Army Aviation Center History, pp. 53-54.

10. (1) Weston and Stephens, *Helicopter Armament*, Pt I, pp. 80-86. (2) Griminger, "The Armed Helicopter Story," Pt III, *United States Army Aviation Digest*, Sep 71, p. 11.

11. Weston and Stephens, *Helicopter Armament*, Pt I, pp. 91-92; Pt II, pp. 18-41; Pt III, pp. 1-A9—1-B5.

12. (1) Weston and Stephens, *Helicopter Armament*, Pt I, pp. 91-95. (2) Griminger, "The Armed Helicopter Story," Pt III, p. 11.

13. The SS-10 was a wire-guided antitank rocket developed by the French.

14. (1) CONARC Summary of Major Events and Problems, FY 59, Vol. III, Army Avn Sec, Jul-Dec 58, pp. 3-4. (2) Vanderpool, "We Armed the Helicopter," pp. 26-27.

15. CONARC Summary of Major Events and Problems, FY 60, Vol. V, Army Avn Sec, Jan-Jun 60, p. 18.

16. (1) CONARC Summary of Major Events and Problems, FY 60, Vol. VI, Cbt Dev Sec Gen Div, Jul-Dec 59, pp. 15-16. (2) Warheads of fractional atomic yield referred to small tactical weapons of less than one kiloton power.

17. CONARC Summary of Major Events and Problems, FY 60, Vol. VI, Cbt Dev Sec Gen Div, Jan-Jun 60, pp. 14-15 (CONFIDENTIAL—Info used is UNCLASSIFIED).

18. (1) OCofT, Summary of Major Events and Problems, FY 60, pp. 102-103. (2) CONARC Summary of Major Events and Problems, FY 60, Vol. V, Army Avn Sec, Jan-Jun 60, p. 18. (3) Griminger, "The Armed Helicopter Story," Pt III, *United States Army Aviation Digest*, p. 10.

19. (1) CONARC Summary of Major Events and Problems, FY 61, Vol. VI, Avn Sec, Jul-Dec 60, pp. 6-7. (2) DA DCSOPS Dir of Army Avn, Summary of Major Events and Problems, FY 61, p. B-II-1 (TOP SECRET—Info used is UNCLASSIFIED).

20. CONARC Summary of Major Events and Problems, FY 57, Vol. VI, USA Cbt Dev Exp Ctr, Jan-Jun 57, p. 20.

21. John L. Romjue, *Combat Developments Questions Answered Through Field Experimentation 1956-1971,* USA CDEC, Aug 72, pp. 112-114 (hereafter cited as Romjue, *Field Experimentation*) (SECRET—Info used is UNCLASSIFIED).

22. CONARC Summary of Major Events and Problems, FY 58, Introductory Narrative, Ch. V, pp. 40-41.

23. REDEYE, man-portable and shoulder-fired, was the smallest guided missile system that gave the soldier an effective defense against low flying aircraft.

24. The VIGILANTE was a 37mm 6-barrel gatling gun mounted on a tank chassis or trailer with a 15,000-foot range and firing rate of 48 rounds per second.

25. CONARC Summary of Major Events and Problems, FY 60, Vol. VI, USA Cbt Dev Exp Ctr, Jul-Dec 59, pp. 9-13.

26. (1) CONARC Summary of Major Events and Problems, FY 60, Vol. VI, Cbt Dev Sec Gen Div, Jan-Jun 60, p. 16. (2) Romjue, *Field Experimentation,* pp. 115-117 (SECRET—Info used is UNCLASSIFIED).

27. (1) CONARC Summary of Major Events and Problems, FY 60, Vol. VI, Cbt Dev Sec Gen Div, Jan-Jun 60, pp. 13-14. (2) CONARC Summary of Major Events and Problems, FY 61, Vol. VII, Cbt Dev Sec CA Div, Jul-Dec 60, p. 7.

28. (1) CONARC Summary of Major Events and Problems, FY 61, Vol. VIII, USACDEC, Jan-Jun 61, pp. 21-23. (2) Romjue, *Field Experimentation,* pp. 118-120.

29. CONARC Summary of Major Events and Problems, FY 61, Vol VIII, CDEC, Jan-Jun 61, pp. 23-25.

30. CONARC Summary of Major Events and Problems, FY 62, Vol. VII, CDEC, Jul-Dec 61, pp. 10-11.

31. CONARC Summary of Major Events and Problems, FY 61, Vol. IV, G-3 Sec Doc & Req Div, Jan-Jun 61, pp. 13-14.

32. (1) Ibid., FY 62, Vol. III, DCSOPS Doc & Req Div, Jul-Dec 61, p. 22, and Vol. VII, DCSCD, Cbt Arms Div Tac Br, Jul-Dec 61, pp. 7-8. (2) DA DCSOPS Dir of Army Avn, Summary of Major Events and Problems, FY 61, p. B-II-1 (TOP SECRET—Info used is UNCLASSIFIED).

33. (1) CONARC Summary of Major Events and Problems, FY 62, Vol. VI, Avn Sec, Jul-Dec 61, pp. 1-5. (2) Ltr ATAVN 350, CONARC to distr, 22 Jan 62, subj: Briefing of CG, USCONARC on Army Aircraft Armament.

34. CONARC Summary of Major Events and Problems, FY 62, Vol. VII, DCSCD Cbt Arms Div Tac Br, Jul-Dec 61, p. 10, and Jan-Jun 62, pp. 1-2.

Chapter XI

THE BEGINNING OF AIRMOBILITY

At the same time that weapons systems were being developed for the armed helicopter, experiments were conducted on airmobile tactical organization and doctrine. These two fields of development were closely interrelated and led eventually to the Army's airmobility concept.

Development of the Air Cavalry Concept

In April 1954, Maj. Gen. James M. Gavin, the Assistant Chief of Staff, G-3, Department of the Army, published an article entitled "Cavalry, and I Don't Mean Horses," which was to have a profound impact on military thinking during the next few years. General Gavin stated that armor was not sufficiently mobile to properly execute the missions historically associated with cavalry. With the introduction of atomic weapons, it was apparent that armies in the future would have to be deployed over a much larger area and that cavalry screening operations would have to be conducted over much greater distances with much greater rapidity.

To achieve the mobility required on the modern battlefield, General Gavin advocated a new type of cavalry: "I mean helicopters and light aircraft, to lift soldiers armed with automatic weapons and hand-carried antitank weapons, and also lightweight reconnaissance vehicles, mounting antitank weapons the equal (or better) of the Russian T-34s." General Gavin concluded, "Today, even the most casual awareness of the historical lesson should suggest that in ground combat the mobility differential we lack will be found in the air vehicle. Fully combined with the armored division, it would give us real mobility and momentum."[1]

Maj. Gen. Hamilton H. Howze became the apostle of this new doctrine after he assumed the position of Director of Army Aviation in early 1956. Speaking before the convention of the Association of the United States Army that year he summarized the following functions of Army aviation in providing aerial mobility as follows: observation; rapid movement of troops and equipment; movement of critical supplies; air mobility for ground reconnaissance—the Sky Cavalry concept; command, control, and liaison; and battlefield casualty evacuation.[2]

By the following year, General Howze was ready to go beyond this somewhat conventional view of the functions of Army aviation. He believed that the use of light aircraft should have a revolutionary effect on the tactics of the Army. The problem was how to convince the Army as a whole that this was true. General Howze wrote:

> *The major part of the solution to the problem must be provided by Army aviation itself. This capability must be developed partly by the creation of new and better aircraft types, and that development must in turn come from a properly conducted research program. We must take our capability, combine it with courage, and display the result to the rest of the Army in such fashion that the utility of aviation will be completely and convincingly obvious.*[3]

It was about this time that General Howze began using the term "airmobile" to describe his concept of the employment of Army aviation. In October 1957, he described his concept in the following terms:

> *In the more distant future looms the probability of large, completely airmobile units—sky cavalry. The possibilities for its employment in the fluid phase of the ground struggle excite the imagination: as covering forces operating in front of heavier ground elements, protecting long, vulnerable flanks of the main forces of the field army, striking enemy formations from unexpected directions with maximum surprise. We are just beginning to investigate these ideas, haltingly and with some trepidation, but with hope.*[4]

Sky Cavalry

Generals Gavin and Howze were not alone in visualizing the potential of Army aviation to provide increased mobility to the ground forces. In the next few years, the Army began to experiment with Sky Cavalry—a term that was descriptive, but because of its differing definitions, not always informative. In fact, there were at least three distinct versions of Sky Cavalry which emerged during this period.

The Fort Rucker concept of Sky Cavalry was discussed in the previous chapter. To avoid confusion with the other forms, the Fort Rucker version in 1957 was redesignated as aerial combat reconnaissance. The Intelligence Corps visualized Sky Cavalry in a completely passive target acquisition role utilizing such devices as television, radar, and infrared. There was no intention to use aggressive tactical efforts to obtain intelligence. The Armor branch developed a Sky Cavalry concept which provided for the addition of a light helicopter company and some fixed wing aircraft to the existing armored reconnaissance battalion of the armored division to obtain additional means for gathering combat intelligence through aerial surveillance, observation, and reconnaissance. It was this concept which was tested in Exercises SAGE BRUSH and SLEDGE HAMMER.

The Army Aviation School's version of Sky Cavalry included the functions contained in the Intelligence and Armor versions, but was not restricted to passive tactical roles. The Fort Rucker unit was intended to be a "completely air-mobile, airmounted, fast moving, hard-hitting, flexible means of searching out, fixing the enemy, and performing the traditional missions of cavalry at an accelerated rate on the battlefield of tomorrow."[5]

Exercise SAGE BRUSH

On 9 July 1954, General Gavin wrote to the Chief of Army Field Forces that the heretofore important function of logistical support by helicopters should be relegated to secondary importance and that the combat arms should develop the application of airlift by helicopter to meet their doctrine and techniques. From this time onward, the Department of the Army became increasingly interested in the tactical applications of the helicopter rather than considering it as just another means of logistical transport.

On 9 March 1955, the Department of the Army proposed to CONARC the organization and training of an experimental reconnaissance troop combining Army aircraft reconnaissance and transport capabilities with ground reconnaissance facilities, integrating the latest electronic surveillance devices. The Department of the Army proposed to test and evaluate such a unit as a replacement for the reconnaissance unit in the infantry and airborne divisions. CONARC concurred in the proposal and recommended phasing. On 27 April, the Department of the Army directed the necessary implementation of the plan and cooperative action by the Chief Signal Officer and the Chief of Engineers.

CONARC furnished instructions and assigned responsibilities for implementation of the plan on 20 May. The plan called for the Commanding General, Third Army, beginning 1 June 1955, to organize, equip, and train the Provisional Reconnaissance Troop (SKY CAV) in accordance with the TOE furnished by CONARC. The provisional troop was to be trained by the 82d Airborne Division during the period June to September, tested as part of the aggressor forces in Exercise SAGE BRUSH in October, and evaluated by the Deputy Director (Army), Exercise SAGE BRUSH, during December 1955 and January 1956.[6]

The Provisional Reconnaissance Troop (SKY CAV) was activated on 1 June by the 82d Airborne Division. The nucleus of the unit was provided by the 82d Airborne Reconnaissance Company. Men and equipment were attached to the troop from the 8th Transportation Battalion (Helicopter), the Army Pictorial Center, the Army Electronic Proving Ground, XVIII Airborne Corps Artillery, the 25th Reconnaissance Battalion at Fort Hood, and miscellaneous other sources. Completely formed in early August, the unit conducted a limited training program at Fort Bragg during August, September, and October.

The primary objective of the test was to determine whether Army aircraft reconnaissance and transport capabilities, ground reconnaissance facilities, and the latest electronic surveillance devices could be combined to form an effective unit with a high degree of mobility and flexibility. The test was also to determine whether a unit so constituted could improve the reconnaissance and target acquisition capabilities of division, corps, and army and if it was suitable either to replace or to become a component of mechanized reconnaissance units.

Exercise SAGE BRUSH, involving 110,000 Army and 30,000 Air Force personnel, was the largest exercise conducted in the continental United States after World War II. Maneuver plans created a theater-scale setting in which atomic, chemical, biological, and electronic weapons were used extensively. The maneuver took place in Louisiana between 31 October and 15 December 1955.[7] The Provisional Reconnaissance Troop (SKY CAV) was composed of 33

THE BEGINNING OF AIRMOBILITY

Friendly infantry troops boarding an H-34 helicopter for movement into the Combat Zone of the Louisiana Maneuver area for Exercise SAGE BRUSH.

officers, 28 warrant officers, and 374 enlisted men with 14 light cargo helicopters, 5 reconnaissance helicopters, 4 utility airplanes, and 5 observation airplanes.

Prior to and during Exercise SAGE BRUSH, the employment of Army aircraft proved to be the most controversial aspect of the SKY CAV concept. The legal controversy stemmed from the 1952 Memorandum of Understanding between the Army and the Air Force concerning the roles of Army aviation in the combat zone. The Air Force desired to limit the Army to the terms of the agreement, while the Army wanted the agreement changed to exploit developments in organic tactical aviation.

An expression of this differing view was contained in a letter from General Dahlquist to Lt. Gen. John H. Collier, Commanding General, Fourth Army. He pointed out that the Army position regarding helicopters was that they were not suitable for joint airborne operations and the Army had no requirement for Air Force helicopter lift. For this reason, the planning for Exercise SAGE BRUSH avoided use of Army helicopters in any operation which might be called a joint airborne operation. The Air Force planned to have a number of helicopters available during the exercise. General Dahlquist told General Collier that, should the Air Force urge Army employment of their helicopters, he could use them provided they were placed under Army command. If this condition were not met, General Collier was to decline the use of Air Force helicopters.[8]

The technical controversies over SKY CAV were related to the limitations in range, speed, and vulnerability of current models of Army aircraft. Aircraft employed by Army units during Exercise SAGE BRUSH were often assigned missions which they were not designed to perform. There was no opportunity during the exercise to conduct a valid test of helicopter vulnerability.

Of much more importance were the tactical controversies resulting from the SKY CAV test which were a direct outgrowth of the manner in which the Army aircraft were employed during Exercise SAGE BRUSH. The tactics of employment of Army aviation during the exercise were generally poor, particularly with regard to helicopters. Some observers were quick to form unfavorable opinions of the potential value of helicopters on the basis of what had been demonstrated.[9]

All phases of the project except evaluation were completed during the maneuver phase of Exercise SAGE BRUSH, and on 19 December the SKY CAV provisional organization was ordered terminated. This was done despite the recommendation by the Commanding General, Third Army, that the troop be retained at Fort Bragg and further developed at corps level in support of the XVIII Airborne Corps.[10]

The final report of the evaluation of the Provisional Reconnaissance Troop (SKY CAV) contained the recommendation that organizational doctrine of the Army provide for the combination of Army aircraft reconnaissance and transport capabilities, certain air transportable ground reconnaissance facilities, and the latest electronic surveillance devices in one unit. The report also recommended that the revised SKY CAV concept of organization and operation be applied to units designed to provide reconnaissance and target acquisition means for division, corps, and the field army. As a result of the problems encountered during the exercise, it was recommended that SKY CAV units not be used to replace, or to become a component of the mechanized reconnaissance units of divisions, corps, and armies.[11]

The test of the SKY CAV concept was not the only aspect of Army aviation to be evaluated during Exercise SAGE BRUSH. An attempt was made to use transport helicopters as an integral part of the transportation support during the exercise. The transport helicopters, however, received limited employment under conditions which made virtually impossible any firm conclusions as to their adequacy or effectiveness. Much of the difficulty resulted from the fact that the transport aviation units were understrength and lacked operating experience with their equipment. Instead of the four companies authorized, the transport helicopter battalion had only one and one-third light helicopter companies. The full company, which had recently been equipped with twenty-one H-34 helicopters was late in arriving in the maneuver area. The company's equipment was immediately grounded for correction of technical difficulty with the fuel systems. As a result, the only available helicopter lift until late in the exercise was a platoon of seven H-21 helicopters.

A tactical airlift operation, scheduled for the third phase of the exercise, was dropped because of insufficient time to coordinate plans with the supported unit. During the final phase of the exercise, the helicopter battalion supported the 3d Infantry Division in its assault across the Red River. As a result of the delays in transmitting the request for the use of the transport helicopters and sporadic liaison between the battalion commander and the division, planning was not completed until immediately before the operation got underway. Because of the training status of the pilots and the absence of facilities for night maintenance, the transport helicopters were made available for only a limited daylight period. Since the infantrymen and the pilots had never worked together, no one at the loading sites knew who should do what. After some confusion, the pilots supervised the slinging of cargo and the infantry provided the labor. Because of refueling limitations, the helicopters were dispatched in "merry-go-round" fashion. A mass lift would have been more efficient and more in keeping with the objective of tactical surprise. In addition, for reasons of safety, the helicopters came in at about 300 feet, a height from which they could be easily spotted, instead of employing contour flying.

The exercise demonstrated that official doctrine regarding the tactics and techniques of Army transport aircraft employment needed clarification. In view of the slow speed, readily identifiable flight noise, and vulnerability to air attack and ground fire, there was need for further study of the suitability of transport helicopters for use over enemy held territory. Other findings indicated the need for improved or additional communications, maintenance and cargo landing equipment, and for a terminal service unit to locate and operate loading and unloading sites. It was urged that greater stress be placed on joint training of transport helicopter and Army combat units.

The controversy between the Transportation Corps and the combat arms over who should control Army aviation surfaced as a result of the findings of the final maneuver report. The portion of the report dealing with transportation concluded that the placing of surface and air capabilities in a single transportation service was sound, while the portion concerned with Army aviation concluded that the arrangement was undesirable. It indicated that the most recent doctrine contained in Department of the Army Training Circular 1-7, 29 March 1955, called for Army transport aviation to be used primarily for combat support, with logistic support as an additional function. It was proposed that until sufficient Army transport aircraft were available for both types of support, the principal emphasis should be placed on their use with tactical elements. To this end, and to simplify channels, it was recommended that transport aircraft be placed under the general staff supervision of the G-3 and the special staff supervision of the Army aviation section, rather than under the G-4. Consideration should be given to the establishment of an Army air arm to provide a career program for the development of necessary specialized aviation personnel.

The Chief of Transportation took exception to these recommendations. He contended that the concept of integrating surface and air transport capabilities was sound. The assignment of the air capability to G-3 would interfere with the G-4 staff responsibility for transportation of units, personnel, and supplies by water, highway, railway, and air. The employment of transport helicopters for either combat or service support missions would provide flexibility, and priority could be given to tactical missions. The Chief of Transportation also nonconcurred in the need for a separate Army air arm although he had already agreed to a proposed Army-wide career development program.[12]

Exercise SLEDGE HAMMER

Following the evaluation of the SKY CAV test in Exercise SAGE BRUSH, CONARC recommended to the Department of the Army that further tests of the concept be conducted in a project designated SKY CAV II. It was planned to add a SKY CAV troop to the 1st Armored Division reconnaissance battalion and conduct further tests of the original concept of improving the capability of ground reconnaissance units by the addition of Army aviation elements and electronic surveillance devices. The testing was to be conducted during Exercise SLEDGE HAMMER in early 1957.[13]

On 23 April 1956, CONARC recommended to the Department of the Army that SKY CAV II be organized as recommended by the test reports of Exercise SAGE BRUSH, with certain modifications and changes deemed appropriate by CONARC. The SKY CAV unit would be combined with, and made organic to, the 1st Armored Division's armored cavalry battalion for tests in Exercise SLEDGE HAMMER. On 19 July, the Department of the Army informed CONARC that it had no objection to the test evaluation of the SKY CAV concept during Exercise SLEDGE HAMMER. It pointed out that the test of the SKY CAV concept could be conducted without major budgetary implications, interference with existing programs, and without the necessity for reorganizing elements of a high priority general reserve division if existing resources and facilities were utilized. The Department of the Army therefore directed that a transportation light helicopter company then available to CONARC be used as the basic unit without reorganization. Additional necessary reconnaissance aircraft and aviators were to be provided to the helicopter company from CONARC resources. A provisional surveillance platoon, to include drone aircraft from signal test resources, was to be attached to the helicopter company on or after 1 February 1957 for the duration of the test. On 21 September, CONARC provided instructions for the organization, testing, and evaluation of the SKY CAV company (SKY CAV II) in Exercise SLEDGE HAMMER. CONARC furnished TOE 17-48T, Sky Cavalry Company, Armored Cavalry Battalion, Armored Division, on 15 October.[14]

The test of SKY CAV in Exercise SAGE BRUSH had shown that the unit was deficient in the non-air-transportable elements of the unit and was therefore not suitable for fulfilling the division's requirement for ground and aerial reconnaissance. SKY CAV II was an effort to accomplish the original objective by utilizing the reconnaissance battalion of an armor division and adding an organic Sky Cavalry company. This company would contain the necessary aerial reconnaissance and transport, and electronic and photographic surveillance devices to enable the battalion to fulfill the division's requirement for greater speed and accuracy in obtaining target information and intelligence, greater terrain coverage, and greater mobility in the performance of all missions of the reconnaissance battalion. SKY CAV II was not only a test of the SKY CAV company itself, but also was a test of a concept for a new division reconnaissance battalion which included aerial reconnaissance and transport capabilities and electronic and photographic surveillance devices.

On 25 October, Fourth Army informed CONARC that if the helicopter company designated for SKY CAV II did not arrive at Fort Polk by 1 December, the test would be invalid due to lack of training with the division. CONARC informed Fourth Army on 10 November that the company would not be available before January 1957, and indicated that this date should provide adequate time to organize and train the unit. Actually, the 64th Transportation Company (Light Helicopter) with its H-34s and attached 544th Transportation Detachment did not move from Fort Sill to Fort Hood until 29 January and did not arrive at Fort Polk to begin training until 10 February. The late arrival of the company at Fort Polk was to have an adverse impact on the effectiveness of the unit during the exercise.[15]

Exercise SLEDGE HAMMER was conducted in the Louisiana Maneuver Area from 6 to 16 May 1957. Because of personnel shortages in the 1st Armored Division, the scope of the exercise was reduced to troop tests of SKY CAV II and the assault pipeline and bulk supply of armor. The final report of Exercise SLEDGE HAMMER was highly critical of the SKY CAV concept. One conclusion stated that the reconnaissance squadron did not have the capability of effectively supporting, operationally or logistically, a Sky Cavalry company. It was also concluded that the reconnaissance squadron was incapable of simultaneously carrying on a ground combat action in one area and planning and conducting airborne reconnaissance activities for the division in another area. Fourth Army felt that the SKY CAV concept of combining reconnaissance and cargo helicopters, reconnaissance aircraft, and armored reconnaissance elements in a single battalion was operationally and administratively unsound. The report contained the recommendation that the concept of Sky Cavalry as an organizational entity be discarded. Instead, in commenting on the final report Fourth Army recommended that the division aviation company be augmented by an additional four fixed wing reconnaissance aircraft and five reconnaissance helicopters to operate in tactical support of the reconnaissance squadron, with nine additional light cargo helicopters assigned to the division aviation company. Pending development of effective electronic and photographic devices, Fourth Army recommended that these items be deleted from the TOE.

Both Fourth Army and CONARC strongly objected to the recommendation to discard the SKY CAV concept. Both believed that the concept of improving reconnaissance capabilities by combining aerial reconnaissance, surveillance, and transport capabilities within the division was basically sound. CONARC, in its comments, pointed out that Exercise SLEDGE HAMMER was not conducted to test the concept but to determine whether the efforts of a SKY CAV unit could be combined with the armored division reconnaissance squadron. CONARC also believed that the electronic and photographic devices should not be deleted from the TOEs, but that issue of such items should be limited to specific tests pending development suitable for general issue. Fourth Army stated that no test had been made of the concept or the effectiveness of Sky Cavalry as a separate organizational entity in a primary role as an information gathering agency in support of a more flexible and timely intelligence effort and urged further exploration of this area.[16]

On 27 September, CONARC forwarded to the Department of the Army an evaluation of the test of SKY CAV II. The evaluation concluded that there was a requirement for continued tests designed to develop doctrine for organization, equipment, and employment of such units, and particularly the units employing surveillance devices. It was uneconomical and unproductive to employ experimental surveillance equipment during maneuvers unless such tests were supported on a sufficient scale to ensure their success and unless the equipment had been through adequate engineering and user tests. CONARC believed that continued experimentation to develop surveillance devices was essential to meet the increased combat surveillance and target acquisition requirements of the field army.

CONARC recommended that the Commanding General, Fourth Army, be directed to develop, through experimentation, the optimum SKY CAV organization and technique of tactical employment, this experimentation to include the feasibility and desirability of including armed helicopters into such organizations. CONARC indicated that the 1st Reconnaissance Squadron (SKY CAV), 16th Cavalry, 2d U.S. Army Missile Command at Fort Hood was the logical unit to serve as the test vehicle.

CONARC also recommended several actions to be taken by the Department of the Army. The Deputy Chief of Staff for Personnel should take action to fill the 1st Reconnaissance Squadron, 16th Cavalry, to authorized strength. The Chief Signal Officer should make available surveillance devices when they had reached a stage of development permitting troop testing of the reconnaissance and surveillance platoon of the reconnaissance squadron. The Director of Army Aviation should provide such additional equipment as was required in connection with the investigation of the desirability and feasibility of including armed helicopters in the SKY CAV organization.

CONARC went on to recommend that a test of a SKY CAV-type unit be included in Exercise GRAND BAYOU, scheduled for the second quarter of FY 1960.[17] Operation and maintenance personnel for the surveillance-type units organic to the new infantry, airborne, and armored divisions, and the missile commands should be trained by the Combat Surveillance and Target Acquisition Training Unit at Fort Huachuca. The U.S. Army Combat Developments Experimentation Center should conduct experiments to test the integral elements of surveillance units scheduled for the PENTOMIC army.

On 26 December, the Department of the Army concurred in the conclusions of CONARC, although designation of the 1st Reconnaissance Squadron, 16th Cavalry, as the organization responsible for further development of SKY CAV concepts was not favorably considered because the availability of special devices and equipment and the requirements of other units would preclude fully equipping these four reconnaissance troops within the foreseeable future. The Department of the Army considered that further testing should be restricted to that which could be accomplished by Troop A, 1st Reconnaissance Squadron, 16th Cavalry, and U.S. Army Combat Developments Experimentation Center as equipment could be made available to these units. Testing within the missile command would be limited to perfecting doctrine and concepts applicable to that type organization, primarily target acquisition, rather than an extension of ground reconnaissance.

The Department of the Army stated that the feasibility of using armed helicopters had been fully established. Whether armed helicopters should be integrated into ground reconnaissance of SKY CAV-type units was considered an appropriate subject for evaluation in a field exercise or maneuver in the near future. The Department of the Army believed that future tests of a SKY CAV unit should be conducted as rapidly as adequate equipment and supervision could be provided and personnel trained. Any test of such a unit must also evaluate the logistical support load thrown upon a field army. The use of CDEC to test the integral elements of surveillance units was considered appropriate; however, in view of the existing requirement for additional information and guidance in this field, tests should be applied to present or near future organizations in addition to those planned for the PENTOMIC army.[18]

The Armair Brigade Study

During 1956 and 1957, the Army Aviation School initiated and largely developed a study entitled "The Armair Brigade." The concept proposed by the Army Aviation School was an extension and enlargement of the SKY CAV organization. The brigade included sky cavalry organizations as subordinate units and provided for a completely airmobile combined arms unit with a capability for sustained operations. The brigade concept provided a high degree of mobility and gave the commander the means of attaining a high degree of freedom of movement.[19]

The organic aircraft of the Armair Brigade provided surveillance information, reconnaissance, and battlefield observation to all echelons of command. The brigade was also able to provide direct application of firepower. The limited Army aviation assigned to the new ROCID division had no appreciable effect on the speed at which the entire ground force moved. In the Armair Brigade, by contrast, movement was geared to the speed of its helicopters and not the pace of the foot soldier.

The Armair Brigade's advantages of faster reaction time, flexibility, high mobility, and direct fire support were offset by some inherent and complex deficiencies. A troop test and evaluation was proposed to study these problems. The major unresolved problem was the vulnerability of helicopters to light enemy ground fire. Another significant problem was the necessity of moving large quantities of aircraft fuels and lubricants to advanced or separate battlefield locations. The adverse effects of bad weather and poor visibility were also important considerations. A serious shortcoming of the helicopter was the extensive and constant need for maintenance and repair.

The Army Aviation School staff planners made certain basic assumptions regarding the vulnerability of helicopters to enemy ground fire. This problem was not investigated in detail until the experiments conducted by the U.S. Army Combat Developments Experimentation

Center in 1959. It was possible at the time of the Armair Brigade study, however, to ascertain with a degree of accuracy the requirements for fuel and lubricants that logistics organizations would have to provide. Everything was to be carried in airmobile vehicles and this imposed a tremendous requirement in regard to forecasting, handling, and delivery of the quantities of petroleum, oil, and lubricants (POL) necessary to support a completely airmobile brigade. The concept devised to solve this problem was the use of bulk delivery from Army supply points to the brigade using a system of aircraft tankers or collapsible fuel cells. Deliveries within the brigade would then be made by the tankers of the aviation POL company. Since the brigade had no facilities to stockpile fuel, deliveries from the tankers of the support group would be made on a rigid schedule whenever the unit was engaged in operations. Refinement of this concept awaited the results of troop tests and organizational development.

Despite the recognized requirement of extensive maintenance of brigade helicopters, no technical service organization was proposed to be included in the unit. This arrangement was in keeping with the principle of reducing to the absolute minimum the service support personnel in the brigade, but was in direct opposition to the requirements for specially trained and highly skilled maintenance men. This contradiction was circumvented by creating within the brigade a pool of technical service personnel. The pool, located in the support group, was expected to provide assistance in major maintenance requirements. The support group was to consist of two emergency repair companies and a rear support company. The rear support company was divided into teams of technical personnel that were to be placed in a direct support or attached basis to each of the combat elements of the brigade.

This concept of maintenance operations was based on restricting equipment down time to a 24-hour limit. Any equipment requiring more time than this to repair would be evacuated by the Army aviation maintenance unit in support of the brigade. Normal maintenance would require the assistance of the combat units' organic personnel as well as the teams from the support group. Although this maintenance concept was a major innovation of the Armair Brigade study, indications that it was feasible were derived from experience gained by the 101st Airborne Division in Operation JUMP LIGHT. The proposed maintenance system was described as the "functionalized" approach.

The maintenance concept contained in the Armair Brigade study received a number of critical evaluations. The functionalization of maintenance would require additional skills from the supporting personnel. This, in turn, would require greater training and experience on the part of technicians, resulting in increased and more complex training requirements. It remained questionable whether the technical service people could perform the variety of work required. The proposed system was also ambiguous as to where the ultimate responsibility for maintenance resided—with the combat unit commander or with the direct support group commander. During noncombat periods, the brigade would depend heavily upon technical service support as its own maintenance capacity would be inadequate unless periodic support was provided. It was obvious that complete consideration of this maintenance concept was not possible until a full scale troop test could be held.

The brigade was organized as much as possible along standard lines. Deviations from existing organizations were made only where the unique requirements of a helicopter mobile combined arms group made them necessary. A major consideration in the design of the Armair Brigade was to ease the transition of troops and equipment into the new brigade.

The Armair Brigade was to consist of a headquarters and headquarters company, a reconnaissance-attack company, a Sky Cavalry group, an infantry battle group, an amphibious artillery battery, and a support group. Certain accepted and proposed units were used in the brigade concept. The existing units adopted for use were:

Sky Cavalry Troop
Aero Infantry Company (ROCID TOE 7-17C)
Infantry Battle Group (ROCID TOE 7-11C)
Field Artillery Battery, 762-mm. Rocket (ROTAD TOE 6-238T-Amphibious)
Airborne Maintenance Battalion (ROTAD TOE 29-657T)
Tactical Transportation Battalion
Artillery Battery, 318-mm. Rocket

The headquarters company performed the normal command, control, staff planning and supervision functions. The reconnaissance-attack company combined aerial maneuver and air-to-ground fire power. The fire power of the company, combined with the other arms in the brigade, provided maximum on-target effect. The Sky Cavalry group was to perform aerial and ground reconnaissance, provide security to the unit to which assigned or attached, and provide delaying actions through offensive and defensive actions. The unit was designed to exploit aerial mobility, surprise, and shock action inherent in its distinctive element. The infantry battle group added aerial mobility to its traditional mission of closing with the enemy. This unit also had the command structure to create and control task forces on independent missions.

To obtain artillery capabilities despite the weight of most existing artillery equipment, the airmobile concept called for the use of the lightweight, air-transportable 318-mm. LITTLE JOHN rocket. This rocket had a nuclear capability. The LITTLE JOHN battery provided long-range aerial artillery support and reinforcing fires to units of the Armair Brigade.

The brigade was manned on an austere basis to enable it to move rapidly over long distances. The matter of limited personnel would present problems only in a sustained combat situation; a role for which the brigade was not designed. Each unit contained the men necessary to perform its combat mission, and reductions were achieved in the normal complement of administrative, mess, and ground vehicle support personnel.

A limitation on the Armair Brigade at the time of its conception in 1956 was the available aircraft. The brigade was to use existing aircraft. Although the study included the use of armed helicopters, the actual development of this armament had just begun. The adaptability of machine guns to helicopters was by this time widely practiced and accepted, but the practicality of heavier armament still had not been proven. The H-34 and H-21 helicopters were used in the

Armair Brigade study as armed troop carriers for tactical operations. The tactical transport battalion contained H-37 helicopters.

The use of fixed wing airplanes was severely limited in the Armair concept. Except for limited command, control, and liaison aircraft, no fixed wing airplane was considered standard for the brigade. The use of fixed wing airplanes was limited because airfield and aircraft requirements were incompatible with those of helicopters. Even though small in number, coordinating the different needs of fixed wing and rotary wing aircraft would add to the complexity in logistics, maintenance, and supply channels.

The H-21 and H-34 helicopters were capable of transporting a full squad, while mounting two machine guns or several aerial rockets. The armed helicopters would be able to deliver troops quickly to the area of the objective. The transport helicopters, in conjunction with the armed reconnaissance and weapons helicopters, would be capable of providing suppressive fire in the landing zone. The weapons helicopters would be available to respond on call to deliver their heavier firepower when needed. The transport helicopters would move using cover and concealment to protect them from ground fire and aid in maintaining the element of surprise.

Although the Armair Brigade proposal never received the troop test and evaluation necessary to properly evaluate and develop the concept, the study is significant in the history of Army aviation. In this 1956 study appear many of the concepts that were to be fully developed in the air assault division tests and organization of the airmobile division in the 1960s and the development of the air cavalry combat brigade in the 1970s.

Helicopter Carrier Tests

The employment by the United States Marine Corps of troop carrying helicopters based on aircraft carriers offered a new dimension to amphibious operations. In 1958, the Army began to investigate the feasibility of operating its helicopters from aircraft carriers.

Exercise ROCKY SHOALS was held in the vicinity of San Simeon Point, California, during the period 1-10 November 1958. Approximately eighty Army aircraft participated in this maneuver. Participating units with Army aircraft included the III Corps Aviation Section, 4th Aviation Company (Infantry Division), 33d Transportation Company (Light Helicopter), 57th Transportation Company (Light Helicopter), and 416th Signal Company (-).

The experience of this exercise pointed to notable advantages of helicopter landings as opposed to amphibious landings, the most apparent of which were the ability to land beyond the beach independent of surf conditions, speed and maneuverability, and increased dispersion of shipping.

An assault helicopter aircraft carrier transported five H-21 helicopters to an off-shore position. Only the top deck of the carrier contained helicopters because the ship's elevator was too small for helicopter storage below deck. Additional Army aircraft participating in this amphibious maneuver were flown to the exercise area because of the limited number of ships. Air traffic control was assumed by the Army forces upon passing corps control ashore.

A reinforced infantry company from the carrier USS *Thetis Bay* landed by helicopter on an objective seven miles inland. Other actual cargo helicopter missions included movement of aggressor forces, delivery of rations to forward units, and delivery of critical ordnance supplies, including a jeep engine. The hilly terrain of the maneuver area indicated a need to plan for aircraft automatic radio relay.[20]

During the period, 13-23 April 1959, one observer from CONARC and seven from Second and Third Armies and the Army Aviation School observed Marine helicopter operations from the USS *Boxer* at Vieques, Puerto Rico. The observer group concluded that special training was necessary for operation of Army helicopters from Navy aircraft carriers and that appropriate field publications should be developed and tested. Recommendations of this group included a directive to the Army Aviation School for development of a training text, a letter to Third Army advising helicopter employment from a carrier during the next spring and summer, and a letter to the Department of the Army requesting direct coordination with the Navy and the Marine Corps for pilot instruction and Navy helicopter carrier utilization.[21]

On 18 August 1959, CONARC pointed out to the Department of the Army that the necessity of dispersion of a landing force and of early seizure of inland objectives had established the role of the helicopter and the helicopter carrier in amphibious operations. Army experience with helicopter carrier operations had been limited to Exercise ROCKY SHOALS, and Army training literature for such operations did not exist.

CONARC proposed the development of a training text for operating helicopters from helicopter carriers during amphibious operations, followed by a training exercise, in coordination with the Navy and the Marine Corps, to test and evaluate this training text. CONARC asked the Department of the Army to obtain from the Navy a suitable helicopter carrier for the training exercise. In addition, a nucleus of approximately twelve Army aviation instructor pilots needed Marine Corps training in helicopter carrier operations.

On 9 November, the Department of the Army approved the proposed action and requested that Navy and Marine Corps support be made available. The Army Aviation School prepared the initial manuscript of TT 1-( ), Helicopter Operations from Helicopter Carriers, and the Commanding General, Third Army, was directed to test and evaluate this training text. To assure an effective evaluation, four each H-37, H-34, H-21, and UH-1A helicopters were to be used and a minimum of two pilots and two crew chiefs for each type of helicopter employed plus selected aviation ground handling personnel were to receive training conducted by Marine Corps instructors.

Temporary duty Marine Corps instructors conducted preliminary carrier training for aircraft crews at Fort Bragg during the period, 25 May-15 June 1960. Actual carrier operations and training exercises were conducted from the USS *Antietam,* 21-24 June, within the Pensacola training area.[22]

Organizational Developments

The potential of aviation gave rise to a number of proposals for its tactical use. Various types of new units were proposed and tests helped develop doctrine for the combat employment of Army aviation.

On 13 December 1957, General Howze briefed General Wyman, the CONARC Commander, on a concept for establishing an armed helicopter unit at Fort Bragg. This unit was to be designated an air cavalry unit and would be approximately battalion (-) sized. Upon completion of the briefing, General Howze requested that General Wyman submit a CONARC position to the Department of the Army on the establishment of this type of unit. On 19 February 1958, CONARC recommended to the Department of the Army that an aerial battalion (infantry) be activated at Fort Benning during the fourth quarter of FY 1959. The proposed unit was to be a TD unit in order to allow for the conduct of experiments. Its mission would be to test the validity of the use of armed helicopters, development of organizational data, tactics, and techniques of employment. The Commanding General, Third Army, would be responsible for the conduct of the tests with assistance from the Army Aviation School.[23]

On 2 July 1958, the Department of the Army requested CONARC prepare a study to develop initial concepts for employment of Army aircraft in conjunction with ground combat forces during the period 1958-1970. In summary, the study group concluded that aircraft with suppressive fire capability could be employed to increase the mobility of ground forces. It also concluded that an aerial combat reconnaissance platoon be included in the cavalry squadrons of the infantry and armored divisions and that an aerial combat reconnaissance company be made organic to the armored cavalry regiment.

The study group recommended that the Department of the Army direct training programs for airmobile operations in overseas theaters. CONARC would be authorized to organize, equip, and train an aerial combat reconnaissance platoon as an organic part of the cavalry squadron of one infantry division and as an organic part of the armored cavalry squadron of one armored division. One aerial combat reconnaissance company was to be an organic part of a cavalry regiment. CONARC forwarded the study to the Department of the Army on 25 July.[24]

Although much progress had been made, some felt in early 1961 that the evolution of organization and tactics involving integrated aviation had been overly cautious. General Clyde D. Eddleman, the Vice Chief of Staff of the Army, told an Association of the United States Army Aviation Symposium at Fort Rucker on 23 March 1961 that the air cavalry troop was a good example of the evolution problem. General Eddleman stated that it would be desirable to add this capability to the ground forces, but in order to form this type of unit other units must be given up. The substitutes had to be carefully considered. There was now a schedule of deployment for air cavalry troops and recent tests had confirmed that the concept was sound. These troops could be substituted for a ground troop of the reconnaissance squadrons of the infantry and armored divisions and might replace one troop of the separate armored cavalry regiments.

General Eddleman realized that there had been sound reasons for proceeding with deliberation in forming air cavalry units, notably the early state-of-the-art in helicopter weapons systems. But he warned not to let development of concepts of employment wait for ideal air vehicles. Alluding to the work of the Rogers Board, General Eddleman stated that a ten year plan had a subtle implication attached to it. He warned that if all attention were focused on 1970, the Army might be in danger of falling short of its intermediate goals. By promising the 1970 soldier everything, little or nothing might be produced for the soldier of the 1960s.[25]

The concerns of General Eddleman were reflected in the shift of national defense policy which began in 1961. This shift was to lead in the following year to the proceedings of the Howze Board and the beginning of a new era in airmobility and Army aviation.

Endnotes
Chapter XI

1. Maj Gen James M. Gavin, "Cavalry, and I Don't Mean Horses," *Harper's Magazine*, Vol. 208, Apr 58, pp. 54-60. The article subsequently was republished in several military journals.

2. Maj Gen H.H. Howze, "The Future Direction of Army Aviation," *Army*, Vol. 7, No. 5, Dec 56, pp. 51-54.

3. Maj Gen H.H. Howze, "Future of Army Aviation," *United States Army Aviation Digest*, Vol. 3, No. 6, Jun 57, pp. 4-6.

4. Maj Gen H.H. Howze, "Combat Tactics for Tomorrow's Army," *Army*, Vol. 8, No. 3, Oct 57, pp. 24-30.

5. Weston and Stephens, *Helicopter Armament*, Pt I, pp. 19-20.

6. (1) CONARC Summary of Major Events and Problems, FY 55, Vol. VIII, Cbt Dev Sec Gen Div, Jan-Jun 55, pp. 5-6. (2) Draft ms, History of Army Aviation, ch VIII, pp. 34-35.

7. For additional information regarding Exercise SAGE BRUSH, see Jean R. Moenk, *A History of Large-Scale Army Maneuvers in the United States, 1935-1964*, HQ CONARC, Dec 69, pp. 205-220 (hereafter cited as Moenk, *Large-Scale Maneuvers*).

8. Ltr, Dahlquist to Collier, 1 Nov 55.

9. (1) Transcript of Joint Critique Exercise SAGE BRUSH, 10 Dec 55. (2) Report of Army Tests, Exercise SAGE BRUSH, 20 Jan 56, App 22, Annex H, Final Report Evaluation of Provisional Reconnaissance Troop (SKY CAV).

10. (1) CONARC Summary of Major Events and Problems, FY 56, Vol. IV, Cbt Dev Sec Gen Div, Jul-Dec 55, p. 2. (2) Msg AJPOD-12-47, CG Third Army to CG CONARC, 151935Z Dec 55. (3) Msg 12354, CG CONARC to CG Third Army, 191835Z Dec 55.

11. Final Report Evaluation of Provisional Reconnaissance Troop (SKY CAV).

12. Army Transportation in Exercise SAGE BRUSH, OCofT, pp. 15-18.

13. CONARC Summary of Major Events and Problems, FY 56, Vol. VIII, Cbt Dev Sec Gen Div, Jan-Jun 56, p. 3.

14. (1) Ltr OPS OT DC, DA DCSOPS to CONARC, 19 Jul 56, subj: Sky Cavalry Company. (2) CONARC Summary of Major Events and Problems, FY 57, Vol. III, G-3 Sec Org & Equip Div, pp. 21-22.

15. (1) Msg 1360 AKADC-E, Fourth Army to CONARC, 041630Z May 57. (2) Ltr ATTNG-D&R 353.01/188(ATT) (21 Sep 56), CONARC to distr, subj: Instructions for Organization, Testing, and Evaluation of Provisional Sky Cavalry Company (SKY CAV II). (3) DF, G-3 to CofS, 10 Nov 56, subj: Helicopter Support for Sky Cav II.

16. (1) Ltr ATTNG-P&O 354 (SLEDGE HAMMER), CONARC to DA DCSOPS, 21 Aug 57, subj: Final Report, Exercise SLEDGE HAMMER. (2) CONARC Summary of Major Events and Problems, FY 57, Vol. IV, G-3 Sec Doc & Req Div, Jan-Jun 57, p. 21.

17. This exercise was cancelled in 1959 due to lack of funds. Moenk, *Large-Scale Maneuvers*, p. 222.

18. CONARC Summary of Major Events and Problems, FY 58, Vol. III, G-3 Sec Don & Req Div, Jul-Dec 57, pp. 26-29.

19. This section is based on Weston and Stephens, *Helicopter Armament*, Pt I, pp. 30-47.

20. CONARC Summary of Major Events and Problems, FY 59, Vol. III, Army Avn Sec, Jul-Dec 58, pp. 17-18.

21. Ibid., FY 59, Vol. III, Avn Sec, Jan-Jun 59, p. 18.

22. Ibid., FY 60, Vol. V, Avn Sec, Jan-Jun 60, pp. 1-2.

23. Ibid., FY 58, Vol. II, Avn Sec, Jan-Jun 58, p. 5.

24. Ibid., FY 59, Vol. VI, Cbt Dev Sec Plans Div, Jul-Dec 58, pp. 2-3.

25. DA News Release No. 241-61, Address by General Clyde D. Eddleman to AUSA Army Aviation Symposium, Ft Rucker, Alabama, 23 Mar 61.

Chapter XII

MATERIEL DEVELOPMENT

The final link in the development of airmobile capability was the provision of suitable aircraft. In 1957, General Howze wrote, "We expect improvement in our aircraft. While what we have are now very useful, we need aircraft that are simpler and easier to maintain, with greater capacities, better performance, and a greater ability to land and take off from very small unimproved fields."[1]

Two years later, Brig. Gen. Clifton F. Von Kann, the Director of Army Aviation, said, "Our goal in the immediate future is to simplify the models and types of Army aircraft to a minimum in order to reduce their cost of procurement, operation, and especially maintenance."[2] General Von Kann went on to say that the Army had a requirement for new light observation aircraft—3,000 aircraft by 1970—and a flying crane. In 1959, the Army had about 5,000 aircraft with a requirement for 6,500. Of this inventory, 68 percent were in the light observation area. General Von Kann believed that the aviation budget must be increased at least threefold to make sure the Army increased its mobility potential rather than experience a steady decline.

Many of the aircraft and equipment developments which took place between 1955 and 1962 have been described in the preceding chapters. The successful implementation of the airmobility concept required much more sophisticated aircraft than were in service in 1955. The introduction of the XG-40 helicopter—subsequently redesignated the UH-1—eventually proved to be the key element in making real airmobility possible. Late in the period, the development of the HC-1 CHINOOK helicopter and the AC-1 CARIBOU fixed wing transport further expanded the Army's ability to move significant forces by air within the combat zone. The search for an adequate reconnaissance aircraft produced the AO-1 MOHAWK, and testing was well underway to choose a new light observation helicopter. Army aircraft during this period are shown in Table 2.

U.S. Army Aviation Board

The Army Aviation Division of Army Ground Forces Board No. 1 had been established in 1945 at Fort Bragg. To facilitate coordination and interchange of ideas, the division—by then known as the Army Aviation Service Test Division—in June 1954 was transferred to Fort

Sill, the location of the U.S. Army Aviation School. In October 1954, the Army Service Test Division followed the school to Camp Rucker. For administrative purposes, the division at Camp Rucker was placed under direct control of Army Field Forces Board No. 5, located at Fort Bragg.

Early in 1955, it became apparent that the test division could not cope with the tremendous amount of testing required by the rapid growth of Army aviation. Consequently, CONARC Board No. 6 was established at Fort Rucker on 1 August 1955. The board was redesignated the U.S. Army Aviation Board on 1 January 1957. The U.S. Army Aviation Board's function was similar to that of other CONARC boards. Items that passed engineering tests were distributed to appropriate CONARC boards for user tests. After examining the items carefully, the boards recommended to CONARC whether or not the items had military potential.

In May 1956, the Chief of Staff of the Army directed the establishment of Transportation Corps and Signal Corps test activities at Fort Rucker. The U.S. Army Transportation Aircraft Test and Support Activity (TATSA) was organized in July as a Class II activity of the Office of the Chief of Transportation. Its primary mission was logistical evaluation of new types of aircraft and equipment. Similarly, the U.S. Army Signal Aviation Test and Support Activity (SATSA) was established in September as a Class II activity under the Chief Signal Officer. Its mission included the evaluation of spare parts, tools, and test equipment used in the avionics field. In August 1962, TATSA and SATSA were combined with the U.S. Army Aviation Board to form the U.S. Army Aviation Test Board.[3]

The Development and Procurement Cycle

When the United States Air Force was established as a separate service in 1947, responsibility for Army aircraft development and procurement was transferred to it. In 1956, the Army was given responsibility for all phases of aircraft planning and disposition of its own aircraft except for procurement and engineering. These two functions could be assigned to either the Air Force or the Navy. The Army in 1960 requested and was given authority to purchase off-the-shelf items, prepare specifications for Army air items, establish and conduct appropriate boards for evaluation and inspection, participate with the services in all phases of testing of Army air items, and to assign qualified personnel to Air Force and Navy development and procuring services. The Air Force objected to the Army assumption of these responsibilities, but the Department of Defense affirmed the new policy.[4]

Responsibilities for research, development, supply and maintenance, and training were assigned and modified by a series of interservice agreements, memoranda of understanding, and Department of Defense directives. By 1962, these responsibilities were distributed as follows:

    a. **Action:** Qualitative Materiel Requirements
       Army: Prepare, approve, publish
       Air Force/Navy:

    b. **Action:** Design Competition
       Army: Conduct, select winner
       Air Force/Navy: Technical assistance

c. **Action:** Specifications
 Army: Prepare, approve, publish
 Air Force/Navy: Technical assistance
d. **Action:** Engineering evaluation specification, review mock-up, developmental engineering inspection, contract technical
 Army: Control
 Air Force/Navy: Technical recommendations and coordination
e. **Action:** Engineering Flight Test
 Army: Review plans, approve
 Air Force/Navy: Prepare test plans, direct and control tests approved by Army
f. **Action:** Logistic and User Flight Tests
 Army: Total responsibility
 Air Force/Navy:
g. **Action:** Type classification
 Army: Total responsibility
 Air Force/Navy:
h. **Action:** Budget and funding
 Army: Total responsibility
 Air Force/Navy:
i. **Action:** Developmental contracting
 Army: Funding
 Air Force/Navy: Award, supervision, control
j. **Action:** Research contracting
 Army: Total responsibility
 Air Force/Navy:
k. **Action:** Modifications
 Army: Final decision except flight safety items
 Air Force/Navy: Technical evaluation and flight safety
l. **Action:** Procurement
 Army: Funding
 Air Force/ Navy: Contract award, supervising program
m. **Action:** Maintenance
 Army: Total responsibility
 Air Force/ Navy:
n. **Action:** Training
 Army: Total responsibility
 Air Force/Navy:

Since 1958, no Army aircraft development had been assigned to the Air Force or the Navy and the following responsibilities were being progressively assumed by the Army with Department of Defense approval on an individual item basis:

a. **Action:** Engineering Flight Tests
 Army: Prepare test plans, select testing agency, fund, control test program
 Air Force/Navy: Technical advice and assistance, conduct test when requested
b. **Action:** Developmental contracting
 Army: Total responsibility
 Air Force/Navy:

c. **Action:** Modification
   Army: Evaluation, final
   Air Force/Navy: Technical assistance and recommendations
   d. **Action:** Procurement
   Army: Total responsibility for aircraft not developed and under procurement for another service, and funding for aircraft under procurement for another service
   Air Force/Navy: Contract award, supervision

Developmental Objectives for Army Aviation

On 22 October 1958, the Department of the Army directed CONARC to conduct a comprehensive study entitled "Study of the Developmental Objectives of Army Aviation." This study was to expand or modify the concepts developed in a previous CONARC study entitled "Army Aircraft and Ground Mobility 1958-1970." As a result of the new study, CONARC materiel requirements for Army aircraft might be materially changed. In December, CONARC advised the Chief of Research and Development, Department of the Army, of the status of CONARC qualitative materiel requirements and military characteristics for Army aircraft. It recommended that the qualitative materiel requirements and military characteristics prepared be used for guidance only, finalization to be held in abeyance pending completion of the study. The new study was to be completed by 31 August 1959 and covered the following areas: type air vehicles (including drones) or a listing of their desirable characteristics to be developed on a phased basis; personnel aspects; provision for reconnaissance and surveillance; integration and pooling of air vehicles; logistical concepts; and optimum organizational concepts for employment of Army aircraft at each echelon at which assignment of aircraft was appropriate.

The study was to be conducted under the overall guidance of CONARC with various agencies contributing to the study by the preparation of sub-studies. Sub-studies were prepared by: Army Aviation School; Transportation Corps Combat Development Group, Fort Eustis; and Army Logistical Management Center, Fort Lee. A working committee, consisting of representatives of cognizant staff sections and responsible for the preparation of the final report, was established at CONARC.

The 1st Logistical Command recommended that the organization, role, and operational concepts relative to Army aviation within the framework of the theater army organization be included in the studies. CONARC determined that the information could be obtained by expansion of the study of Army aviation developmental objectives. Accordingly, the Transportation Corps Combat Development Group and the Army Aviation School were requested to include in their respective sub-studies comments and recommendations on the general role of Army aviation within the framework of the theater of army organization.

During the last half of FY 1959, the Infantry School received CONARC approval for a sub-study aimed primarily at determining infantry requirements for aerial vehicles in the 1959-1979 period. Sub-studies were received during this period from the Army Aviation School, the Infantry School, and the Transportation Corps Combat Development Group. The second phase of the Infantry School study, covering the period 1965-1970 was withheld by the school pending additional guidance from the MOMAR-70 Study.[5]

Additional sub-studies were submitted during the first half of FY 1960 by the Army Artillery and Missile School, the Transportation Corps Combat Development Group, and the Army Aviation School. The Infantry School also completed the second part of its study during this period. The entire study was completed and approved by the Commanding General, CONARC, and forwarded to the Department of the Army on 9 May 1960. Although CONARC distributed the report throughout the combat development system in CONUS, copies were not furnished to agencies outside the Army since the report had not yet been approved by the Department of the Army.[6]

The Army Aircraft Development Plan which began to take shape during this period provided for an orderly aviation development through the decade of the 1960s. According to the plan, the L-19, H-13, and H-23 observation aircraft were obsolete and should be replaced. After approving the plan, the Chief of Staff of the Army created the Army Aircraft Requirements Review Board (Rogers Board) whose deliberations have been discussed above.[7]

Helicopter Development

UH-1 IROQUOIS

The Army Equipment Development Guide of 1952 had stated a requirement for a helicopter for medical evacuation, instrument trainer, and general utility missions. As a result of changes made at this time and advances in the state of the art, revised military characteristics were prepared and forwarded to the Department of the Army in November 1953. Existing utility helicopters either were too large for operations in anticipated conditions or they had inadequate performance levels. Furthermore, they were more complex and difficult to maintain than was desired and some were not satisfactory as an aircraft ambulance because of the difficulty of litter stowage and handling.

In June 1955, Bell Aircraft Corporation won a contract to select a new utility helicopter for the Army. The Bell XH-40 was designed specifically to meet Army military characteristics and requirements. It was a closed cabin helicopter of all metal construction, employing one two-bladed main rotor and a two-bladed anti-torque tail rotor. Powered by one Lycoming gas turbine engine, it was the Army's first turbine-powered engine, either fixed wing or rotary. The XH-40 was designed for a pay-load, excluding fuel, oil, and pilot, of 800 pounds. Development progressed sufficiently so that the Mock-up Inspection Board conducted an inspection in mid-November 1955. As a result, 106 minor changes were proposed of which 96 were approved by the board for incorporation in the three experimental aircraft.[8]

The first of the three prototype XH-40s was flown on 22 October 1956, less than sixteen months after design work began. Even before the first flight, a service test batch of six YH-40s had been ordered and were delivered by August 1958.[9] One remained with Bell, together with the XH-40s, one went to Eglin Air Force Base for climatic and cold weather testing, one to Edwards Air Force Base for testing, and three to Fort Rucker for Army trials. Numerous small changes were made in the YH-40s, including a 13-inch lengthening of the fuselage to increase cabin capacity to four stretchers, an increase of ground clearance by four inches, wider crew door, and changes in the controls.

In December 1958, it was determined, subject to satisfactory completion of the remainder of the service test, that the YH-40 was suitable for Army use under desert conditions. CONARC forwarded the results of the service test to the Department of the Army in March 1959. Various deficiencies in the YH-40 were listed for correction when the aircraft went into production as the UH-1. Subject to the results of further service testing of the UH-1, the aircraft was considered suitable as a utility helicopter.

In October 1958, CONARC directed the Army Aviation School to troop test the UH-1A. The objectives of the test were to determine changes in organization and equipment required for operation and maintenance of the UH-1A, when issued as a replacement for the H-19 utility helicopter, and to develop and prepare for publication new and revised operational instructions. In March 1959, the Army Aviation School pointed out to CONARC that the YH-40 service test conducted by the Army Aviation Board had already answered the objectives of the proposed troop test of the UH-1A and recommended that the test be canceled.

In May, CONARC agreed to cancel the UH-1A troop test. The Army Aviation School, however, was to review the interim and final reports of the service test of the YH-40 to determine necessary changes in Army Aviation doctrine, publications, and TOEs when the UH-1A replaced the H-19. The Army Aviation School submitted its recommendations in these areas to CONARC in June.[10]

While the final steps were being taken in the adoptions of the UH-1, CONARC began preparation of the training program for the new helicopter. On 3 October 1958, CONARC approved the program of instruction for the UH-1A maintenance course. The purpose of this two week course was to train enlisted men in organizational maintenance of the UH-1A. The first class, consisting of eleven 101st Airborne Division mechanics, reported on 24 June 1959. One hundred and fifteen mechanics were programed for the course in FY 1960. On 14 January 1959, CONARC approved the program of instruction for the UH-1A Instructor Pilot Transition Training Course. The purpose of this five week course—which was reduced to four weeks on 22 June—was to train commissioned and warrant officer Army aviators as unit instructors in the UH-1A. The first class, consisting of two 101st Airborne Division aviators, reported on 10 June. Twenty-two aviators were programed for the course in FY 1960.[11]

Delivery of the first nine pre-production UH-1As took place on 30 June. A contract for 100 of the helicopters had been announced in March. These helicopters were generally similar to the YH-40s, with a 700 HP Lycoming turbine engine. In July, CONARC furnished the Department of the Army with its requirements for UH-1As. CONARC concurred in a proposal to retain H-34 helicopters in the airborne divisions until an adequate tactical transport helicopter became available. CONARC recommended that eight H-13 helicopters in each airborne division be replaced by a like number of UH-1As. CONARC also recommended that the number of utility helicopters in the infantry and armored divisions not be increased until evaluation of the proposed D series of aviation company TOEs.

Of the original order, fourteen UH-1As were delivered to the Army Aviation School as instrument trainers with dual controls and provision for blind flying instrumentation. The priority distribution schedule for the first forty-seven UH-1As included four instrument trainers for the Army Aviation School and provided for filling the requirements of the 82d Airborne Division.[12]

Following delivery of a UH-1A to the Army Aviation Board in July, deliveries were made to the 82d Airborne Division, 101st Airborne Division, and 57th Medical Detachment (Helicopter Ambulance). During the first half of 1960, the airborne divisions conducted tactical evaluations. The primary purpose of this evaluation was to provide information to determine the suitability of the UH-1A for assignment to the TOE of the airborne division as replacement for the H-34s. As a result of these evaluations, CONARC recommended the replacement of twenty light transport helicopters in each division with thirty-two UH-1As.[13]

Prior to FY 1961, production deliveries of the UH-1 had reached a rate of ten aircraft per month. During FY 1961, actions taken in the development of the FY 1962 budget enabled the production rate to be increased to thirty aircraft per month. Distribution to the field placed these helicopters in the hands of the troops in the Pacific, Europe, and Alaska as well as the STRAC units in CONUS.

Deliveries of the UH-1A were completed in June 1961. An improved model appeared in 1960 with the successful flight of the first of four UH-1Bs. This model had a 1,000 HP Lycoming engine and accommodated eight passengers. The first series UH-1Bs were delivered in March 1961 and successfully passed their service test. Late in 1961, a further contract for 274 UH-1Bs was announced. Still another model, the UH-1D, had a 1,100 HP Lycoming engine and an enlarged cabin to accommodate twelve fully equipped troops. The first UH-1D flew on 16 August 1961, and eight were ordered later in the year.[14]

Light Observation Helicopter

In July 1953, as a result of a requirement in both the Combat Development Objective Guide and the Army Equipment Development Guide, OCAFF submitted military characteristics for a two-place reconnaissance helicopter to the Department of the Army. In May 1954, OCAFF again emphasized the need for such an aircraft and recommended procurement of troop test quantities of the YH-32 helicopter for evaluation. The YH-32 was a small ultra-light helicopter with a two blade rotor powered by a ramjet at each blade tip. Engineering tests, however, subsequently indicated that the YH-32 possessed so many inherent deficiencies that it could not meet the requirements. CONARC therefore recommended that procurement and troop tests be canceled.

On 11 October 1955, CONARC recommended the initiation of a development project to produce a new standard two-place reconnaissance helicopter as a replacement for the command, liaison, and reconnaissance functions performed by the H-13s and H-23s. The H-13 and H-23 had been used to perform aeromedical evacuation as well. The H-19s were used in increasing numbers for aeromedical evacuation, and the introduction of the H-40 was expected to eliminate any further need for the H-13 and H-23 for this purpose.

On 19 March 1956, CONARC pointed out to the Department of the Army that the need for an inexpensive reconnaissance helicopter was not being recognized in the current research and development programs. Unless a replacement for the H-13 and H-23 was developed, the Army would be confronted with continued expensive and marginal product improvements of obsolete aircraft or the procurement of off-the-shelf aircraft, neither of which would be capable of adequately fulfilling the Army's needs.

CONARC believed that the availability of a suitable replacement for the H-13 and H-23 would help the widespread integration of aircraft at the lower echelons of all arms and services. Such a goal could be achieved only if the aircraft were inexpensive in mass production, had a high availability rate, and could be readily maintained at the echelon used. The Chief of Research and Development, Department of the Army, agreed to include the requirement for a new reconnaissance helicopter in the Transportation Corps research and development budget for FY 1957.[15]

The new military characteristics prepared by CONARC called for a reconnaissance helicopter which would be used by battalion and separate unit commanders of all arms and services for command transportation, route and position reconnaissance, and observation of assigned areas of operations. The helicopter should not require a prepared airfield. It should operate on standard vehicle rules, be easy to camouflage and maintain, and simple to operate. The helicopter would normally be employed singly, carrying a pilot and passenger or observer, in the forward areas at low altitudes and within friendly lines. In addition, the helicopter should be suitable for use in the primary training of helicopter pilots.[16]

To meet this requirement for a reconnaissance helicopter, three different models were initially considered. Completed in October 1958 was the service test of the French YHO-1 DJ, a reconnaissance helicopter powered by a gas turbine compressor. The desert and temperate testing of the Hughes YHO-2 HU was completed in October 1959. This helicopter was found to be the most suitable of the light 2-place helicopters tested, but not suitable as a replacement for the H-13H due to its limited load carrying capability. User tests of the YHO-3 BR were canceled due to design deficiencies revealed by engineering tests.[17]

No immediate action was taken to adopt a new reconnaissance helicopter following the failure of the first three models to meet Army requirements. In answer to a request from the Office of the Chief of Transportation on 27 March 1960, the Bureau of Naval Weapons on 31 March consented to let contracts for the competition for a new light observation helicopter. The Office of the Chief of Transportation furnished the Navy with the military characteristics of the proposed new helicopter on 18 May, and the Navy passed this information on to industry. Clarification of the military characteristics came on 16 June at a meeting between thirty-six representatives of industry and a panel of Army and Navy officers at the Bureau of Naval

Weapons. Invitations went out to twenty-five companies on 14 October. Of these, twelve sent in nineteen designs by the end of January 1961.

Six committees established by CONARC during the first week of February examined the designs to determine which ones met operational requirements. On 13 April, the Joint Army-Navy Technical and Operational Evaluation Groups met to combine their findings. The Navy had narrowed its choice to the Hiller model while the Army selected the Bell model first and the Hiller second. Further joint meetings on 18 April and 3 May resulted in a recommendation to the Light Observation Helicopter Design Selection Board that both the Bell and Hiller designs should be developed.

The Light Observation Helicopter Design Selection Board, established by the Chief of Staff of the Army on 17 April and chaired by General Rogers met on 3 and 4 May. On 6 May, the board notified the Chief of Research and Development that it accepted the findings of the joint groups. DCSOPS, Department of the Army did not concur, suggesting that the Hughes design should also be developed. The Army members of the board met on 17 May and recommended that the Chief of Staff of the Army authorize the Chief of Research and Development to procure the Hughes design separately. The manufacturers were notified on 19 May.

Ordinarily the Navy would have carried this program to completion. However, a ruling by the Department of Defense on 10 December gave the Army permission to procure off-the-shelf aircraft directly from industry rather than through the Air Force or the Navy after 1 July 1961. On 12 June 1961, the Chief of Research and Development informed the Chief of Transportation that the test models from Bell and Hiller could be procured directly as permitted.

Contrary to all previous contracts for aircraft procurement, the manufacturers were free to draw the detailed designs and make all decisions on subsequent design and engineering matters. The Army would introduce no changes as long as the designs complied with Federal Aviation Agency Specifications for airworthiness. The Transportation Corps hoped that the time interval between design and procurement would be six and a half years—a goal which eventually was surpassed. Tests of the Bell HO-4, Hiller HO-5, and Hughes HO-6 had not yet taken place at the close of 1962.[18]

Cargo Helicopters

Army interest in heavy cargo helicopters had centered on the development of the H-16B. This helicopter could carry forty-seven troops or 8,500 pounds of cargo. The program encountered many problems, but in March 1955, CONARC recommended that the development of the H-16B be continued with the objectives of obtaining a flying test aircraft by mid-calendar year 1958. In September, the Senior Research and Development Board indicated that the requirement for a heavy helicopter was not questioned. But in view of its size, cost, and complexity, the board doubted the utility of the H-16B in forward combat areas. It therefore recommended cancellation of the H-16B project; development funds were to be used to determine a better method of meeting the requirement.[19]

Despite CONARC's objections, the Department of the Army canceled the H-16B program in April 1956. In June, the department informed CONARC that it was exploring alternate courses of action to achieve the heavy lift capability which was to have been met by the H-16B. It requested CONARC review the Army requirement for a heavy lift helicopter and to furnish the general operational requirement. CONARC responded that its Combat Development Objective Guide of February 1956 contained a requirement for a heavy transport helicopter which should have a normal payload of 5 tons at an operating radius of 100 nautical miles, an overload capacity of 8 tons, and substantially greater payloads at shorter distances. The helicopter would be employed as a basic transport of troops, supplies, and equipment in the combat zone, including aeromedical evacuation, and heavy lift in the field army area.[20]

Consideration was given to the HCH-1 flying crane being developed by the Navy, an optimized configuration of the H-37A, a flying crane version of the H-37, and the British Fairey Rotodyne. No further significant progress was made in the development of a heavy cargo helicopter as interest shifted to light and medium cargo aircraft. On 30 September 1958, the Department of the Army requested that CONARC reevaluate and restate the requirements for light and medium cargo aircraft to furnish guidance for the Army staff in support of a revised 5-year materiel program. The recommendations of CONARC were to include the relative priority of procurement of the Vertol CHINOOK helicopter (3-ton payload) and/or a 3-ton short takeoff and landing (STOL) airplane, and the relative priority of procurement of an improved light cargo helicopter.

On 9 October, CONARC recommended priorities for procurement of the light transport 3-ton STOL, the light transport helicopter, and the CHINOOK in that order. A strong stand was taken that if the CHINOOK could not be procured because of budgetary limitations, it was necessary that both the 3-ton STOL and a new or improved light transport helicopter be developed and placed in service as soon as feasible. It was further recommended that none but essential decisions be made in the aircraft developmental field pending the outcome of a Department of the Army directed study on developmental objectives for Army aviation.[21]

The Army placed a contract in July 1958 for ten YHC-1A CHINOOK helicopters. The CHINOOK was a tandem rotor transport helicopter with two turbine engines. It could carry twenty men or fifteen litters. Development of the much larger YHC-1B resulted in reducing the order for the YHC-1A to three aircraft. Five YHC-1Bs were ordered in June 1959 for service tests and the first aircraft flew in September 1961. The Army ordered five more HC-1Bs in 1960, 18 in February, and another 24 in December 1961. While basically similar to the YHC-1A, the HC-1B was able to carry a maximum of forty troops with full equipment, and the fuselage was large enough to contain all the components of the PERSHING missile system. A 6,000 pound payload could be carried a distance of 100 nautical miles or a maximum external load of some 6 tons could be carried 20 nautical miles. The CHINOOK had several novel features, including a rear loading provision and the fuel tanks located in the fuselage side blisters. The HC-1B was developed to meet the requirement for a new transport helicopter and was expected to replace the H-21, H-34, and H-37 helicopters.[22]

Flying Crane

On 27 August 1958, CONARC approved a Qualitative Materiel Requirement for a flying crane and forwarded it to the Department of the Army. As a result of staffing with field agencies and within the CONARC headquarters, it was determined that the payload be specified at twelve tons. Military characteristics were prepared and forwarded to the Department of the Army on 14 November 1958. CONARC recommended that the military characteristics be approved, but in view of the limited application of the vehicle and high cost of development and production, development items to meet the requirement be held in abeyance.[23]

In October 1961, the Department of the Army requested CONARC conduct a preliminary review covering operational and organizational concepts, essentiality, and priority of the aerial crane development. The department proposed a 5-year program aimed at the development of a 20-ton payload aerial crane. The program would require 15 percent of the research, development, test, and evaluation funds earmarked for improving Army mobility for the years 1962-1967. The program included purchase and evaluation of six S-64 Sikorsky flying cranes of 8-ton capacity. On 24 November, CONARC affirmed its position that it had never stated a requirement for an aerial crane. CONARC considered that the HC-1 CHINOOK could fulfill the essential requirements for tactical lift of heavy equipment and that the development of an aerial crane should not be accorded a priority which would jeopardize or significantly affect development of more critical requirements. CONARC recommended that the Department of the Army monitor West German evaluation of the S-64, and if further testing were required, efforts be made to procure not more than two aircraft on a rental or loan basis from Sikorsky.

CONARC felt that continued research was necessary to lead to development of heavy transmissions and hot cycle pressure jet motor systems for aerial crane applications. It also recommended that consideration be given to product improvement of the HC-1 helicopter with the ultimate goal of achieving an 11-ton payload capacity for external lift. CONARC further stated that it could not agree to a high priority for such a qualitative materiel requirement when more critical programs were inadequately funded. It recommended that more funding emphasis be placed on development of the Lockheed rigid rotor system and evaluation of the British Hawker Siddeley P1127 V/STOL aircraft (XV-6A).[24]

Despite CONARC's objections, the Department of the Army continued with the development of the Sikorsky flying crane. The first flight of the twin-engine CH-54A took place on 9 May 1962. The CH-54A carried a 10-ton payload and was designed to carry its cargoes externally. By means of a hoist it could pick up or deposit loads without landing.[25]

Development of Fixed Wing Aircraft

The development of a high performance observation airplane received considerable attention during the period under review. The Army Equipment Development Guide for 1954 had stated a requirement for development of a high performance aircraft for observation, long range adjustment of fire, reconnaissance, command, and utility use. Army experiments with borrowed Air Force T-37 jet trainers were of considerable help in the development of doctrine and organization for the use of higher performance aircraft. Up to this time, Army experience in fixed wing observation aircraft had been limited to the O-1 (L-19) BIRD DOG, which had been introduced during the Korean War. In 1959, the AO-1 MOHAWK entered Army service to fill the observation role. Although the O-1 continued to be used for artillery spotting missions, the radar equipment of the MOHAWK gave the Army a much more sophisticated reconnaissance capability.

T-37 Troop Test

On 21 June 1954, OCAFF requested that the Department of the Army procure ten T-37 jet aircraft for testing in the Army aerial observation/reconnaissance role.[26] The Army formally requested procurement of the aircraft on 23 November. In making the original request, General Dahlquist admitted that the aircraft might accomplish a portion of the tactical reconnaissance for which the Air Force was responsible, nonetheless, he called for an Army expansion in this area.

General Gavin, the Army Assistant Chief of Staff, G-3, doubted that the Air Force had complete primary responsibility for tactical air observation, but he could not officially agree with General Dahlquist's suggestion that the Army intrude into an area which was clearly the Air Force's responsibility. He pointed out, however, that the agreements with the Air Force in 1951 and 1952 had given the Army responsibility for conducting aerial observation to amplify and supplement other methods in locating, verifying, and evaluating targets, adjusting fire, terrain study, or obtaining information on enemy forces not obtained from the other services. General Gavin therefore felt that the request for the T-37s could be justified in accomplishing these missions under the changed conditions of the modern battlefield.

The Army staff interpreted the wording of the agreements to mean that observation, a short range activity, was clearly the province of Army aviation. Reconnaissance, which was the undisputed mission of the Air Force, involved long range, deep penetration of enemy air space. In order to avoid Air Force contention of mission duplication, General Taylor, soon after he succeeded General Ridgway as the Chief of Staff of the Army, directed that the word observation be used rather than reconnaissance when discussing the need of the Army for the T-37. Another term which caused problems was "high performance aircraft," which meant jet combat aircraft to the Air Force. The Army staff was directed to refer to the function of the T-37 as higher performance, which meant higher than the existing liaison aircraft.[27]

The Army did not make public its intention of procuring the T-37s until May 1955, when General Ridgway announced to the Armed Forces Policy Council that a test quantity of ten aircraft would be purchased from the manufacturer. General Twining, the Chief of Staff of the Air Force, immediately objected to General Ridgway's definition of the mission of the T-37s. The Army received no support at this time from the Navy or the Marine Corps. On 14 June, Harold E. Talbott, the Secretary of the Air Force, charged that the procurement of the aircraft was a distinct infringement upon an Air Force function, that the T-37 could not survive over enemy territory, and that it was uneconomical and duplicative of Air Force missions.

At this point, Secretary Wilson ordered the Army to stop procurement of the T-37 and referred the entire matter to the Joint Chiefs of Staff. In August, after lengthy deliberations, the Joint Chiefs directed the loan of T-37s to the Army from Air Force stocks to test their suitability as light observation aircraft. To support the Army position before the Joint Chiefs, CONARC had revised its concept of the use of the T-37 in July. At the same time, CONARC urged that once the procurement of the T-37 had been approved, it was vital that the troop test for this aircraft be designed to determine and exploit its maximum capabilities.

The Joint Chiefs of Staff did not specify the number of aircraft to be loaned by the Air Force, and the Army assumed that it would be the original request for ten. When the Army asked for ten aircraft for two years, the Air Force replied that informal agreements by the Joint Chiefs of Staff had stipulated only two aircraft for one year. After lengthy negotiations with the Air Force, General Twining finally agreed to loan three T-37s for one year, with an option to extend the loan for an additional year. General Taylor, rather than prolonging the argument and possibly endangering the test, reluctantly agreed to the Air Force terms.[28]

While the Department of the Army and the Air Force argued over the T-37, CONARC continued to plan for the troop test. On 12 July, CONARC requested that the aircraft be modified to include electronic and photographic equipment for test purposes. At the request of CONARC, the Department of the Army partially concurred in modification of the aircraft and on 21 November requested the Air Force furnish delivery schedules, training of personnel, and modifications of the aircraft.[29]

On 7 January 1956, CONARC directed the Army Aviation School to prepare an outline test plan for ten T-37 aircraft to determine organization and operational concepts for higher performance observation aircraft. CONARC forwarded the approved outline test plan, with recommended changes, to the Department of the Army on 13 March. On 31 May, the Department of the Army informed CONARC that the number of aircraft had been reduced from ten to three and that the delivery date had been slipped from September 1956 to February-April 1957. The department requested a revised plan based on the reduction in aircraft and the change in delivery dates.[30]

The Army Aviation School submitted the revised plan on 12 June. The test was designed to determine organizational and operational concepts for the employment of higher performance observation aircraft to supplement the L-19 and was not to determine the suitability of the T-37 as the specific aircraft for these missions. The test was to be conducted in three phases. During Phase I, the test detachment would be organized and the pilots and maintenance personnel trained. Phase II would be conducted by the test detachment at the Infantry, Armor, and Artillery and Guided Missile Schools and would be concerned with developing operational procedures for support of the various combat arms. Phase III envisaged employment of the test detachment in Exercise GULF STREAM which was scheduled to be conducted at Fort Polk in April 1958.[31]

On 14 September, the Department of the Army approved the plan, subject to additional changes. CONARC then asked the Army Aviation School to submit personnel requisitions for the test unit, a detailed budget estimate, detailed plans for Phase II of the test, and a proposed

TA for the test unit. The test unit for Project LONG ARM, as the T-37 test program was called, was activated by Third Army as the 7292d Aviation Unit on 5 November.

A conference was held at the Pentagon on 10 December to complete the modification program and delivery schedule for the aircraft. Delivery of three aircraft with KA-20 cameras and DPN-31 radar beacons was changed from March 1957 to 15 July 1957, necessitating a rescheduling of the test program. Discussions were also held with the Air Force concerning transition of pilots. On 26 December, CONARC approved the proposed Air Force training program. Cessna conducted the transition training for the Air Force under contract.[32]

The troop test of the T-37, as prepared by the Army Aviation School, had five objectives. First, to determine the most effective organization, training, and logistical implications for higher performance Army observation aircraft within the field army, and to prepare tentative training literature. Second, to obtain an evaluation of higher performance observation aircraft vulnerability and survival probability when operating at various speeds and altitudes in the vicinity of enemy ground weapons, antiaircraft weapons, and surface-to-air guided missiles. This evaluation was to be based on the limitations of present and planned radar and weapons systems, and the reaction time of troops manning the weapons. Third, to determine the relative observation capabilities at various altitudes and speeds in both day and night operations. This objective would include determination of the capabilities for target identification, observer visibility transition training requirements, and observer adaptability from low to high speed aircraft and other factors affecting observation. Fourth, to develop and test operational procedures for target acquisition, damage assessment, surveillance, and adjustment of fire by higher performance Army observation aircraft. Finally, to recommend performance characteristics for a higher performance Army observation aircraft.[33]

The test unit completed its unit training at Fort Rucker and then took part in tests covering employment with artillery and armor units at Fort Sill and Fort Knox, respectively, during the first half of FY 1958. In Phase III of the test program, the unit participated in Exercise CUMBERLAND HILLS at Fort Bragg from 19-30 May 1958. The test unit returned to Fort Rucker on 4 June.[34]

On 28 March 1958, the Department of the Army approved the extension of the T-37 test detachment through FY 1959 and extended the loan of the T-37 aircraft until January 1959. Long before the aircraft were returned to the Air Force, however, the Army had lost interest in Project LONG ARM. The Department of the Army was convinced that Air Force opposition had so influenced the thinking of the Joint Chiefs of Staff and the Department of Defense that it was not feasible to pursue the project. Additionally, the success in the development of the AO-1 MOHAWK airplane had met most of the observation requirements being studied in the tests. At the conclusion of the loan of the T-37s from the Air Force, it was anticipated by DCSOPS, Department of the Army, that the test detachment would be equipped with SLAR L-26 aircraft and eventually with the MOHAWK.[35]

The Army Aviation School submitted the interim report on Phase III on 22 October 1958 and Third Army submitted on 30 July the report of the tests conducted during Exercise

CUMBERLAND HILLS. Both of the reports were forwarded by CONARC, along with copies of the Phase II report of Project LONG ARM, to its interested staff sections. As a result of the staffing, CONARC positions were furnished to Third Army on the CUMBERLAND HILLS tests and to the Department of the Army on the Phase III interim report. On the CUMBERLAND HILLS report, CONARC acknowledged the desirability of a medium observation aircraft organization in the field army. Third Army was advised that the size of a test unit to continue this program would be established after consideration of current limitations on personnel spaces and equipment. CONARC stated that it was premature to initiate courses of instruction for operation and use of medium observation aircraft. Instead, the Army Aviation School would be directed to integrate instruction for the employment of the medium observation aircraft into current programs of instruction. Field manuals would be revised to reflect doctrine resulting from Exercise CUMBERLAND HILLS and previous testing.

In regard to the Phase III interim report, CONARC recommended to the Department of the Army that approval be given for further testing to determine mission requirements for the medium observation aircraft at army, corps, division, and missile commands. It favored approval of the organization of a TD experimental medium observation aircraft test unit at the Army Aviation School to conduct necessary tests, using the T-37 test unit to form the basis for the new experimental test unit. At the same time, CONARC recommended disapproval of the retention of the three T-37 aircraft by the Army Aviation School in view of the limited value which would accrue from further testing. It suggested that the T-37 aircraft be returned to the Air Force on 31 December 1958. CONARC recommended that negotiations be entered into with the Department of the Navy to procure, on a loan basis, three T-28 propeller aircraft to support the new experimental test unit.[36]

The final report and comments of the various reviewing agencies on Project LONG ARM were received at CONARC during the first half of FY 1960. Testing of combat surveillance equipment and aircraft was a continuing process conducted under a program established by CONARC on 8 May 1959. The final report of Project LONG ARM was used as background information in the conduct of these tests.

CONARC initiated action relative to the assignment of medium observation aircraft, training of crews, preparation of training literature, determination of appropriate avionics equipment, and tests of combat surveillance equipment. It felt that the Project LONG ARM test and actual troop testing of the medium observation aircraft would further develop support requirements and would indicate any changes considered necessary.

The purpose of the troop test was to determine the organization, tactics, and techniques of employment of medium observation aircraft in support of tactical operations of the field army. The objectives were: to determine the most effective organization, the training and logistical implications for higher performance observation aircraft within the field army, and to prepare tentative training literature; to obtain an evaluation of higher performance observation aircraft vulnerability and survival probability; to determine the relative observation capabilities at various altitudes and speeds in day or night operations; and to develop and test operational procedures for target acquisition, damage assessment, surveillance, and adjustment of fire by higher performance Army observation aircraft. The test was not conducted as an evaluation of the merits of the T-37, but of the concept of operation of an aircraft which generally performed in a manner similar to the T-37. Completion of the Project LONG ARM tests completed action on this project.[37]

Despite the completion of the T-37 tests, the Army still maintained an interest in the possible adoption of jet aircraft. In April 1961, the Office of the Chief of Research and Development directed CONARC to conduct a comparative flight evaluation of three types of jet airplanes. The Army Aviation Board was directed to conduct the evaluation between the Fiat G-91, the Northrop N156 (F-5), and the Douglas A4D-2N. Testing was accomplished throughout the last quarter of FY 1961. CONARC recommended on 20 September 1961 that further evaluation be conducted prior to final selection of an Army close support airplane. In the event of an emergency requiring an immediate selection, the A4D aircraft was probably the most suitable of the types tested.[38]

AO-1 MOHAWK

The Army Equipment Development Guide of 1954 included a requirement for development of a high performance aircraft for observation, long range adjustment of fire, reconnaissance, command, and utility use. A conference was held by the Office, Chief of Research and Development, Department of the Army, on 15 February 1956, at which time six manufacturers presented design studies for an Army-Navy (USMC) higher performance observation airplane. Because this airplane had to be operationally available during calendar years 1958-1960, its plans needed to be of an inherently simple design, with no special complicated high lift device, which would ease development and production at the lowest possible cost in dollars and time. At the direction of the Department of the Army, CONARC prepared military characteristics for an Army higher performance observation aircraft which it submitted on 12 March 1956. Immediately following Secretary Wilson's decision in November 1956 regarding weight restrictions on Army aircraft, the Department of the Army forwarded a memorandum requesting two exceptions to the 5,000 pound limitation on fixed wing aircraft. The first exception was for procurement of the de Havilland DHC-4 light transport and the second was for authorization to continue participation with the Marine Corps in the development of an improved observation airplane. Secretary Wilson approved both the exceptions.[39]

The AO-1 MOHAWK fixed wing observation airplane was originally developed to meet joint Army and Marine Corps requirements. The Marines withdrew from the project before the first flight, leaving the Army to continue development alone. The requirement was for an aircraft capable of rough field operation with short take-off performance and equipped for tactical observation and battlefield surveillance missions.

The first Army contract—placed in 1957 through the Navy Bureau of Aeronautics which administered the program on behalf of the Army—was for nine test items, designated as the YAO-1AF. The first flight took place in April 1959. Later that year, the Army contracted for thirty-five production model MOHAWKs to be used for the test, training, and assignment to high priority units. The order was later increased to a total of seventy-seven airplanes, to be delivered in three models. First were thirty-six AO-1AFs, with a KA-30 camera in the fuselage, which could be rotated from the cockpit to left or right oblique positions. Upward ejecting flares were carried for night photography, with 104 flares mounted in two pods. The AO-1BF was similar, but carried side-looking airborne radar (SLAR) in a long external pod. This equipment provided a permanent radar photographic map of the ground on each side of the flight path, with a developed photograph available in the cockpit within seconds of the film being exposed. Seventeen of the first seventy-seven MOHAWKS were ordered as AO-1BF models; the first flew in 1960. The third MOHAWK series was the AO-1CF, of which twenty-four were ordered from the initial contracts. This model differed from the AO-1AF only in having UAS-4 infrared mapping equipment.[40]

On 25 October 1960, an interim report was submitted based upon the Army Aviation Board's participation in the Navy trials and approximately 200 hours of flight time at Fort Rucker. The report recommended that the distribution of AO-1 airplanes be limited to CONUS activities pending the correction of discrepancies described in the report. CONARC concluded in June 1961 that the AO-1 was suitable for Army use as a combat surveillance airplane, provided that appropriate engines were furnished and the deficiencies and shortcomings disclosed by the service test were corrected. CONARC recommended that action be taken to extend the service life and improve the reliability of the T-53 turbine engine.[41]

Planning for MOHAWK training began even before the first aircraft flew. In July 1958, Brig. Gen. Ernest F. Easterbrook, the Director of Army Aviation, requested that CONARC prepare plans for specialized training. On 7 October, CONARC submitted a plan for initiating training for operational and maintenance personnel and recommendations on actions required by the Department of the Army. Personnel to support the test activities and initiate school training on the MOHAWK would be given specialized training by Grumman and Lycoming on a contract basis.

Before attending these factory training courses, pilots had to undergo indoctrination training in high altitude flying and ejection seat operation. Because the Army did not have the capability to conduct this training, CONARC recommended that arrangements be made with the Air Force or the Navy to provide this type of training for Army personnel.[42]

Major problems developed as a result of the multiplicity of systems involved in the MOHAWK and delays in qualification and production of acceptable turbine engines, radar and infrared surveillance sensors, photographic systems, and ground support equipment. CONARC crew training was originally scheduled to begin in May 1960, but slippage in the availability of aircraft required repeated rescheduling. As a result, training did not start until April 1961. CONARC representatives attended systems management meetings at the Department of the Army on 24 August and 15 November 1960 in order to coordinate corrective actions with all agencies involved.

Forty MOHAWKs had been produced by the end of FY 1961; two were issued to the Army Aviation School, the balance were involved in tests or were at the Grumman plant awaiting the results of tests to establish a firm electronic configuration. Ground support equipment generally was not in existence or was in short supply. Small items, such as oxygen masks and attachments, photographic flares, and ejection seat cartridges, had not been programmed. During the year, actions continued in the development of a distribution schedule for the AO-1 to CONUS and overseas commands. Problems centered around the establishment of pipeline support of spare parts to overseas areas and CONUS posts for the airframe, engine, the new camera, signal electronics, and avionics equipment.[43]

Because of the numerous deficiencies, CONARC conducted an additional series of confirmatory tests on the MOHAWK which disclosed that not all the problems previously reported had been corrected. On 26 March 1962, CONARC recommended that corrective action be taken. The problems, however, did not prevent the deployment of the first AO-1s to Vietnam. During FY 1962, the Department of the Army developed a surveillance concept using armed AO-1s. In addition to their normal surveillance mission, the aircraft were armed and capable of attacking ground targets or could be used to provide close air support. The use of the MOHAWK in this role was to cause serious problems with the Air Force in the following years. The 23d Special Warfare Aviation Detachment was equipped with the armed MOHAWK and deployed to Vietnam during FY 1962.[44]

Even as the MOHAWK entered service, the Army began development of the next generation of observation aircraft. In September 1961, CONARC began active participation in the development of a new manned surveillance aircraft by designating a representative to the U.S. Army Transportation Research Command System Phasing Group which was conducting the research on the project. The objective of the group was to provide and coordinate the essential elements of information for defining the technical and operational characteristics of the aircraft configuration. The group findings would be provided as input into an Office of the Chief of Research and Development study being done by Canadair on survivability of the manned surveillance aircraft. This type aircraft had been recommended for development by the Rogers Board. In December, the Department of the Army directed CONARC to furnish a member of the Project Advisory Group for the new surveillance aircraft. The group would provide advisory and coordinating functions with respect to the overall objectives of the Systems Phasing Group.[45]

AC-1 CARIBOU

Immediately after Secretary Wilson's memorandum of November 1956 reconfirmed the 5,000-pound weight limitation of fixed wing aircraft, the Department of the Army requested an exception in order to procure five de Havilland DHC-4 airplanes for evaluation of their suitability to meet the requirement for a 3-ton payload transport having a short take-off and landing capability. Secretary Wilson approved this request, and the aircraft were delivered in February 1959. DCSOPS, Department of the Army, recommended the purchase of an additional twenty aircraft to organize and equip a company for test purposes.[46]

Distribution of the troop test directive for the AC-1 CARIBOU, the Army designation given to the de Havilland transport, had been made on 18 June 1959. The troop test was to be conducted in four phases beginning in the spring of 1960. Final responsibility for the troop test was assigned to the Commanding General, Third Army. The Commanding Generals, Second and Fourth Armies, had responsibilities for the conduct of certain phases of the test as well as for comments in the final report. The 1st Aviation Company was designated as the test unit and was reorganized under TOE 1-107T with initial equipment of four AC-1 CARIBOU and eight U-1A OTTERs. The final phase of the test provided for participation in Exercise BRIGHT STAR employing the maximum number of CARIBOU aircraft that could be made available to the unit.

The objectives of the troop test of the AC-1 were to develop doctrine, tactics, techniques, and operational and organizational concepts for Army 3-ton short take-off and landing transport aircraft units. These objectives were to be accomplished through operational experience in four phases over a 7-month period. The initial training of the 1st Aviation Company and the first phase of the troop test were to be conducted at Fort Benning.

The initial phase of the training was originally scheduled to start on 1 April 1960 and last for three months. The first phase of the troop test was scheduled for one month. The second phase was also scheduled for one month, beginning 1 August, and was to be conducted at Fort Sill, followed by a third phase of one month at Fort Knox. The fourth and last phase provided for participation in Exercise BRIGHT STAR for a 15-day period beginning in October. Phase IV was to be conducted at Fort Bragg and Fort Campbell. A provisional maintenance unit was provided by the Chief of Transportation to accomplish third echelon maintenance and supply functions in support of the test unit.[47]

The start of the troop test was delayed as a result of late receipt of the aircraft. Also, the test director made recommendations that certain test objectives be revised to permit accomplishing the test within specified periods. CONARC published a new test directive in early January 1961 which provided for five phases of testing. Phase I would take place 1 September 1960-15 January 1961 at Fort Benning and would include pretest training as well as the Army Training Test. Phase II, 22 January-22 February at Fort Sill, and Phase III, 1-31 March at Fort Knox would accomplish the test objectives. Phase IV, 1-31 July at Fort Benning would cover the logistical test objectives. The troop test concluded with Phase V, which consisted of participation in Exercise SWIFT STRIKE.[48]

Delays continued to affect the start of the troop test. In February 1960, the phase at Fort Benning was slipped to February-April 1961, and in December it was slipped further to April-June 1961. Interim doctrine for employment of fixed wing aviation companies was submitted by the Army Aviation School as a revision to Chapter 5 of FM 1-5, Army Aviation Organizations and Employment, and was approved for test purposes by CONARC on 1 June 1960. A Pretest Training Schedule and an Army Training Test, submitted by the Army Aviation School for use in attaining training objectives by fixed wing aviation companies, were approved for troop test purposes by CONARC on 19 May 1960.[49]

Despite the delays in troop testing, sufficient aircraft were obtained to conduct the service tests of the CARIBOU. Three YAC-1s were turned over to the Army on 8 October 1959, followed by two more in November. Extensive service tests were conducted which uncovered numerous deficiencies which needed correction before the aircraft went into production.[50]

The service tests of the AC-1 had proved so promising by February 1960 that the Transportation Corps was ready to request a Standard A classification in order to procure greater quantities of the aircraft. Seven additional aircraft were on order at that time and procurement had started for fifteen more to be delivered by the end of FY 1960.

A request for a Standard A classification ran into trouble from two sources when brought before the Transportation Corps Technical Committee on 17 March. The Surgeon General did not like the number of litters being fitted into the aircraft and objected to the type of supports being inserted for them. The Surgeon General consulted with de Havilland and the Transportation Corps to resolve the difficulties. CONARC wanted to extend the limited production classification until after the completion of service tests. Such action need not prevent procurement of the fifteen additional aircraft and would ensure that any deficiencies found in the test would be corrected by the manufacturer. The Chief of Research and Development agreed with this view on 7 April, commenting that the AC-1 would undoubtedly qualify as Standard A at the end of testing in June. The fifteen aircraft were purchased with FY 1960 funds under the limited production classification.

As the service tests continued, reports constantly indicated that the AC-1 performed well. On 13 May, the Transportation Corps Technical Committee coordinating subcommittee reopened the subject of type classification. Approval of the Standard A classification came on 21 July. The Federal Aviation Agency certified the AC-1 to be airworthy on 23 December and, in the same month, the Transportation Corps contracted through the Air Force for thirty-four additional aircraft.[51]

From early February to mid-June 1961, the Commanding General, Third Army, conducted a thorough series of troop tests with four AC-1s at Fort Benning. The general objectives were to test and evaluate TOE 1-107T, Aviation Company, Fixed Wing, Light Transport, modified to accommodate sixteen AC-1s, and to determine the adequacy and suitability of organization, equipment, missions, doctrine, tactics, procedures, and techniques for the support of combat units of the field army. Each exercise evolved from a tactical problem played out on maps. Distances, timing, and restrictions to air corridors had meaning when tied to a definite combat situation. The 124th Terminal Service Detachment of the 11th Transportation Battalion made all weight and balance computations and loaded and unloaded the cargo, personnel, and equipment. The transport aviation company landed the transports on partially prepared fields and in open meadows within landing zones which varied in length from 1,600 to 4,000 feet. Flights at night and during heavy weather added to the realism.

The troop test was conducted by the Infantry School using the 1st Aviation Company, equipped with four AC-1s and eight U-1A OTTERs. The final report of the test, submitted on 12 July by Third Army, recommended that TOE 1-107T be changed to an organization of three flight platoons of eight AC-1s each, with an aggregate personnel strength of 210. The report also recommended that aviation companies equipped with AC-1s be assigned on the basis of one company per corps and one company per field army and that a field maintenance detachment be developed to provide on site support to the unit.

Third Army forwarded the report on 26 July, concurring in recommendations for minor revisions. At the time this report of troop test was under consideration at CONARC, the final positions were established on the RODAC-70 study and on an aviation unit TOE prefix study. These actions, plus the conclusion that a 24- aircraft company structure was too large for use in a tactical or logistical role, prompted a modification of the troop test recommendations. CONARC informed the Department of the Army on 16 February 1962 that a requirement existed within the field army for two types of AC-1 aviation companies, one (built around approximately nine aircraft) to support tactical operations and the other (built around approximately eighteen) to support logistical operations. Assignment of AC-1 equipped units was to be in accordance with organizational concepts contained in the RODAC-70 concept. Field maintenance support would be provided by the existing transportation aircraft direct support companies.[52]

Convertiplanes and Vertical Lift Research Vehicles

In addition to the development of the fixed wing and rotary wing aircraft for immediate tactical use, the Army participated in numerous experimental developments of convertiplanes and vertical lift research vehicles. It was hoped that the various convertiplane designs tested would eventually lead to the development of a fixed wing aircraft which could take off vertically like a helicopter. The vertical lift vehicles generally fell into the class of providing the individual soldier a limited flying ability or to provide a flying jeep.

Convertiplanes

Typical of the convertiplanes was the McDonnell XV-1, which made its first conversion flight in March 1955. The Army procured two of these aircraft which had a helicopter rotor for lift and a small jet engine for horizontal flight. The Bell XV-3 also combined the characteristics of the helicopter and the airplane. The project started in 1951 under a joint Army-Air Force contract which called for Bell Helicopter Company, Doak Aircraft Company, and Ryan Aeronautical Company to develop a convertiplane for Army consideration.

Bell began extensive testing, and later the other two companies dropped out of the program. Bell completed two XV-3s in February 1955 and placed them in a ground test program. The initial flight of an XV-3 took place on 23 August, but the aircraft was destroyed on 25 October 1956 in an accident caused by instability of the 3-bladed prop-rotor. The prop-rotors were replaced on the second XV-3 with a 2-bladed, semi-rigid model which proved satisfactory.

The XV-3 achieved 100 percent in-flight conversion of its tilt rotors on 18 December 1958. The full conversion was the world's first by a tilt-rotor fixed wing aircraft. The XV-3 conversion took about ten seconds if done continuously or it was accomplished by a gradual step-by-step basis. This process entailed transferring the lift from the rotors to the wings without loss of altitude. The XV-3 ultimately went through more than 100 full conversions, but the project was terminated at the conclusion of the tests.[53]

Flying Saucer

A briefing by representatives of Aircraft Armaments, Inc., of Cockeysville, Maryland, on the flying combat vehicle was given to senior officers and representatives of the CONARC staff sections on 21 August 1957. As a result of this briefing, a letter was sent to the Chief of Research and Development, Department of the Army, on 22 October, stating CONARC interest in the flying saucer concept and requesting initiation of a feasibility study of a manned flying saucer. The Chief of Research and Development replied on 21 November, advising that he had reviewed a current Air Force project with AVRO Aircraft, Ltd., of Canada, which was similar to the Aircrafts Armaments proposal and which appeared promising. CONARC was invited to attend an AVRO presentation at the Pentagon on 29 November. After this briefing, the Chief of Research and Development forwarded copies of an AVRO brochure to CONARC, requesting review and recommendations on the AVRO proposal. This project was considered important because the impact of a successful flying saucer concept could revolutionize the Army's aircraft development and vehicle program and might be capable of reducing the Army's inventory of aircraft and vehicles to a minimum.[54]

On 22 January 1958, CONARC representatives visited the Chief of Research and Development to determine the status of the AVRO proposal to build two Avromobiles for research purposes and to determine the schedule of availability of test items. The Commanding General, CONARC, had concurred in purchasing two items at a cost of $2,028,670. Manufacture of the two vehicles would be in accordance with the following schedule: mock-up of first model in late September or early October; first vehicle rolled out twelve months after date of contract; ground and flight testing by the contractor six to nine months after roll-out of first vehicle; second vehicle rolled out twenty months after date of contract; availability of several models for testing by Army troops estimated to be mid-1962.

The Chief of Research and Development commented that the Avromobile, with a payload of 1,000 pounds, would satisfy the requirement for a utility helicopter and a utility fixed wing airplane with VTOL capabilities. The Avromobile would replace the H-40 helicopter after 1962. A requirement would still exist for a simple 2-place reconnaissance helicopter and possibly for small observation airplanes. The aerial jeep was basically a research vehicle and was considered as a stepping stone from ground surface pressure vehicles to the AVRO or zero ground pressure vehicles. If the AVRO concept proved successful, the aerial jeep would be abandoned.

The Chief of Research and Development went on to say that there still would be a possible requirement for a flying crane device since it was not known if the AVRO concept would be operationally suitable as an external load carrying vehicle. Eventually, the larger versions of the AVRO would replace the medium and light transport helicopters and airplanes. The AVRO vehicle would satisfy all requirements for reconnaissance drones and possibly the other drone systems, including cargo.

The Office of the Chief of Transportation advised CONARC that the signed AVRO contract had been returned to the Air Force for their signature on 23 June 1958.[55]

The saucer-shaped craft, designated as the VZ-9V by the Army, was powered by three Continental J69 turbojet engines. These drove the central fan which provided a peripheral air curtain and ground cushion for VTOL operation. The air intakes for the engine were in the center, while the focusing ring control was located around the bottom edge. The body of the saucer was designed for aerodynamic lift in forward flight, and the craft was intended to have a maximum speed of 300 mph at high altitudes and a range of 1,000 miles. Two craft of this type were built by AVRO for the Army and tested from 1959 to 1961. The project was discontinued in late 1961 due to problems with internal aerodynamic losses and uncontrollable pitching.[56]

The Status of Aircraft Development

By 1961, most of the types of aircraft needed by the Army to implement fully the airmobile concept had been developed. The early expectations regarding the numerical expansion of Army aircraft however, had not been achieved. In 1955, it had been estimated that the Army would be operating 8,500 aircraft in 1959. By 1961, the Army was still 3,000 aircraft short of this goal and inventory forecasts for 1970 also fell short of the target. Twelve helicopter battalions had been estimated for 1959, including a heavy lift capability. There were only twenty helicopter companies in existence in 1961, and the H-37 helicopter—the largest in the Army inventory—was limited to about a 3-ton capacity.

Planning in the mid-1950s had assumed a larger Army and larger budgets than were actually provided. The Army had also proved over-optimistic in forecasting certain technical advances in the area of all-weather flight and advances in speed, range, and load carrying capacity of helicopters. Development had not progressed at the anticipated pace.[57]

Despite these shortfalls, the progress made during the period was remarkable. In the next few years, the numbers of aircraft and aviation units would increase far beyond anything imagined in the 1950s. This rapid expansion was made possible by the accomplishments of the late 1950s. The aircraft developed during this period were to prove far more versatile than had been expected and were to meet fully the requirements of airmobility.

Endnotes
Chapter XII

1. Howze, "Combat Tactics for Tomorrow's Army."

2. Address by Brig Gen Clifton F. Von Kann to the Senior Officers Army Aviation Logistics Course, Ft Eustis, 26 Oct 59.

3. (1) US Army Aviation Center and Army Aviation School History, 1954-1964, p. 50. (2) CONARC GO 14, 15 Jul 55. (3) CONARC GO 1, 1 Jan 57.

4. This section is based on Fact Sheet, OACSFOR/AV MPF, 24 May 63, subj: Development and Procurement of Army Aircraft, w/3 incls.

5. CONARC Summary of Major Events and Problems, FY 59, Vol. III, Mat Dev Sec Army Avn & Avn Div, Jul-Dec 58, p. 5; Vol. VI, Cbt Dev Sec Gen Div, Jul-Dec 58, pp. 11-12, and Jan-Jun 59, p. 10.

6. Ibid., FY 60, Vol. V, Trans Sec, Jul-Dec 59, p. 3; and Vol. VI, Cbt Dev Sec Gen Div, Jul-Dec 58, pp. 11-12, and Jan-Jun 60, p. 14.

7. OCofT, Summary of Major Events and Problems, FY 61, p. 21.

8. (1) CONARC Summary of Major Events and Problems, FY 56, Vol. III, Dev & Test Sec Army Avn & Abn Div, Jul-Dec 55, pp. 1-2. (2) F.G. Swanborough, *United States Military Aircraft Since 1907* (New York: Putnam, 1963), p. 59 (hereafter cited as Swanborough, *Military Aircraft*).

9. The X designation normally indicated a prototype, while the Y designation was given to indicate service test status.

10. (1) CONARC Summary of Major Events and Problems, FY 59, Vol. III, Avn Sec, Jan-Jun 59, p. 1; Mat Dev Sec Army Avn & Abn Div, Jul-Dec 58, p. 5, and Jan-Jun 59, p. 6. (2) Swanborough, *Military Aircraft*, p. 59.

11. CONARC Summary of Major Events and Problems, FY 59, Vol. III, Avn Sec, Jan-Jun 59, p. 10.

12. (1) Ibid., FY 60, Vol. V, Avn Sec, Jul-Dec 59, p. 7. (2) Swanborough, *Military Aircraft*, p. 59.

13. CONARC Summary of Major Events and Problems, FY 60, Vol. V, Trans Sec, Jul-Dec 59, pp. 6-7; FY 61, Trans Sec, Jan-Jun 61, p. 5.

14. (1) Ibid., FY 62, Vol. V, Mat Dev Sec Army Avn & Abn Div, Jul-Dec 61, p. 7, and Jan-Jun 62, p. 6. (2) Swanborough, *Military Aircraft*, pp. 59-60. (3) DA DCSOPS Dir of Army Avn, Summary of Major Events and Problems, FY 61, p. B-II-5 (TOP SECRET—Info used is UNCLASSIFIED).

15. (1) Ltr ATSWD-G 452.1 (C), CONARC to DA Chief of R&D, 19 Mar 56, subj: Development of New Reconnaissance Helicopter. (2) Swanborough, *Military Aircraft*, p. 512.

16. Ltr ATSWD-G 452.1 (C), CONARC to DA, 19 Mar 56, Incl 3.

17. (1) CONARC Summary of Major Events and Problems, FY 58, Vol. V, Mat Dev Sec Army Avn & Abn Div, Jan-Jun 58, p. 2. (2) CONARC Summary of Major Events and Problems, FY 59, Vol. III, Mat Dev Sec Army Avn & Abn Div, Jul-Dec 58, p. 2. (3) CONARC Summary of Major Events and Problems, FY 60, Vol. V, Mat Dev Sec Army Avn & Abn Div, Jul-Dec 59, pp. 5,6.

18. (1) OCofT Summary of Major Events and Problems, FY 61, pp. 22-24. (2) Swanborough, *Military Aircraft*, p. 576. (3) *Army Aviation*, Feb-Mar 64, pp. 62-65.

19. (1) Ltr ATDEC-5 452.1, CONARC to CofT, 10 Mar 5f5, subj: H-16B Helicopter Program. (2) Ltr ATDEC-6 452.1, CONARC to DA R&D, 1 Oct 55, subj: Heavy Transport Helicopter, H-16B.

20. Ltr OPS AV OR-3, DA DCSOPS to CONARC, 26 Jun 56, subj: H-16 Replacement, w/1st Ind.

21. CONARC Summary of Major Events and Problems, FY 59, Vol. VI, Cbt Dev Sec Gen Div, Jul-Dec 58, p. 14.

22. (1) Swanborough, *Military Aircraft*, pp. 116-117. (2) CONARC Summary of Major Events and Problems, FY 59, Vol. III, Mat Dev Sec Army Avn & Abn Div, Jan-Jun 59, p. 6.

23. CONARC Summary of Major Events and Problems, FY 58, Vol. VI, Cbt Dev Sec Gen Div, Jan-Jun 58, p. 14; FY 59, Vol. III, Mat Dev Sec Army Avn & Abn Div, Jul-Dec 58, p. 4, and Vol. VI, Cbt Dev Sec Gen Div, Jul-Dec 58, p. 9.

24. Ibid., FY 62, Vol. VII, DCSCD Cbt Arms Div Tac Br, Jul-Dec 61, pp. 10-12 (SECRET—Info used is UNCLASSIFIED).

25. *Army Aviation,* Feb-Mar 64, p. 57.

26. The T-37 was a jet trainer designed and built by the Cessna Aircraft Company. The first prototype had flown in October 1954 and the first Air Force models were flown in September 1955. The aircraft was a simple, low-mid wing all metal monoplane, having two turbojet engines and side-by-side seating.

27. (1) CONARC Summary of Major Events and Problems, FY 55, Vol. IV, Cbt Dev Sec Gen Div, Jul-Dec 54, pp. 3-4 (CONFIDENTIAL—Info used is UNCLASSIFIED). (2) DA ACofS G-3, Army Avn Div, Summary of Major Events and Problems, FY 55, p. 2 (TOP SECRET—Info used is UNCLASSIFIED). (3) Draft ms, History of Army Aviation, ch VII, pp. 34-37.

28. (1) Draft ms, History of Army Aviation, ch VIII, pp. 37-40. (2) Memo for Brig Gen H.H. Howze, Army Avn Div, G-3, 26 Jul 55, subj: T-37 Troop Test Program.

29. CONARC Summary of Major Events and Problems, FY 56, Vol. IV, Jul-Dec 55, pp. 6-7.

30. (1) CONARC Summary of Major Events and Problems, FY 56, Vol. VIII, Cbt Dev Sec Gen Div, Jan-Jun 56, p. 2 (SECRET—Info used is UNCLASSIFIED). (2) DA DCSOPS Army Avn Dir, Summary of Major Events and Problems, FY 56, p. 1 (TOP SECRET—Info used is UNCLASSIFIED).

31. Ltr ATSWD-G 452.1, CONARC to Oklahoma Air Materiel Area, Tinker AFB, 6 Jul 56, subj: T37A Project.

32. (1) CONARC Summary of Major Events and Problems, FY 57, Vol. VI, Cbt Dev Sec Sp Div, Jul-Dec 56, pp. 1-3 (SECRET—Info used is UNCLASSIFIED). (2) DA DCSOPS Army Avn Dir, Summary of Major Events and Problems, FY 57, p. 1 (TOP SECRET—Info used is UNCLASSIFIED). (3) Ltr TTOTT-A, Technical Training Air Force to CONARC, 3 Dec 56, subj: T-37A Aircraft Pilot Training, w/1 incl.

33. HQ CONARC, Troop Tests FY 57 Review and Analysis, 29 Jan 58, pp. 39-40.

34. Exercise GULF STREAM had been cancelled in November 1957 because of a curtailment of funds.

35. (1) CONARC Summary of Major Events and Problems, FY 58, Vol. VI, Cbt Dev Sec Sp Div, Jul-Dec 57, p. 4, and Gen Div, Jan-Jun 58, pp. 16-18 (CONFIDENTIAL—Info used is UNCLASSIFIED). (2) Draft ms, History of Army Aviation, ch VII, p. 40.

36. CONARC Summary of Major Events and Problems, FY 59, Vol. VI, Cbt Dev Sec Gen Div, Jul-Dec 58, pp. 15-17.

37. Ibid., FY 60, Vol. VI, Cbt Dev Sec Gen Div, Jul-Dec 59, pp. 20-22.

38. Ibid., FY 61, Vol. VI, Mat Dev Sec Army Avn & Abn Div, Jan-Jun 61, p. 12; FY 62, Vol. V, Mat Sec Army Avn & Abn Div, Jul-Dec 61, p. 7.

39. (1) Ibid., FY 56, Vol. VII, Dev & Test Sec Army Avn & Abn Div, p. 1 (SECRET—Info used is UNCLASSIFIED). (2) DA DCSOPS Army Avn Dir, Summary of Major Events and Problems, FY 57, p. 2 (TOP SECRET—Info used is UNCLASSIFIED).

40. (1) DA DCSOPS Dir of Army Avn, Summary of Major Events and Problems, FY 58, p. 1 (TOP SECRET—Info used is UNCLASSIFIED). (2) Swanborough, *Military Aircraft,* pp. 272-273.

41. CONARC Summary of Major Events and Problems, FY 61, Vol. VI, Mat Dev Sec Avn & Abn Div, Jul-Dec 60, p. 6, and Jan-Jun 61, p. 11 (SECRET—Info used is UNCLASSIFIED).

42. Ltr OPS AV OR-6, DA Dir of Army Avn to CG CONARC, 7 Jul 58, subj: Initial Crew Training for MOHAWK Observation Airplane, w/1st Ind, CG CONARC to DA DCSOPS, 7 Oct 58.

43. (1) CONARC Summary of Major Events and Problems, FY 61, Vol. VI, Army Avn Sec, Jul-Dec 60, p. 11 (CONFIDENTIAL—Info used is UNCLASSIFIED). (2) DA DCSOPS Dir of Army Avn, Summary of Major Events and Problems, FY 61, p. B-II-3 (TOP SECRET—Info used is UNCLASSIFIED).

44. (1) CONARC Summary of Major Events and Problems, FY 62, Vol. V, Mat Dev Sec Army Avn & Abn Div, p. 8 (SECRET—Info used is UNCLASSIFIED). (2) DA DCSOPS Dir of Army Avn, Summary of Major Events and Problems, FY 62, p. B-II-1 (TOP SECRET—Info used is UNCLASSIFIED). (3) Tolson, *Airmobility 1961-1971,* pp. 40-44.

45. CONARC Summary of Major Events and Problems, FY 62, Vol. VII, DCSCD Cbt Arms Div Tac Br, Jul-Dec 61, pp. 8-10 (SECRET—Info used is UNCLASSIFIED).

46. (1) DA DCSOPS Army Avn Dir, Summary of Major Events and Problems, FY 57, p. 2. (2) DA DCSOPS Dir of Army Avn, Summary of Major Events and Problems, FY 58, p. 1 (Both TOP SECRET—Info used is UNCLASSIFIED).

47. CONARC Summary of Major Events and Problems, FY 59, Vol. III, Avn Sec, Jan-Jun 59, pp. 2-3.

48. Ibid., FY 60, Vol. V, Avn Sec, Jul-Dec 59, p. 3.

49. (1) CONARC Summary of Major Events and Problems, FY 60, Vol. V, Avn Sec, Jan-Jun 60, pp. 5-7. (2) CONARC Summary of Major Events and Problems, FY 61, Vol. VI, Avn Sec, Jul-Dec 60, pp. 4-5 (CONFIDENTIAL—Info used is UNCLASSIFIED).

50. (1) Swanborough, *Military Aircraft*, p. 546. (2) CONARC Summary of Major Events and Problems, FY 60, Vol. V, Mat Dev Sec Army Avn & Abn Div, Jan-Jun 60, pp. 4-5 (SECRET—Info used is UNCLASSIFIED), and Trans Sec, pp. 3-4.

51. OCofT, Summary of Major Events and Problems, FY 61, p. 25.

52. (1) CONARC Summary of Major Events and Problems, FY 62, Vol. VI, Avn Sec, Jan-May 62, pp. 6-12. (2) OCofT Summary of Major Events and Problems, FY 61, p. 25.

53. (1) DA ACofS G-3 Army Avn Div, Summary of Major Events and Problems, FY 55, p. 2 (TOP SECRET—Info used is UNCLASSIFIED). (2) Tierney and Montgomery, *Army Aviation Story*, pp. 272-283. (3) *Army Aviation*, Vol. 12 (Feb-Mar 64), pp. 65-68. (4) *Army Aviation*, Vol. 8, No. 9 (Sep 60), p. 546.

54. CONARC Summary of Major Events and Problems, FY 58, Vol. VI, Cbt Dev Sec Sp Div, Jul-Dec 57, p. 3.

55. Ibid., FY 58, Vol. VI, Cbt Dev Sec Gen Div, Jan-Jun 58, pp. 12-14.

56. Info furnished by Transportation Museum, Fort Eustis, 17 Nov 75.

57. DA News Release No. 241-61.

Chapter XIII

DEVELOPMENT OF AVIATION TRAINING

The Army had developed a firm foundation for its aviation training with the establishment of the United States Army Aviation School at Fort Rucker. As 1955 began, the most aggravating training problem was the continued sharing of Army aviation with the Air Force. The efforts to consolidate all training under Army control bore fruit during the next two years. At the same time, the Army Aviation School continued to grow, and new unit training commands were established.

Transfer of Training from the Air Force

Early Interest in Training Consolidation

Attempts had been made to consolidate all Army aviation training under Army control since before the Korean conflict. Financial problems and Air Force reluctance to transfer the responsibility had aborted the effort of early 1954. In November, the Secretary of the Army noted in a memo to the Secretary of Defense that the increased Army use of helicopters and fixed wing aircraft made it essential to maintain maximum efficiency and flexibility in the training of Army personnel. The Army was convinced that by managing all aviation training, its personnel would be better utilized and more responsive to special needs. The Secretary of the Army therefore urged that the Secretary of Defense transfer to the Army the primary pilot and mechanic training of aviation personnel then being conducted by the Air Force at Gary Air Force Base.

The Secretary of the Army presented two possible solutions. The Army could use contractor-furnished facilities for primary fixed wing training and for primary helicopter training, thus freeing Gary Air Force Base for Air Force use. Or, as an alternative, Gary Air Force Base could be transferred to the Army for primary helicopter and fixed wing training if the Air Force had no other requirements for the base. Either solution provided full utilization of existing facilities without duplication.

Because the Air Force successfully contracted with civilian flying schools for all primary pilot training of Air Force pilots, the Secretary of the Army believed that contract training was economical and effective. If full responsibility for Army aviation training were assigned to the

Army, the Army would propose to conduct all primary flight training by contract with civilian flying schools.[1]

As a follow-up to the request of the Secretary of the Army, in January 1955, Assistant Secretary of Defense for Manpower and Personnel Carter L. Burgess reported to the Deputy Secretary of Defense that disagreement between the Air Force and the Army over training responsibilities had resulted in duplicate requests for funds to conduct primary flight training in the FY 1956 program. The Army insisted that control of all aviation training would be more efficient and economical and that it in no way duplicated Air Force training. The Air Force disagreed, claiming that duplication already existed. The Assistant Secretary of Defense therefore proposed a detailed study of the problem to determine appropriate training responsibility for aviation personnel required by the Army. A study of the flight and technical training programs of both the Air Force and the Army would be conducted to determine Air Force capability to provide trained personnel. The relative costs involved in the separation of Army aviation courses as against Army utilization of Air Force facilities to meet Army needs would also be compared.[2]

The Department of the Army informed CONARC that action had been taken to include $1.8 million in the FY 1956 budget for civilian contract primary flight training for cargo helicopter pilots. On 25 March, the Department of the Army requested that CONARC establish and supervise the training. Final proposals were received from the Army Aviation School on 31 May, and CONARC submitted its recommendations to the Department of the Army on 6 June. Ten days later, the Department of the Army designated Third Army as the negotiator of the contract and established 1 October as the starting date.[3] Because of funding and negotiating difficulties the tentative date of the contract was delayed from 1 October to 1 May 1956. The original contract would continue through fiscal year 1957 for a total of fourteen months.[4]

In late 1955, the Air Force requested that part of the Army's input to primary fixed wing classes conducted at Gary Air Force Base be directed to Spence Air Force Base, Moultrie, Georgia. The twenty-seven students in Class 56-7 began training on 3 January 1956 and became the first Army students to receive training in the L-19 from a civilian contractor.[5]

Army Assumption of Training Responsibility

After thorough consideration of all factors involved in Army aviation training, and discussions with the Secretaries of the Army and the Air Force, the Department of Defense concluded on 19 April 1956 that the Department of the Army should have responsibility for the aviation training required to support Army activities. This responsibility was to include the four aviation training courses then being conducted for the Department of the Army by the Air Force.

As a matter of economy and of operational efficiency, existing facilities and in-place equipment was to be utilized to minimize additional and highly specialized construction. Those purposes would best be served by using existing facilities at Wolters and Gary Air Force Bases rather than establishing and operating those activities on additional nongovernmental facilities. Both of the bases were surplus to Air Force requirements and had been scheduled for

Headquarters, U.S. Army primary helicopter school and Camp Wolters, Texas.

inactivation. The Army was to conduct primary fixed wing pilot training by civilian contractor at Gary Air Force Base, San Marcos, Texas, and primary helicopter pilot training by civilian contractor at Wolters Air Force Base, Mineral Wells, Texas.

The transfer of program and command responsibilities would relieve the Air Force of providing maintenance personnel support for elements of Army aviation training. The Secretary of the Army, in coordination with the Secretary of the Air Force, was directed to formulate plans for the orderly, effective, and timely assumption of the transferred responsibilities and submit such plans to the Secretary of Defense for approval. The Secretaries of the Army and the Air Force were directed to develop guidelines for the transfer agreement and submit them jointly to the Secretary of Defense for approval by 1 May 1956.[6]

CONARC assisted in the development of an Army position through participation in a conference conducted by the Deputy Chief of Staff for Operations, Department of the Army, 23-25 April. Other participants included representatives of the Air Force, the Army Aviation School, and Fourth Army. On 27 April, CONARC assigned to the Commanding General, Fourth Army, the command of Gary and Wolters at such time as the transfer became effective and designated the Commandant, Army Aviation School, as technical adviser to assist Fourth Army in the development and consummation of the necessary planning.

On 2 May, the Department of the Army directed CONARC to initiate planning and to take necessary action to accomplish the transfer of training. This included the phasing in of contract training for fixed wing pilots at Gary Air Force Base with the target date of 15 November, and the initiation of mechanics courses and officer courses at Fort Rucker. CONARC would initiate contract primary training for cargo helicopter pilots at Wolters Air Force Base with a target date of 1 January 1957.

In order to accomplish the required detailed planning at all levels of command, the Department of the Army requested that it be furnished military and civilian personnel space requirements, identified by grade and MOS, and Maintenance and Operation funds required by project, giving details and indicating bases and method of computation. The Department also requested that CONARC report the capability of the CONUS armies to meet enlisted personnel requirements from their own resources. Maintenance and Operation repairs and utilities projects which would require Department of the Army approval would also be reported, indicating costs. Construction line item priority lists and detailed justification sheets for construction projects recommended for inclusion in the FY 1958 Military Construction, Army (MCA) program would be in integrated sequence to indicate their appropriate priority within line items previously submitted.

On 9 May, CONARC directed Fourth Army to furnish directly to the Department of the Army information pertaining to personnel spaces and Maintenance and Operation fund requirements for Gary and Wolters and estimated costs of repairs and utilities projects. Fourth Army would complete detailed plans and implement them by joint coordination between its headquarters and the Air Training Command or the Continental Air Command of the Air Force. On 10 May, CONARC assigned the Army Aviation School the responsibility for the Officer Rotary Wing Pilot Course and the two enlisted mechanics courses then being conducted at Gary Air Force Base and directed that phased plans for the orderly assumption of these additional missions be submitted.[7]

A major concern of CONARC during this transition period was the optimum distribution of the various Army aviation training courses among the three installations soon to be at its disposal. Another problem was the orderly phasing out of the various types of training being conducted for the Army by the Air Force and the timely rescheduling of this training, in some cases at new locations, in others, under civilian contract. CONARC submitted its plan for the accomplishment of these objectives to the Department of the Army on 9 June. Both the Department of the Army and the Department of the Air Force approved the CONARC plan.

The plan provided that the Fixed Wing Officer Pilot Course (Army Primary Flight Training) would be retained at Gary. By terminating Air Force instruction as of 1 December 1956 and resuming instruction under civilian contract beginning on or about 1 January 1957, the scheduled course input could still be maintained. The Officer Rotary Wing Pilot Training Course would be transferred from Gary to Fort Rucker. Input to this course at Gary was to terminate in June 1956, with the last students phasing out in August. The first class scheduled for Fort Rucker would begin on 13 July 1956. The Enlisted Fixed Wing Maintenance Course and the Enlisted

Rotary Wing Maintenance Course would also be transferred from Gary to Rucker. Inputs to these courses at Gary were to terminate on or about 1 September, with the remaining students phased out by December. The new classes at the Army Aviation School would begin on or about 1 October.

The Army Aviator Transport Pilot Course (Phase II) was to be implemented at Camp Wolters as an 18-week contract primary helicopter flight training course on 7 January 1957. This training was to be followed by a 12-week Army Aviator Transport Pilot Course (Phase III) at the Army Aviation School starting in May 1957. The more advanced training in utility and cargo helicopters would be implemented at the Army Aviation School to qualify students in transport helicopters. Army aircraft and helicopters assigned to the Air Force for the training of Army students would be turned over to the Army by 1 January 1957.

The Department of the Air Force would still be responsible for the completion of funding of projects under construction at the time of the transfer. The Department of the Army would be responsible for justification and funding of any modification of projects under construction and for new projects that might be required after the assumption of command.

Since the enlisted students would be sent to Wolters on permanent change of station, it was decided, in the interest of economy, to transfer the 4-week preflight officer candidate school training being conducted at the Army Aviation School to Camp Wolters. The transfer was to be effective with the establishment of contract training at Wolters, with the first pre-flight class scheduled to begin in November 1956. The shifting of courses was designed to provide maximum utilization of facilities and minimize travel and temporary duty (TDY) costs. On 21 June 1956, the Department of Defense approved the guidelines which had been submitted jointly by the Army and the Air Force. A Department of the Army message on 22 June constituted authority to implement the transfer.[8]

On 1 July, Army training at Spence Air Force Base was terminated and the two classes in residence were transferred to Gary Air Force Base to complete their primary fixed wing training. In the short time that Spence Air Force Base was used, 128 Army students completed their primary training.[9]

As a result of the assumption of training responsibility by the Army, it became necessary to move primary helicopter training for rated pilots from Gary Air Force Base to Fort Rucker while negotiations were completed for the Army take over of Wolters Air Force Base. Wolters Air Force Base passed to Army control on 1 July and officially became Camp Wolters. The first primary rotary wing pilot course conducted under Army sponsorship began at Fort Rucker on 13 July 1956. Because of a shortage of rotary wing instructor pilots, the Army began to look for new sources of qualified helicopter pilots. The Marine Corps permitted the resignation of twenty-four pilots who were accepted in the Army as chief warrant officers. The men reported to Fort Rucker in early August and were given an accelerated course as rotary wing instructor pilots.

Camp Wolters became the U.S. Army Primary Helicopter School on 26 September 1956. A contract was negotiated with Southern Airways Company to provide flight instruction, ground school instruction, and the maintenance of government aircraft and equipment at the school. During August and September, twenty-seven civilian instructor pilots were sent to Fort Rucker for standardization training. Problems of support for the course and the orderly transfer of equipment and training aids involved the Fourth Army and the Army Aviation School under the guidance of CONARC.[10]

The phase-out of Air Force activity at Gary Air Force Base—which was redesignated Camp Gary—and the phase-in of instruction by contract was completed by December. Camp Gary officially became an Army installation on 15 December. Five classes were canceled to facilitate this transfer, and the first contractor supported course started in January 1957. CONARC transferred the responsibility for the conduct of Phase I and Phase II of the Army Aviator Transport Pilot Course from the Commandant, Army Aviation School, to the Commanding General, Fourth Army. The latter was directed to establish a contract school for this training at Camp Wolters. A contract was negotiated and training under this new arrangement began on 26 November.[11] To support this course, H-23 helicopters were moved from Fort Rucker to Camp Wolters.

On 7 January 1957, the first class began training at Camp Gary with W. J. Graham and Sons, Inc. conducting primary fixed wing flight instruction. A staff of twenty-two officers and twenty-two enlisted men were responsible for the military operations and provided quality control of the contractor's job performance. By 1 July 1959, 2,151 student pilots had successfully completed primary training.[12]

On 29 January 1957, the Department of the Army informed CONARC that the requirements for warrant officer pilots and student inputs into Camp Wolters were being reduced because of rescheduling and reduction in the number of helicopter units. The Department of the Army requested that CONARC consider the feasibility of transferring some of the training from the Army Aviation School to Camp Wolters to ensure that the training load commitments at Camp Wolters were maintained. To meet this requirement, CONARC requested that Fourth Army and the Army Aviation School consider conducting the primary phase of the Army Helicopter Aviation Tactics Course at Camp Wolters and the tactics phase at Fort Rucker. When the Army Aviation School objected to this split, CONARC informed the Department of the Army on 26 March that the mission of training one-half of the scheduled input into the course for FY 1958 would be transferred from Fort Rucker to the Primary Helicopter Training Unit at Camp Wolters. This vertical rather than horizontal split of the course satisfied the objections of the Army Aviation School.[13] Both Camp Wolters and Fort Rucker continued to conduct primary helicopter training until 1958. The last primary class trained at Fort Rucker graduated on 6 September 1958, at which time the entire course was consolidated at Camp Wolters.[14]

On 20 April 1959, the Department of the Army directed that CONARC inactivate Camp Gary by 30 September 1959, and terminate all Army aviation training there not later than 30 June. The Army Aviation School, in conjunction with Third and Fourth Armies, Camp Gary, and CONARC, had previously prepared and obtained Department of the Army approval of a plan for the transfer of primary fixed wing training to Fort Rucker. There were 988 Active Army officers either on orders or programmed for fixed wing training between the cut-off class at Camp Gary and 30 June 1960. The Army Aviation School only had an FY 1960 input capability of 780 officers. It was anticipated by the Department of the Army that this consolidation of training would save the Army approximately $2 million annually.[15]

The last fixed wing primary class in residence at Camp Gary moved to Fort Rucker where students received the remainder of their advanced training. Camp Gary was inactivated on 30 September 1959. Most of the instructor pilots from Camp Gary moved to Fort Rucker along with approximately 190 L-19 aircraft. On 11 September, the first primary fixed wing class with seventy-eight students began training at Lowe Army Air Field with the Hawthorne School of Aeronautics conducting the primary phase of training. The contractor conducted both the officer Fixed Wing Aviator Course and the Fixed Wing Qualification Course.[16]

Army Aviation Unit Tactical Training

On 19 October 1954, OCAFF had recommended to the Department of the Army that two Army Aviation Unit Training Commands (AAUTC) be established in two phases. These AAUTCs had the mission of activating and training aviation companies. Phase I would utilize the commander and staff of an assigned headquarters and headquarters detachment, transportation helicopter battalion, as the commander and staff of the AAUTC. During Phase II, a separate TD unit would be established. OCAFF recommended that one command be established at Fort Sill for single rotor training and one command at Fort Riley for tandem rotor helicopter and transport airplane training.[17]

On 6 December, the Department of the Army stated that personnel shortages prevented the establishment of TD units, but recommended that the mission be assigned to the 71st Transportation Battalion at Fort Riley and the 45th Transportation Battalion at Fort Sill, CONARC assigned the training mission to the 71st Transportation Battalion on 24 January 1955. On 31 May, CONARC directed that Fifth Army establish a Provisional Training Command at Fort Sill by using the 45th Transportation Battalion and a TD augmentation of fourteen officer and enlisted spaces provided by the Department of the Army.[18]

The AAUTC at Fort Sill was activated and became operational on 1 July 1955. H-19s and H-34s were used at this center. Slippage of helicopter production at the Sikorsky plant during the first half of fiscal year 1956 created a shortage of aircraft at the Fort Sill AAUTC. This slippage seriously curtailed the AAUTC's training mission because it delayed transition flight training for a large number of pilots. CONARC recommended to the Department of the Army that the assignment of flight personnel be scheduled to coincide with the actual delivery of aircraft and also took action to divert some of the pilots at Fort Sill to duty with exercise SAGE BRUSH.

The AAUTC at Fort Riley became operational on 18 February 1955, although it was not formally organized until 1 August. This AAUTC used H-25 and H-21 helicopters and U-1A OTTERs. Production slippage on the U-1As, due to a labor strike at the de Havilland plant, delayed development of the U-1 training program.[19]

In early April 1956, CONARC noted that warrant officer cargo helicopter pilots, upon completion of training at the Army Aviation School, were not properly prepared for duty in a helicopter company. It was estimated that by the end of fiscal year 1957, twenty-five companies would be operational. The normal assignment for new helicopter pilots would be as replacements in operational companies. To prepare the graduate to serve as a replacement, it was necessary that action be taken to revise the current course to include familiarization training to the degree necessary to qualify the graduate as a co-pilot in a cargo helicopter and to permit him to continue flight transition in a company training program.

CONARC desired that the change be made with the establishment of the civilian helicopter training program. Limited experience in helicopter transition training at Fort Riley indicated that the warrant officer graduate would qualify for a cargo helicopter more rapidly by going directly from the reconnaissance to the cargo helicopter and omitting training in the utility helicopter. The Army Aviation School was considering that procedure in the preparation of a study to provide the following information by 15 May 1956: amount of flying time in the cargo helicopter which was required to familiarize the graduate only to the degree necessary to act as copilot in H-21s or H-34s and to be capable of continuing training under a company training program; the time during the 12-week basic training phase when the cargo helicopter would be introduced; the amount, type, and schedule of equipment required to support the revised training program; the amount of lead time required to implement training on receipt of the equipment; personnel impact, if any, of the program recommended; and the estimated increase in costs and where these costs could be included in the FY 1957 budget.[20]

Revision in Helicopter Company Activation Schedule

The aviation training requirements placed on CONARC intimately related to the aviation unit activation schedule. In August 1952 the Chief of Staff of the Army had approved the organization of twelve helicopter battalions. This program was modified in the following years, but it did provide the basis on which the aviation training program was developed.

Early in 1956, one class of the H-34 Helicopter Pilot Transition Course had to be canceled because of a shortage of H-34s at Fort Sill and the urgent need for completion of training newly activated and organized helicopter companies. Organizations which had quotas canceled were authorized to transition pilots into H-34s if qualified instructor pilots were available locally.[21]

Originally twenty-one rotary wing companies had been scheduled for activation by the end of FY 1956. Shortages of equipment—mainly resulting from delays in deliveries of H-34s—and training facilities resulted in a stretch-out of the training schedule. Deliveries of the H-34s were back on schedule by the third quarter of FY 1956, but the limited training facilities precluded overcoming the delay in training new companies. By the end of FY 1956, fourteen rotary wing companies had been activated.[22]

On 18 January 1956, the Deputy Chief of Staff for Operations, Department of the Army, directed that CONARC review a revised schedule for the activation of helicopter companies. CONARC did not agree with the Department of the Army proposed program due primarily to facility limitations at Fort Riley and on 10 March forwarded its own activation and stationing program based on facilities capabilities.

Meanwhile, on 10 February, the Department of the Army directed CONARC to take necessary action to ensure that construction requirements, based upon the Department of the Army's proposed helicopter stationing plan, were included in the FY 1958 MCA program of the CONUS armies to provide airfield facilities. CONARC recommended that planned stationing of helicopter units at Forts Ord and Polk be deferred until hangar and shop space was constructed, and that special consideration not be given to aviation facilities for FY 1958, but be left to the discretion of the CONUS army commanders. On 12 April, the Department of the Army requested CONARC comments on a revised helicopter stationing schedule which incorporated previous CONARC recommendations. CONARC submitted its concurrence, in general, with the Department of the Army program and further stationing recommendations on 14 May. On 15 June, the Department of the Army forwarded the activation and deployment schedule of transportation helicopter battalions and the aviation unit activation and stationing schedule.[23]

On 18 September 1956, a conference was held at CONARC with Col. H.D. Edson, the Deputy Director of Army Aviation, and other Department of the Army staff representatives, to discuss several problems regarding the transportation helicopter program. Three major subjects were discussed at the conference. Deficiencies existed in and mitigated against the attainment of the objectives of the program involving aviation unit activation and the stationing schedule. Short range requirements had to be determined for transportation helicopter unit support during the remainder of FY 1957. Finally, consideration needed to be given to projected unprogrammed future requirements established in regard to ROTAD and the SKY CAV tests and the impact of these requirements upon the Army aviation and transportation helicopter unit programs.

The Army Aviation Unit Training Commands at Fort Riley and Fort Sill were unable to organize, activate, train, and deploy fixed wing tactical transport and transportation helicopter units in accordance with the activation and stationing program due to a lack of trained personnel. Among the major requirements for helicopter support was the ROTAD organization, training and testing of the 101st Airborne Division, and the support of the division during Exercise JUMP LIGHT. It was also necessary to provide organic TOE aircraft and aviation personnel on an assigned basis to the 101st Airborne Division to ensure the division's full operational capability by 1 March 1957. Finally, helicopter support of the SKY CAV II test unit, which was to be provisionally organized and trained at Fort Polk as of January 1957 was an additional requirement.

Projected and unprogrammed new requirements for aircraft, pilots, and maintenance personnel for the new organizations were estimated at approximately 900 aircraft of all types, 900 additional fixed and rotary wing pilots, and 1,500 maintenance personnel. These new and unprogrammed requirements superimposed on the current lagging program indicated that a complete review and revision of the aviation and helicopter programs was essential.

As a result of the conference, on 28 September CONARC recommended to the Department of the Army that the current activation program for Army aviation and transportation helicopter units be temporarily suspended. CONARC also recommended that a new program be developed with consideration given to requirements for equipment and trained personnel to support an accelerated activation and testing program for new units. CONARC requested at the same time that action be taken to provide necessary cargo helicopter support for Exercise JUMP LIGHT, the SKY CAV II test in Exercise SLEDGE HAMMER, and to provide aircraft and aviation personnel to the 101st Airborne Division to ensure full operational capability upon its assumption of the Western Hemisphere reserve mission.

The Department of the Army reply on 25 October failed to fully support the CONARC recommendations. Pending the completion of a revised Army Aviation Plan, the Department of the Army agreed to temporarily suspend the activation schedule. The revised activation schedule coincided with scheduled aircraft production receipts and output of pilot personnel. It was recognized that men and equipment might be diverted on occasion from assignment to new units. The Department of the Army considered such diversions preferable to the transfer of men and equipment from units in the process of formation.

On 26 November, CONARC reminded the Department of the Army of the immediate requirements and commitments for transportation helicopter units for which there were no adequate means of support. A conference in Washington on 4 November between Lt. Gen. Clyde D. Eddleman, the Department of the Army DCSOPS, and Lt. Gen. Edward T. Williams, the Deputy Commanding General of CONARC, reached several decisions regarding specific units which to a great extent met CONARC's requirements.

On 7 December, another conference with Department of the Army representatives was held at Fort Monroe on 7 December to determine a system of priorities for the allocation of light cargo helicopters to support the reorganization of airborne and armored divisions to the ROTAD and ROCAD organization structure and to support the activation of Field Artillery Atomic Support Commands. CONARC recommended that priority for the assignment of light cargo helicopters and allied personnel should be established to support the reorganization of divisions and the activation of Atomic Support Commands. In the event that the activation of additional helicopter companies and helicopter field maintenance detachments competed with these reorganizations and activations for personnel and equipment, CONARC recommended that the activation of the helicopter companies and helicopter field maintenance detachments competed with these reorganizations and activations for personnel and equipment, CONARC recommended that the activation of the helicopter companies should be delayed accordingly. CONARC also recommended that the activation of additional helicopter companies should be accomplished at the two existing Army Aviation Unit Training Commands to take maximum advantage of these existing and experienced organizations.[24]

On 5 March 1958, the Department of the Army recommended the discontinuance of the Army Aviation Unit Training Commands at Forts Riley and Sill due to a reduction in the number of aviation units required under the FY 1959 troop structure. CONARC concurred in this proposal on 14 April and recommended that the Fort Riley AAUTC be discontinued on or about 30 June and that the Fort Sill AAUTC be discontinued on or about 31 December. CONARC requested retention of the 45th and 71st Transportation Battalions for support of the Fourth and Fifth Army aviation programs. On 3 June, the Department of the Army informed CONARC that it planned to reduce the TD augmentations of the Headquarters and Headquarters Detachments, 45th and 71st Transportation Battalions, by sixty-seven military and six civilian spaces. The effective reduction dates were in the first quarter and second quarter of FY 1959 respectively.[25] The mission of conducting individual training was transferred to the Army Aviation School at the beginning of FY 1959.

Growth of the Army Aviation School

Formal aviation training had begun at the Field Artillery School during World War II. When the rapid growth of Army aviation began during the Korean conflict, the U.S. Army Aviation School was officially established on 1 January 1953 at Fort Sill as a Class I activity under the Commanding General, Fourth Army. Congestion and inadequate facilities at Fort Sill led to the selection of Camp Rucker as the permanent school location in 1954. The Army Aviation School completed the transfer from Fort Sill to Camp Rucker during the last half of 1954.

Organization

Within the concept guidance furnished by CONARC, the Army Aviation School developed doctrine, organization, procedures, tactics, and techniques relating to the operation and employment of Army aviation, up to and including the Army Aviation Group, in joint and unilateral operations, airborne operations, and amphibious operations. The school instructed and trained officers, warrant officers, and enlisted men of all components, branches, and services of the Army in the functions of Army aviation, and in the relationship of Army aviation between branches and services within the Department of Defense. Instruction included normal employment, capabilities, and limitations of Army aviation at all levels. The school also conducted, coordinated, and supervised instruction in flight training of officers, warrant officers, and enlisted men in primary, basic, and advanced flight training in fixed and rotary wing aircraft and such other specialized flight courses as might be required.

In addition to its training mission, the Army Aviation School developed Army aviation doctrine, tactics, logistics, and techniques. It assisted in the development of Army aviation equipment and prepared statements of requirements for new equipment or improvement of existing equipment. The school developed proposed organizations as directed by CONARC. It evaluated and made recommendations on Army extension course revisions as directed; administered the Army extension course aviation program, and assisted in the development and production of training aids.[26]

The Army Aviation School was organized with the usual Commandant, Assistant Commandant, and Office of the Secretary. The Aviation Medical Advisor provided technical advice and conducted training on matters pertaining to aviation medicine. The Combat Development Office provided for early integration of the latest concepts of Army aviation organizations, equipment, doctrine, tactics, techniques, and procedures into the Army structure. Among the functions of the office was the development, revision, and evaluation of doctrine, tactics, techniques, organizations, and equipment as they affected Army aviation. The office determined new requirements concerning equipment, materiel, and new systems. It monitored troop testing of organization, tactics, techniques, and materiel. The office also supervised and coordinated feasibility tests of organization and equipment assigned to the Army Aviation School for that purpose.

Upon the movement of the Army Aviation School from Fort Sill to Camp Rucker in 1954, the Director of Instruction was established as the principal assistant to the assistant commandant. The Director of Instruction planned, supervised, and coordinated all resident and nonresident instruction, arranged for special training of students, staff, and faculty, and formulated instructional standards.

The Department of Fixed Wing Training conducted flight training in fixed wing aircraft and academic instruction for fixed wing and rotary wing students. The Department of Rotary Wing Training conducted all flight training in rotary wing aircraft.

The Department of Tactics prepared, conducted, and presented advanced, intermediate, and basic level instruction in organization and tactical employment of Army aviation units. Among the department's functions was the preparation and conduct of field exercises, demonstrations, and special presentations in support of instructional activities.

The Department of Maintenance conducted personnel training of all components of the Army in subjects relating to pilot maintenance phases of instruction and enlisted maintenance courses designed to support rotary and fixed wing aircraft.

The Department of Publications and Nonresident Instruction was responsible for the preparation, editing, and revision of Department of the Army type publications and special texts pertaining to Army aviation; the preparation of extension courses; and the publication of the *U.S. Army Aviation Digest*. It was also responsible for the storage and distribution of training publications and instructional material for the Army Aviation School, including requirements for issue to outside agencies and nonresident students.

Operations

During the first few months of operations at Camp Rucker, fixed wing training fell behind schedule primarily due to a lack of facilities. Only Ozark Air Field was available on the post, necessitating the use of civilian airfields. By mid-1955, engineers had completed three fixed wing stage fields and ten surfaced strips. Following these improvements, fixed wing training began to meet the programmed schedule. By late 1955-1956, thirty-seven off-post tactical strips had been constructed on leased property. The first field exercises were conducted from makeshift field strips located on the post. In March 1955, two large tactical sites were opened and field exercises improved.

A class of twenty-five officer and warrant officer candidates, which had begun training in October 1954, was the first rotary wing class at Camp Rucker. This class graduated on 30 April 1955. The first Army Helicopter Aviation Tactics Course class reported to Camp Rucker on 11 January, having received primary helicopter training from the Air Force at Gary Air Force Base.

As more aircraft arrived at Camp Rucker, heliports were established in abandoned motor parks. By mid-1955, the flight training was confined to three small stage fields. The school consequently selected various off post tactical sites for use in rotary wing training and began negotiations with the Mobile District Engineer to acquire training sites. With a shortage of instructors and inadequate facilities, flight training fell behind schedule. Despite a 6-day week, classes remained behind schedule until the fall of 1955. Late in 1955, negotiations began to acquire real estate for off post tactical sites and the first was made available to the Department of Rotary Wing Training early in 1956.[27]

The Army Aviation Center was authorized forty utility helicopters for aviation training during FY 1956. On 28 July 1955, the center requested that the Department of the Army furnish seventy-four additional utility helicopters to support the program of instruction and to provide the POI Flight Section with three flyable aircraft daily. The need for the additional utility helicopters was based on a new training program that would be initiated due to the CONARC approved program of instruction for Phase III of the Army Helicopter Aviation Tactics Course. On 24 February 1956, CONARC stated that if certain additional factors were met the requirement could be reduced from 74 to 48 additional aircraft or a total of 92 utility helicopters.

This reduction could be made only if there was strict Department of the Army cooperation with the implementation of the CONARC policy of disapproval of any loan of aircraft or support of any Army aviation demonstration which would seriously interfere with training. Revision of contractual negotiation procedures would be necessary to permit the Army Aviation School to negotiate a civilian maintenance contract more favorable to the Army. An improved supply of spare parts was also required.

Utility helicopters needed for the training mission assigned to the Army Aviation School by CONARC were included in a proposed revision of TA 60-4, with the following bases of issue: 1 per 1.26 students for the Cargo Helicopter Pilot Course, 1 per 1.77 students for the Basic Flight Training course, and 2 per Army Aviation School (class 012 or 26). The proposed authorization was concurred in by the Chief of Transportation.[28]

In September 1957, Lowe Army Air Field at Fort Rucker was completed. The new field had a modern flight instructor building, maintenance hangers, fire stations, control tower, and four 2,000 foot runways. At this time, all fixed wing flight training moved to Lowe Army Air Field with the exception of the instrument flights which continued to use the Ozark facility. In early 1959, the Department of Primary Fixed Wing Training was formed at Fort Rucker and located at Lowe Field, while advanced contact training moved to Cairns Army Air Field, the former Ozark Army Air Field. On 6 June 1959, the first class of rated officers began a fixed wing qualification course. Previously, warrant officers had been limited to rotary wing training. A prerequisite for selection for the course was that pilots have a minimum of 350 flying hours.

On 5 October 1959, the Department of Rotary Wing Training of the Army Aviation School moved into its new home at Hanchey Army Air Field. With ample parking space, maintenance facilities, and modern classrooms located on the field, the department was centralized for the first time. By this time, the department had complete control of the eastern portion of the Fort

Ozark Army Airfield, Fort Rucker, 1955. The field was renamed Cairns Army Airfield in 1959.

Rucker reservation and had expanded off-post with one stagefield and sixty-five tactical training sites. On 24 July 1961, another modern stagefield was acquired.

The roles and missions being assigned to Army aviation and development of new hardware and tactics pointed out the need for an Army Aviation Staff Officers Course. The first class started on an 8-week program of instruction on 23 October 1957 and was composed of twenty senior company grade and field grade officers. On 24 October 1960, the length of the course was changed to six weeks, with an average input of thirty-five officers per class. On 12 January 1962, the course was reduced to three weeks.

The Department of Rotary Wing Training organized the H-37 transition course in 1957, with the first class beginning on 8 July 1957. On 1 April 1959, it was necessary to organize a transition course of the UH-1A. In 1962, the CH-21 transition course was organized with the first class beginning on 6 July 1962. The Army's acceptance of the CH-47A helicopter necessitated a transition course which was established on 29 April 1962.

The Army Aviation School submitted an initial staff study to CONARC in May 1959 which recommended, among other things, that an aerial gunnery program be established at the school. In August 1959, CONARC indicated that the recommendations were premature, but directed the school to keep the matter under review. The study continued throughout 1960, with the

Department of Tactics reviewing troop test results and making liaison visits to nearby installations in an effort to locate adequate range facilities and training areas. In the fall of 1960, the Rogers Board recommended that aerial gunnery training using machine guns, missiles, and rockets be incorporated into the Rotary Wing Aviator Course beginning in FY 1963.

The school prepared another staff study on aerial suppressive fire which was submitted, along with a proposed program of instruction, on 27 July 1961. The Army Aviation School received the mission to train twenty-six officers on the UH-1B/SS-11 missile system, with training to begin on 1 February 1962. During the next few months, programs of instruction and lesson plans were written, training areas located, and instructor pilots trained. On 12 September, CONARC informed the school that the SS-11 project would be delayed, but that preparations should continue.

During the second week of October 1961, the school received a commitment to train six officers in observation helicopter machine gunfire techniques. Another crash program was set in progress preparing for the class. Training was scheduled to be completed prior to Christmas 1961, but the class was delayed until early 1962, and the first Rotary Wing Machine Gunners Instructor Course was not graduated until 20 April. Then the Department of Tactics again turned its attention to SS-11 training. The first special course began on 28 May 1962 with eight students graduating on 8 June. The first training class in the UH-1B/XM-6 system graduated on 28 September.[29]

Training Developments

By 1955, the Army aviation program had gone through a significant expansion. In addition to the regular flight and maintenance training programs being conducted, additional training requirements became necessary. A milestone in the history of Army aviation was the 1955 program to train senior officers as Army aviators. For the aviation program to continue to expand it was imperative that it have the highest caliber of senior leadership. Another vital concern impacting on expansion was the provision of an instrument flight capability.

Courses for Senior Officers

On 16 February 1955, the Department of the Army advised CONARC that plans had been developed to annually train from nine to twelve senior colonels as aviators to give the program depth and prestige. The scope, purpose, and course length were to be recommended by CONARC. The Army Aviation School and CONARC prepared a recommended 35-week course consisting of 25 weeks of fixed wing and 10 weeks of rotary wing training. The first class, consisting of twelve colonels and lieutenant colonels, started training on 6 September 1955.[30]

During FY 1956, a requirement was established for a course of instruction to acquaint senior Army officers with pertinent aspects of Army aviation personnel, organization, and procurement problems, doctrine, tactics, and employment techniques, capabilities and limitations, training considerations, and research and development trends. Officers taking the course had to be assigned to a position which required knowledge of the subject matter covered in the course. The first class, originally canceled because of undersubscription by Army commands, got underway on 5 February 1956.[31]

Mountain Flight Training for Army Helicopter Pilots

The Chief of Transportation on 2 June 1955 advised CONARC that funds and training spaces had been provided for eighteen Army aviators to take a 4-week course in helicopter operations in mountain terrain. The course was conducted by Okanagan Helicopter Limited, Vancouver, British Columbia. CONARC allocated these spaces to instructor pilots at the Army Aviation School and the Army Aviation Unit Training Commands at Fort Sill and Fort Riley. In efforts to evaluate the training, the students were required to submit critiques of the course. Based upon student comments, CONARC directed the Commandant, Army Aviation School, to study the subject of high altitude mountain flying techniques, and if appropriate, submit to CONARC recommended changes in helicopter pilot training courses and publications reflecting these techniques. In September 1956, CONARC asked Fifth Army about the feasibility of using Fort Carson as a helicopter mountain training site. One suggestion by CONARC was the assignment of a helicopter mountain training command mission to the helicopter company which was scheduled to be stationed at Fort Carson.[32]

Instrument Training

The Army Aviation School in December 1954 had begun investigating helicopter instrument flying. In March and April 1955, an evaluation was conducted of the H-19 and H-25 helicopters. Stability characteristics varied between the single rotor H-19 and the tandem rotor H-25, and the H-19 proved to be more stable in straight and level flight. It also had less tendency to pitch, roll, and yaw. Another factor was that excessive vibrations on the H-25 instrument panel during climbs, descents, autorotations, and airspeed transitions caused instrument interpretations to be difficult. The H-19 was determined to be the more suitable instrument trainer and was the only helicopter used in the early months of the program.[33]

The first helicopter instrument class began on 3 May 1955. The students were selected at random from the H-19 instructor pilots at the school and were scheduled to become instrument instructors.

A CONARC study revealed that approximately 2,000 Army aviators had to be instrument qualified at the beginning of FY 1956 to meet the requirements of SR 95-15-5. On 8 June 1955, CONARC outlined to the Department of the Army an instrument training program to train 540 aviators per year until the backlog was eliminated. On 26 June, the Department of the Army indicated that no funds were available, but requested that plans be prepared to include training and TDY costs, the agency to conduct the training, the type of aircraft to be used, and the number of personnel per class. In October, the Department of the Army provided guidelines indicating the FY 1957 budget limitations in travel, per diem, training costs, and number of students. The information was forwarded to the CONUS armies to be used in the revision of plans previously submitted for possible implementation during FY 1957.[34]

The Department of the Army approved the CONARC plan in October and provided the necessary budgetary guidelines. The CONUS armies had indicated that fixed wing instrument training could be conducted by contract within existing budget guidelines. CONARC requested that the Department of the Army advise it of any funds available from the FY 1957 budget.[35]

Another part of the test and evaluation program conducted by the Army Aviation School consisted of the Instrument Helicopter Experimental Course, which began on 26 March 1956 with fourteen students and lasted four weeks.

While experimentation continued with the ability to fly helicopters under instrument conditions, steps were taken to improve the fixed wing instrument training program. The Department of the Army, CONARC, and the Army Aviation School worked together to make all Army aviators fully instrument qualified. Additional instrument training was added to the fixed wing pilot course as a prerequisite for fully qualified instrument aviators. Civilian contract training in the CONUS armies was also conducted to reduce the backlog of unqualified pilots.[36]

Recognizing the inadequacy of existing equipment and the urgency of the helicopter instrument requirement, the Army Aviation School and CONARC Board No. 6 agreed to join in a mutual effort to expedite the entire program. The school determined operational procedures and requirements for helicopter instrument flight while the board concurrently determined the suitability and adequacy of the equipment. CONARC approved equipping the two H-21s and two H-34s belonging to the board for instrument flight.[37]

On 29 June 1956, CONARC requested that a special electronic and instrument configuration be provided for H-21s and H-34s for use in integrated instrument-visual flight training. This request was approved by the Deputy Chief of Staff for Military Operations, Department of the Army, with delivery scheduled for June 1957. No helicopters modified in accordance with the request, however, were available for student training at the end of FY 1958. Vigorous follow-up action showed that engineering change proposals and contract change notices were not negotiated to incorporate these requirements in current production H-21s and that retrofit kits would have to be installed. An engineering change proposal for modification of the H-34s was received at the Department of the Army during February 1958 and was not approved in time to ensure delivery during the calendar year. The Army Aviation School capability was limited to eight students per class until additional equipment was available.[38]

Despite the equipment shortages, the Army Aviation School had continued to press the development of helicopter instrument flight. On 7 May 1957, it had reported to CONARC that up to that date there had been approximately 2,635 hours of simulated instrument flight time flown and approximately 126 hours of actual flight. The actual flights were conducted by H-19, H-25, and H-34 helicopters, an H-19 being the first helicopter to be flown under actual instrument conditions on 19 January 1956. The Army Aviation School requested that Army regulations be revised to allow the operation of helicopters under instrument conditions. A set of proposed changes were drawn up by the school and submitted for approval on 19 May 1958. Generally, they involved the rewording of regulations to include helicopters in a number of existing regulations. Specifically, the proposals requested that rotary wing take-off minimums be made lower than those applied to fixed wing aircraft and also that helicopters be allowed lower minimums at destination and alternate airports. Most of these changes were approved in late 1958.

By mid-1958, CONARC had approved a helicopter instrument flying course and the first class began on 14 July. Immediately following the graduation of this class, a helicopter instrument examiner course was established and the graduates began training on 22 September.[39]

Army ROTC Flight Training Program

At a Department of the Army conference on 29 November 1955, a CONARC representative was advised of an immediate requirement for a tentative plan to initiate flight instruction as part of the ROTC program. CONARC developed such a plan and presented it to the Department of the Army on 21 December. The plan was used as a basis for a Department of the Army briefing of the Senate Armed Services Committee in January 1956. Public Law 879, 84th Congress, established authority to initiate and conduct the Army ROTC Flight Training Program during school year 1956-1957.

CONARC planned to implement the Army ROTC Flight Training Program in selected institutions as soon as practicable in FY 1957. Selection of institutions for the program was based on the following criteria: best qualified; wide geographical spread throughout the United States; the availability of a Civil Aeronautics Administration approved flying school in close proximity to the institution; and budgetary limitations.

The Army ROTC Flight Training Program was offered on an extracurricular basis and did not alter the prescribed ROTC program. The following criteria applied to the selection of students for the program; enrolled in Military Science IV ROTC instruction and scheduled to graduate in one academic year; volunteer for flight training; parental or guardian approval obtained in writing; pass a Class I physical examination; pass a flight aptitude test; agree to volunteer for Army aviation training and assignment while on active duty; agree to an extended period of active duty (three years) or two years subsequent to completion of the Army Aviation School, whichever was the shorter period; and have an academic standing the upper half of the class.[40]

Due to unforeseen difficulties encountered in negotiating contracts and completing physical examinations, only twenty-five of the selected institutions elected to commence the program during the first year. From these institutions, 464 applications for flight training were received. Of this number, 162 were disqualified for physical reasons. A total of 202 students successfully completed the course prior during the 1956-1957 school year. A quota of 800 had originally been allocated by the Department of the Army.

A survey of interested students, conducted in the spring of 1957, indicated that the Department of the Army quota of 650 for the 1957-1958 school year would not be met unless the number of participating institutions was increased. During the period June to December 1957, ten more were authorized, bringing the total to fifty-eight participating institutions.

Successful completion of the ROTC Flight Training Program prepared ROTC seniors to qualify for private pilot's licenses, though receipt of such a license was not considered by the

Army as a requirement for successful completion of the course. Graduates of the program were qualified, following completion of officer basic branch courses, to attend the Army Primary Flight Training Course at Camp Gary. The program created a pool of Army pilots which might be used in the event of national emergency.[41]

In the summer of 1958, the CONARC training memorandum on the Army ROTC Flight Training Program was revised, coordinated with the Civil Aeronautics Board and the Civil Aeronautics Administration, and published. The new memorandum removed the requirement for a specific number of hours to be devoted to the various subcourses of the in-flight training, giving the flight instructor more flexibility in the conduct of the course. The number of hours for in-flight instruction was increased from thirty-six and one half to thirty-nine and one half when considered necessary to improve the flying proficiency of the student. The memorandum also authorized further expansion of the program as deemed necessary by the CONUS army commanders to ensure a sufficient base to fulfill assigned quotas. CONARC retained final approval of all schools entering the program.[42]

Ten additional institutions, including the University of Alaska, were authorized to conduct the program during FY 1959. This brought the number of institutions participating to sixty-nine. An evaluation of reports on the progress of the Army ROTC Flight Training Program indicated that fifty-six institutions participated in the program in 1957-1958, and 436 students successfully completed the course of instruction. Reports of performance of graduates attending the Primary Fixed Wing Course at Camp Gary indicated that only 4 percent of the graduates of the program failed to successfully complete this course during their active duty tour. The quota for the program during school year 1958-1960 was reduced to 450 students.[43]

During school year 1958-1959, sixty-six institutions actually participated in the program, producing 349 completions with commissions and 133 completions who were not commissioned, due primarily to failure on their part to meet requirements for a baccalaureate degree. The majority of these were later commissioned upon completion of their academic requirements. Due to the success of the program, the Department of the Army increased the student quota to 500 spaces for school year 1961-1962 and to 600 spaces for school year 1962-1963.[44]

Endnotes
Chapter XIII

1. Memo, Sec of the Army to Sec Def, 22 Nov 54, subj: Transfer of Residual Aviation Training of Army Personnel from Air Force to the Army.

2. (1) Memo, Asst Sec Def to Dep Sec Def, 21 Jan 55, subj: Transfer of Residual Aviation Training of Army Personnel from the Air Force to the Army. (2) DA ACofS G-3 Army Avn Div, Summary of Major Events and Problems, FY 55, p. 2 (TOP SECRET—Info used is UNCLASSIFIED).

3. CONARC Summary of Major Events and Problems, FY 55, Vol. VI, G-3 Sec Tng Div Sp Tng Br, p. 14.

4. Ibid., FY 56, Vol. II, G-3 Sec Tng Div Sp Tng Br, pp. 5-6.

5. *History of the US Army Aviation Center and Army Aviation School, 1954-1964*, p. 6.

6. (1) Memo, Dep Sec Def to Secs Army and Air Force, 19 Apr 56, subj: Responsibility for the Conduct and Administration of Army Aviation Training. (2) CONARC Summary of Major Events and Problems, FY 56, Vol. VI, G-3 Sec Tng Div Sp Tng Br, Jan-Jun 56, pp. 2-4. (3) DA DCSOPS Army Avn Dir, Summary of Major Events and Problems, FY 56, p. 1 (TOP SECRET— Info used is UNCLASSIFIED).

7. (1) Ltr OPS AV OR 7, DA to CONARC, 2 May 56, subj: Transfer of Responsibility for Army Aviation Training, and 1st Ind ATTNG-TNG 322.011, 9 May 56. (2) CONARC Summary of Major Events and Problems, FY 56, Vol. VI, G-3 Sec Tng Div Sp Tng Br, Jan-Jun 56, pp. 4-5.

8. (1) Departments of the Army and Air Force Agreements on General Guidelines for the Transfer of Responsibility for the Conduct and Administration of Army Aviation Training, nd. (2) CONARC Summary of Major Events and Problems, FY 56, Vol. VI, G-3 Sec Tng Div Sp Tng Br, Jan-Jun 56, pp. 5-7.

9. *History of the US Army Aviation Center and Army Aviation School, 1954-1964*, p. 6.

10. (1) *History of the US Army Aviation Center and Army Aviation School, 1954-1964*, pp. 10-11. (2) Tierney and Montgomery, *The Army Aviation Story*, pp. 97-98. (3) DA GO 29, 11 Jul 56.

11. (1) CONARC Summary of Major Events and Problems, FY 57, Vol. II, Avn Sec, Oct-Dec 56, pp. 7-8. (2) DA GO 53, 10 Dec 56.

12. *History of the US Army Aviation Center and Army Aviation School, 1954-1964*, p. 6.

13. (1) Ltr OPS AV OR-1, DA DCSOPS to CONARC, 29 Jan 57, subj: Helicopter Training Requirements—Camp Wolters. (2) Msg ATAVN 3150, CONARC to Third and Fourth Armies and Army Avn School, 5 Feb 57. (3) Msg AASAC 2-1, Army Avn Center to CONARC, 111700Z Feb 57. (4) Msg ATAVN 3282, CONARC to Third and Fourth Armies and Army Avn School, 042127Z Mar 57. (5) CONARC Summary of Major Events and Problems, FY 57, Vol. II, Avn Sec, Jan-Jun 57, p. 2.

14. *History of the US Army Aviation Center and Army Aviation School, 1954-1964*, p. 11.

15. (1) CONARC Summary of Major Events and Problems, FY 59, Vol. III, Army Avn Sec, Jan-Jun 59, p. 12. (2) DF, Army Avn Sec to CofS, 26 May 58, subj: Transfer of Fixed Wing Training. (3) DA DCSOPS Dir of Army Avn, Summary of Major Events and Problems, FY 59, p. 1 (TOP SECRET—Info used is UNCLASSIFIED).

16. (1) CONARC Summary of Major Events and Problems, FY 60, Vol. V, Army Avn Sec, Jul-Dec 59, p. 5. (2) *History of the US Army Aviation Center and School, 1954-1964*, p. 7. (3) Tierney and Montgomery, *Army Aviation Story*, pp. 91-93. (4) DA GO 29 Jul 59.

17. CONARC Summary of Major Events and Problems, FY 55, Vol. II, G-3 Sec Doc & Req Div, Jul-Dec 54, p. 6.

18. (1) Ltr ATTNG-TNG 322(S), CONARC to Fourth Army, 31 May 55, subj: Advanced Transport Aviation Training. (2) CONARC Summary of Major Events and Problems, FY 55, Vol. VI, G-3 Sec Tng Div Sp Tng Br, Jan-Jun 55, p. 16, and Vol. V, G-1 Sec Manpower Control Div, Jan-Jun 55, p. 4.

19. (1) Ltr ATTIS 322, CONARC to Fourth and Fifth Armies, 29 Jun 55, subj: Activation of Army Aviation Unit Tactical Training Commands. (2) CONARC Summary of Major Events and Problems, FY 56, Vol. II, G-3 Sec Tng Div Sp Tng Br, Jul-Dec 55, pp. 7-8.

20. Ltr ATTNG-TNG 352 (Army Avn Sch), CONARC to Army Avn School, 5 Apr 56, subj: Integration of H-21 and H-34 Flight Transition in Cargo Helicopter Pilot Course.

21. Ltr ATTNG-TNG 452.1, CONARC to DA DCSOPS, 18 Jan 56, subj: Shortage of Helicopters for Training Purposes at Fort Sill.

22. DA DCSOPS Army Avn Dir, Summary of Major Events and Problems, FY 56, p. 1 (TOP SECRET—Info used is UNCLASSIFIED).

23. CONARC Summary of Major Events and Problems, FY 56, Vol. VI, G-3 Sec P&O Div Ops Br, Jan-Jun 56, pp. 13-14.

24. (1) Ltr ATTNG-P&O 360(S), CONARC to DA DCSOPS, 28 Sep 56, subj: Army Aviation and Transportation Helicopter Program, w/4 ind. (2) Ltr, Lt Gen Edward T. Williams to Lt Gen Clyde D. Eddleman, 26 Nov 56. (3) CONARC Summary of Major Events and Problems, FY 57, Vol. III, G-3 Sec P&O Div Ops Br, Jul-Dec 56, pp. 4-5.

25. (1) CONARC Summary of Major Events and Problems, FY 58, Vol. II, Avn Sec, Jan-Jun 58, p. 1. (2) DA DCSOPS Dir of Army Avn, Summary of Major Events and Problems, FY 58, p. 1 (TOP SECRET—Info used is UNCLASSIFIED).

26. This section is based on Organization and Functions Manual, US Army Aviation School, 29 Oct 58.

27. *History of the US Army Aviation Center and Army Aviation School, 1954-1964*, pp. 6, 10, 15.

28. CONARC Summary of Major Events and Problems, FY 56, Vol. VI, G-3 Sec Org & Equip Div, Jan-Jun 56, pp. 36-37.

29. *History of the US Army Aviation Center and Army Aviation School, 1954-1964*, pp. 7, 11, 15-16.

30. CONARC Summary of Major Events and Problems, FY 56, Vol. II, G-3 Sec Tng Div Sp Tng Br, Jul-Dec 55, pp. 3-4.

31. (1) CONARC Summary of Major Events and Problems, FY 57, Vol. II, Avn Sec, Oct-Dec 56, p. 8. (2) *History of the US Army Aviation Center and Army Aviation School, 1954-1964*, p. 6.

32. (1) CONARC Summary of Major Events and Problems, FY 56, Vol. II, G-3 Sec Tng Div Sp Tng Br, Jul-Dec 55, p. 4. (2) Msg 25193, CONARC to Fifth Army, 072016Z Sep 56.

33. (1) Tierney and Montgomery, *Army Aviation Story*, pp. 102-103. (3) *History of the US Army Aviation Center and Army Aviation School, 1954-1964*, p. 11.

34. CONARC Summary of Major Events and Problems, FY 56, Vol. II, G-3 Sec Tng Div Sp Tng Br, Jun-Dec 55, p. 5.

35. (1) Ibid., FY 56, Vol. II, G-3 Sec Tng Div Sp Tng Br, Jan-Jun 56, pp. 7-8. (2) Ltr ATTNG-TNG 353, CONARC to DA DCSOPS, 13 Jun 56, subj: Instrument Training for Army Aviators.

36. (1) Tierney and Montgomery, *Army Aviation Story*, p. 104. (2) Ltr OPS AV OR-6, Maj Gen Hamilton H. Howze to CG CONARC, 7 Sep 56, subj: Instrument Training (Army Aviation). (3) Ltr, General W.G. Wyman to Lt Gen Thomas F. Hickey, CG Third Army, 13 Nov 56.

37. Ltr ATBG-DG 452.1, CONARC Board No. 6 to CONARC, 15 Jun 56, subj: Request for Equipment for Helicopter Instrument Flight.

38. CONARC Summary of Major Events and Problems, FY 58, Vol. II, Avn Sec, Jan-Jun 58, p. 17.

39. (1) Ltr AASRW 360.02, Army Avn School to CONARC, 7 May 57, subj: Feasibility of Helicopter Instrument Flight. (2) Tierney and Montgomery, *Army Aviation Story*, pp. 105-106. (3) *History of the US Army Aviation Center and Army Aviation School, 1954-1964*, pp. 11-12.

40. (1) CONARC Summary of Major Events and Problems, FY 56, Vol. II, G-3 Sec RC Div, p. 6. (2) CONARC Summary of Major Events and Problems, FY 57, Vol. III, G-3 Sec RC Div, p. 4. (3) Ltr ATTNG-RC 353, CONARC to CONUS Armies, 18 Aug 56, subj: Army ROTC Flight Training Program.

41. (1) CONARC Summary of Major Events and Problems, FY 57, Vol. IV, G-3 Sec RC Div, Jan-Jun 57, p. 6. (2) CONARC Summary of Major Events and Problems, FY 58, Vol. III, G-3 Sec RC Div, Jul-Dec 57, pp. 4-5.

42. CONARC Summary of Major Events and Problems, FY 58, Vol. IV, G-3 Sec RC Div, Jan-Jun 58, p. 9.

43. CONARC Summary of Major Events and Problems, FY 59, Vol. IV, G-3 Sec RC Div, Jul-Dec 58, pp. 6-7, and Vol. V, G-3 Sec RC Div, Jan-Jun 59, pp. 5-6.

44. (1) CONARC Summary of Major Events and Problems, FY 60, Vol. III, G-3 Sec RC Div, Jul-Dec 59, pp. 44-45. (2) CONARC Summary of Major Events and Problems, FY 62, Vol. III, DCSOPS RC Div, Jul-Dec 61, p. 7.

Chapter XIV

SUPPLY AND MAINTENANCE

Prior to 1955, the responsibility for supply and maintenance of Army aircraft was split between the Department of the Army and the Department of the Air Force. The Army was responsible for field maintenance of aircraft, computation of requirements, and funding for spare parts. The Air Force was responsible for depot storage of aircraft and parts, and for major overhaul maintenance. Because of this dual responsibility in a single logistics area, the Army encountered several major problems which retarded proper support for Army aircraft. The lack of adequate and timely stock status information required the Department of the Army to employ an excessive administrative lead time in computing its anticipated requirements for replenishment procurement. The nonavailability of inventory status reports made it impossible to integrate properly the stocks on hand with requirements for provisioning spare parts support for new aircraft coming into the system.

Another problem was the lack of issue experience and clear delineation between recurring and nonrecurring issues that prohibited proper budgeting for procurement of aircraft parts returned to Air Force depots from Army installations for rebuild. The excessive administrative lead time between the critical supply situations at the depots and the reporting of such situations to the Army agency competent to take corrective supply action resulted in additional difficulties. There was no worldwide inventory report including quantities of available Army supplies in overseas depots due to the lack of information from Air Force reports.

The Army maintenance concepts contained three echelons of maintenance—organizational, field, and depot—located separately, while the Air Force, although recognizing these three echelons, merged organizational and field maintenance at base shops. This dissimilarity in the two maintenance systems caused difficulty in computing allowable lots of parts, technical order compliance requirements for deport maintenance of parts, and funding for spare parts consumption. The division of responsibility for aircraft maintenance and budgeting made it impossible to develop reliable operational and cost accounts on the effectiveness and efficiency of Army aircraft maintenance.[1]

Transfer of Depot Responsibility

During 1954, the Army had come to the conclusion that adequate logistical support of its aviation could not be attained under the existing alignment of responsibilities. The Air Force, which had earlier opposed the idea, exhibited willingness to go along with a transfer of depot functions. The Transportation Corps immediately began planning for the assumption by the Army of the depot support mission. The initial Transportation Corps plan, prepared by Transportation Corps Army Aviation Field Service Office in September 1954, laid down the broad outlines for the Army assumption of depot support responsibilities over a two year period, beginning 1 July 1955.

On 14 March 1955, the Army and the Air Force signed a memorandum of agreement laying down the general principles for the transfer of depot support functions. By the terms of the agreement, the Army would store and issue Army aircraft and all common and peculiar spares and spare parts to include airframes, engines, instruments, accessories, communications and electronics equipment, ground handling equipment, overhaul and maintenance tools, paint, hardware, raw materials, and other supplies and equipment used in direct support of Army aircraft.

The transfer of storage, issue, and depot maintenance responsibilities would begin on 1 July 1955 and be accomplished progressively according to a schedule devised by a joint working committee. Army equities of serviceable items in Air Force depot stocks were to be exhausted by normal attrition, physical transfer from Air Force depots to Army depots, or transfer to the Air Force of those items excess to Army requirements. Stocks purchased by the Air Force for the depot maintenance of Army aircraft and allied equipment would be turned over to the Army. The Air Force would continue to process overhaul reparable items pending the date of transfer of this responsibility. And it would continue to budget for the support of depot supply and maintenance of Army air items for FY 1957, with the Army assuming responsibility in FY 1958.[2]

In May 1955, a Department of Defense decision suspended action on the transfer of the depot support functions. Planning by both services was temporarily suspended pending the submission and evaluation of the total recommended adjustments between the departments in the materiel field. On 26 October, Assistant Secretary of Defense Thomas P. Pike approved the transfer in principle and the general plan for effecting it, as presented by the Chief of Transportation. The Department of Defense approval of the plan, it was made clear, would not preclude later reexamination and changes dictated by fund readjustments and changes in construction requirements as implementation proceeded. The Army was not to create any depot facilities, either in CONUS or overseas, where adequate facilities existed. All CONUS maintenance would be performed by contract or by cross servicing with the Air Force or the Navy. On 26 November, the Assistant Secretary of the Army requested a periodic progress statement on the status of the assumption of the depot functions. The Deputy Chief of Staff for Logistics, Department of the

Army, formally assigned the responsibility for Army aviation depot support to the Chief of Transportation on 13 December.[3]

Army Aviation Depot Plan

Provisions of the Plan

As soon as the depot responsibility was assigned to the Chief of Transportation, work began on updating and revising the Army implementation plan. A revised Army Aviation Depot Plan was completed on 15 January 1956. It was necessary to make changes in the time phasing of the transfer of functions and in resource requirements. As a result of a restudy of the depot sites, the Transportation Corps decided to have four, rather than three, Transportation Sections located at depots. Adjustments also had to be made in the plan as a result of the restrictions imposed on depot maintenance by the Department of Defense. Requests for additional construction funds were turned down, and the strength of depot support battalions, planned for overseas service, was reduced. The Deputy Chief of Staff for Logistics, Department of the Army, approved the revised Army Aviation Depot Plan on 30 March.

The supply system developed in the plan was based on normal Army supply procedures, with centralized accountability maintained at the Transportation Supply and Maintenance Command (TSMC) and with stocks held at Transportation Sections of New Cumberland General Depot, Pennsylvania; Atlanta General Depot, Georgia; Sharpe General Depot, California; and Fort Worth General Depot, Texas. The supplies currently stocked at fourteen Air Force depots would be used for supply actions to reduce levels by attrition. Receipts from procurement and returns from overhaul would be placed in Army depots beginning 1 April 1956. The Transportation Corps anticipated supplies in the Air Force depots would be negligible by 1 July 1958.

The Department of the Air Force would continue to budget through FY 1957 for depot maintenance. Major repair and overhaul of aircraft components, except for limited capability prior to 1 July 1957, would be performed by contract or cross-servicing agreements entered into by TSMC. The maintenance facilities established at the depots would enable the Transportation Corps to perform the following functions: fourth echelon maintenance, beyond the capability of field maintenance centers, and contingency maintenance; technical order compliance on reparables and serviceable stock; area support of crash damaged aircraft; and minor unscheduled maintenance by appropriate contracts.

Overseas, supplies would be placed in Army Supply Centers, with requisitions passing through normal Army supply channels at a date to be determined by the theater commanders. Maintenance facilities overseas were to be established in FY 1956, with TD personnel, using available tools and equipment, until replaced by TOE units when they became available.

Implementation of the plan would proceed on a phased basis, beginning on 1 April 1956, with the diversion of supplies under procurement to Army depots until independence from the Air Force depot system was virtually achieved by 30 June 1958. During the third and final year, efforts would be made toward completing construction, obtaining final personnel allocations, cleaning up residual Army assets in Air Force depots, and attaining a full area maintenance support capability at the Army depot shops.[4]

Army Regulation 700-210, 14 August 1956, described the phased transition of depot support for Army aircraft from the Air Force to the Army. On 17 September, CONARC requested information from the Department of the Army for planning and budgetary purposes. The Department informed CONARC that it would continue the liberal aircraft assembly exchange policy which existed for support of Army aircraft. The Army Aviation Depot Plan contemplated absorbing from the existing CONUS army field maintenance shops that portion of fourth echelon requirements above the capability of the Army shops. No additional funds, personnel spaces, tools, and equipment or facilities would be required. Depot support would be accomplished by cross-servicing agreement, contractual services, and depot facilities. The specific target date for the transfer of responsibility for the depot support of Army aircraft was 1 April 1957, but the program was phased in as requirements existed.[5]

Implementation of the Plan

The air materiel capabilities of the Army depots had to be developed from scratch. Warehouse and storage space was acquired at the four depots and new procurement and excess supplies from the CONUS army areas were brought in as initial stock. Arrangements were made for construction during FY 1957 and FY 1958 of area support fourth echelon shops, including hangars, runways, and related facilities.

Although the timing of the changeover in supply support proceeded according to plan, the expected improvements in the accuracy and responsiveness of the support did not immediately materialize. Recovery from the expected slow down which resulted from transition from the Air Force to the Army supply system was slow. Increasing workloads, limitations in resources and manpower, excessive and improper requisitioning, difficulties in item identification, and other problems necessitated concentration of overcoming backlogs and on meeting current needs.

The rapid growth of Army aviation had been one of the basic causes of the problems which developed. The original 1954 plan was based on a worldwide fixed and rotary wing aircraft population of approximately 3,500. By the end of 1957, this number had increased to approximately 4,500, and more increases were certain in the years to come. The number of air support spare parts to be managed was originally estimated at 36,000, but by the end of 1957 had reached nearly 70,000, with 100,000 expected in 1959. Original plans were based on receiving requisitions for 14,000 air line items per month, while rate of receipt had reached 22,000 per month in 1957. The estimated workload was expected to increase to 40,000 during 1958. The plan contemplated that approximately 1,000 air line items per month would be purchased by TSMC. During 1957, the figure was closer to 3,000 per month.[6]

The Deputy Chief of Staff for Logistics directed in August 1957 a time-phased program to improve the Transportation Corps supply effectiveness. Intended to correct both short and long range problems, the program had several major objectives. To reduce the need for time-consuming procurement actions on requisitions, the Transportation Corps sought to assure a greater correlation between stockage and demand. Existing provisioning procedures, which had been intended primarily for Air Force use, were replaced. Attempts were made, through CONARC and the CONUS army commanders, to achieve standardization of types and models of aircraft at installations, and, where possible, on an area-wide basis. Problems of requisition identification and processing were to be eliminated and improper requisitions reduced.

As a result of this program, the Transportation Corps made steady, if sometimes slow and erratic, progress in improving its supply system. While neither its overseas nor domestic supply performance had come up to the DCSLOG criteria by the end of 1958, definite improvement was evident. The Transportation Corps expected steady progress toward the objective of meeting Army standards of supply effectiveness as a result of continuing the existing program, together with benefits drawn from increased experience and expanded automatic data processing operations.[7]

During the transition period, many exceptions to Army regulations had to be requested and many regulations peculiar to aviation were published. These measures were due in part to assuming practices which had been common to the Air Force and could not be quickly changed, in part to the large number of technicians employed by the Transportation Supply and Maintenance Command who were former Air Force employees trained in the Air Force method of doing business. TSMC expended much effort in revising procedures and practices to conform to standard Army patterns, and, as time went on, fewer and fewer exceptions to Army regulations had to be requested. By early 1960, the only regulations which dealt exclusively with aviation equipment were based on the peculiarities of that equipment and not upon Air Force practices.

The transition period culminated in calendar year 1959. The attrition of Air Force stocks had taken place much more quickly than expected. Anxious to clear Army equities from its depots, the Air Force pressed for earlier transfer of stocks and offered to pay certain transportation costs. The Army also placed increased emphasis on expediting the transfer of disposal of its assets in Air Force depots. By 30 June 1958, almost $78 million worth of stock had been issued by or transferred from Air Force depots. Residual stocks, valued at about $1.6 million, were subsequently transferred or disposed of as rapidly as possible.[8]

During FY 1960, the Transportation Materiel Command was responsible for the supply and maintenance of 5,461 Army aircraft with a value of $427,000,000. The Master Authorized Stockage List (MASL) reflected the efficiency of supply stockage and supply distribution. During FY 1960, the list was expanded to embrace all items in the Transportation Corps supply system to be provided within a relatively short time, as contrasted with items supplied on an "as required" basis. The expansion of the MASL along with improved management techniques raised the number of requisition line items matching the MASL from 60 percent in FY 1959 to 80 percent in FY 1960. Slow procurement action, and the expansion itself, also kept a large percentage of items at a zero balance, which was improved after the close of the fiscal year. A 50 percent reduction in the number of critical air items to only 13 was encouraging even though it did not meet the target of zero. Measured by the Department of the Army DCSLOG criteria that at least 80 percent should be delivered on time, the Transportation Materiel Command met the target for CONUS troop support, an improvement of 12 percent over 1959, though it still lagged for overseas troop support. These improvements in supply effectiveness could be ascribed to the perfecting of internal controls over the MASL and to the correction of errors in depot inventories.

Warehouse refusals at the beginning of FY 1960 were well above the target of 3 percent, causing the Transportation Materiel Command to attack the problem by examining the inventory of depot stocks, by purifying them, and by emphasis on correct identification and cataloging. The Transportation Corps sections of the four general depots were closed in turn between April and November 1959, and nearly 40,000 line items were adjusted by proper identification, classification, or correction of balances.

During the first half of FY 1960, procurement lagged because of a lack of funds, resulting in many priority item requests and a decline in the filling of requisitions. Additional funds for the last half of the year reversed these trends. Some 60,000 stock replacement items were procured during the year, a decrease of 25 percent from the previous year.[9]

Army Procurement of Aircraft

In September 1959, at the direction of the Office of the Secretary of Defense, the Chief of Transportation submitted a plan for direct engineering and procurement of Army aircraft to begin on 1 July 1961. During 1960, the Transportation Corps obtained 122 fixed wing aircraft and 304 helicopters through interservice procurement actions with the Air Force and the Navy. The Office of the Secretary of Defense did not believe that the Transportation Corps had the capability in engineering fields to undertake direct procurement of aircraft, therefore the Transportation Corps submitted a revised plan in January 1961 omitting this area. On 1 July 1960, the Office of the Secretary of Defense refused to permit full procurement of all aircraft, but indicated that a beginning could be made by the Transportation Corps in purchasing off-the-shelf items, including aircraft and components certified by the Federal Aviation Agency. The Transportation Corps could also prepare specifications, establish evaluation boards, conduct mock-up inspections, and participate with the other developing services in engineering and functional flight tests.[10]

Maintenance Personnel Problems

Maintenance was a major continuing problem of Army aviation. The maintenance of Army aircraft grew steadily more difficult and costly. Despite efforts at standardization and simplification, aircraft, particularly helicopters, increased in complexity as well as in size and number. Design deficiencies and modifications, short service life of components, the necessity for frequent tear down, inspection, and overhaul, and the wide dispersion of aircraft combined to complicate maintenance. Even the simplest aircraft required approximately ten hours of maintenance per hour of flight.[11]

On 4 May 1955, G-3, Department of the Army had requested the assistance of CONARC in the solution of certain problems concerning the adequacy of the enlisted grade structure of helicopter mechanics in the transportation helicopter company and other TOE units that contained aircraft. At an Aviation Conference conducted at the Department of the Army on 29 April 1955, the adequacy of the rank of helicopter mechanics in the transportation helicopter company had been questioned, and the desirability of designing a specific position as crew chief so as to retain capable and competent maintenance personnel in the service was proposed.

A related problem was cited on 23 May in a letter from the Chief of Transportation to the Commanding General, CONARC, which stated that an evaluation of experience data clearly indicated the inadequacy of the method for computing aircraft mechanic requirements as established in SR 310-30-15, which contained organization and equipment authorization tables. The normal availability of helicopters assigned to transportation helicopter companies was 57 percent instead of the 66 and two-thirds percent planned for in the TOE. This availability objective was not being attained because of a lack of men to meet the high maintenance requirements. The Chief of Transportation recommended that the aircraft mechanic authorization contained in SR 310-30-15 be changed to increase the number of aircraft mechanics authorized in aviation units.

A CONARC study of the aircraft maintenance authorizations and the grade structure concluded that the number of mechanics authorized in existing TOEs was not adequate to perform required maintenance, and that the present grade structure for aircraft maintenance personnel should be raised one grade under the new specialist grade system. These measures would provide the incentive to encourage competent and highly trained mechanics to remain in the service.

On 3 June, CONARC recommended to the Department of the Army that the method of computing aircraft mechanics by SR 310-30-15 be changed. In order to raise the grades of aircraft maintenance personnel one grade, CONARC recommended that it would be necessary to change the standards of grade authorization contained in AR 611-201. CONARC proposed the following changes in titles for aircraft mechanics: aircraft mechanics helper be changed to airfield service crewman; senior helicopter mechanic be changed to helicopter crew chief (mechanic); and helicopter mechanic helper in field maintenance organizations be changed to aircraft maintenance apprentice. CONARC also recommended that the position of crew chief be authorized on the basis of one per aircraft.

CONARC representatives participated in a conference at the Department of the Army on 16 September concerning the requirements for additional mechanics for transportation helicopter companies. The G-3 representatives stated that they were in agreement with recommendations made by the Chief of Transportation and the Commanding General, CONARC, concerning a need for an increased number of mechanics in helicopter companies. It was indicated, however, that CONARC's proposed change to SR 310-30-15 would increase the number of fixed wing aircraft mechanics as well as rotary wing mechanics in various TOEs. The G-3 representatives felt that there was ample evidence presented to support an increase of rotary wing mechanics, but not to increase the number of fixed wing mechanics. Because there was an immediate requirement to increase the number of mechanics in TOE 55-75R, Transportation Helicopter

Company, this TOE should be revised accordingly and the Department of the Army would grant a waiver of the provisions for SR 310-30-15 for this revision. When sufficient factors were available for both fixed and rotary wing mechanic equivalents, a change would be published to SR 310-30-15. The conferees concluded that CONARC should publish a revision of TOE 55-75R, to include the increased number of mechanics required based on statistical data of operation experience to be furnished CONARC by the Chief of Transportation. The Department of the Army G-1 was instructed to furnish CONARC with an advance copy of the MOS and grade structure revision for aircraft mechanics to include in the revision of TOE 55-75R.

The Department of the Army on 23 September formally directed CONARC to make the revision. CONARC forwarded the revised TOE to the Department of the Army on 15 November for approval and publication. This revision increased the number of helicopter mechanics from 33 to 61 based on a maintenance workload of 7 hours of maintenance for each hour of flying time for H-21 light cargo helicopters and 4 hours of maintenance for each hour of flying time for H-13 reconnaissance helicopters. The position of crew chief on the basis of one per helicopter was also included in this revision. This action was considered an initial step in improving the Army Aircraft Maintenance Program. When all the actions recommended to the Department of the Army were completed, an increase in aircraft mechanics in forty-five TOEs would be required.[12]

Depot Maintenance Support

Fifth Echelon Maintenance

On 1 July 1955, the Transportation Supply and Maintenance Command assumed the depot level maintenance responsibility after making a preliminary survey of commercial facilities and negotiating initial contracts. While cross-service agreements were employed where feasible, the bulk of the fifth echelon work on Transportation Corps air items was performed by commercial contract.[13]

To accomplish the contractual maintenance of aircraft end items, the Transportation Corps established a new Standard Configuration and Modernization Program (SCAMP). While retaining the concept of scheduling aircraft through the depots on a three year cycle, as under Air Force programs, SCAMP was intended to avoid the difficulties which had been experienced earlier. SCAMP consisted of the inspection of aircraft, the performance of all maintenance work which had fallen due, the installation of product improvement and modification kits, and the restoration of aircraft to their scheduled level of depreciation. This program was expected to maximize maintenance effectiveness, correct deficiencies and discrepancies left unremedied at lower echelons, and simplify parts support. At the same time, reparable components were removed from aircraft and after restoration to serviceable condition were returned to depot stocks for reissue.

The Transportation Corps experienced great difficulty during FY 1958, the first complete year in which it had the depot maintenance responsibility, in assuring timely and efficient negotiation and execution of contracts for aircraft component overhaul and repair. Despite difficulties, TSMC did make progress in the program. It was apparent, however, that the accomplishment left much to be desired. Contract awards lagged and long delays were experienced in getting aircraft through and out of maintenance facilities.

Steps were taken by the Transportation Corps to assure that the situation would be more orderly in FY 1959. Efforts were made to obtain the early release of funds and promptly to obtain bids and make awards of contracts. Indefinite quantity contracts were used to facilitate adjustments to changes in funds and workloads. Implementation of the FY 1959 depot maintenance program, however, was adversely affected by delays in obtaining Department of the Army approval of contracts and by shortages of contractor-furnished and government-furnished parts. New Department of the Army restrictions on the scope of the SCAMP program caused additional difficulties. With the establishment of fourth echelon maintenance at the depot sites, TSMC was directed to eliminate from SCAMP contracts any provision for performance of lower echelon maintenance tasks that should have been accomplished prior to delivery to the contractor. The Transportation Corps believed that it was both logical and economical to perform at the SCAMP site all aircraft repairs which had fallen due or would shortly become due. The deferral or omission of these repairs would probably lead to the grounding of aircraft on their return to using activities.[14]

Under cold war plans, mobilization capabilities and training facilities were essential for an instant readiness posture. Consequently, the Office of the Secretary of Defense on 22 December 1959 authorized Transportation Corps in-house assumption of about 40 percent of fifth echelon maintenance to be phased in over the next three years. The Transportation Materiel Command immediately established a Directorate of Maintenance Operations to move ahead on a two phased plan. The first phase consisted of inaugurating fifth echelon maintenance in general depots on components, excluding engines, transmissions, and aircraft themselves. The second phase—fifth echelon maintenance of engines, transmissions, and aircraft—required more extensive facilities than the Army had available. After careful analysis of available facilities of the Air Force and the Navy, the Naval Air Station at Corpus Christi, Texas, seemed to be the most promising.

Just as the Transportation Corps supply and maintenance sections in the general depots were getting ready for increased maintenance duties, the Quartermaster General on 2 September 1959 announced plans for a new concept which would eliminate the technical service sections. The technical service staff would be limited to staff guidance in the accomplishment of the depot's mission. This concept would remove the Transportation Corps staff officer from direct control over the aircraft supply and maintenance operations. The Chief of Transportation requested that Transportation Corps aircraft maintenance be set up in each of the general depots as a Class II activity. On 1 February 1960, the Department of the Army DCSLOG agreed to this proposal. The Quartermaster General desired to test this concept in one depot; the year's trial began at Sharpe General Depot in July 1960.[15]

Fourth Echelon Maintenance

The Army Aviation Depot Plan provided for shops as part of the Transportation Sections at the general depots to handle fourth echelon maintenance workloads beyond the capabilities of field maintenance activities. It was contemplated that the shops would have limited capabilities by 1 July 1958 and be fully operational by the end of the following year.

By late 1956, it had become evident that delays in the construction program for the shops, along with the lead time involved, would preclude completion of the aircraft maintenance facilities until at least mid-1958. The limited capability of the field maintenance shops, coupled with the delay in completing the new depot facilities, threatened to affect the maintenance support of Army aircraft. Because of the urgency of the situation, the Department of the Army DCSLOG directed the Chief of Transportation in December 1956 to establish a limited interim fourth echelon capability using available existing facilities at the depots.

The unanticipated acceleration in the scheduled buildup of fourth echelon capabilities at the depots caused difficulties. The CONUS army commanders were reluctant to submit estimates of work beyond the capabilities of their field maintenance shops, making it impossible to develop firm workloads for the depot shops. Considerable lead time was also necessary to secure the tools and equipment needed for the depot shops.

At the suggestion of the Transportation Corps, facilities construction at the depots was deferred for eighteen months or until such time as a definite idea of the amount of work that would be accomplished at the shops could be obtained. This decision made it impossible for the depots to absorb the load in excess of the capabilities of the field maintenance shops and caused CONARC to resort to expensive contractual maintenance.

As a result of this deteriorating situation, the DCSLOG, Department of the Army, in February 1958 ordered the facilities construction program reinstated. On 19 March, the Chief of Transportation was directed to assume responsibility for all fourth echelon maintenance support of Active Army, National Guard, and Army Reserve aircraft on 1 July 1958. With the exception of large contracts at Fort Rucker, Camp Wolters, and Camp Gary, which had large aircraft populations, the CONUS armies would be responsible for only third echelon maintenance.

The Transportation Corps took action to speed up the delivery of tools, shop equipment, and supplies to the depot sites. Plans were developed for the phased transfer of fourth echelon workloads from the CONUS armies to the depots, beginning on 1 July 1958, with the depots achieving a 100 percent capability by 1 January. Resources shortages continued and backlogs tended to grow. This, in turn, made it necessary to give priority to the repair of aircraft and components to be returned to users at the expense of reconditioning items for depot stock. Problems continued with the construction program.

The successful accomplishment of the CONUS field maintenance mission required a close correlation of the CONUS army and depot shop capabilities. The Transportation Corps, CONARC, and other interested agencies developed a coordinated plan for aircraft maintenance support in CONUS. Task groups were established to devise a program tailored to current peacetime conditions. The plan was expected to provide for efficient utilization of available dollar, manpower, and facility resources, to assure the necessary back-up of overseas command with military personnel spaces and units; to determine the types, missions, strengths, and command control of required maintenance units; and to establish means for coordinating and budgeting and programing of funds for maintenance support.[16]

Maintenance Training

In May 1954, the Department of the Army considered the consolidation of all Army aviation maintenance instruction at the Transportation School. Both the Army Field Forces and the Army Aviation School voiced objections to the proposal. The Army Aviation Program approved in 1955 retained organizational aircraft maintenance instruction at the Army Aviation School and field and depot aircraft maintenance instruction at the Transportation School. In May 1959, the transfer of organizational maintenance instruction to the Transportation School again came under study. The Transportation School study to determine its capability to assume the additional workload concluded that it could be done provided programmed construction and limited improvements of existing facilities were completed. Once again, the proposed transfer was dropped from consideration. A year later, the Transportation School again studied the feasibility of consolidating aviation maintenance training at one installation. This study summarized savings in training time, instructor manpower capabilities, aircraft requirements, facility analysis and classroom requirements, shop space, and temporary and permanent construction at Fort Eustis and Fort Rucker. No changes resulted from this study. Finally, the Transportation School in 1962 once more studied the possibility of consolidation at the direction of CONARC. Again, no changes in maintenance training were made.[17]

The major maintenance courses taught at the Army Aviation School and the Transportation School from 1954 to 1962 are shown in tables 5 and 6.

Army Aviation School

The Department of Aviation Maintenance of the Army Aviation School, which began to move from Fort Sill to Camp Rucker on 20 November 1954, began the first instruction at the new site on 26 November. Two courses were conducted at this time: the Army Helicopter Maintenance Course (sixteen weeks) and the Twin-Engine Transition Maintenance Course (two weeks).

The actual move to Camp Rucker was conducted in phases and completed on 17 December. During the move, one class from each course was canceled and the first Helicopter Maintenance class, with twenty-four students, was scheduled for graduation on 8 January 1955. Due to the enthusiasm of the instructors and students, however, the class was accelerated and graduated before Christmas. Like all the other departments of the Army Aviation School, the Department of Aviation Maintenance at first suffered with inadequate facilities at Camp Rucker. An old vehicle shop building was used as a classroom. The Department of Academics was formed in September 1955 in an effort to consolidate general subjects and maintenance training. The new department was headed by the former director of the Department of Aviation Maintenance. In August 1957, the Department of Academics was discontinued and the Department of

Maintenance was formed. At this time, general subjects instructors were transferred to the Department of Fixed Wing Training.[18]

The Department of the Army in mid-April 1956 had reported to CONARC in its analysis of the program of instruction of airplane repair, reconnaissance helicopter repair, and tandem rotor helicopter repair courses that course content was consistent with the MOS and skill level for which each course trained and that course purpose statements conformed to established procedures. The department emphasized that course titles should, whenever possible, be expressed in terms of the subject matter taught. Course titles should be revised for the single rotor helicopter repair and for tandem rotor helicopter repair course to utility and cargo tandem rotor helicopter repair. The Department of the Army believed that prior experience in airplane repair activity was essential and should be included in the prerequisites for the courses.[19]

In mid-March 1956, CONARC approved the proposed program of instruction for the Aircraft Maintenance (Entry) Course and revised the course purpose to read: "to provide enlisted personnel with basic fundamentals required to enable them to participate in the operation of Army airfields and airstrips and in the servicing and maintenance of fixed wing and rotary wing aircraft." With the implementation of a new MOS system, certain aviation mechanics courses were added and others deleted. At Gary Air Force Base, the Army Helicopter Mechanic and the Army Airplane Mechanic courses were deleted and the Army Maintenance (Entry) Course was added. At the Army Aviation School, the Army Helicopter Maintenance, Twin Engine Transition Maintenance, Army Helicopter Maintenance (H-25), Army Helicopter Maintenance (H-19), Army Helicopter Maintenance (H-21), and Army Helicopter Maintenance (H-34) were deleted, and Airplane Maintenance, Reconnaissance Helicopter Maintenance, Utility and Cargo Single Rotary Wing Helicopter, and Utility and Cargo Tandem Rotor Helicopter courses were added. Implementation of training under the new courses and deletion of the old courses was effective on 1 July 1956.[20]

Third Army in June 1956 desired that schools be established to transition train automotive maintenance and other available personnel to aircraft maintenance crewmen (MOS 670) and to more specialized MOSs. The high number of aircraft in the Army area were causing increasing maintenance problems. It was recommended that those schools include a minimum of two hours per day of organized classroom instruction in addition to on-the-job training. Following a period of attendance at local transition schools combined with on-the-job training, individuals who demonstrated the necessary aptitudes and skills would be awarded with MOS. Local schooling would be continued following the awarding of the MOS until the mechanic reached a sufficiently high degree of skill for the awarding of MOSs 671, 672, 673, as appropriate. If advanced training could not be given at the station or unit level, quotas would be obtained from Third Army to send those men requiring such training to the Army Aviation School. Excess individuals who could not be absorbed into the locally established transition schools would be carefully screened and sent to the Army Aviation School to pursue a course for the award of MOS 670 followed by the specialized course in the type of aircraft assigned to their units.

Third Army reported on 6 August that aircraft maintenance transition schools were established at Third Army stations as a stop gap measure only because the replacement system was not providing enough trained aircraft mechanics to enable aviation units to maintain assigned aircraft. Third Army felt that aircraft maintenance was too complex a subject to be taught at station level only. It was intended that retained automotive mechanics eventually would attend formal training in aircraft maintenance. Third Army recommended that the input to aircraft maintenance schools be increased in order to provide sufficient fully qualified aircraft mechanics for assignment to aviation units.

In August 1956, the Fixed Wing Maintenance Course conducted at Camp Gary began moving to Fort Rucker. By January 1957, the move was completed with many of the civilian instructors from Camp Gary making the move to Fort Rucker. A labor dispute in November temporarily grounded the school's aircraft fleet. With the contract personnel on strike, students and instructors moved from the classrooms to the flight line and performed the necessary maintenance.

The Army Aviation School in May 1956 had suggested to CONARC that it would be feasible to establish an organizational aircraft maintenance officers course at the school and recommended that it be of fourteen weeks duration. The school also suggested that the course should have a minimum class of eight and a maximum class of sixteen dual rated officers, with a minimum annual input of 48. Based on two classes in residence, 5 additional primary instructors, 10 practical maintenance instructors, and 2 classrooms (1 conference type and 1 laboratory type) would be required. These additional resources would cost $86,200.

The Army Aviation School requested 120 days lead time for implementation of the course. The school also determined that there was a need for two additional courses—organizational aviation supply and technical inspector—for officer and enlisted students. These courses would each be 3 weeks in length, have a minimum class size of 8 students, and have a minimum course annual input of 128. Each course would require 3 additional instructors, 2 conference-type classrooms, and a lead time of 120 days.[21]

CONARC reported to the Department of the Army early in July that the establishment of the aircraft organizational maintenance officer course would have little or no effect on the existing aircraft maintenance officer course conducted at the Transportation School. Present input into that course came primarily from agencies engaged in field and depot, rather than organizational maintenance activities. Furthermore, the program of instruction for the existing course was slanted toward field and depot maintenance. Under the circumstances, CONARC would take necessary action to establish the aircraft organizational maintenance course at such time as the additional funds and instructor spaces were made available by the Department of the Army. The existing aircraft maintenance officer course would be continued at the Transportation School.

On 10 April 1957, CONARC gave interim approval to the program of instruction for the 10-week Organizational Maintenance Officer Course. Final approval came on 17 August. The purpose of the course was to provide officers with basic knowledge and fundamentals required to enable them to supervise and instruct the mechanics of aviation units in all forms, records, and technical publications, and to provide officers with a thorough knowledge of aircraft maintenance, organizational (first and second echelon) through limited field maintenance (limited third echelon). Formal announcement of the course was made by CONARC on 5 September. The course length was subsequently reduced to five weeks in December 1957.[22]

On 10 April 1959, the Department of the Army approved a recommendation by CONARC to eliminate the Organizational Maintenance Officer course. Unit commanders could not spare the personnel, time, and funds, and—especially in small units—needed the potential students on the job, as trained in previous flight courses. Because everyone agreed that officer organizational maintenance training was essential to reduce overall maintenance costs and to increase the availability of aircraft for operational use, CONARC and the Army Aviation School studied a proposal to integrate more maintenance training in the initial flight training course.[23]

CONARC announced in May 1957 the prerequisites for the eight week Flight Simulator Operations and Maintenance Course, the purpose of which was to train enlisted men to operate and maintain those flight simulators needed to provide instruction in instrument flight techniques to rated Army aviators. These prerequisites included normal color perception, normal use of both hands, good hearing, twelve months or more of service remaining following the completion of the course, and a standard score of 100 or higher aptitude area GT.

CONARC informed the Army Aviation School in October that it was revising school loads for the third and fourth quarters of fiscal year 1958. The revision was based on budget cuts and revised MOS requirements, and would in some instances affect inputs into certain school courses. The Aircraft Maintenance Course was to continue to be offered until a revised schedule of classes reflecting new inputs was submitted to CONARC. The revised schedule was to be in conformance with the school's recommendation for a weekly flow of students.[24]

The introduction of new aircraft resulted in the development of new maintenance courses at the Army Aviation School. During July 1958, the Department of Maintenance organized a transition course for crew training on the H-37 MOJAVE. Because of the many complicated systems of the aircraft, the training was conducted for complete crews including the pilot, copilot, and crew chief. This course continued until February 1959, when it was replaced by the H-37 Helicopter Maintenance Course for mechanics only. With the introduction of the UH-1 IROQUOIS, a mechanics course for that aircraft was adopted on 1 April 1959. A year later, the first class of AO-1 MOHAWK mechanics met with twelve students. This was followed on 10 May 1960 with a new maintenance course of instruction for AC-1 CARIBOU mechanics. In July 1961, a course was organized by the Department of Maintenance to provide instruction on the automatic stabilization equipment which was installed on some H-34s and all H-37s. This course was discontinued in July 1962, and the instruction integrated into the regular maintenance course for H-37 mechanics.

In April 1960, the Department of Maintenance organized the first U.S. Army Aviation School Organization Aircraft Maintenance Supervisors Mobile Instruction Team whose mission was assistance for unit commanders in training maintenance personnel on station. The three teams organized from military instructors within the Department of Maintenance presented forty hours of instruction at major installations throughout the CONUS army areas.[25]

Transportation School

The major emphasis in resident instruction at the Transportation School shifted in 1954 to the aviation maintenance training program. Rail and marine subjects made up over 60 percent of the courses given by the school in 1954, while aviation maintenance courses accounted for almost 60 percent of the courses in 1958. The first aviation maintenance course began in late June 1954 with the opening of six classes. An additional course began that July.

Late in 1955, the Defense Department studied the feasibility of having all nontactical Army aviation training, including aviation maintenance, conducted by the Air Force. The Department of the Army strongly recommended that the Army be given responsibility for all Army aviation training, and the proposed change was not made.

Attrition rates were a matter of concern in both the advanced and specialist aviation maintenance courses. In order to improve the qualifications of enlisted men attending the advanced maintenance courses, the Transportation School recommended that the Department of the Army School Catalog be revised to provide for formal examination by the Aviation Department. If found deficient, a man would then be required to attend MOS 680 entry training or be returned to his unit. CONARC concurred in this recommendation.

When the Transportation School began instruction in aviation maintenance, certain items of equipment were still in critically short supply. These included special tools required for assembly and disassembly of aircraft components, major items of shop equipment, and L-20 and L-23 aircraft. Due to nonreceipt of major items of shop test equipment, the first class of the Aircraft Instrument and Electrical System Repairman Course (MOS 3559) was sent to the Norfolk Naval Air Station for two weeks, and the second class was rescheduled. The lack of these special tools and major items of equipment continued as a major problem for the next two years. With respect to aircraft components and special tools, the aviation supply process, linked with provisioning, procurement, production, storage, and priority field distribution, imposed unreliable delivery dates ranging from one to twenty-four months. The shortage of aircraft also continued to be a limiting factor on maintenance training for the next several years.[26]

In November 1956, CONARC approved a draft program of instruction for the Aircraft Maintenance Officer Course. The revised program of instruction increased the course length from fourteen to fifteen weeks. The increase in the course length was necessary to provide greater emphasis on supply production control, management, and other subjects which had increased in importance with the assumption of Army aviation depot maintenance.

On 7 January 1957, CONARC formally announced the prerequisites for the revised Aircraft Maintenance Officer Course which would train officers to coordinate and supervise field, depot, and organizational maintenance, including technical maintenance inspection of Army aircraft. The officer could be Regular Army or Reserve Component whose assignment, actual or anticipated, was to a position involving direction of organizational or higher level aircraft maintenance activity or to a staff position.[27]

In early 1956, CONARC requested the Chief of Transportation to comment on the feasibility of establishing a Special Aircraft Officer Maintenance Course. Acting on the request of the Chief of Transportation, the Transportation Training Command announced that a special course of instruction for National Guard officers had been established at the Transportation School. The two week course would emphasize procedures, forms, and records of aircraft maintenance and would be based on programs of instruction then being utilized in the Aviation Officers Maintenance Course. Items common to both organizational field maintenance would be stressed, with inspection methods predominant. The Transportation Training Command recommended that the starting date be 14 May 1956, with a reporting date at Fort Eustis of 10 May.

The National Guard Bureau in January 1957 requested the establishment of the special aviation officer maintenance course, estimating that sixty officers would be available to attend such a course, provided it would be conducted in May. CONARC approved the course in March 1957, provided that training could be conducted within school facilities. Since the training would be on a one-time basis, submission of a program of instruction was not required. The Transportation Center at Fort Eustis proposed a starting date of 13 May with the closing that being 18 May. The anticipated attendance was forty-five students.[28]

In the summer of 1959, the Aviation Department of the Transportation School provided six instructors for aviation maintenance support training of U.S. Army Reserve and National Guard units at Camp Drum, New York, for nineteen days, and two instructors of National Guard units at Fort Ripley, Minnesota. This experiment evolved into the Mobile Aviation Maintenance Training Teams, as directed by the Office of the Chief of Transportation, which officially became part of the school's mission in December 1959. The program was enlarged in 1961 when two teams of eleven men each were sent out by the school. When the 1962 teams were organized, the Aviation Maintenance Training Branch had 222 military instructors authorized, but only 92 assigned. Because of this, it was decided to cut each team to six men. The Transportation School felt that units did not take full advantage of the instruction available because of field training and support requirements.

The Army Aircraft Maintenance Management Course had been given three times in 1959-1960. In 1960, in order to comply with a change to AR 600-201, this course was dropped and replaced by three separate courses designed to train qualified personnel in accordance with the new MOS structure. The new courses were Fixed Wing Technical Inspector (679.4), Rotary Wing Technical Inspector (679.5), and Aircraft Maintenance Supervisor (679.6). Because previously aviation maintenance personnel had been trained either in fixed wing or rotary wing aircraft and the new 679.6 MOS required the supervisor to be qualified in both, the Transportation School had to train its own instructors in order to qualify them for the MOS conversion. To do this, the school set up a training course for its instructors which followed closely the 679.6 supervisor course.

In FY 1960, the emphasis on MOS enlisted training at the Transportation School shifted further toward aviation as all rail courses were stopped and several marine courses were canceled. In 1958, 55 percent of the enlisted training courses had been in aviation maintenance; by the end of 1962, this figure had risen to slightly over 80 percent. The increases in the aviation courses were primarily in MOS 673.2, Single Rotor Helicopter Repair, and MOS 685.1, Aircraft Electrical Repair. While the actual input of students into the aviation maintenance courses in FY 1960 represented only a 15 percent increase over FY 1959, these courses required a lower instructor-student ratio and more intricate and expensive equipment. In FY 1959, FY 1961, and FY 1962, the input into the aviation courses at the Transportation School averaged about 1,225; in FY 1960 it reached 1,425.[29]

Endnotes
Chapter XIV

1. (1) Detailed Information to Support Report on Army Aircraft Maintenance and Supply Presented to the Assistant Secretary of the Army, 20 Dec 57, pp. 1-2. (2) *The Army Aviation Depot System: Its Origins and Development*, pp. 1-3.

2. (1) Report on Army Aircraft Maintenance and Supply, Sec. I, App. I, pp. 5-8. (2) *The Army Aviation Depot System: Its Origins and Development*, pp. 8-9.

3. (1) Report on Aircraft Maintenance and Supply, p. 3. (2) *The Army Aviation Depot System: Its Origins and Development*, p. 9.

4. (1) Revised Army Aviation Depot Plan, 15 Jan 56, TSMC. (2) *The Army Aviation Depot System: Its Origins and Development*, pp. 10-11.

5. CONARC Summary of Major Events and Problems, FY 57, Vol. V, G-4 Sec, Jul-Dec 56, pp. 5-6.

6. (1) *The Army Aviation Depot System: Its Origins and Development*, pp. 16-23. (2) Report on Army Aircraft Maintenance and Supply, pp. 12-13. (3) By 1960, there were about 6,000 aircraft in the Army inventory.

7. *The Army Aviation Depot System: Its Origins and Development*, pp. 23-25, 28-30.

8. (1) Army Aircraft Repair Parts Management Report-1959, TMC, 5 Feb 60, p. 6. (2) *The Army Aviation Depot System: Its Origins and Development*, p. 19.

9. OCofT Summary of Major Events and Problems, FY 60, pp. 58, 61-114.

10. Ibid., FY 60, p. 64.

11. (1) Bykofsky, *The Support of Army Aviation 1950-1954*, pp. 71-72. (2) Tolson, *Airmobility 1961-1971*, p. 88.

12. CONARC Summary of Major Events and Problems, FY 56, Vol. II, G-3 Sec Org & Equip Div, Jul-Dec 55, Item 9; and FY 58, Vol. II, Army Avn Sec, Jul-Dec 57, pp. 6-7.

13. There were five Army maintenance categories. First echelon was maintenance performed by the user or operator of the equipment. Second echelon was performed by specially trained personnel in the using organization and was beyond the capabilities and facilities of the first echelon. Third echelon was performed by specially trained units in direct support of the using organization. The first two echelons were performed in the using units, while the third echelon was performed by attached aviation maintenance units. Fourth echelon was performed by units organized as semifixed or permanent shops to serve lower echelon maintenance usually for return to supply channels. Fifth echelon involved the rebuilding of major items, assemblies, parts, accessories, tools, and test equipment.

14. (1) *The Army Aviation Depot System: Its Origins and Development*, pp. 32-37. (2) Report on Army Aircraft Maintenance and Supply, pp. 51-55.

15. OCofT, Summary of Major Events and Problems, FY 60, pp. 66-68.

16. (1) *The Army Aviation Depot System: Its Origins and Development*, pp. 37-43. (2) DF LOG B/3, DA DCSLOG to CofT and QMG, 7 Mar 58, subj: Fourth Echelon Maintenance of CONUS Army Aircraft. (3) Ltr AGAM-P (M) 400.402 (7 Mar 58) DCSLOG DA, DA TAG to distr, 19 Mar 58, subj: Fourth Echelon Maintenance of Army Aircraft in the Continental United States.

17. (1) Weinert, Army Aviation, p. 131. (2) *History of the United States Army Transportation School, 1942-1962*, USA Trans Sch, Oct 67, pp. 253, 256.

18. *History of the US Army Aviation Center and Army Aviation School*, p. 14.

19. Ltr AGTP-M 352.11, DA to CONARC, 20 Apr 56, subj: Proposed Program of Instruction for Aircraft Repair Courses.

20. (1) Ltr ATTNG-TNG-352.11, CONARC to Army Aviation School, 19 Mar 56, subj: Program of Instruction for Aircraft Maintenance Entry Course MOS 670. (2) Ltr ATTNG-TNG-352 (Army Aviation School), CONARC to Army Aviation School, 30 Mar 56, Army Aviation Maintenance Course under New MOS System.

21. Ltr AASDI 352.11, Gen Army Avn School to CONARC, 10 May 56, subj: Organizational Aircraft Maintenance Officer's Course.

22. Ltr ATTNG-TNG-352/54 (Army Avn Sch) (5 Sep 57), CONARC to distr, 5 Sep 57, subj: Announcement of the Organizational Maintenance Officer Course (1A-F-13).

23. CONARC Summary of Major Events and Problems, FY 59, Vol. III, Army Avn Sec, Jan-Jun 59, pp. 11-12.

24. (1) Ltr ATTNG-TNG-352/16 (Army Avn Sch) (2 May 57), CONARC to distr, 2 May 57, subj: Announcement of the Flight Simulator Operations and Maintenance Course. (2) Ltr AASDI 352.11 AMC, Army Avn Sch to CONARC, 25 Sep 57, subj: Revised Schedule for Aircraft Mechanic Course, w/1st Ind, CONARC to Army Avn Sch, 10 Oct 57.

25. *History of the US Army Aviation Center and Army Aviation School*, pp. 14-15.

26. *History of the United States Army Transportation School, 1942-1962*, pp. 202-203, 217-218, 235-236.

27. (1) Ltr TCTTC-TS-DOI-3, Trans Sch to Trans Tng Cmd, 21 Aug 56, subj: Program of Instr for Aircraft Maint Officer Course (55-0-16) MOS 4823, w/3 Ind. (2) Ltr ATTNG-TNG 352/1 (TC Sch) (7 Jan 57), CONARC to distr, 7 Jan 57, subj: Announcement of the Aircraft Maintenance Officer Course.

28. (1) Ltr NG AROTS, National Guard Bur to CONARC, 23 Mar 56, subj: Special Aircraft Officer Maintenance Course, w/5 Ind. (2) Ltr TCTTC-G3-AIR 360, Trans Tng Comd to CofT, 26 Apr 56, subj: Special Aircraft Officer Maintenance Course, w/1 incl.

29. *History of the United States Army Transportation School, 1942-1962*, pp. 253, 256, 264, 267, 281.

CHAPTER XV

SUMMARY

Army aviation, as it is known today, has undergone a significant metamorphosis since its inception in World War II. Its origins lie in the reconnaissance mission of the field artillery. Field artillerymen, flying small fixed wing aircraft, established and validated the aviation mission approved in June 1942. Since that time, Army aviation has made its mark under the watchful eye of at least two Army branches and a sister service.

The National Security Act of 1947 separated the Air Force from the Army and formally established Army aviation as a separate entity. Separate, however, was not equal, and Army aviation shared an uneasy airspace with the developing Air Force. For instance, while the Air Force provided primary fixed and rotary wing training for Army pilots, for many years advanced training was conducted by the U.S. Army Department of Air Training at the Artillery School at Fort Sill.

The separation of the Army and the Air Force naturally caused considerable organizational flux, and both services spent time and effort attending the accompanying changes. The role of Army aviation was of paramount interest to both. Joint Army and Air Force Regulation 5-10-1, published in 1949, set forth the utilization criteria for Army aircraft and imposed weight limitations on both fixed and rotary wing Army aircraft. Publication of AR 700-50 and AFR 65-7 on 23 March 1950 confirmed that basic understanding and officially assigned the major responsibility for logistical support of Army aviation to the Ordnance Corps.

The procedures and responsibilities contained in the Joint Army and Air Force regulations were the subject of continual discussions from the date of publication. The basic problem stemmed from the two services' divergent views on close air support. By 1951, discussions of the function and role of Army aircraft had reached the highest administrative levels of the two services. As a result of these discussions, on 2 October 1951, a special Memorandum of Understanding was signed which eliminated the aircraft weight limitations and substituted a definition of organic Army aircraft in terms of the functions to be performed.

The need for further clarification of Army and Air Force viewpoints on Army aviation, particularly regarding helicopters, required additional consideration and discussion at the Department level. The discussions, which began in November 1951 and continued throughout the fall of 1952, included those problems encountered during the Korean conflict. On 4 November 1952, the Army and the Air Force concluded a second Memorandum of Understanding which superseded the special agreement of 1951. This second document favored the Army point of view on Army aviation. It reestablished a maximum weight limitation of 5,000 pounds on Army fixed wing aircraft, but left helicopters unrestricted. The document stipulated that the weight restriction would be the subject of review by the Secretary of Defense upon the request of either service secretary. A most significant feature of the second memorandum was the clear delineation made between the functions to be performed by Army aircraft and those operated by the Air Force.

Responsibility for logistical support of Army aviation was transferred from the Ordnance Corps to the Transportation Corps on 11 August 1952. At the same time, the Army Field Forces organized and trained the first transportation helicopter companies. Beginning in 1951, several of these companies participated in large-scale maneuvers which, while not involving fully equipped companies, conclusively demonstrated the value of helicopters in combat. During the exercises the first tactical movement of combat units by helicopter was achieved.

The rapid expansion of Army aviation which began in 1950 resulted in a commensurate increase in training operations. The Air Force had continued to train pilots and mechanics for the Army. Tactical training continued at Fort Sill, and in 1953 the Army Aviation School was established. Primary flight training by the Air Force was gradually phased out and the subsequent overcrowding of facilities at Fort Sill led to the transfer of the school to Camp Rucker in 1954. The Transportation School began field maintenance training of mechanics on 1 July 1954.

By the end of 1954, Army aviation was firmly founded. Its dependence on the Air Force for training and logistical support was rapidly being phased out. A strong and flexible training base had been provided with the establishment of the Army Aviation School and the assumption of maintenance training by the Transportation School. Tactical units were formed and a few saw combat in Korea.

Basic to the rapid expansion of Army aviation during this period was the formulation of the first coherent long range plan for future development. The impetus for this plan came from General Ridgway's call for a comprehensive review of Army aviation. Its implementation was carried out within the framework of policies adopted by the Department of Defense. Continued disputes between the Army and the Air Force over mission and function led Secretary of Defense Charles E. Wilson to modify the 1952 Memorandum of Understanding in 1956. The agreement maintained the weight restrictions on Army aircraft, but left the door open for continued expansion. In addition, the Wilson memorandum expanded the size of the combat zone within which Army aircraft could operate. No restrictions were placed on their performance within that zone.

Despite—or often because of—the Department of Defense ruling, the Army encountered Air Force opposition to their proposed expansion. At the root of this dispute were the widely differing viewpoints on the proper role and means of employment of aviation assets. The Army believed that aviation assets, both combat and transport, existed primarily to support ground combat forces. In order to be responsive to the needs of the ground units, the commander had to exercise a relatively high degree of control over aviation units. The Air Force, as the Army Air Force before it, believed that the most efficient and economical use of air power could be attained only with centralization of command and control under the air commander.

While admitting Air Force responsibility in most areas of aviation, the Army faced the problem of securing air support for ground units. Air Force interest in the 1950s focused primarily on strategic bombardment. Little attention and few resources were devoted to tactical transport or close air support. Recognizing the value of aviation in the accomplishment of its mission, the Army moved in to close the gap. Light tactical transports were developed—both rotary and fixed wing—and eventually armament was installed on the aircraft.

To meet the more complex demands of the expanded aviation program, organizational changes took place at all levels of the Army. At the Department of the Army level, all activities relating to Army aviation—except those of a purely logistical nature and some aspects of the research and development program—were drawn together into a Directorate of Army Aviation. The appointment of Maj. Gen. Hamilton H. Howze as the first Director of Army Aviation had a profound effect on the development of the program. General Howze became the apostle of airmobility. Not only in his official activities as Director of Army Aviation, but also in countless speeches and articles, General Howze advocated the expansion of the Army aviation program and the introduction of airmobility into combat operations.

The Transportation Corps, which at the beginning of the period had undisputed responsibility for aviation, also underwent a significant reorganization. The assumption of supply and maintenance responsibilities from the Air Force resulted in the establishment of the Transportation Supply and Maintenance Command. The staff of the Office of the Chief of Transportation was reorganized to reflect the fact that the majority of Transportation Corps activities centered around aviation. CONARC also adjusted its organization to provide for increasing involvement in aviation activities. The command believed that it should have greater responsibility for overall direction of the aviation program. The Department of the Army remained firm, however, that direction and guidance would originate in the Directorate of Army Aviation. To complement the Directorate, CONARC created a focal point in its headquarters with the Army Aviation Section. As tactical combat uses for Army aviation became increasingly important, responsibility for more of the Army aviation program shifted to CONARC.

During the period, the ground army underwent an extensive reorganization as well. Acceptance of Army aviation was reflected in the AFTA experiment and the increased number of aircraft in the PENTOMIC divisions. But these were only interim solutions to the Army's combat problems, and with the adoption of the ROAD division organization the number of Army aircraft in divisions approximately doubled. In addition to the expansion of Army aviation in divisional organizations, separate aviation units also multiplied. New company organizations were developed for improved fixed wing transports and medium helicopters. In response to the combat situation in Southeast Asia, Special Warfare Aviation Detachments were formed.

Perhaps in the long run the most significant advance during this period was the successful development of aircraft armament. Beginning with an unsuccessful attempt to find a flying tank destroyer during Project ABLE BUSTER, rapid strides were made in the development of armament. A few officers at the Army Aviation School had faith in the ability of the helicopter to carry weapons. Under the guidance of Brig. Gen. Carl I. Hutton, and with the tacit consent of CONARC, the Army Aviation School conducted a series of experiments with various types of armament which eventually led to several practical weapons systems. The imagination and dedication of the officers and men of the school helped prove that weapons could be fired from rotary aircraft. The success of the efforts of the Army Aviation School and CONARC resulted in official approval of the armed helicopter by the Department of the Army in 1960.

The arming of the helicopter was to have a profound effect on both Army organization and combat doctrine. Various types of Sky Cavalry were organized and tested. While Sky Cavalry units were primarily reconnaissance oriented, the possibilities of much broader application were quickly seen. The Armair Brigade Study by the Army Aviation School, although never really field tested, pointed the way to the airmobile employment of infantry supported by helicopter gunships.

An underlying result of this growth of tactical employment of Army aviation was the continuing friction between the Transportation Corps and CONARC. Brig. Gen. William B. Bunker warned in the late 1950s that the Transportation Corps was doing nothing to develop aviation doctrine for the PENTOMIC army and had made no progress in aviation unit organization since 1951. As a consequence, the Combat Development Group at Fort Rucker, the Army Aviation School, and many other agencies took over responsibility for the fulfillment of the future transportation mission of the Army.

The frustrations of the Transportation Corps surfaced again in late 1961 when DCSOPS, Department of the Army, recommended on the advice of CONARC that two separate types of companies be formed to fly the HC-1 and two separate types to fly the AC-1. This action would distinguish logistical and tactical units. Maj. Gen. Frank S. Besson, the Chief of Transportation, charged that some elements of the Army intended to eliminate the flying role of the Transportation Corps and urged that the corps have an aviation mission in the combat zone. Happily for the future of Army aviation, this internal dispute over the control of aircraft ended with the 1962 Army reorganization that abolished the Office of the Chief of Transportation. As a result of this reorganization, CONARC assumed most responsibilities for aviation except combat and materiel developments.[1]

The progress made by Army aviation between 1955 and 1962 was made possible by development of new aircraft. The search for a utility helicopter led to the adoption of the UH-1. This aircraft quickly proved adaptable for medical evacuation, as a gunship, and as a transport for small units. Using a turbine engine, the UH-1 proved to be more rugged and reliable than the earlier utility helicopters. The search for a cargo helicopter produced the H-37 as a temporary solution and eventually the adoption of the tandem rotor HC-1. Teamed together, the UH-1 and HC-1 became the workhorses in the evolving airmobility concept. Fixed wing transport aviation came of age with the adoption of the U-1. As the period ended, the AC-1 offered even greater possibilities in the use of fixed wing transports from unimproved airfields. The search for an improved reconnaissance aircraft resulted in extensive tests to find a new light observation helicopter. At first unsuccessful, by 1962 the program began to show results. A concurrent search for a higher performance observation aircraft led to troop tests with the T-37 jet. Strong Air Force opposition resulted in the termination of the project without significant results. At the same time, the Army developed the propeller driven AO-1 which proved suitable for Army requirements.

Aviation training made steady progress during the period under CONARC. Consolidation of all flight training under Army direction was a notable accomplishment. The Department of Defense ordered the transfer of primary flight training from the Air Force in 1956, bringing to an end several years of Army efforts to achieve consolidation. Primary helicopter training was established at the U.S. Army Primary Helicopter School at Camp Wolters, while primary fixed wing training was conducted at Camp Gary until the eventual shift to Fort Rucker. Advanced training for both fixed wing and rotary wing pilots took place at the Army Aviation School at Fort Rucker.

In order to properly train the large number of aviation units being activated, CONARC established Army Aviation Unit Training Commands at Fort Sill and Fort Riley. Difficulties beset the operation of these centers because of slow delivery of aircraft, shortages of maintenance personnel, and changes in the number of units included in the troop program. The Department of the Army discontinued the two commands during FY 1959 with the concurrence of CONARC.

The Army Aviation School at Fort Rucker steadily expanded to meet the growing training requirements. New courses reflected changes in doctrine and equipment. The physical facilities of the school were improved and enlarged. The instrument qualification of most pilots enhanced the capabilities of aviation units.

The Army encountered numerous problems because of the split that existed in supply and maintenance responsibility between the Army and the Air Force. Approval for the transfer to the Army of all supply and maintenance responsibilities finally came in 1955. The Transportation Corps developed an Army Aviation Depot Plan to govern its new responsibilities. To oversee the operations in this field, the Transportation Supply and Maintenance Command—redesignated the Transportation Materiel Command in 1959—was established. Although there were many growing pains in the development of depot operations, by 1962 the Transportation Corps oversaw a functioning system.

The Berlin Crisis of 1961 resulted in an immediate and unexpected expansion of Army aviation. The partial mobilization disrupted the orderly development of aviation, but provided valuable experience for the much larger growth which was soon to take place as a result of the Vietnam war. The deteriorating situation in Southeast Asia imposed additional requirements upon the aviation structure. By the end of 1962, Army aviation units were beginning to arrive in South Vietnam.

The sudden contingency requirements in both Europe and Asia coincided with the Army's new programs for aviation expansion. In early 1960, the Army Aircraft Requirements Review Board (Rogers Board) had formulated plans for aircraft development and acquisition for the coming decade. Immediately thereafter, the Rogers Committee on Army Aviation developed a training program to support this expansion. In 1961, the CONARC Ad Hoc Committee to Study Aircraft Armament made recommendations to expedite the procurement and distribution of the new aircraft weapons systems. Although many of the findings of these three groups were soon overtaken by events, they provided a valuable background for the Howze Board in 1962.

Many of the Army's plans and proposals for future expansion were severely limited by Department of Defense policies. Since 1954, the Army had been working under the grave handicap of the national defense policy of massive retaliation. This policy was strategically nuclear in orientation, and left little money or attention for conventional forces. In 1961, President Kennedy directed Secretary of Defense McNamara to undertake a thorough reappraisal of strategic plans, force levels, and military programs. A policy emerged that called for an American force structure designed to provide strong limited capability as well as general war forces.[2]

Secretary McNamara was dissatisfied with the existing program for attaining tactical mobility. He wanted the Army to reexamine its quantitative and qualitative requirements for aviation through an extended program of analyses, exercises, and field tests in order to evaluate revolutionary new concepts of tactical mobility. The Army was to recommend actions which would provide it with maximum mobility in the combat area. He pointed out that Army studies of airmobile divisions, airmobile reconnaissance regiments, aerial artillery, and similar units indicated the type of doctrinal concepts which could be evolved. Results of the Army study were to be presented in terms of both cost and transport effectiveness.[3] To initiate these studies, Secretary McNamara established the Army Tactical Mobility Requirements Board (Howze Board) in April 1962. The recommendations of the Howze Board were to open a new era in the history of Army aviation.[4]

Endnotes
Chapter XV

1. (1) Speech by Brig Gen William B. Bunker to First Senior Officers Aviation Maintenance Indoctrination Conference, no date. (2) Memo TCCAD-SP, Maj Gen F.S. Besson to DCSLOG, 29 Nov 61, subj: Prefix Numbers for Army Aviation Units.

2. U.S. Army Expansion, 1961-1962, pp. 9-10.

3. (1) Informal memo, Sec Def to Sec Army, 19 Apr 62. (2) Memo, Sec Def to Sec Army, 19 Apr 62, subj: Army Aviation.

4. For the recommendations of the Howze Board, see Barbara A. Sorrill and Constance J. Suwalsky, The Origins, Deliberations, and Recommendations of the U.S. Army Tactical Mobility Requirements Board (Howze Board), USACDC CAG, Fort Leavenworth, Apr 69.

LIST OF ABBREVIATIONS

AAOD	Army Aviation Operating Detachment
AATRI	Army Air Traffic Regulation and Identification
AAUTC	Army Aviation Unit Training Command
ACofS	Assistant Chief of Staff
AGF	Army Ground Forces
AR	Army Regulation
ARST	Aerial Reconnaissance and Surveillance Unit
ASR	Army Study Requirement
ATFA	Atomic Field Army
ATP	Army Training Program
CDEC	Combat Development Experimentation Center
CONARC	Continental Army Command
CONUS	Continental United States
CORG	Combat Operations Research Group
DA	Department of the Army
DCSLOG	Deputy Chief of Staff for Logistics
DCSOPS	Deputy Chief of Staff for Operations
DCSPER	Deputy Chief of Staff for Personnel
FAA	Federal Aviation Administration
FASCOM	Field Army Support Command
FECOM	Far East Command
FM	Field Manual
FOC	Flight Operations Center
FW	Fixed Wing
JCS	Joint Chiefs of Staff
LASSO	Light Aviation Special Support Operations
MASL	Master Authorized Stockage List
MCA	Military Construction Army
MOMAR	Modern Mobile Army
MOS	Military Occupational Specialty
OCAFF	Office of the Chief of Army Field Forces

LIST OF ABBREVIATIONS

OCofT	Office of the Chief of Transportation
OCS	Officer Candidate School
PENTANA	Pentagonal Atomic-Nonatomic Army
POL	Petroleum, Oil, and Lubricants
POM	Preparation Overseas Movement
POR	Preparation Overseas Replacement
QMR	Qualitative Materiel Requirement
ROAD	Reorganization Objective Army Divisions
ROCAD	Reorganization of the Armored Division
ROCID	Reorganization of the Combat Infantry Division
ROTAD	Reorganization of the Airborne Division
ROTC	Reserve Officer Training Corps
SATSA	Signal Aviation Test and Support Activity
SCAMP	Standard Configuration and Modernization Program
SKY CAV	Sky Cavalry
SLAR	Side-Looking Airborne Radar
STOL	Short Takeoff and Landing
STRAC	Strategic Army Corps
TA	Table of Allowances
TAAM	Transportation Army Aircraft Maintenance
TAAR	Transportation Army Aircraft Repair
TATSA	Transportation Aircraft Test and Support Activity
TD	Table of Distribution
TOE	Table of Organization and Equipment
TSMC	Transportation Supply and Maintenance Command
USABAAR	U.S. Army Board for Aviation Accident Research
USAF	U.S. Air Force
USAREUR	U.S. Army Europe
USARPAC	U.S. Army Pacific
USMC	U.S. Marine Corps
V/STOL	Vertical/Short Takeoff and Landing

APPENDIX

Tables and Charts

TABLE 1	Fixed Wing Aircraft 1942-1962
2	Rotary Wing Aircraft 1942-1962
3	Convertiplanes and Vertical Lift Vehicles 1953-1962
4	Army Aviation School Courses
5	Army Aviation School Maintenance Courses
6	Transportation School Maintenance Courses
CHART 1	Headquarters, CONARC 1 February 1955
2	Headquarters, CONARC 10 October 1957
3	Headquarters, CONARC 1 January 1959
4	Aviation in the ROAD Division
5	United States Army Aviation School
6	Army Aviation Organization

Directors of Army Aviation

Maj Gen Hamilton H. Howze	1 January 1956 - 15 December 1957
Maj Gen Ernest F. Easterbrook	16 December 1957 - 9 December 1958
Maj Gen Clifton F. van Kann	20 July 1959 - 16 October 1961
Maj Gen Delk M. Oden	17 October 1961 - 10 March 1963

Pictoral Display of Army Aircraft

TABLE 1
FIXED WING AIRCRAFT, 1942-1962

Designation	Name	Manufacturer	Weight (Gross)[a]	Capacity[b]	Remarks
L-4	Grasshopper	Piper	1,220	2	Observation/reconnaissance
L-5	Sentinal	Vultee-Stinson	2,020	2	Observation/reconnaissance 1 litter capacity
L-13		Consolidated-Vultee	2,900	3	Observation
L-14		Piper	1,800	3	Observation/reconnaissance
L-15	Scout	Boeing	2,116	2	Observation/reconnaissance
L-16		Aeronica	1,300	2	Observation/reconnaissance
L-17	Navion	Ryan No. American	3,050	4	Utility
L-18		Piper	1,500	2	Observation/reconnaissance improved L-4
L-19 (0-1)	Bird Dog	Cessna	2,100 (L19A) 2,400 (L19E)	2	Observation/reconnaissance
L-20 (U-6)	Beaver	deHavilland	4,820	6	Utility
L-21	Super Cub	Piper	1,500	2	Observation/reconnaissance
L-23 (U-8)	Seminole	Beech	7,000	6	Utility
L-24	Courier	Helio	3,000	4	Observation/reconnaissance
LC-126		Cessna	3,350	4	Trainer/utility
U-1	Otter	deHavilland	7,600	10	Light tactical transport 2000lb payload
U-9 (L26)	Commander	Aero Design	7,000	5	Utility
CV-2 (AC1)	Caribou	deHavilland	26,000	30	Tactical transport (To Air Force 1969)
OV-1 (AO-1)	Mohawk	Grumman	12,800	2	Combat surveillance
T-37		Cessna	6,250	2	Jet observation airplane on Air Force loan

Sources: (1) Montgomery and Tierney, *The Army Aviation Story*, pp 235-46. (2) "Controversial Fifties," *Army Aviation*, Sep 60, pp 477-90, 499, 502. (3) Brigadier General John J. Tolson, "Aircraft Hardware: Aviation Milestones," *Army Aviation*, Feb-Mar 64, pp 11-24, 25-29. (4) F. G. Swanborough, *United States Military Aircraft Since 1909*, (London & New York: Putnam, 1963), pp 33, 42-44, 121, 400-03, 480, 485, 486, 489, 512, 522, 542, 544-47.

Legend:
    a = In pounds
    b = Including crew

TABLE 2
ROTARY WING AIRCRAFT, 1942-1962

Designation	Name	Manufacturer	Weight (Gross)[a]	Capacity[b]	Remarks
H-13	Sioux	Bell	2,450	3	Observation/reconnaissance training, 2 litter capacity
XH-15		Bell	2,800	4	reconnaissance, utility
XH-16		Piasecki	46,700	50	First heavy cargo
XH-17		Hughes	46,000	3	First flying crane
XH-18		Sikorsky	2,400	4	Utility
H-19	Chickasaw	Sikorsky	7,522 (H19D) 6,767 (H19C)	12	Utility, 6 litters
XH-20		McDonnell		1	Observation/reconnaissance
H-21	Shaunee	Piasecki (Vertol)	13,300	22	Utility, 12 litters
H-23	Raven	Hiller	2,800	3	Observation/reconnaissance, training, evacuation
YH-24		Sibel	1,540	2	Reconnaissance/evacuation
H-25	Army Mule	Piasecki	5,500	5 to 8	Utility
XH-26		American	810	1	Observation/reconnaissance
YH-30		McCulloch	2,000	2	Observation, training cargo, evacuation
YH-31		Doman	5,200	4 to 8	Utility
YH-32		Hiller	1,080	2	Reconnaissance
H-37	Mojave	Sikorsky	30,342	26	Medium cargo, 24 litters
H-39		Sikorsky	3,560	4	Observation - one model obtained
UH-1 (H40)	Iroquois	Bell	8,500	13	Tactical transport, armed or w/litters
H-41	Seneca	Cessna	3,000	4	Observation, 10 models used for high altitude eval.
H-42 (HO-2)		Hughes	1,550	2	Observation, training reconnaissance (5 obtained)
CH-46 (HC-1A)	Chinook	Vertol	15,550	23	Medium cargo, 15 litters
CH-47 (HC-1B)	Chinook	Boeing/Vertol	27,921	36	Medium cargo, 24 litters
H-51A		Lockheed	3,500		Experimental rigid rotor, high speed
CH-54	Skycrane	Sikorsky	38,000	2	Heavy lift flying crane, passenger refit
HO-1	Djinn	Sud	1,671	2	Observation/reconnaissance 3 obtained, eval.
HO-3		Brantly	1,600	2	Observation/reconnaissance, 5 obtained, eval.

Sources: (1) Montgomery and Tierney, *The Army Aviation Story*, pp 256-66. (2) "Controversial Fifties," *Army Aviation*, Sep 60, pp 490, 492- 512. (3) Brigadier General John J. Tolson, "Aircraft Hardware: Aviation Milestones," *Army Aviation*, Feb-Mar 64, pp 32-45, 49-50, 53, 55-57, 61. (4) F. G. Swanborough, *United States Military Aircraft Since 1909*, (London & New York: Putnam, 1963), pp 56-58, 116-117, 274-76, 398-99, 432-33, 436-37, 512, 525.

Legend:
a = In pounds
b = Including crew

TABLE 3
CONVERTIPLANES AND VERTICAL LIFT RESEARCH VEHICLES, 1953-1962

Designation	Manufacturer	Type	Remarks
XV-1	McDonnell	Convertiplane	Rotor and fixed wing. One obtained.
XV-3	Bell	Convertiplane	Tilting rotor type. One obtained.
VZ-1	Hiller	Vertical Lift	Ducted propeller flying platform.
VZ-2	Vertol	Aircraft	Tilt-wing. One obtained in 1957.
VZ-3	Ryan	Aircraft	Vertiplane, deflected slipstream. One obtained in 1959.
VZ-4	Doak	Aircraft	Tilting duct fans. One obtained.
VZ-5	Fairchild	Aircraft	Deflected slipstream. One obtained.
VZ-6	Chrysler	Vertical Lift	Flying jeep, ducted propellers. Two built.
VZ-7	Curtiss-Wright	Vertical Lift	Flying jeep, direct lift, four propellers.
VZ-8	Piasecki	Vertical Lift	Flying jeep, direct lift, two ducted rotors.
VZ-9	AVRO Canada	Vertical Lift	Flying saucer with fan lift. Two built.
XV-4 (VZ-10)	Lockheed	Aircraft	Twin jet VTOL. Jet-ejector lift. Two built.
X-19	Curtiss-Wright	Aircraft	VTOL research with radial lift force propellers. Two obtained.
X-22	Bell	Aircraft	VTOL research with four tilting duct airscrews. Two obtained.
XV-8	Ryan	Vertical Lift	Flex wing utility vehicle.

Source: Richard Tierney and Fred Montgomery, *The Army Aviation Story*, pp. 266-67, 272-73, 278-82.

APPENDIX

TABLE 4
ARMY AVIATION SCHOOL COURSES

OFFICER COURSES		
Course	Number	Remarks
Army Aviation Tactics	1-0-7	Became Officers Fixed Wing Aviator Course—1-A-1980
Army Helicopter Aviation Tactics	1-0-8	
Helicopter Transition Flight Training (H-21)	1-0-10	
Twin-Engine Transition Flight Training	1-0-11	
Instrument Flying	1-0-12	
Instrument Flight Examiner	1-0-13	
Senior Officer Flight Training	1-0-14	
Army Aviation Orientation	1-0-15	Renumbered 1-A-F3
Air Observer Officer	1-0-17	
Army Aviation Medicine	1-0-18	
Advanced Aviation Officer	1-0-19	Renumbered 1-A-F2
U-1A Transition Flight Training	1-0-21	
Army Aviation Primary and Tactical Flight Training	1-0-22	
H-13/H-19 Transition Flight Training	1-0-23	
H-13/H-21 Transition Flight Training	1-0-24	
H-13/H-34 Transition Flight Training	1-0-25	
Army Primary Flight Training	1-0-26	
H-37 Pilot Transition		
Transportation Helicopter Transition		
Army Aviation Safety		
OV-1 Transition Training		
CV-2 Transition Training		
Army Cargo Helicopter Pilot	6-OE-18	
Army Helicopter Aviation Tactics		
Primary Helicopter Training		Temporary 1956-1958
HU-1A Transition Training		
CH-21 Transition Training		
ENLISTED COURSES		
Army Aviation Pre-Flight Training (Helicopter)	1-E-4	
Army Aviator Transport Pilot (Rotary Wing) Phase II	1-OE-5	
Army Aviator Basic Flight Training (Helicopter) Phase III	1-OE-6	
Warrant Officer Rotary Wing Aviator	1-R-1981C	

281

TABLE 5
ARMY AVIATION SCHOOL MAINTENANCE COURSES, 1955-1962

Course	Remarks
Organizational Maintenance Officer	Initiated Jul 57; dropped 1959
Twin-Engine Transition Maintenance	Dropped Jul 56
Army Helicopter Maintenance H-19	Dropped Jul 56
Army Helicopter Maintenance H-21	Dropped Jul 56
Army Helicopter Maintenance H-23	Dropped Jul 56
Army Helicopter Maintenance H-25	Dropped Jul 56
Army Helicopter Maintenance H-34	Dropped Jul 56
Flight Simulator Operation and Maintenance	Initiated Jul 57
Army Helicopter Maintenance	Dropped Jul 57
Aircraft Maintenance (Entry)	Initiated Jul 56
Airplane Maintenance	Redesignated Aircraft Mechanic, 1957
Reconnaissance Helicopter Maintenance	Initiated Jul 56
Utility and Cargo Single Rotor Helicopter Maintenance	Initiated Jul 56
Utility and Cargo Tandem Rotor Helicopter Maintenance	Initiated Jul 56
Army Helicopter Maintenance H-37	Initiated Jul 58
Army Helicopter Maintenance HU-1	Initiated Apr 59
AO-1 Maintenance	Initiated Apr 60
AC-1 Maintenance	Initiated May 60

Source: History U.S. Army Aviation Center and Army Aviation School, 1954-1964, pp. 14-15.

TABLE 6
TRANSPORTATION SCHOOL MAINTENANCE COURSES, 1955-1962

Course	Remarks
Aircraft Maintenance	
Aviation Logistics	Initiated Sep 59
Airplane Repair	Dropped Oct 59
Single Engine Airplane Repair	Initiated Aug 59
Army Aviation Maintenance Management	Oct 59 to Jul 60
Helicopter Repairman	Dropped Dec 56
Reconnaissance Helicopter Repair	Aug 56 to Oct 59
Multi-Engine Airplane Repair	Initiated Sep 60
Single Rotor Helicopter Repair	Aug 56 to Jun 60
Utility and Cargo Single Rotor Helicopter Repair	Feb 60 to Dec 60
Utility and Cargo Tandem Rotor Helicopter Repair	Aug 56 to Oct 60
Reconnaissance, Utility, and Cargo Helicopter Repair	Initiated Jul 60
Tandem Rotor Helicopter Repair	Initiated Jul 60
Helicopter Repair (Twin-Engine)	Mar 59 to Jun 60
Medium Cargo Helicopter Repair	Initiated Jul 60
Rotary Wing Technical Inspector	Initiated Jul 60
Aircraft Maintenance Supervisor	Initiated Aug 60
Aircraft Component Repair	Jun 56 to Jul 58
Aircraft Power Train and Engine Repair	Dropped Oct 55
Engine Repair	Initiated Oct 55
Aircraft Carburetor Repair	Oct 56 to Aug 57
Aircraft Power Train Repair	Initiated Aug 56
Aircraft Rotor and Propeller Repair	
Aircraft Instrument and Electrical System Repairman	Dropped Aug 56
Aircraft Electrical Repair	Sep 56 to May 60
Aircraft Electrician	Initiated Mar 60
Airframe Repair	
Aircraft Hydraulic Repair	Initiated Oct 56
Aircraft Instrument Repair	Initiated Sep 56
HU-1A Helicopter Transition Repair	Initiated Jan 60
OV-1 Aircraft Repair Transition	Initiated Apr 61
CV-1 Aircraft Repair Transition	Initiated May 61

Source: History of the United States Army Transportation School, 1942-1962, pp. J-46 - J-63.

APPENDIX

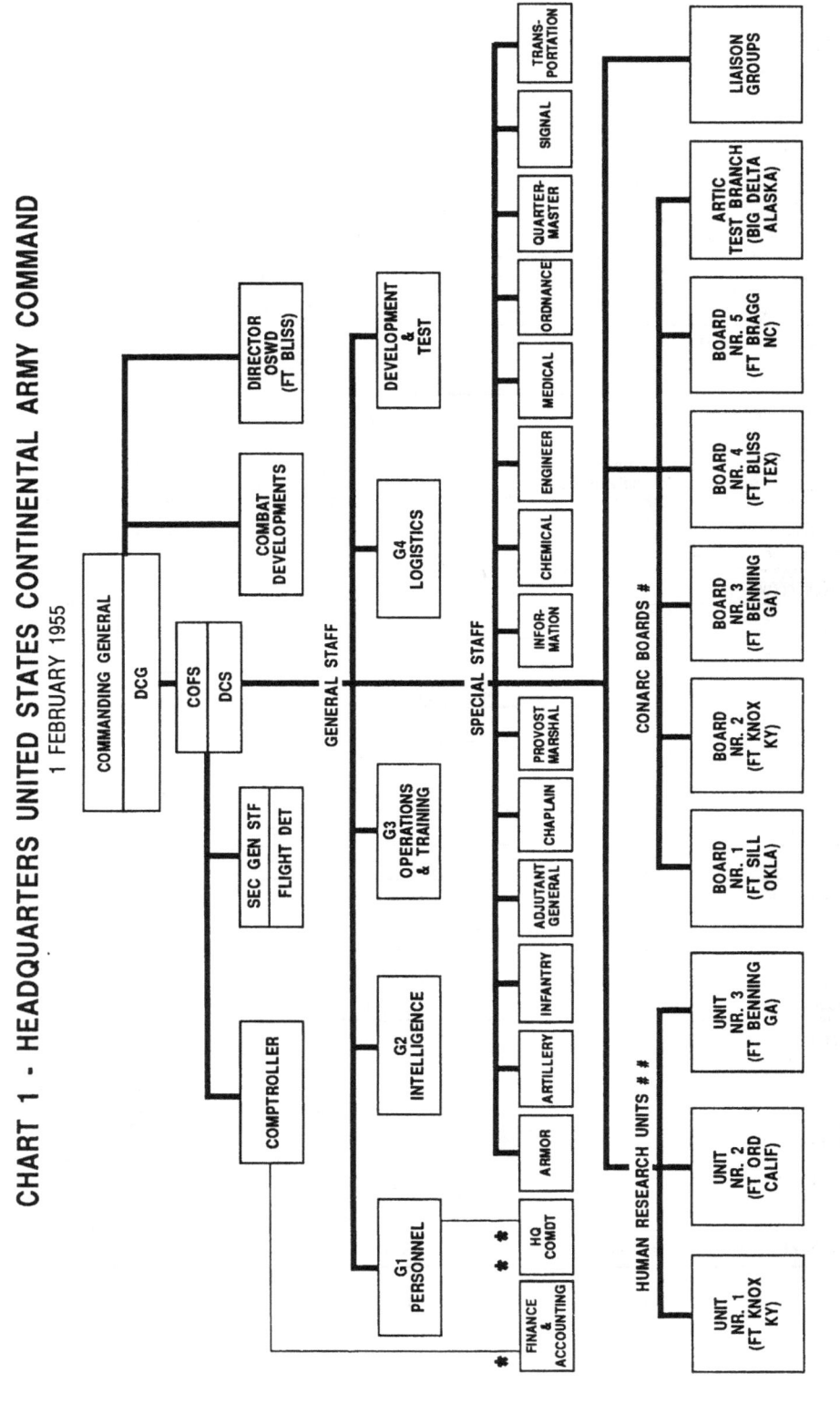

284

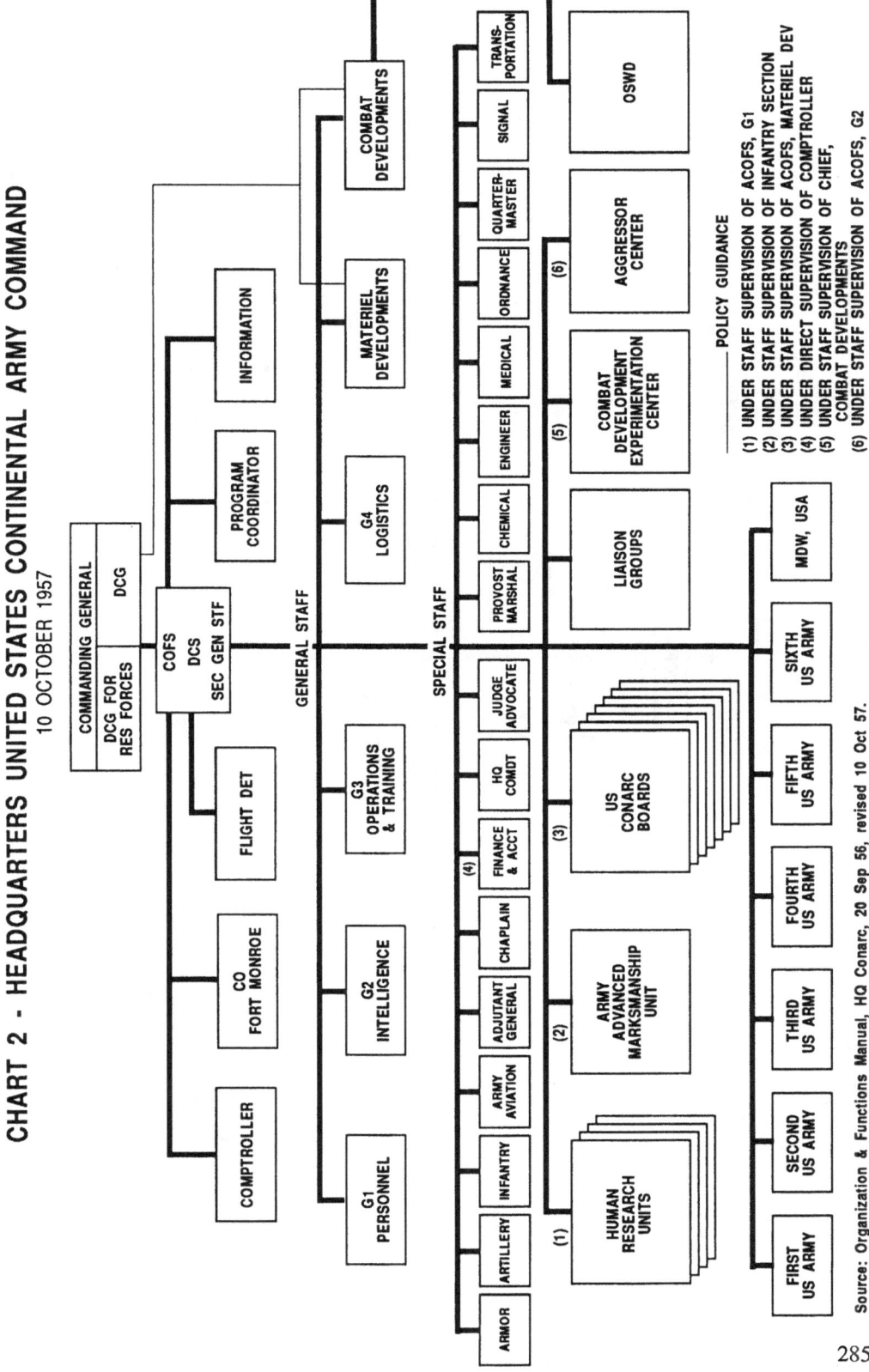

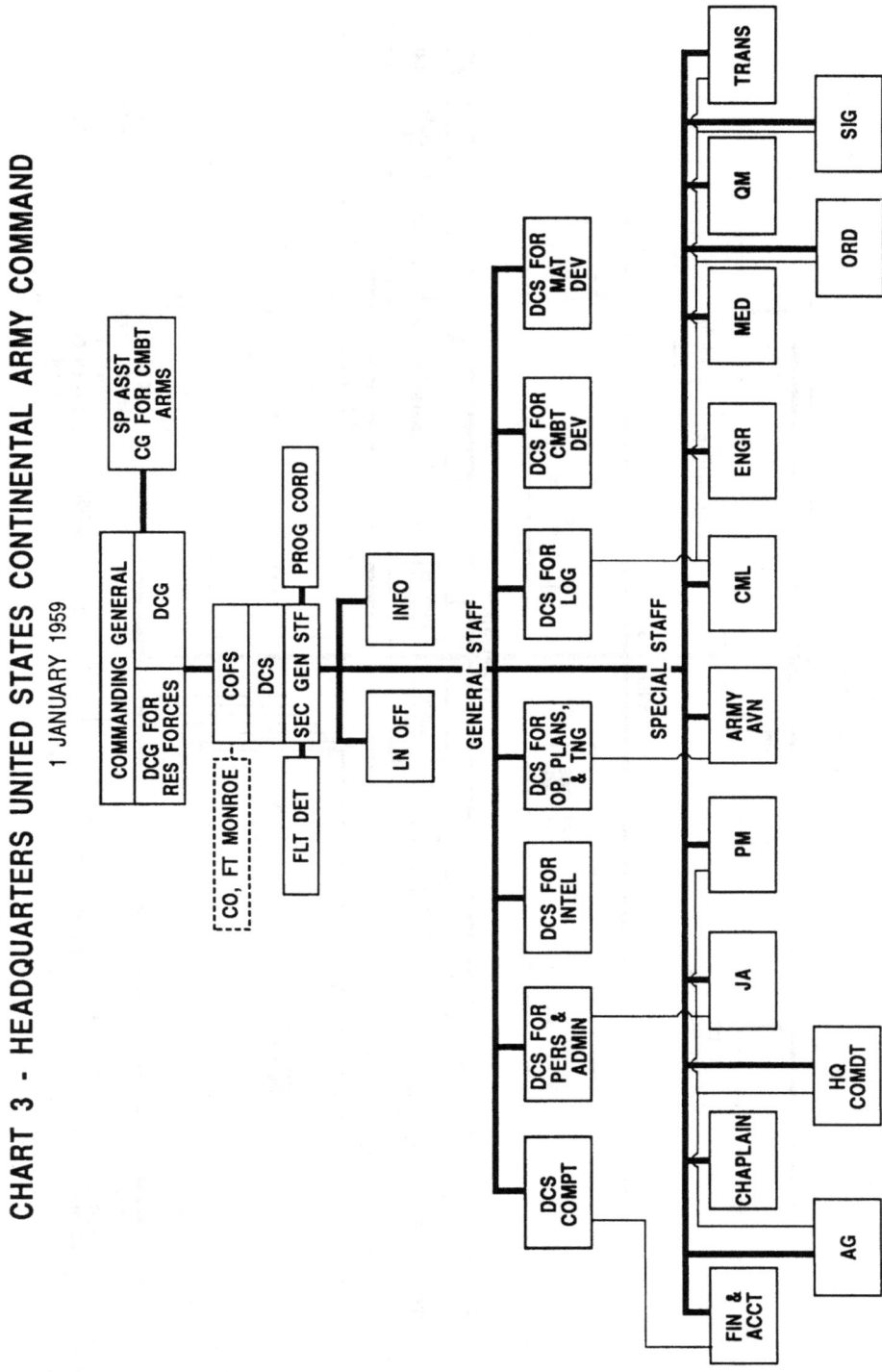

CHART 3 - HEADQUARTERS UNITED STATES CONTINENTAL ARMY COMMAND
1 JANUARY 1959

Source: Organization & Functions Manual, HQ Conarc, 1 Jan 59.

APPENDIX

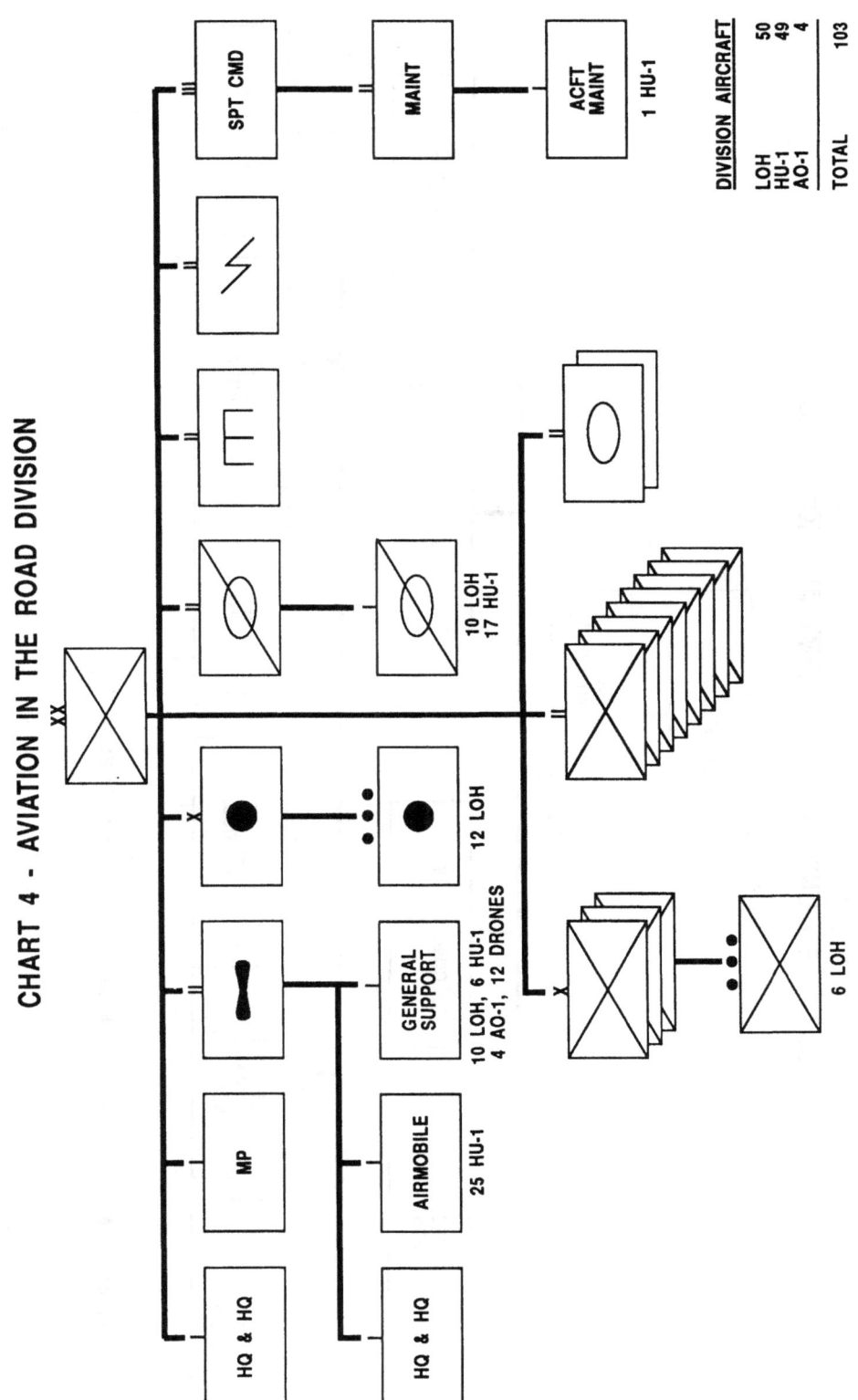

Source: Lt. Col. Morris G. Rawlings, "Army Aviation and the Reorganized Army Division," *United States Army Aviation Digest*, Vol. 8, No. 2 (Feb 62), p. 2.

APPENDIX

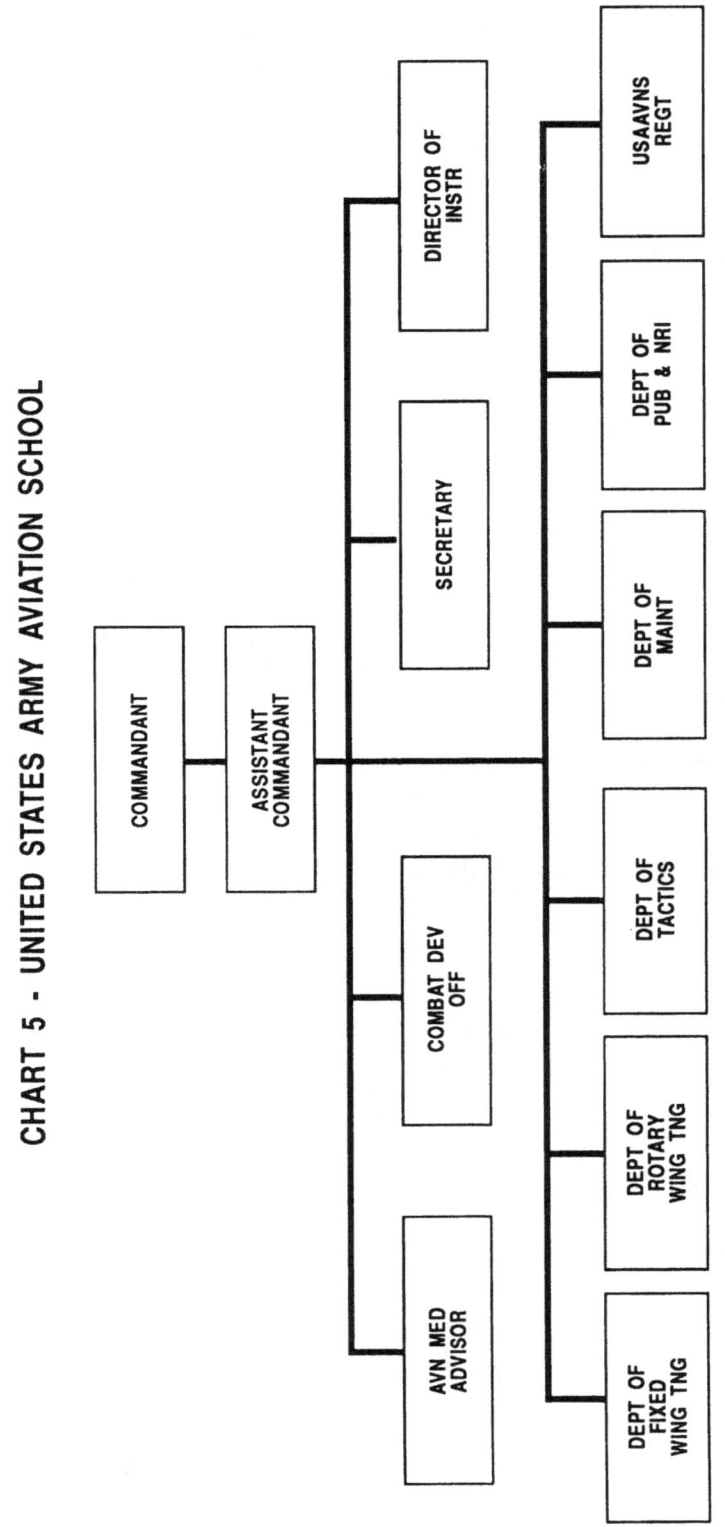

CHART 5 - UNITED STATES ARMY AVIATION SCHOOL

Source: Organization & Functions Manual, U.S. Army Aviation School, 29 Oct 58.

APPENDIX

CHART 6 - ARMY AVIATION ORGANIZATION
Office, Chief of Army Field Forces
(10 August 1953)

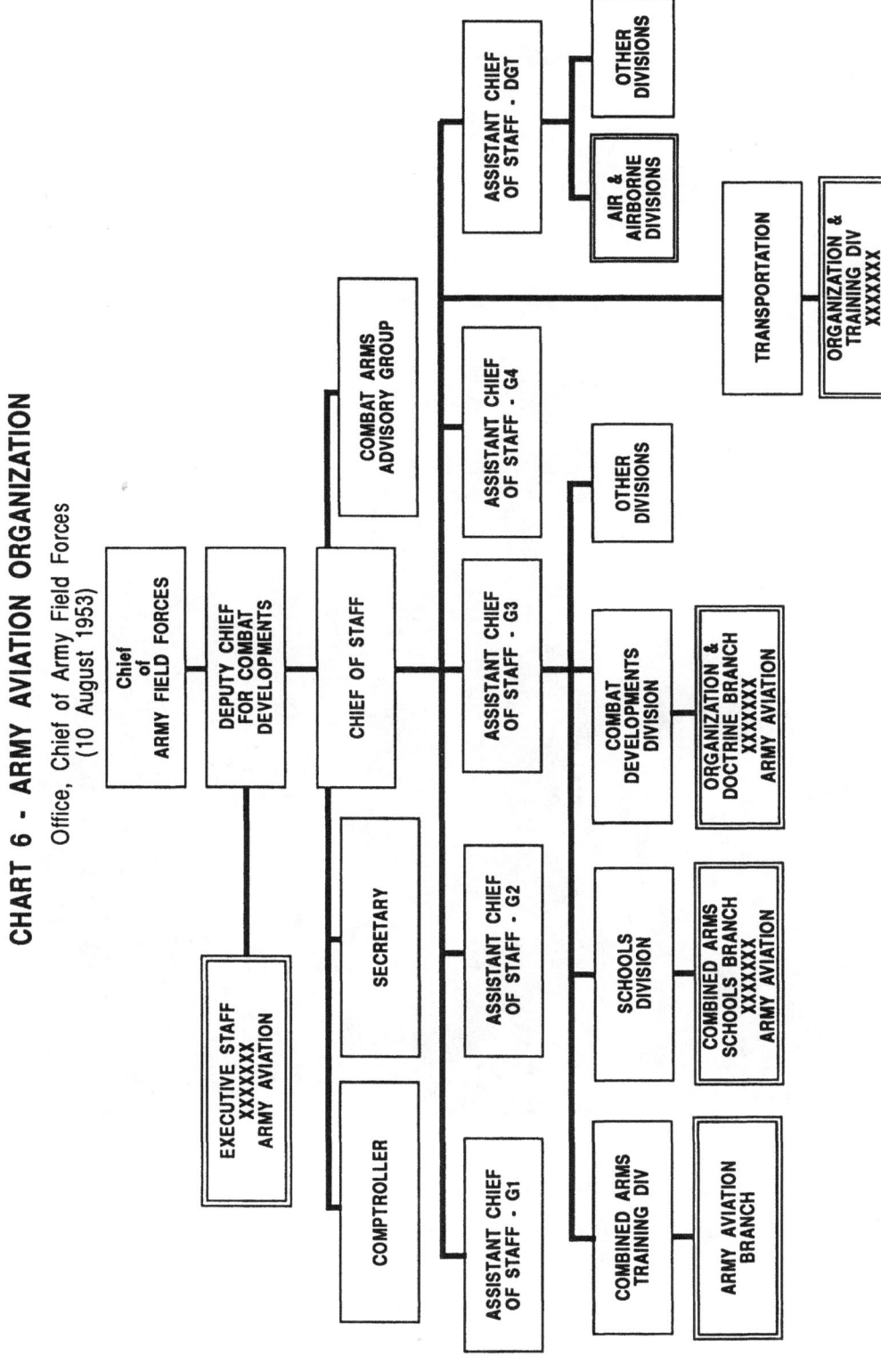

Source: Ltr ATTNG-52 360(S), OCAFF to DA ACofS G-3, 29 Aug 53, Annex A to Incl 3.

Maj Gen Hamilton H. Howze
1 January 1956 - 15 December 1957

APPENDIX

Maj Gen Ernest F. Easterbrook
16 December 1957 - 9 December 1958

Maj Gen Clifton F. van Kann
20 July 1959 - 16 October 1961

APPENDIX

Maj Gen Delk M. Oden
17 October 1961 - 10 March 1963

L-4 Grasshopper Observation Airplane

L-5 Sentinal Liaison and Observation Airplanes

APPENDIX

L-20 Beaver Observation Airplane

L-15 Scout Observation Airplane

APPENDIX

L-16 Observation Airplane

L-17 NAVION Light Utility Airplane

APPENDIX

L-18 Improved Observation Airplane

L-19 BIRD DOG Observation Airplane

APPENDIX

L-13 Utility Airplane

L-21 SUPER CUB Observation Airplane

APPENDIX

L-23 SEMINOLE Utility Airplane

L-24 COURIER Observation Airplane

LC-126 Light Cargo Airplane

U-1A OTTER Light Transport Aircraft

U-9 COMMANDER Utility Airplane

AC-1 (CV-2) CARIBOU Tactical Transport Airplane

APPENDIX

AO-1 (OV-1) MOHAWK Combat Surveillance Airplane

T-37 Jet Observation Airplane

APPENDIX

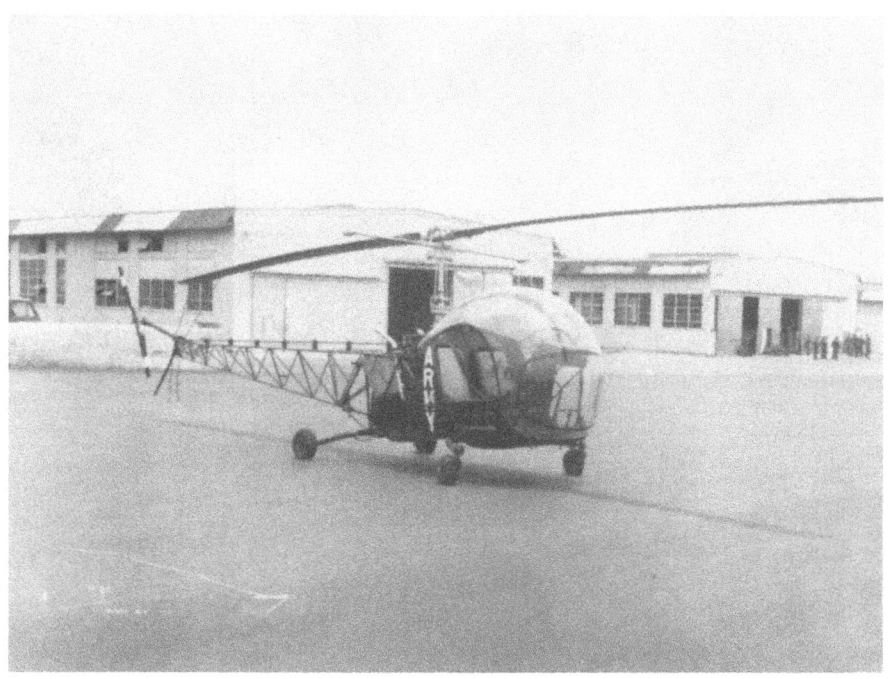

H-13 SIOUX Observation and Training Helicopter

XH-15 High Altitude Reconnaissance Helicopter

APPENDIX

YH-16 First Heavy Cargo Helicopter

XH-17 Heavy Lift Research Helicopter

APPENDIX

YH-18 Utility Helicopter

H-19 CHICKASAW Utility Helicopter

XH-20 Experimental Ram-Jet Helicopter

H-21 SHAWNEE Transport Helicopter

H-23 RAVEN Observation and Training Helicopter

YH-24 Experimental Observation Helicopter

APPENDIX

H-25A ARMY MULE Utility Helicopter

YH-30 Reconnaissance Helicopter

APPENDIX

YH-31 Utility Helicopter

H-34 CHOCTAW Light Tactical Transport Helicopter

H-37 MOJAVE Medium Cargo Helicopter

H-39 Observation Helicopter

UH-1 IROQUOIS Tactical Utility Helicopter

H-41 SENECA Observation Helicopter

APPENDIX

CH-47 CHINOOK Transport Helicopter

H-51A Lockheed's Experimental Rigid Rotor Helicopter

APPENDIX

CH-54 SKY CRANE Heavy Lift Helicopter

INDEX

Adams, Paul D., 105
Aerial evacuation, 29-33, 50-52, 66, 67, 69, 110, 139, 148, 181, 206
Aerial gunnery, 239
AFF Helicopter Pilot Course, 12, 13, 79, 86
AGF Air Training School, 11
Air cavalry, 115, 118, 119, 163, 181
Air cavalry combat brigade, 193
Air Force Helicopter School, 12
Air Mechanic Course, 12
Air observers, 174
Air Service, 3
Air traffic operations, 150-152
Air Training Command, 81, 228
Air Training Department, 79, 82, 86, 93, 94
Air Training Detachment, 7
Aircraft Accident Review Board, 137
Aircraft Armaments, Inc., 220
Aircraft Maintenance Officer Course, 261
Aircraft strength, 47, 62
Airmobility, 159, 181-196
Airplane and Engine Mechanic Course, 83
Antiaircraft Command, 5
Armair Brigade, 190-193
Armor Association, 164
Army Air Corps, 3, 4
Army Air Forces Liaison Pilot Course, 11, 12, 77, 81, 84-85
Army Airborne Center, 16
Army Aircraft Maintenance Program, 254
Army Aircraft Requirements Review Board, 115-119
Army Airplane Mechanic Course, 96, 228
Army Aviation Battalion, 147-148
Army Aviation Board, 106, 151, 167, 176, 177, 200, 204, 205, 214, 215
Army Aviation Center, 104, 105, 129, 138, 163, 237
Army Aviation Corps, 63, 65
Army Aviation Depot Plan, 249-252, 256
Army Aviation Electronics Program, 154
Army Aviation Flight Safety Board, 137-138
Army Aviation Instrument Course, 86, 96
Army Aviation Plan, 41- 44, 104-109, 234
Army Aviation Program, 119, 120
Army Aviation Safety Program, 136
Army Aviation School, 35, 78, 80, 86, 89-101, 122, 123, 137, 140, 142, 152, 155, 159-163, 167, 168, 170, 177, 182, 190, 194, 195, 202-205, 211-213, 216, 217, 225-232, 235-239, 257-260
Army Aviation Staff Officers Course, 238
Army Aviation Tactics Course, 85, 86, 99, 100, 230, 236, 237
Army Aviation Test Board, 200
Army Aviation Training Program, 119
Army Aviation transport company, 67, 70
Army Aviation Unit Training Commands, 29, 231, 233-234, 240
Army Board for Aviation Accident Research, 138
Army Field Forces Board No. 1, 18-19, 35, 48, 49, 50, 52, 54, 55, 61-3
Army General School, 91
Army Ground Forces Pilot Course, 12

315

INDEX

Army Helicopter Mechanic Course, 96, 98, 101, 228

Army Helicopter Transport Class, 79, 229

Army Helicopter Transport Mechanics Class, 79

Army Materiel Command, 137

Army Regulation 95-5, 10-59

Artillery observers, 8

Association of the United States Army, 163, 181

Atomic Field Army, 53, 67, 112, 113, 129, 140-145, 154

Atomic Support Commands, 234

Autogiros, 3, 4

Aviation Officer Career Program, 114

AVRO Aircraft, Ltd., 220

Baldwin, Thomas S., 2

Balloon Corps, 1-2

Balloons, 1-2

Basic flight training, 6, 9, 11, 43, 59, 77-86, 89, 90, 96, 225-231, 236

Bell Helicopter Company, 12, 53, 203, 219

Berlin build-up, 121-124

Brucker, Wilbur M., 110

Burgess, Carter L., 226

Cannon, J. K., 11

Cargo helicopter program, 21, 69-72, 207, 209

Carrier tests, 193-194

Chief of Transportation Study, 22-24

Clark, Mark W., 5, 17, 78, 89

Clarke, Bruce C., 119

Close air support, 106-108, 111, 165, 216

Cold weather operations, 30, 32

Collier, John H., 184, 185

Collins, J. Lawton, 16, 17

Combat Developments Command, 137

Combat Operations Research Group, 172

Convertiplanes, 47, 53, 219

Dahlquist, John E., 98, 105-107, 184, 185, 210

Danford, Robert M., 4

Decker, George H., 146

Department of Air Training, 8, 11

Depot maintenance, 248

Devers, Jacob L., 11

Director of Army Aviation, 107, 108, 129, 130, 133, 181, 189, 199, 215

Division combat aviation company, 67

Doak Aircraft Company, 219

Dulles, John F., 103

Easterbrook, Ernest F., 215

Eddleman, Clyde D., 195-196, 234

Edson, H. D., 233

Enlisted pilots, 114

Exercise BLUE BOLT, 140

Exercise BLUE BOLT II, 113

Exercise BRIGHT STAR, 217

Exercise CUMBERLAND HILLS, 212-213

Exercise DESERT ROCK, 33

Exercise FLASHBURN, 33, 159

Exercise FOLLOW ME, 140

Exercise GRAND BAYOU, 189

Exercise GULF STREAM, 211

Exercise JUMP LIGHT, 141, 191, 233-234

Exercise KING COLE, 141

Exercise LONGHORN, 30-32, 34

Exercise ROCKY SHOALS, 152, 193-194

Exercise SAGE BRUSH, 113, 160, 182-187, 231

Exercise SLEDGE HAMMER, 108, 182, 187-190, 234

Exercise SNOWFALL, 30

Exercise SNOWSTORM, 32, 33, 159

Exercise SOUTHERN PINE, 29

Exercise SWIFT STRIKE, 217

INDEX

Federal Aviation Act 1958, 152
Field Army-75, 146
Field Artillery Air Mechanic Course, 82
Field Artillery School, 7, 8, 9, 11-2, 16, 17, 48, 49, 63, 78-86, 89, 91, 94, 235
Fifth echelon maintenance, 254-255
First Aero Squadron, 2
First Corps Observation Group, 3
First Helicopter Company, 17, 27-30, 32
First Transportation Helicopter Company, 70
Fixed Wing Maintenance Course, 259
Fixed Wing Training Plan, 106
Fixed wing training, 82, 225-231, 236
Fixed wing utility aircraft, 49-51, 216-219
Flight Simulator Operations and Maintenance Course, 260
Flight training installations, 11, 90
Flying crane, 209
Flying saucer, 220
Ford, W. W., 7
Fourth echelon maintenance, 256-257
Gavin, James, 178, 181, 183, 210
General Electric Company, 165
Grasshopper Squadron, 4
Hart, Charles E., 98
Heileman, Frank A., 22-23
Helicopter detachments, 66-67
Helicopter Maintenance Course, 260
Higgins, G. J., 36
Howze, Hamilton H., 108, 118, 119, 130, 134, 178, 181, 182, 195, 199
Human Research and Operations Research Office, 136
Hutton, Carl I., 100, 160, 163, 178
Instrument Flight Examiners Course, 86, 96, 242
Instrument training, 84-86, 95, 240-242
Jet aircraft, 210-214

Joint regulations, 10, 17
Key West Agreement, 10, 109
Louisiana Maneuvers, 4
Lowe, Thaddeus, S. C., 1
Magruder, Carter B., 165
Maintenance and supply support, 72-74
Maintenance personnel, 252-254
Maintenance training, 257-263
Marshall, George C., 4
Materiel Requirements Review Board, 34, 38, 39, 54, 63, 66, 73, 92
McNair, Lesley J., 4
Mechanic training, 82-84, 225-231, 236
Medical Field Service School, 67
Medical service helicopter ambulance detachments, 66-67, 80
Memorandum of Understanding 1951, 19-21, 34-36, 109, 210
Memorandum of Understanding 1952, 38-39, 63, 109, 111, 184, 210
Mexican Punitive Expedition, 2
Mitchell, William, 3
Mobile Army Surgical Hospitals, 66-67
Mobile Aviation Maintenance Training Teams, 262
Modern Mobile Army I Study, 145-146
Mountain flight training, 240
National Security Act, 10, 109
Navy Bureau of Aeronautics, 214
Observation aircraft, 48-49, 205, 207, 210-216
Okanagan Helicopter Limited, 240
Organizational Maintenance Officer Course, 259, 260
Overman Act, 3
Pace, Frank M., 17, 19, 23, 109
Palmer, W. B., 134
PENTANA, 140-145, 161
Pike, Thomas P., 248

317

Piper Aircraft Corporation, 48
Powell, Herbert B., 174, 175, 176
Primary Flight Training Course, 96, 99, 228
Project ABLE BUSTER, 106, 159-160, 162
Project LONG ARM, 212-214
Ridgway, Matthew B., 103, 104, 110, 112, 124, 125, 130, 140, 178, 210
ROAD, 121, 129, 145-150, 155
RODAC-70, 149
Rogers, Gordon B., 115, 119, 174
Rogers Board, 115-119, 125, 196, 203, 216, 239
Rogers Committee, 119-121, 125
Rotary wing aircraft, 51-53
Rotary wing training, 12, 43
ROTC flight training program, 242-243
Ryan Aeronautical Company, 219
Seaplane training, 9, 11
Signal Aviation Test and Support Activity, 200
SKY CAV, 108, 160, 183-187, 233
SKY CAV II, 187, 233-234
Sky Cavalry Platoon, 163
Sky cavalry, 181, 182, 188, 190, 192
Southern Airways Company, 229
Spanish American War, 1-2
Spartan School of Aeronautics, 95
Springfield Armory, 165
Stahr, Elvis J., 146
Standard Configuration and Modernization Program, 254, 255
Strategic Army Corps, 117
Tactical Air Navigation and Landing Aids System, 153-154
Tactical helicopter course, 79
Tactical training, 6, 9, 11, 43, 59, 77-86, 89, 90, 231-232, 236
Talbott, Harold E., 210

Taylor, Maxwell D., 108, 141
Townsend Company, 165
Transport helicopter companies, 15, 18
Transportation Aircraft Test and Support Activity, 200
Transportation Army aircraft maintenance companies, 71
Transportation Army aircraft repair teams, 71
Transportation Corps Army Aviation Field Service Office, 72, 131
Transportation helicopter companies, 70, 79
Transportation Helicopter Mechanic Course, 80
Transportation Materiel Command, 132, 133
Transportation Research Command, 133
Transportation Supply and Maintenance Command, 131, 132, 250, 251
Trudeau, Arthur, 154, 165
Truman, Louis W., 174
Twelve helicopter battalion program, 56
Twining, Nathan, 110, 210
Twin-Engine Maintenance Course, 101
Utility helicopters, 52-6, 69-72, 203-5
Van Natta, T. F., 175
Vandenberg, Hoyt S., 17, 20
Vanderpool, Jay D., 160, 162, 163, 178
Von Kann, Clifton F., 199
Warrant officer aviators, 70, 80, 112-114, 120-122, 204, 232, 236
Warrant officer pilot training, 20
Weight limitations, 10, 16, 17, 18, 19, 39, 50, 109, 110-111
Williams, Edward T., 234
Wilson, Charles E., 110, 111, 124
Wright, Orville, 2
Wyman, Willard G., 107, 134, 161, 162, 195

Richard P. Weinert, Jr.

Mr. Richard P. Weinert, Jr., who entered federal service in 1958 with the National Archives, served as a military historian with the United States Army from 1963 until his retirement in 1988. He was born in Illinois, and completed a baccalaureate degree in international relations at the University of Florida and a master's degree in history at American University. He served as a historian in the Office of the Chief of Military History, Department of the Army and in the Historical Office of the U. S. Continental Army Command, then from 1973, as Deputy Chief Historian of the U. S. Army Training and Doctrine Command. He is the author of *Defender of the Chesapeake: The Story of Fort Monroe*, and the forthcoming *The Confederate Regular Army,* and thirty journal articles on Civil War and other historical topics. Mr. Weinert has written historical monographs on the Army's Vietnam buildup and reserve mobilization and numerous studies of Army training. A member of several professional organizations, he serves on the Board of Directors of the Council on America's Military Past. In addition to professional and Department of the Army commendations, he has received the Moncado and Gondos awards from the American Military Institute.

www.ingramcontent.com/pod-product-compliance
Lightning Source LLC
Chambersburg PA
CBHW081913170426
43200CB00014B/2723